# WITCH HUNTING
## AND
# WITCH TRIALS

The Indictments for Witchcraft from
the Records of 1373 Assizes held for
the Home Circuit A.D. 1559–1736

Collected and edited by
### C. L'ESTRANGE EWEN
With an Introduction

LINCOLN MAC VEAGH
THE DIAL PRESS
NEW YORK : MCMXXIX

**Kessinger Publishing's Rare Reprints**
**Thousands of Scarce and Hard-to-Find Books!**

.         .         .
.         .         .
.         .         .
.         .         .
.         .         .
.         .         .
.         .         .
.         .         .
.         .         .
.         .         .
.         .         .
.         .         .
.         .         .
.         .         .
.         .         .
.         .         .
.         .         .
.         .         .
.         .         .

We kindly invite you to view our extensive catalog list at:
http://www.kessinger.net

A WITCH AND HER IMPS. A.D. 1621
(From a contemporary drawing, Brit. Mus., Add. MS. 32496

PRINTED IN GREAT BRITAIN BY
STEPHEN AUSTIN AND SONS, LTD., HERTFORD.

# CONTENTS

# LIST OF ILLUSTRATIONS

# PREFACE

WITCHCRAFT is a subject which has appealed to many writers, and a large number of books and essays recording facts and fiction relating to the practices of sorcery and enchantment have been published.

Of the volumes relating to witchcraft in England, the most useful for reference appear to be the following :—

Scot (Reginald). The discoverie of witchcraft, Wherein the lewde dealing of witches and witchmongers is notablie detected, the knaverie of conjurors, the impietie of inchantors, the follie of soothsaiers, the impudent falshood of cousenors, the infidelitie of atheists, the pestilent practises of Pythonists, the curiositie of figurecasters, the vanitie of dreamers, the beggerlie art of Alcumystrie . . . the vertue and power of naturall magike, and all the conveiances of Legierdemaine and juggling are deciphered . . . Heereunto is added a treatise upon the nature of substance of spirits and devils, etc. Black letter. pp. 560. *W. Brome* : London, 1584. 4°.

Hutchinson (Francis). *Bishop of Down and Connor.* An historical essay concerning Witchcraft, with observations . . tending . . . to confute the vulgar errors about that point. *London,* 1718. 8°.

Notestein (Wallace). *Professor of English History at Cornell University, Ithaca, N.Y.* A History of Witchcraft in England from 1558 to 1718. pp. xiv, 442. 1911. 8°.

Kittredge (George Lyman). *Professor of History, U.S.A.* English Witchcraft and James the First. pp. 65. *Macmillan Co.* : New York, 1912. 8°.

Murray (Margaret Alice). *Assistant-Professor of Egyptology at University College, London.* The Witch-Cult in Western Europe. A study in anthropology. pp. 303. *Clarendon Press* : Oxford, 1921. 8°.

Summers (Rev. Augustus Montague). The History of Witchcraft and Demonology, pp. xv, 353, pl. viii. *Kegan Paul and Co* : London, 1926. 8°

—— The Geography of Witchcraft. pp. xi, 623. pl. viii. *Kegan Paul and Co.* : London, 1927. 8°.

Of these writers, Reginald Scot, a Kent gentleman, as indicated by his title-page, gives a very full and entertaining exposition of the subject, his opinions being marked by outstanding intelligence and unusual independence of vision. Dr. Hutchinson in 1718 was, however, the first inquirer to compile statistics, and he notes (p. 49) that from the time of the Act of Henry VIII until the year 1644 about fifteen sorceresses or enchantresses were executed in England, and in his chronological table he mentions (quoting Scot, p. 543) seventeen or eighteen witches condemned at St. Osyth in 1676 (neither date nor number is borne out by the official records now presented), and fifteen hanged in Essex in 1645 (an under-estimate). These are the only cases in the Home Circuit for the period 1588–1718 which he was able to trace. For two centuries Hutchinson's statistics were the only data available. and his figures were used as late as 1883 by Sir J. F. Stephen (*History of Criminal Law*, ii, 431–5). Professor G. L. Kittredge, who made diligent search for records of executions for witchcraft throughout England during the reign of James I, found mention of less than forty (p. 65). As, unfortunately. he gives neither list nor index it is not possible to say whether any one of the fourteen cases for the Home Circuit now given is an addition to his list. The present researches support his view that the time of James I was not the period of greatest persecution, although I shall shew that the early part of that reign was the time of greatest danger to the arraigned witch in Middlesex and the five counties of the Home Circuit.

Professor W. Notestein, another twentieth century investigator, in a list of cases of witchcraft 1558–1718, mentions about 400 cases in all in England, about 100 of the suspects or accused being persons in Essex, Herts., Sussex, and Kent, of whom approximately one-half were convicted and suffered the death penalty.

Assistant-Professor Murray, in her book on the Witch-Cult, gives a bibliography of the subject, as does the Rev. A. Montague Summers in his first-named work. The most recent volume is the latter writer's *Geography*, forming with his *History*, a comprehensive survey of the subject, but one which is unfortunately marred by the author's religious venom. In the second volume the chapter on witchcraft in England consists of 121 pp., of which 15 pp. relate to Ireland. This authority rests content with the statistics of Professor Notestein. So much energy has been expended in this sphere of literature that it is surprising to find that no writer (not even Mr. Summers, who has given " more than thirty years close attention to the subject of witchcraft ") has made any use whatever of the records of Assizes. It is hoped, therefore, that the notes now brought together and presented for the first time may serve as an addendum to the works already in print and be of value to future students of the history of the magic arts.

Now, instead of the fifteen executions discovered by Hutchinson for the period 1541–1644, proof is provided of no less than eighty from five counties only, and during a shorter period. The hundred cases of Professor Notestein are now swelled to 513 persons accused (790 indictments) in the same five counties, and that from about 77 *per centum* of the original rolls, and an even smaller proportion of original indictments, as many bills returned with an ignoramus were destroyed.

The figures now given will correct the statement of the authors of *History of English Law* (p. 556) that " very few people were done to death by the laws of Henry VIII and Elizabeth ". These eminent lawyers (Sir F. Pollock and Dr. F. W. Maitland), misled by Hutchinson, erred further in stating that the " days of the Commonwealth were the worst days for witches in England ". Attention may also be drawn to the views advanced by Sir J. F. Stephen (*History of Criminal Law*, 1883, ii, 432), that trials were "most common in the seventeenth century", and by Mr. N. W. Thomas (*Encyclopædia Britannica*), who states that they were most numerous during the same period. As the seventeenth century covered more than two-thirds of the period during which the trials were in progress the remark is somewhat pointless; moreover, it is inaccurate. So far as can be estimated from existing records, there were more trials in forty-two years of the reign of Elizabeth than during the entire century to which these two authorities point as the most active period.

The present essay is not intended to be a popular account of the witch-cult and description of the disgusting habits and filthy orgies commonly ascribed to the devil-worshippers. Many able pens have already written up these subjects. Reference to the contents will show that my remarks are confined solely to an account of the official machinery of conviction and punishment and statistics of the results of its functioning which, although they should form the sub-stratum of any history of witchcraft, have not hitherto attracted more than passing attention. For instance, I cannot trace a single writer on witchcraft who makes reference to the laws of William the Conqueror and Henry I on the subject.

The search of the Home Circuit indictments alone occupied the writer for four months. Doubtless a more leisured examination would have revealed further details. Looking through the last thirty or forty bundles was a dreary dirty business, and had a negative result. Some of these later files were scanned hurriedly and others still more hopeless were passed over entirely.

The indictments have been abstracted as briefly as possible and the manner in which this has been done can be ascertained by comparing one of the complete forms given pp. 77–92 with its corresponding précis. Baptismal names have, in general, been modernized. I have endeavoured to give references to all contemporary pamphlets and literature.

In the appendices will be found a collection of instructive and interesting extracts, most of which have not been printed before. As an example of a gaol delivery roll I have selected that for the famous assizes at Chelmsford in 1645 when nineteen women were sentenced to death. The two Upper Bench actions see the light of day for the first time, and the Suffolk and Leicester depositions are likewise new. Dalton's Discovery of Witches, the Scottish indictment, and the Chelmsford examination have appeared before, but will be found of sufficient interest to bear repetition. I include a list of additional witches compiled from various sources.

My own search of the public records is by no means complete; a thorough examination of the Coram Rege and De Banco rolls (a lengthy undertaking) would reveal many cases of persons who had been publicly accused, if not officially charged with the crime. A complete catalogue of witches is yet far from being an accomplished fact.

C. L. E.

# WITCH HUNTING AND WITCH TRIALS

## INTRODUCTION

### Ancient Laws against Witchcraft

Witchcraft, enchantment, sorcery, invocations of evil spirits, and other phases of the black arts have been recognized and practised in England, as elsewhere, from time immemorial. At all times magic in all forms appears to have been considered to be a public danger, and was punished by both ecclesiastical and civil courts. The Church, blindly following biblical behests, believed that the slaughter of wizards and witches was in accordance with the wishes of the Almighty.

" Thou shalt not suffer a witch [sorceress R.V.] to live." (*Exodus* xxii, 18.)

" A man also or woman that hath a familiar spirit, or that is a familiar spirit, or that is a wizard, shall surely be put to death : they shall stone them with stones." (*Leviticus* xxi, 9.)

" There shall not be found among you anyone . . . that useth divination or an enchanter or a witch or a charmer or a consulter with familiar spirits or a necromancer." (*Deuteronomy* xviii, 10, 11.)

Roman treatment of magicians and practisers of the occult was equally drastic. By the Twelve Tables, a collection of the earliest known laws of the Roman people, it was ordained that a man should not remove his neighbour's crops to another field by incantations, nor conjure away his corn. For practising incantations or administering poisonous drugs [the penalty was death].[1] Various offences in respect of witchcraft were severely noticed by the *Sententiæ* of Julius Paulus.[2] Prophets were to

[1] *Roman Law*, by A. W. Hunter, 1903, pp. 20, 21.
[2] *Ibid.*, p. 1068.

be beaten and expelled from the city ; if they came back, they were to be imprisoned or deported. Persons consulting with reference to the life of the Emperor were punished with death. Those who took part in the exercise of magical and diabolical arts were to be crucified ; the magicians themselves, to be burnt alive. Even to keep books on the subject was a crime , the books were to be burned and the owners severely punished.

Under the *lex Cornelia de Sicariis*, those who offered sacrifices to injure their neighbours, even if no evil result followed, were punished.[1]

Punishment of witchcraft was likewise ordained by the Church of Rome, but at first the penalties were not severe. The *Liber Pœnitentialis* of Theodore, Archbishop of Canterbury (668–690), the most venerable compendium of ecclesiastical laws for England, is divided into fifty chapters, of which the twenty-seventh deals with idolatry and sacrilege and the penances for offending.[2] Of the twenty-six heads the following selection of punishments is made :—

1. Anyone who has sacrified to demons: 1 to 10 years' penance.

6. The consulter of those who divine by birds : 3 years' penance, one of which he shall fast on bread and water.

8. The layman or cleric practising as a magician or enchanter : expulsion from church.

9. Anyone who has destroyed another by evil spells : 7 years' penance, three of which he shall fast on bread and water.

10. The frequenter of soothsayers or makers of divinations : 5 years' penance, three of which he shall fast on bread and water.

13. The woman who uses divinations or devilish witchcrafts : 1 year's penance.

20. Astrologers, that is those who by the invocation of demons have turned a man's reason : 5 years' penance, one of which he shall fast on bread and water.

21. Anyone who has raised storms : 5 years' penance, one of which he shall fast on bread and water.

[1] *Roman Law*, p. 1068.
[2] *Ancient Laws and Institutes of England*, p. 292.

As early as the time of King Wihtraed (690–731), consulting
and rewarding evil spirits appears to have been a civil offence in
England, and duly noticed in a code of laws.

> If a husband, without his wife's knowledge, make an offering
> to devils [or idols], let him be liable in all his substance and
> his " heals-fang " [i.e. a fine].  If both make offering to devils,
> let them be liable in their " heals-fang ", and all their substance.
>     If a " theow " make an offering to devils or idols, let him
> make a " bōt " of vi shillings, or his hide.[1]

The eighth century Northumbrian digest, the Confessional of
Ecgberht, Archbishop of York (735–766), also provides that if a
woman exercised the magic art, witchcrafts. and evil-spells she
should fast, and if by her spells she should slay any person, her
fast should continue for 7 years.   Also if anyone sacrifice to
demons, he should fast 1 to 10 years.[2]

The punishment for witchcraft became much more severe by
the laws of Edward and Guthrum.

> If witches (*wiccan*) or diviners (*wigleras*), perjurers or
> " morth "[3]-workers, or foul, defiled, notorious adulteresses,
> be found anywhere within the land ; let them then be driven
> from the country and the people cleansed, or let them totally
> perish within the country, unless they desist, and the more
> deeply make " bot ".[4]

King Æthelstan (925–940) ordained respecting witchcrafts,
and " lyblacs ", and " morthdæds " :—" if any one should be
thereby killed, and he could not deny it, that he be liable in
his life.  But if he will deny it, and at the threefold ordeal
shall be guilty ; that he be cxx. days in prison : and after
that let his kindred take him out. and give to the king cxx.
shillings, and pay the ' wēr ' to his kindred, and enter into
' borh ' [i.e. surety] for him, that he evermore desist from the
like."[5]

---

[1] *Ancient Laws and Institutes*, p. 18, sections 12, 13.
[2] *Ibid.*, p. 355, sections 29, 32.
[3] Secret homicide.
[4] *Ancient Laws and Institutes*, p. 74, section 11.
[5] *Ibid.*, p. 86, section 6.

The ecclesiastical laws of King Edmund (940–946) also forbade the working of " lyblac ", i.e. *veneficium* or the compounding and administering of drugs and philtres.[1]

King Edgar (958–979) enjoined " that every priest zealously promote Christianity, and totally extinguish every heathenism ; and forbid well-worshipings, and necromancies, and divinations, and enchantments, and man-worshipings, and the vain practices which are carried on with various spells, and with ' frith-splots ' [i.e. sacred spots], and with elders, and also with various other trees, and with stones, and with many various delusions, with which men do much of what they should not ".[2]

The Witan of King Ethelred (975–979) followed the laws of Edward and Guthrum :—

> And if witches or soothsayers, magicians or whores, " morth "-workers or perjurors, be anywhere found in the country, let them diligently be driven out of this country, and this people be purified : or let them totally perish in the country, unless they desist, and the more deeply make " bot ".[3]

The secular digest of King Cnut (1014–1038) followed on similar lines, and also forbade the love of witchcraft or the promotion of " morth "-work in any wise ; or by " blot " [i.e. offering to idols], or by " fyrht " ; or the performing of anything pertaining to such illusions.[4] By another code, the Northumbrian priests also fined those who were found in any way to love witchcraft.[5]

William the Conqueror (1066–1087), in a summary of laws, recorded that perpetual banishment was the punishment for killing *veneno*, which may mean by " venom " or " poison ", but more probably the " magic art ", having regard to the wording of a later law.[6] Witchcraft was much mixed up with poisoning, and in one indictment of date 1567 shortly to be

---

[1] *Ancient Laws and Institutes*, p. 105, section 6.
[2] *Ibid.*, p. 396, section 16.   [3] *Ibid.*, p. 135, section 7.
[4] *Ibid.*, p. 162, sections 4, 5.   [5] *Ibid.*, p. 419, section 48.
[6] *Ibid.*, p. 207, section 36.

transcribed, " *incantatione et venefica* " occurs, but sometimes there was little difference between the meaning of the two words, *veneficium* as well as *incantatio* being used to express witchcraft. The latter was also used as well as *incantamentum* to express enchantment or charm.[1]

Henry I (1100–1135) ordained touching homicide or other witchcrafts (*maleficiis*) : " Si quis veneno, vel sortilegio, vel invultuacione, seu maleficio aliquo, faciat homicidium, sive illi paratum sit sive alii, nichil refert, quin factum mortiferum et nullo modo redimendum sit. Reddatur utique qui fuerit reus hujusmodi parentibus et amicis interfecti, ut eorum misericordiam aut judicium senciat, quibus ipse non pepercit."[2] Sortilegium is here evidently " sorcery ", and *invultuacio*, according to Thorpe,[3] a species of witchcraft, the perpetrators of which were called *vultivoli*, and are thus described by John of Salisbury : " Qui ad affectus hominum immutandos, in molliori materia, cera forte vel limo, eorum quos pervertere nituntur effigies exprimunt."[4] To this superstitution Virgil alludes—

" Limus ut hic durescit, et haec ut cera liquescit,
    Uno eodemque igni, sic nostro Daphnis amore."[5]

Public records which are extant, with few exceptions, do not commence until the thirteenth century. The earliest reference to any of the magical arts which can now be traced is a Norfolk plea of Hilary term, 10 John (1209) brought into the *Curia Regis* by Agnes, wife of Odo, the merchant, who appealed (i.e. accused) Galiena of sorcery (*sorceria*) who was, however, delivered by the ordeal of iron (*judicium ferri*).[6]

---

[1] See p. 22.
[2] Leges Regis Henrici Primi. lxxi. *Ibid.*, p. 251.
[3] *Ancient Laws*. Glossary.
[4] *Polycraticus*, lib. i, c. 12 (ed. Giles).
[5] At all times, this superstition was practised, both in England and Scotland. I have known the pricking of waxen images done in all seriousness, in Wales, in the twentieth century.
[6] Curia Regis Roll 51, m. 8*d*. (P.R.O.).

For several centuries very few prosecutions for witchcraft took place in any of the civil courts of justice. Magicians and witches were classed as heathen and heretics, and except for a few offences which were dealt with under the *lex non scripta* or common law, were punished by the ecclesiastical authorities.

Little on the subject of witchcraft is to be gathered from the early legal writers, Glanvill (Hen. II), Bracton (Hen. III), Britton (Edw. I), and " Fleta " (Edw. I). Britton compiled a compendium of the laws of England, apparently by the express desire of Edward I. which gives the position as it existed in the thirteenth century, from which the following notes are translated.

Let inquiry also be made of those who feloniously in time of peace have burnt others' corn or houses, and those who are attainted thereof shall be burnt. so that they may be punished in like manner as they have offended. The same punishment shall be passed upon sorcerers, sorceresses, renegades, sodomites, and heretics publicly convicted.[1]

If anyone be indicted by presentment of robbery, . . . or of enchantment, as those who send people to sleep,[2] . . our will is that such be apprehended ; or if they cannot be found they shall be demanded, and their lands and chattels be seized into our hands, and if, when they are tried, they cannot acquit themselves of the felony, whether at our suit or another's, let them be condemned to be hanged, or to lose an ear, or to the pillory, according to the greatness of their crime, and according as they have been habitual offenders or not.[3]

---

[1] *Britton*, by F. M. Nichols, i, 42. French.
[2] Mr. Nichols observes that " this seems to give some support to the conjecture, that the experiments of mesmerism and animal magnetism, which have created so much interest in our times, were not unknown in the thirteenth century. *Endormeurs de genz* are mentioned as offenders in the *Consuet. S. Genov.*, f. 34. MS. cited in Ducange, Gloss. s.v. *Dormitabilis.* It is possible that the effect may have been produced by drugs ". One such case occurred in the Northern Circuit in 1652 where a woman undertook to drive out an evil spirit from a man. She endeavoured to effect the cure by plying him with drink, and putting him into a trance (if it was not a drunken slumber). P.R.O., Assizes 44/5. Paper packet of informations.
[3] *Britton*, i, 60.

Among the articles which were to be inquired of at the Sheriff's tourns and at views of frankpledge is noticed " of sorcerers and sorceresses ; of apostates and heretics ".[1]

Mr. Nichols notes that as to the offences of sorcery, sodomy, etc., though the king's court was in general ancillary to the ecclesiastical tribunal, it sometimes acted independently.[2] The following note is from an early MS. copy of Britton's work :—

> Burners of corn and houses, wives guilty of treason against their husbands, sorcerers, sodomites, renegates, and misbelievers, run in a leash (*currunt en une leesse*) as to their sentence of being burned. But the inquirers of Holy Church shall make their inquests of sorcerers, sodomites, renegates, and misbelievers ; and if they find any such, they shall deliver him to the king's court to be put to death. Nevertheless, if the king by inquest find any persons guilty of such horrible sin, he may put them to death, as a good marshal of Christendom (*come bon Mareschal de la Chrestieneté*).[3]

It is perfectly clear, therefore, that in the thirteenth century a suspected witch might be arrested and examined by either secular or ecclesiastical authority and upon conviction in either case punished by death, the sentence being carried out by the civil executioners. It is probable that the greater number of cases came under the jurisdiction of the church.

Dr. Kurtz, the eminent German authority on church history, observes that in the thirteenth century witchcraft came more and more to occupy the attention of the ecclesiastical authorities. " Heresy and sorcery were regarded as correlates like two agencies resting on and serviceable to the demoniacal powers, and were treated in the same way as offences to be punished with torture and the stake."[4]

A fourteenth century set of rules, based upon the constitution of Pope Clement V prohibits—

---

[1] *Britton.* i, 179.    [2] *Ibid.*, i, 40.    [3] *Ibid.*, i, 40.
[4] *Church History*, by Professor Kurtz, edited by the Rev W R. Nicoll, M.A., vol. ii, p. 195.

Alle that knoweth eresye, coniuracyons, nygramancye, enchaunttementes, wychecraftes other any other false byleue aȝen the feyth of holycherche bote hy dystrwye hyt by here power & alle that beth y-ordeyned to enquere therof hyf they leue here swte & suffre hem.[1]

The activity of the ecclesiastics in the fourteenth century has been noticed by Chaucer in the Friar's Tale.[2]

> Hylom there was dwellynge in my countre
> An archedeken, a man of hye degre,
> That boldly dyd execution
> Or punisshyng of fornycation
> Of witchcrafte, and eke of baudrie
> Of defamacion and advoutrie.

Wycliffe, the fourteenth century religious reformer, in his *Apology*, quotes the Mosaic law and the prophet Isaiah, St Austin and the Decretum, in support of his doctrine that " charmis on no maner are leful " and that " it is supersticious to hang wordis at the nek ".[3] He shews by his authorities that witchcraft, charms, enchantments, and divinations in every form are unlawful, both by the law of God, and by the law of the Church.[4] He defines the various kinds of charmers, as enchauntors, phitoners, ariolers, ruspiceris, augurreris, dremridars, nigramauncers, geomanceris, idromauncers, ayeromauncers, piromauncers, and sortilegers.[5] In conclusion the Reformer observes that, since God hath " forfendid " these things, and " holi doctoris both and the kirk " it is vain and superstitious, and a kind of idolatry to use such things against so many " biddingis, autoritees, witnes and counseilis ".[6]

---

[1] Burney MS., 356, p. 100.      [2] Godfray, 1532.

[3] *An Apology for Lollard Doctrines*, attributed to Wicliffe. (J. H. Todd, Camden Society, p. 92.)

[4] *Ibid.*, p. 1.

[5] *Ibid.*, p. 95. Enchanters, phytoners (perhaps diviners who use plants), ariolers (soothsayers), aruspicers (those who foretell the future from inspection of the entrails of animals), geomancers (diviners by figures and lines), hydromancers (by water), aeromancers (by air), pyromancers (by fire), and sortilegers (diviners by lots).

[6] *Ibid.*, p. 96.

It seems probable that in general practice, in the fourteenth century, punishments were less severe than are indicated by the laws cited above. In many cases the Church called for little more than a penance from the convicted or confessed sorcerer.[1] A record of several civil prosecutions held in London in 1382 shews that an hour in the pillory was held to be sufficient punishment, the articles used in the enchantments being usually hung about the neck of the discredited magician.[2] The following rendering of a contemporary Latin record gives an illustration of the views held in a big city, touching the enormity of the practice of the black arts.

" On Tuesday, the third day of March, 13 Rich. II, [1390] . . . by assent of the Mayor and Aldermen, deliberation having been held thereon, because that such soothsaying, art magic, and falsities, are manifestly against the doctrine of holy writ, and a scandal and disgrace to the whole commonalty of the city aforesaid, and through such doings murders might easily ensue, and good and lawful men be undeservedly aggrieved and defamed in their name and reputation, etc., it was awarded that the said John [Berkyng] should on the same day be put upon the pillory on Cornhulle, there to stand for one hour of the day. And precept was given to the Sheriffs of London, to have the cause for the same punishment proclaimed. And afterwards, they were to take him back to prison, there to remain until the said Mayor and Aldermen should give other orders as to his release. Afterwards on Saturday the 19th day of March, the said John Berkyng was sworn that he would depart from the liberty of the City, and would never return to the same ; and that such soothsaying should not be practised by him for the future." [3]

In England, in the fifteenth century, upon the ecclesiastical court certifying a conviction of heresy, a writ *de hæretico comburendo* issued, and the heretic was handed over to the

---

[1] See, for instance, *Cistercian Statutes*, A.D. 1256-7, edited by Rev. J. T. Fowler, M.A., p. 56.
[2] *Memorials of London*, by H. T. Riley, pp. 462, 472.
[3] *Ibid.*, p. 519.

secular power for punishment.[1] Presumably witches were treated in the same manner.[2]

On 2 Jan., 1406, Henry V sent letters patent to the Bishop of Lincoln. drawing attention to the many *sortilegi* in his diocese. "who perpetrate daily many horrible and detestable crimes to the damage of the people and scandal of the church, and directing him to seek them out, examine them, and detain them until they repent, etc." [3]

That the ecclesiastical authorities continued to be satisfied with moderate punishment or purgation appears from the following extract from a book containing the judicial proceedings of the Official of the Prior and Convent of Durham.

> 1447/8, 16 Feb. Mariot Jacson. Personaliter. Imponitur sibi quod est incantatrix, et quod utitur arte incantatricis. Et habet ad purgandum se in prox. cum v$^{ta}$ manu, et restituta est pristinæ famæ.[4]

Another example of light punishment may be taken from Archbishop George Neville's register at York for the year 1467. William Byg *alias* Lech of Wombwell, was convicted of professing to find out thieves by a crystal stone. He had to do penance with a paper scroll about his head, inscribed *Ecce sortilegus*, and on his breast and back *Invocator spirituum* and *Sortilegus*.[5]

The practice of magic is referred to in the Act of 3 Hen. VIII, c. 11, prohibiting persons exercising as physicians or surgeons unless first examined and approved. "The science and conning of physyke and surgerie being exercised by a grete multitude of ignorant persons and that artificers as smyths wevers and women

---

[1] *Statutes of the Realm*, 2 Hen. IV, c. 15. A more severe statute was 2 Hen. V. c. 7. Proceedings on the writ *de hauretico comburendo* and all punishments by death in pursuance of any ecclesiastical censures, were taken away by Statute, 29 Chas. II, c. 9.

[2] The witch of Eye. burnt at Smithfield. 27 Oct.. 1440. is mentioned in a later extract.

[3] Patent Rolls, 7 Hen. IV.

[4] *Depositions*. Surtees Soc.. 1845, p. 29.

[5] f. 69 See *Cistercian Statutes*, edited by Rev. J. T. Fowler, p. 56.

boldely and custumably take upon theim grete cures and thyngys of great difficultie in the which they partely use socery, etc."[1]

Later in the same reign a serious attempt was made to stamp out the supposed growing evil by Act of Parliament. A savage statute passed, which, however, does not appear to have extensively operated,[2] and in the first year of the following reign (1547) was repealed.[3]

In 2 Edw. VI [1549] Archbishop Cranmer issued " articles to be inquired of, in visitations to be had within the Diocesse of Canterbury". Among the questions may be noticed, " Whether you know any that use charmes, sorcery, enchantments, witchcraft, southsaying, or any like craft invented by the Devil."[4]

Delusions fostered by the Church, became the beliefs of the people. If the Devil existed, it was a small step to the supposition that personal acquaintance was possible and that agreements and liaisons could be made. Protestants were as superstitious as the Catholics, and the Reformation is no way lessened the persecution arising from these ridiculous beliefs.

Common law procedure cannot have been very effective in suppressing the magicians, at any rate a month after the accession of Elizabeth (1558) the Queen's Attorney sent a letter to the Bishop of London with the examinations of some that practised conjuring in the City of London " wherin he is willed to procede by suche severe punischment against them that shalbe proved culpaple herein, according to thorder of thecclesyasticall lawes, as he shall thinke mete".[5] Neither can the episcopalian jurisdiction have been functioning very

---

[1] *Statutes of the Realm*, iii, p. 31.
[2] The only case I have noticed is that of John Morris of Brampston (Leic.), yeoman, who was pardoned for all felonies, being crimes of the magic arts, divinations, and witchcraft (*offensiones ariolarum*). (*Letters and Papers of the Reign of Henry VIII*, xvii, 567.) It must not, however, be forgotten that few indictments for the years 1542–7 are now in existence.
[3] See p. 14.
[4] *Articles of the Church of England* (A. Sparrow), 1661, p. 31.
[5] *Acts of the Privy Council*, vii 22.

satisfactorily because about the same time, according to Strype, the Bishop of Salisbury in a sermon before the Queen prayed that the laws touching witches and sorcerers might be put in due execution.[1]    Elizabeth "ministered unto her loving subjects" sundry "godly injunctions", among them being noticeable—

> "That no persons shall use charms, sorceries, enchantments, witchcraft, soothsaying, or any such like divillish device, nor shall resort at any time to the same counsel or help."[2]

Among the articles to be inquired at the visitation in 1559 was the following :—

> "Whether you know any that do use charmes, sorceries, inchantments, invocations, circles, witchcrafts, soothsaying, or any like crafts or imaginations invented by the Devil, and specially in the time of women's travel."[3]

At this time a statute was in draft form for it is recorded that on 27 Apr., 1559, a bill making enchantments, etc., felony was preferred in the Upper House.[4]    In 1560 witches were again being arraigned at the Assizes.

The growth of cases in the secular courts did not terminate the activity of the commissaries and ordinaries, although their charges seem to have been confined more to the employers and consultants of the witches than to the actual practisers of the magic arts.    Archdeacon Hale, who culled from the records of the diocese of London a collection of causes tried in the ecclesiastical courts in the sixteenth century, gives several examples which illustrate this view.[5]

[1] *Annals of the Reformation*, vol. i, pt i, p. 11.
[2] *Articles of the Church of England*, p. 73.
[3] *Ibid.*, p. 238.
[4] *Annals of the Reformation*, vol. i, pt. i, p. 87.    See note, p. 15.
[5] *Precedents and Proceedings*, by W. H. Hale, 1847.    Witches of the Home Circuit mentioned are Margery Skelton of Wakering, 1566, p. 148 ; Mrs. Mason of Borah, 1566, p. 147 ; Mother Persore of Navestock, 1576, p. 163 ; Father Parfoothe of Romford, 1585, p. 185 : Tailer, a wizard of Thaxted, 1599, p. 219 ; Mary Cutford of Raynham, p. 255, who wished herself to be a witch, p. 255. All of Essex.

The slight punishment enforced may be gathered from an entry in Hart (Durham) parish register which records under date 28 July, 1582, that Allison Lawe, " a notorious sorceror and enchanter was sentenced to do penance once in the market-place at Durham ' with a papir on her head ', once in Hart church, and once in Norton church." [1]

The Act of Elizabeth was repealed in 1 Jas. I by a statute of more severity, but one which was not so harsh as that of 1541. The various English statutes are as follow :—

### A.D. 1542.[2]  33 Hen. VIII, c. 8

The Bill ayēst conjuraċõns & wichecraftes and sorcery and enchantments.

Where dyvers and sundrie persones unlawfully have devised and practised Invocaċõns and conjuraċõns of Sprites, ꝓtendyng by such meanes to understande and get Knowlege for their owne lucre in what place treasure of golde and Silver shulde or mought be founde or had in the earthe or other secrete places, and also have used and occupied wichecraftes inchauntement' and sorceries to the distrucċõn of their neighbours persones and goodes, And for execuċõn of their saide falce devyses and practises have made or caused to be made dyvers Images and pictures of men women childrene Angelles or develles beastes or fowles, and also have made Crownes Septures Swordes rynges glasses and other thinges, and gyving faithe & credit to suche fantasticall practises have dygged up and pulled downe an infinite nombre of Crosses wᵗin this Realme, and taken upon them to declare and tell where thinges lost or stollen shulde be becōme ; whiche thinges cannot be used and excersised but to the great offence of Godes lawe, hurt and damage of the Kinges Subjectes, and losse of the sowles of suche Offenders,

---

[1] *Local Records,* by John Sykes, p. 79.
[2] The bill was read in the House of Lords for the first time on 28 Feb., 1542, and sent to the House of Commons on 6 Mar. (*Journal of the House of Lords,* i. p. 185), being returned on 21 Mar. (i, p. 189a).

to the greate dishonoᵣ of God, lnfamy and disquyetnes of the
Realme : For reformac͠on wherof be it enacted by the Kyng
oure Soveraigne Lorde wᵗ thassent of the Lordes sp͠uall and
temporall and the Comons in this p͡sent Parliament assembled
and by auctoritie of the same, that yf any persone or persones,
after the first daye of Maye next comyng, use devise practise or
exercise, or cause to be used devysed practised or exercised, any
Invocac͠ons or conjurac͠ons of Sprites wichecraftes enchauntmentes or sorceries, to thentent to get or fynde money or treasure,
or to waste consume or destroy any persone in his bodie membres
or goodes, or to pvoke any persone to unlawfull love, or for
any other unlawfull intente or purpose, or by occac͠on or coloᵣ of
suche thinges or any of them, or for dispite of Cryste, or for
lucre of money, dygge up or pull downe any Crosse or Crosses,
or by suche Invocac͠ons or conjurac͠ons of Sprites wichecraftes
enchauntementes or sorcerie or any of them take upon them
to tell or declare where goodes stollen or lost shall become,
That then all and ev⁹y suche Offence and Offences, frome the
saide first day of May next comyng, shalbe demyde accepted
and adjuged Felonye ; And that all and ev⁹y persone and
persones offendyng as is abovesaide their Councelloᵣs Abettoᵣs
and Procuroᵣs and ev⁹y of them from the saide first day of
Maye shallbe demyde accepted and adjuged a Felon and Felones ;
And thoffender and offenders contrarie to this Acte, being therof
lawfullie convicte before suche as shall have power and auctoritie
to here and determyn felonyes, shall have and suffre such paynes
of deathe losse and forfaytures of their lands teñtes goodes and
Catalles as in cases of felonie by the course of the C͠omon lawes
of this Realme, And also shall lose pⁱvilege of Clergie and
Sayntuarie.[1]

## A.D. 1547.  1 Edw. VI, c. 12

An Acte for the Repeale of certain Statutes, etc.

Sect. 3.    And be it further ordeyned and enacted by
thauctoritie aforesaide, that all offences made felonye by anny

[1] *Statutes of the Realm*, vol. iii, p. 837.

Acte or Act℮ of plament Statute or Statut℮ made sithens the xxiij<sup>th</sup> daie of Apryll in the first yere of the Reigne of the saide late King Henry theight, not beinge felonye before and allso all and everye the br<sup>a</sup>unches and articles mentioned or in anny wise declared in anny of the same Statut℮ concerninge the making of anny Offence or Offences to be felonye not being felonye before, and all paynes and forfaitures concerninge the same or anny of them, shall from hensfurthe be repealed and utterlye voyde and of none effecte.[1]

### A.D. 1563.[2]  5 Eliz., c. 16

An Act agaynst Conjuraĉõns Inchantments and Witchecraftes.

Where at this present, there ys no ordinarye ne condigne Punishement provided agaynst the Practisers of the wicked Offences of Conjuraĉõns and Invocaĉõns of evill Spirites, and of Sorceries Enchauntmentes Charmes and Witchecraftes, the w<sup>ch</sup> Offences by force of a Statute made in the xxxiij yere of the Reigne of the late King Henry the Eyghthe were made to bee Felonye, and so continued untill the sayd Statute was repealed by Thacte and Statute of Repeale made in the first yere of the Reigne of the late King Edwarde the vjth ; sythens the Repeale wherof many fantasticall and devilishe psons have devised and practised Invocaĉõns and Conjuraĉõns of evill and wicked Spirites, and have used and practised Wytchecraftes Enchantementes Charms and Sorceries, to the Destrucĉõon of the Psons and Goodes of their Neighebours and other Subjectes of this Realme, and for other lewde Intentes and Purposes contrarye to the Lawes of Almighty God, to the Perill of theyr

---

[1] *Statutes of the Realm*, vol. iv, pt. i, p. 19.

[2] The bill was read in the House of Commons for the first time on 15 Mar., 1559, engrossed on 4 Apr., and passed on 25 Apr., (*Journal of the House of Commons*, i, 57–60). In the following year I find the Act to have been in force (*see* Indictments 1 and 2). Nevertheless it was again read in the House of Commons on 8 Feb., 1563 (J.H.C., i, 65), and in the Upper House a week later (J.H.L., i, 591a), and passed in both Houses in Mar., 5 Eliz. (1563).

owne Soules, and to the great Infamye and Disquietnes of this
Realme : For REFORMAĈON wherof bee it enacted by the Quenes
Ma^tie w^th thassent of the Lordes S̃puall and Temporall and the
Cōmons in this p̃nte Pliament assembled, and by thaucthoritee
of the same, That yf any p̃son or p̃sons after the first daye of
June nexte cōming, use practise or exersise any Invocaĉons
or Conjuraĉons of evill and wicked Spirites, to or for any Intent
or Purpose ; or els if any p̃son or p̃sons after the said first daye
of June shall use practise or exercise any Witchecrafte Enchantment Charme or Sorcerie, wherby any p̃son shall happen to
bee killed or destroyed, that then aswell every suche offendo^r
or offendo^rs in Invocaĉons or Conjuraĉons as ys aforesayd,
their Concello^rs & Aidours, as also every suche offendo^r or
offendo^rs in Witchecrafte Enchantement Charme or Sorcerie
wherby the Deathe of anny p̃son dothe ensue, their Aidours
and Concello^rs, being of either of the said Offences laufully
convicted and attainted, shall suffer paynes of Deathe as a
Felon or Felons, and shall lose the Priviledg and Benefite of
Sanctuarie & Clergie : Saving to the Wief of such parsone
her Title of Dower, and also to the Heyre and Successour of
suche p̃son his or theyr Tytles of Inheritaunce Succession and
other Rightes, as thoughe no suche Attayndour of the Auncestour
or Predecessour had been hadd or made.

And further bee yt enacted by thaucthoritee aforesayd,
That if any p̃son or p̃sons, after the saide first daye of June
nexte cōmyng, shall use practise or exercyse any Wytchecrafte
Enchauntement Charme or Sorcerie, wherby any p̃on shall
happen to bee wasted consumed or lamed in his or her Bodye or
Member, or wherby any Goodes or Cattelles of any p̃son shalbee
destroyed wasted or impayred, then every suche offendour
or Offendours their Councelloures and Aydoures, being therof
laufully convicted, shall for his or their first Offence or Offences,
suffer Imprisonment by the Space of one whole Yere, w^thout
Bayle or Mayneprise, and once in every Quarter of the said
Yere, shall in some Market Towne, upon the Market Daye or

at such tyme as any Fayer shalbee kepte there, stande openly upon the Pillorie by the Space of Syxe Houres, and there shall openly confesse his or her Erroure and Offence ; and for the Seconde offence, being as ys aforesayd laufully convicted or attaynted, shall suffer Deathe as a Felon, and shall lose the Privilege of Clergie and Sanctuarye : Saving to the Wief [*as above*].

Provided alwaies, That yf the Offendour, in any of the Cases aforesayd for whiche the paynes of Deathe shall ensue, shall happen to bee a Peere of this Realme, then his Triall thereyn to be hadd by hys Peeres, as yt ys used in cases of Felonye or Treason and not otherwyse.

And further to thintent that all maner of practise use or exercise of Witchecrafte Enchantement Charme or Sorcerye shoulde bee from hensforthe utterly avoyded abolished and taken awaye ; Bee it enacted by thaucthoritee of this p̄nte Pliament, That yf any p̄son or p̄sons shall from and after the sayd first daye of June nexte cōming, take upon him or them, by Witchecrafte Enchantement Charme or Sorcerie, to tell or declare in what Place any Treasure of Golde or Sylver shoulde or might bee founde or had in the Earthe or other secret Places, or where Goodes or Thinges lost or stollen should bee founde or becume, or shall use or practise anye Sorcerye Enchantement Charme or Witchcrafte, to thintent to provoke any p̄son to unlaufull love, or to hurte or destroye any p̄son in his or her Body, Member or Goodes ; that then every suche p̄son or p̄sons so offending, and being therof laufully convicted, shall for the said offence suffer Imprysonement by the space of One whole yere w^{th}out Bayle or Mayneprise, and once in every Quarter of the said yere shall in some Market Towne, upon the Marcket day or at suche tyme as any Fayer shall bee kept there, stande openly upon the Pillorie by the space of Sixe Houres, and there shall openly confesse his or her Error and Offence ; And yf anye p̄son or p̄sons, beyng once convicted of the same Offences as ys aforesayd, doo eftesones p̄petrate and cōmitt the lyke

c

Offence, that then every suche Offendour beyng thereof the seconde tyme convicted as ys aforesaid, shall forfaitee unto the Quenes Majestie her heires and successoures, all his Goodes and Cattelles and suffer Imprysonement during Lyef.[1]

## A.D. 1580-1.   23 Eliz., c. 2

An Acte against sedicious Wordes and Rumors uttered againste the Queenes moste excellent Majestie.

[Clause 5] And for that divers persons wickedlye disposed, and forgetting their Duetie and Allegiaunce, have of late not onlye wisshed her Ma^ties Deathe, but also by dyvers meanes practised and sought to knowe howe longe her Highenes should lyve, and who should raigne after her Decease, and what Chaunges and Alteracōnes shoulde therebye happen ; To the entent that suche Mischeifes and Inconveniences as maye thereby growe in the Cōmon Weale, to the greate Disturbance of the same, maye be cut of and p⁹vented ; Be yt also enacted by the aucthoritie aforesaid, That yf any person or psons, of what Estate Condicōn or Degree soever he or they bee, at any tyme, after the ende of the said fortie dayes, and during the lief of our sayde Soveraigne Ladye the Queenes Ma^tie that nowe ys, eyther within her Highenesses Dominions or without, shall by setting or erecting of any Figure or Figures, or by casting of Nativities, or by calculacōn, or by any Prophecieng Witchcrafte Cunjuracōns or other lyke unlawfull Meanes whatsoev⁹, seeke to knowe, and shall set forth by expresse Wordes Deedes or Writinges, howe longe her Ma^tie shall lyve or contynue, or who shall raigne as King or Queene of this Realme of England after her Highenesse Decease, or els shall advisedlye and with a maliciouse intent againste her Highenes, utter any manner of directe Pphecies to any suche Intent or Purpose, or shall malitiouslye by any Wordes Writing or Printing wishe will or desier the Deathe or Deprivacōn of our Soveraigne Ladye the Queenes Ma^tie (that nowe ys,) or any Thing directlye to the same Effecte, That

---

[1] *Statutes of the Realm*, vol. iv, pt. i, p. 446.

then everye suche offence shalbe Felonye, and everye Offendour
and Offendours therein, and also all his or their Aydours Procurers
and Abettors in or to the said Offences, shalbe judged as Felons,
and shall suffer paynes of Deathe and [Forfeyte] as in Case of
Felonye ys used, without any Benefite of Cleargie or Sanctuarye.[1]

The general pardon of 23 Eliz., c. 16, excepted *inter alia* " all
offences of Invocations Conjurations Witchcrafts Sorceries
Inchauntments and Charmes, and all offences of procuring
abetting or comforting of the same, and all persons now attainted
or convicted of any of the said offences." [2]

## A.D. 1604.[3] 1 Jas. I, c. 12

An Acte against Conjuration Witchcrafte and dealinge with
evill and wicked Spirits.

Be it enacted by the King our Sov⁹aigne Lorde the Lordes
Spirituall and Temporall and the Comons in this p̃sent Parliament
assembled, and by the authoritie of the same, That the Statute
made in the fifte yeere of the Raigne of our late Sov⁹aigne Ladie
of moste famous and happie memorie Queene Elizabeth, intituled
An Acte againste Conjurations Inchantmentℓ and Witchcraftℓ,
be from the Feaste of St Michaell the Archangell nexte cōminge,
for and concerninge all Offences to be cōmitted after the same
Feaste, utterlie repealed.

And for the better restrayninge the saide Offenses, and more
severe punishinge the same, be it further enacted by the authoritie
aforesaide, That if any p̃son or persons, after the saide Feaste

[1] *Statutes of the Realm*, vol. iv, pt. i, p. 659.
[2] *Ibid.*, p. 700.
[3] The bill was read in the House of Lords for the first time on
27 Mar., 1604, and committed on 29 Mar. (*Journal of the House of
Lords*, ii, 267b, 269a). The bill having been considered and found
to be imperfect, a new bill was brought in on 2 Apr. (J.H.L., ii,
271a). On 7 May amendments were read and the bill appointed
to the engrossed (J.H.L., ii, 239a). On 11 May it was read in the
House of Commons for the first time (J.H.C., i, 207, 970). A month
later the bill passed and was returned to the Lords (J.H.L., ii,
316b).

of Saint Michaell the Archangell next cōminge, shall use practise or exercise any Invocation or Conjuration of any evill and wicked Spirit, or shall consult covenant with entertaine employ feede or rewarde any evill and wicked Spirit to or for any intent or purpose ; or take up any dead man woman or child out of his her or theire grave, or any other place where the dead bodie resteth, or the skin bone or any other parte of any dead person, to be imployed or used in any manner of Witchcrafte Sorcerie, Charme or Inchantment ; or shall use practise or exercise any Witchcrafte Inchantment Charme or Sorcerie, wherebie any pson shalbe killed destroyed wasted consumed pined or lamed in his or her bodie, or any parte thereof ; that then everie such offendor or offendors, theire Ayders Abettors and Counsellors, being of any the saide Offences dulie and lawfullie convicted and attainted, shall suffer pains of deathe as a Felon or Felons, and shall loose the priviledge and benefit of Cleargie and Sanctuarie.

And further, to the intent that all manner of practise use or exercise of Witchcrafte Inchantment Charme or Sorcerie should be from henceforth utterlie avoyded abolished and taken away, Be it enacted by the authoritie of this p᷎sent Parliament, That if any pson or psons shall from and after the saide Feaste of Saint Michaell the Archangell next cōminge, take upon him or them by Witchcrafte Inchantment Charme or Sorcerie to tell or declare in what place any treasure of Golde or Silver should or might be founde or had in the earth or other secret places, or where Goode or Thinge loste or stollen should be founde or become ; and to the intent to pvoke any person to unlawfull love, or wherebie any Cattell or Goods of any pson shall be destroyed wasted or impaired, or to hurte or destroy any pson in his or her bodie, although the same be not effected and done ; that then all and everie such pson & psons so offendinge, and beinge thereof lawfullie convicted, shall for the said Offence suffer Imprisonment by the space of one whole yeere, without baile or maineprise, and once in everie quarter of the said yere, shall in some Markett Towne, upon the Markett Day, or at such tyme as any Faire shalbe kepte there, stande openlie upon the Pillorie by the space of sixe houres, and there shall openlie confesse his or her error and offence ; And if any pson or psons beinge once convicted of the same offences as is aforesaide, doe eftsones ppetrate and cōmit the like offence, that then everie such Offender, beinge of any the saide offences the second tyme lawfullie and duelie convicted and attainted as is aforesaide, shall suffer paines of death as a Felon or Felons, and shall loose the benefitt and priviledge of Clergie and Sanctuarie : Savinge to the wife of such person as shall offend in any thinge contrarie to this Acte, her title of dower ; and also to the heire and successour of everie such person his or theire titles of Inheritance Succession and other Rights, as though no such Attaindor of the Ancestor or Predecessor had been made : Provided alwaies, That if the offendor in any the Cases aforesaide shall happen to be a Peere of this Realme, then his Triall therein to be had by his Peeres, as it is used in cases of Felonie or Treason and not otherwise.[1]

Like that of 23 Elizabeth the general pardons of 21 Jas. I (c. 35) and 12 Chas. II (c. 11) excepted all offences of invocations, conjurations, witchcrafts, etc.[2]

### Definition of Terms

It is evident from the foregoing recital of the various laws, that the prohibited science or art of black magic was described by a number of distinct words or phrases such as, conjuring of spirits, divination, necromancy, soothsaying, compounding of philtres, entertainment of spirits, enchantment, invocation, sorcery, witchcraft, etc. All of these practices were largely mixed up with treason, heresy, poisoning, coining, and other crimes. It would serve no practical purpose and would, in fact, be difficult, if not impossible, to define each of these terms

[1] *Statutes of the Realm*, vol. iv, pt. ii, p. 1028.
[2] *Ibid.*, vol. iv, pt. ii, p. 1271 ; vol. v, p. 228.

in a manner which could be satisfactorily applied in every case. In all the earlier codes the originals were in Anglo-Saxon, Latin, or French, and the choice of an English equivalent for any particular word is left to the discretion of the translator. For instance : A.S. *wicce-cræft* can be rendered " witchcraft " or " sorcery ", which may be the same thing, and Lat. *veneficium*, may be Englished, " sorcery " or " poisoning ", which are not verbal equivalents. The difficulty of rendering English satisfactorily into Latin was recognized in legal circles and both languages were often used together, an illustration of which is afforded by the following extract from a record of the year 1702. Sarah Morduck, an honest and pious woman and not " sagam (Anglice a witch) " nor using " magiam (Anglice witchcraft) incantamentum (Anglice inchantment) incantamentum (Anglice charm) fascinationem (Anglice sorcery) ".[1] *Fascinatio* was also used to express " witchcraft " as a comparison of indictments Nos. 679 and 727 shews,[2] in the former of which *præcantatio* may be noticed as an equivalent of " charm ".

The following definitions, culled from *Symbolæographie*,[3] a legal treatise written by William West of the Inner Temple in 1594, give an insight into the distinctions which were made between the various classes of the black arts in the time of Elizabeth :—

*Magicke.*—Magitions be those which by uttering of certein supstious words conceiued, aduenture to attempt things aboue the course of nature, by bringing forth dead mens ghosts, in showing of things either secret or in places farre off, and in showing them in any shape or likenesse. These wicked persons by othe or writing written with their owne blood, hauing betaken themselues to the diuill, haue forsaken God, and broken their couenant made in baptisme, and detest the benefits thereof, and worship the deuil onely, And setling their whole hope in

[1] *A Complete Collection of State Trials*, by T. B. Howell, xiv, 641.
[2] See p. 91 post.
[3] Sections 168–173.

him, do execute his commandements, and being dead, commend both their bodies and soules vnto him.

*Southsaying Wizards.*—Of this kinde of Magitians be all those which ensue, as Southsayers or Wizards which diuine and foretell things to come and raise vp euill spirits by certein supersticious and conceiued formes of words. And vnto such questions as be demanded of them, do aunswere by voice, or else set before their eies in glasses, christall stones, or rings, the pictures or images of things sought for.

*Diuination.*—The professors of thart of diuination which be puffed vp with prophesing spirits. And can manifest who hath stollen thinges, and tell where things lost or stollen be.

*Iuggling.*—Iudglers and sleightie Curers of diseases which for the curing of all sicknesses and sores of man and beast, vse eyther certeine superstitious words or writinges called charmes or spelles hanged about the necke or some other part of the body.

*Inchanting and Charming.*—Inchaunters or charmers through certeine words pronounced and characters or images, herbs, or other things applyed, thinke they can do what they list, the deuil so deceiueth them, or in verie deede dispatcheth those thinges which the Inchantors would haue done, from these somewhat differ witches or hagges, and Augurers or south-sayers by birdes, diuinors, by seeing thintrals of beastes sacrificed.

*Witcherie.*—A Witch or hagg is she which being eluded by a league made with the deuil through his perswasion, inspiration and iudgling, thinketh she can designe what maner of euil things soeuer, either by thought or imprication, as to shake the aire with lightnings and thunder, to cause hail and tempests, to remoue grene corne or trees to an other place, to be caryed of her familiar which hath taken vpon him the deceiptful shape of a goate, swine, or calfe &c. into some mountaine farre distant, in a wonderfull short space of time, And sometimes to flie vpon a staffe or forke, or some other instrument. And to spend all the night after with her sweete hart, in playing, sporting, bankqueting, dauncing, daliance, and diuerse other deuelish lustes, and lewd desports, and to shew a thousand such monsterous mockeries.

On this point it will be. sufficient for practical purposes to say that, from the drafting of the first Act of Parliament relating to witchcraft in 1533, the various indictable offences were definitely arranged in two classes of different degree.

    1.   Invocations, conjurations of evil spirits.

    2.   Witchcrafts, enchantments, sorceries, charms.

### Punishments for Invocation and Witchcraft

By all the three Acts of Parliament the penalty for invoking (Class 1) was death, the punishments for witchcraft (Class 2), for convenience of reference, will be given in tabular form on the opposite page.

The Act of Hen. VIII considered as offences of equal magnitude the use of either art with the *intent* of killing and harming persons, destroying and wasting goods, provoking unlawful love, discovering treasure or things lost or stolen. and punished all found guilty by death. In the time of Elizabeth and James the invocation or conjuration of evil spirits was considered to be the more heinous magic, and the practisers of such for any intent or purpose, upon conviction, were sent to the gallows.

With regard to the lesser crime of practising witchcraft, enchantments, charms, and sorcery, the severity of the Act of Hen. VIII was modified by that of 5 Eliz. Anyone using such means with the intent of hurting a person in his body, destroying goods, provoking unlawful love or discovering treasure or lost and stolen goods was liable to one year's imprisonment with four periods of six hours' duration in the pillory, etc. A second conviction of exercising the forbidden arts, with the intent of harming a person or destroying goods. was punishable by death, and of provoking unlawful love and discovering treasure, etc., by imprisonment for life.

# TABLE OF PUNISHMENTS FOR THE FELONIES OF USING (DEVISING), PRACTISING, OR EXERCISING¹ WITCHCRAFT, ENCHANTMENTS, CHARMS, OR SORCERIES.

| Act. | To kill or destroy persons. | To waste, consume or lame persons in body or members or to waste, destroy. or impair goods. | To the intent to waste, consume, or destroy any person in his body and members, or goods | To the intent to get, find, or tell of money, treasure, or goods lost or stolen, etc. | To the intent to provoke any person to unlawful love or for any other unlawful intent or purpose. | REPEAL. |
|---|---|---|---|---|---|---|
| 33 Hen. VIII, c. 8, 1541–1547. *Statutes of the Realm*, vol. iii, p. 837. | Death. Forfeiture of lands, etc., and goods, etc. Loss of clergy and sanctuary. | Death. Forfeiture of lands, etc., and goods, etc. Loss of clergy and sanctuary | Death. Forfeiture of lands, etc., and goods, etc., Loss of clergy and sanctuary. | Death. Forfeiture of lands, etc., and goods, etc. Loss of clergy and sanctuary. | Death. Forfeiture of lands, etc., and goods. etc. Loss of clergy and sanctuary. | 1 Edw. VI, c 12. |
| 5 Eliz., c. 16, 1562–1603. *Statutes of the Realm*, vol. iv, pt. 1, p. 446. | Death. Loss of clergy and sanctuary. Saving dower, inheritance, etc. | 1st Offence :— Imprisonment 1 year Pillory 4 times and confession of error. 2nd Offence :— Death. Loss of clergy and sanctuary. Saving dower and inheritance. | 1st Offence :— Imprisonment 1 year. Pillory 4 times and confession of error. 2nd offence :— Imprisonment for life. Forfeiture of goods. | 1st Offence :— Imprisonment 1 year. Pillory 4 times, and confession of error. 2nd Offence :— Imprisonment for life. Forfeiture of goods. | 1st Offence :— Imprisonment 1 year Pillory 4 times and confession of error. 2nd Offence :— Imprisonment for life. Forfeiture of goods. | 1 Jas I, c. 12. |
| 1 Jas. I, c. 12, 1603–1736. *Statutes of the Realm*, vol iv, pt 2, p 1029. | Death. Loss of clergy and sanctuary. | Death. Loss of clergy and sanctuary. | 1st Offence :— Imprisonment 1 year. Pillory 4 times, and confession of error. 2nd Offence :— Death. Loss of clergy and sanctuary. Saving dower and inheritance. | 1st Offence .— Imprisonment 1 year Pillory 4 times and confession of error. 2nd Offence :— Death. Loss of clergy and sanctuary. Saving dower and inheritance. | 1st Offence .— Imprisonment 1 year Pillory 4 times, and confession of error. 2nd Offence .— Death. Loss of clergy and sanctuary. Saving dower and inheritance. | 9 Geo. II, Statute Law Revision Act, 1863. |

In addition to the penalties tabulated, the Act of Hen. VIII makes punishable by death the pulling down of any cross for the furtherance of any unlawful purpose, and the Act of James I made it a capital felony to exhume dead bodies, etc., for the purpose of witchcraft. Counsellors, abettors, and procurers are considered equally culpable with the principals by the above statutes.

¹ The Act of Hen. VIII adds "or *cause* to be used, devised, practised, or exercised".

By the Act of James I the consulting. covenanting with, entertaining, employing, feeding, or rewarding any evil spirit was added to class number one and punished equally with invocation.

The Act of James I was also designed to punish more severely the users of witchcraft, etc., and anyone found guilty of harming a person in his body again suffered death, which penalty also superseded the sentences of imprisonment for life given in the case of second convictions of provoking unlawful love and discovering treasure.

In Scotland an Act passed in 1563 forbidding the use of " witchcraftis. sorsarie and necromancie . . . vnder the pane of deid alsweill to be execute aganis the vsar abusar as the seikar of the response or consultation ".[1]   Notwithstanding the holocaust around them, in 1641 the Commissionaries of the Kirk petitioned Parliament *inter alia* that the Acts " anent charmers, sorcerers & consulters with witches be renewed ".[2]   In 1649 the above-mentioned Act of Queen Mary was ratified, special notice being taken of persons who consult with devils.[3]

With regard to Ireland. Richard Cox states that in 1578 witches were condemned by the law of nature because there were no positive laws against witchcraft in those days.[4]   In 1586 the application of the English statute was extended to Ireland.[5]

## Condition of Gaols

In England the death sentence for a convicted witch or invoker was " to be hanged by the neck until he or she be dead ".   More rarely the punishment was one year's imprisonment with four periods of six hours' duration each in the pillory, etc.   This

---

[1] Mary, 9. *Acts of the Parliaments of Scotland*, ii, 539.
[2] *Ibid.*. v. 646a.
[3] Chas I, 44. *Ibid.*, vi, pt. ii, 152.
[4] *History of Ireland*, 1689, i, 354.
[5] *Irish Witchcraft and Demonology*. by St. John D. Seymour, p. 61.

punishment sometimes meant death in a more lingering form. Confinement in sixteenth and seventeenth century goals often had a fatal termination from cold, disease, starvation, and cruelty.[1] Occasionally considerable numbers died during their term of incarceration, for instance, in a Guildford Castle gaol delivery roll for 1598, no less than twenty deaths are entered, being twelve *per centum* of the prisoners calendared.[2] The condition of the gaols and the suffering of the prisoners may be gathered from the following presentment.

The Presentments of the Inquest for the boddy of the County att the Assizes holden att Brentwoode the xvijth daye of March, 1630.

Imprimis we doe p̃sent that the Castell of Colchester in the Borrough of Colchester hath ben tyme out of memory of man reputed & knowne to be the Comon Goale for this County but that the said Castell is nowe soe ruinated & in soe great decay that it is not sufficientlie strong & safe to rettine the prisoners there comitted w'hout continuall danger of escapes nor fitt to keepe the prisoners free from winde and weather whereby their healthes are contynually much impaired.

Next we are crediblie informed that the miseries of the poore prisoners are soe great & lamentable ptlie by reason of the crueltie of the Gaoler & ptlie by reason of the extreame wantẽ they suffer that many of them are famished. Whereas if the

---

[1] In 1545 a monk appealing for the prisoners said " their lodging is too bad for hoggys, and as for their meat it is euil enough for doggys ". (*Complaint of Boderwyck Mors*, by Henry Brinklow. E.E.T. Society, 1874.)

[2] Stow, writing in 1598, stated that in the six years preceding 1579 nearly 100 prisoners died through contagion in the King's Bench prison. (*Survey*, ii, 18.) On several occasions at Oxford, Exeter, Taunton, and elsewhere, nearly every court official from the judges downwards died of the gaol distemper. Nearly 200 years later, when the prison reformer John Howard commenced his great work, his " attention was principally fixed by the gaol fever, and the small pox, which he saw prevailing to the destruction of multitudes, not only of felons in their dungeons, but of debtors also ". (*The State of the Prisons*, 1780, p. 2.)

Gaole might be placed about the middle of the Countie and the meanes thereunto belonging & due from the right ho^ble the Lo : Stanhoppe (as we are informed) conferred uppon it & an honest & fitt Gaoler chosen wee conceive then the Countrey would be verry forward & willing to helpe pfect the worke.[1]

## Further Punishments

Women as well as men arraigned for felony and standing mute and refusing to plead directly to the fact or to put themselves on trial by the country suffered death by the *peine forte et dure*. Many criminals elected to undergo this horrible punishment to prevent attainder, corruption of blood, and forfeiture of lands. As silence would have saved nothing, no case of a person accused of witchcraft being pressed to death was noticed in the records of the Home Circuit, but Dr. Cotton Mather, writing in 1693, mentions the case of Giles Cory of Salem, U.S.A., who suffered the " hard pain ".[2] Seventeen years previously he had been charged with murder, but had bought himself off.[3] In 1692 he was under suspicion of sundry acts of witchcraft which at his examination he denied, but was committed to gaol.[4] Presumably at his trial he stood mute. The court records for 1692 have been lost, and it is not known where Giles Cory met his horrible end.[5] The following account of the sentence, in the case of a man indicted for murder and robbery, is taken from a gaol delivery file for the Kent Summer Assizes held at Maidstone, 24 July, 1654.

" hee stands mute & rufuseth to plead therefore hee must bee sent to the prison from whence hee came & put into a meane house stopped from light & there must bee layed vppon the bare ground w^thout any litter straw or other Covering & w^thout any garment about him saving something to cover

[1] Assizes, 35/73.
[2] *The Wonders of the Invisible World.* 1693, p. 147.
[3] *Ibid.*, p. 148.
[4] *Salem Witchcraft*, by Robert Calef, 1861, p. 371.
[5] *Ibid.*, p. 449.

his privy members & that hee must lye vppon his backe & his head must bee Covered & his feete bare & that one of his armes shal bee drawne w$^{th}$ a Cord to one side of the house & the other arme to the other side & that his leggs shalbee vsed in the same manner & that vppon his body must be layed soe much yron & stone as hee can beare & more & that the first day after hee must have three morsells of barley bread w$^{th}$out any drinke. And the second day hee must drinke soe much as hee can three tymes of the water w$^{th}$ is next the prison dore saving running water w$^{th}$out any bread & this must bee his dyett vntill hee dye."[1]

Terrible as the hard and strong pain was, this punishment was not so revolting as others in force at the time.

In Scotland where the persecution was much more severe, the convicted witch was burnt, occasionally after being strangled, but more often alive. The sentence was entered in the following form :—

> The judge acceptis the determinatioun of the assyse and ordanis the panell to be tane be the lockman, hir hands bund, and be caried to the head of the lon.[2] the place of executioun, and thair to be knet[3] to ain staik, wiried[4] to the death and brunt in asses, quhilk . . ., dempster, gave for dome.[5]

Occasionally a modified sentence was given, the panel being ordered to be " brunt on the cheik ".

The scenes at the burnings were sometimes terrible, and on one occasion at Brechin the horrors so moved the Earl of Mar that he declared to the Privy Council. 1 Dec., 1608. that the women " albeit thay perseveirit constant in thair denyell to the end, yit thay wer brunt quick efter sic ane crewell maner that sum of thame deit in dispair, renunceand and blasphemeand, and utheris, half brunt, brak out of the fyre and wes cast in quick in it agane quhill thay wer brunt to the deid ".[6]

---

[1] Assizes 35/95, Kent file. The usual entry was. " He refuseth to plead and is to be pressed to death ", or " premend ad mortem ".
[2] A lane or common.      [3] Knotted.     [4] Strangled.
[5] *The Register of the Privy Council of Scotland*, 1624, p. 360.
[6] *Ibid.*, vol. xiv, p. 605.

It is a popular supposition that women convicted of the crime of witchcraft in England were also burnt to death. Although many witches were undoubtedly burnt and possibly some boiled also, it will be found that in such cases it was because their crime was classed as heresy, poisoning, or treason.[1] By Act of 22 Hen. VIII, c. 9, poisoning was made treason and punishable by " deth by boylynge ".[2] A wife murdering her husband, or servant her master or mistress by witchcraft or otherwise, was held to have committed petty treason, and so was liable to be burnt to death.[3] No case of a witch being sent to the stake or to the pot has been noticed in the records of the Home Circuit.[4]

## Military Action

There is little evidence pointing to action by the military authorities in the suppression of witchcraft, but if we are to believe a pamphleteer of 1643, at least one brutal murder was committed by order of army officers. Soldiers of the Earl of Essex's army having taken a woman at Newbury, whom they alleged had been walking on the water by means of a plank, she was brought to the Commanders who promptly told off a couple of soldiers to shoot her. The lady, however, we are told, caught their bullets in her hand and chewed them, whereupon one set his carbine close to her breast, but upon discharge the bullet rebounded like a ball, and narrowly missed his face. " This so enraged the gentleman, that one drew out his sword & manfully run at her with all the force his strength had power to make, but it prevailed no more than did the shot, the woman still though speechless, yet in a most contemptible way of scorn, still laughing at them, which did the more exhaust their furie against

---

[1] P. Browne (*History of Norwich*, p. 38), mentions two women burnt about 1648, and Mother Lakeland was burnt at Ipswich, 9 Sept., 1645, for bewitching her husband to death.

[2] *Statutes of the Realm*, vol. iii, p. 326.

[3] *History of Criminal Law*, i, 477.

[4] In Scottish accounts a certain notorious wizard William, Lord Soulis, is said to have been boiled to death by his enemies. (Summers, *Geography*, p. 205.)

her life, yet one amongst the rest had heard that piercing or drawing blood from forth the veins that cross the temples of the head, it would prevail against the strongest sorcery, and quell the force of witchcraft. which was allowed for trial ; the woman hearing this, knew then that the Devil had left her and her power was gone, wherefore she began aloud to cry, and roar, tearing her hair, and making piteous moan, which in these words expressed were · And is it come to passe, that I must die indeed ? why then his Excellency the Earl of Essex shall be fortunate and win the field, after which no more words could be got from her, wherewith they immediately discharged a pistol underneath her ear, at which she straight sunk down and died. leaving her legacy of a detested carcass to the wormes, her soul we ought not to judge of, though the evils of her wicked life and death can scape no censure." [1]

## Ratio of Death Sentences to Arraignments

It will be shewn from the information now gathered together, and from the statistics which have been prepared, that in the Home Circuit the chance of a witch suffering the death penalty, when arraigned before the regular justices, was small, 81 persons out of every 100 escaping the rope. The most dangerous period was the decade 1598–1607. being the last six years of the reign of Elizabeth and the first four years of James I, "the demonologist," when 41 *per centum* of persons indicted were sent to the gallows. The greatest slaughter occurred in the summer of 1645, when the victims of the campaign of Hopkins, the witch-finder, were brought before Justices of the Peace headed by the Earl of Warwick, 19 out of 29 women receiving the death sentence. There is reason to suppose that the death rate was equally as high at Norfolk assizes. but probably less in other parts of the country.

Although all the judges believed in the existence of witch-

[1] *A most Certain, Strange, and true discovery of a Witch*, pr. by George Hammond, 1643.

craft they do not seem to have been so easily gulled as was
Justice Winch, who is said to have condemned nine women to
death at Leicester assizes on the evidence of one boy ! [1]  Nevertheless, sentences of hanging were occasionally passed in what
appear to be very mild cases.  For instance, at the Kent Lent
assizes in 1649, before Roger Hill, serjeant-at-law, and Thomas
Lee, J.P., Mary Allen, the elder, and Mary Allen, the younger
(Nos. 727–8), possibly mother and daughter, were both condemned to death for feeding and employing an evil spirit in the
likeness of a black dog " with intent and purpose that " they
" by the aid and help of the said evil and wicked spirit certain
evil and devilish arts, etc., might use, practice, and exercise,"
etc.  Yet there was nothing irregular in the sentence (see 629,
630, etc.).

### Reprieves

English records show that reprieves and respites, both
temporary and absolute, were granted to convicted witches upon
various considerations, both at the judge's discretion and
*ex necessitate legis*.  Common annotations found upon the
indictments and gaol books are : reꝑ ꝑ preg, reꝑ ꝑ anno,
reꝑ quousq, reꝑ sine tri, reꝑ sine judic, reꝑ post judm,
reꝑ ante judm, reꝑ in ꝑsona, repri vsq ad px, repri ad gaol,
repr' in gaol sine ball, repri ꝑ ball, etc   Rep', repr', or repri'
may be extended to *reprivatur* or *reprisonetur*.[2]  To be reprieved
or reprisoned meant that the accused returned to prison until he
should be delivered by due course of law.  In indictment No. 104
the verb *retornari* seems to be used.  " Remanere in gaolem "
was noticed in gaol books of the Oxford and Northern Circuits.
" Delivery by due course of law " might cover ultimate hanging
as in the case of Judith Sawkins (No. 730), or indefinite imprisonment as in the case of five women convicted at the Essex Summer

<hr/>

[1] Leicester Records, MSS   See *Biog. Dict. of the Judges of
England*, by E. Foss.

[2] Mr. J. C. Jeaffreson (*Middlesex County Records.* ii. 243) has
some notes on the word " reprieve ".

Assizes, 1645, who were still in gaol nearly three years later (Nos. 613, 618, 624, 637, and 647). In some cases, however, such as that of Mary Hurst (No. 712) the term of incarceration could not legally have been more than one year. In these days discharge depended largely upon the gaoler receiving financial satisfaction.

A woman sentenced to death for witchcraft or other felony might, *after* pronouncement of sentence, plead pregnancy, whereupon the Clerk of the Assize ordered the Sheriff to return an inquest of twelve women. If this jury of matrons found the prisoner quick with child of a quick child, her execution was stayed, and it was usually ordered that " she remain in goal until delivered of the child, and within one month thereafter he hanged by her neck until she be dead ". Judges, however, differed in their practice and sometimes the temporary respite thus granted was till the next sessions, or for a period of one year (e.g. No. 287). In one case, at least, a woman reprieved for child-birth received an absolute pardon after two years in prison.[1] Even if the jury of matrons was unable to certify the woman to be in the condition alleged, the sentence does not seem to have been immediately carried out. Alice Adcock, convicted of murder by witchcraft in July, 31 Eliz., and found not to be enceinte, was not sent to the gallows until July of the following year (No. 307).

Rep̃ quousq̃ (she is reprisoned until) is equivalent to the English entry " to be kept in gaol without bail until delivered by due course of law ". Rep̃ post judm generally indicates that the capital sentence is commuted to a term of imprisonment. For instance Mary Holt (No. 545) sentenced to be hanged, and reprieved after judgment, was, according to the gaol delivery roll, in gaol without bail. The length of the term of imprisonment is not stated, and the longest period noticed by the writer was

---

[1] Elizabeth Lightbone found guilty at Chester Assizes, 27 Sept., 11 Jas. I, on two counts of witchcraft, pleaded pregnancy and was respited. She was proclaimed 25 Sept., 13 Jas. I (Gaol Book, Chester 21/2, pp. 91, 104, 109).

about three years. Sometimes the entry is vsq ad px (see No. 578 and gaol delivery roll). This does not, however, indicate that the prisoner would be released at the next assizes, for instance, Coppinge. Mayers, Thurston, Johnson. and Starlinge, who, according to the gaol delivery roll (Appendix I), " were reprieved after judgment and must remain in gaol without bail until the next gaol delivery," were still in prison nearly three years later. Non-payment of fees to the gaoler may have had something to do with the detention.

Sometimes the reprieve *post judicium* is stated to be on account of " weak evidence " (Nos. 248 and 394).

Repr' ante judic' (No. 664). Reprisoned before sentence is occasionally met with on the indictments (see Nos. 695 and 712). The corresponding entry on the gaol delivery roll is " reprieved by the Court before judgment, but must be safely kept in gaol till she be thence delivered by due course of law " (see Mary Browne guilty of murder by witchcraft, No. 695, and Mary Hurst guilty of hurting a person, No. 712). A curious Englished version of repr' ante judic' noticed in a gaol book of the Northern Circuit was " reprieved before judgment for hangman ".

Rep sine judicio likewise indicates an indefinite sentence. Ellen Bett, convicted of murder on two counts and reprieved without judgment at Summer Assizes, 31 Eliz. was still in gaol two years later (Nos. 283–4).

A common annotation and a more definite one is rep p anno. This is the record of a sentence of one year's imprisonment with four spells in the pillory of six hours' duration each. Sometimes the sentence is written in at greater length as in Nos. 50 and 350.

In one case a reprieve was granted upon the desire of the Minister (see Coppine in gaol delivery roll, Appendix I). Indictment No. 730 provides an example of a temporary suspension of the judgment for no stated reason. Judith Sawkins sentenced to death at the Kent Summer Assizes, 1657, was, according to the gaol delivery roll, " to be kept in gaol without bail until delivered by due course of law," which in this case was by the gallows, the sentence being duly carried out on 30 Mar.. 1658. This delay in execution did not necessarily have any connection with an " expected event ", the same words being often used in delaying the hanging of male felons. The case of Joan Neville (744) may be similar.

The annotations to indictments Nos. 695–6 record a tragedy. " Hanged and reprieved after by order of Parliament." The gaol delivery roll records that both Mildred Wright and Anne Wilson were duly executed, no mention being made of the pardon.

It may be noted that rep is sometimes entered only on the delivery roll and not on the indictment (e.g. Nos. 248, 624).

## Lesser Punishments

What is an apparent miscarriage of justice or a case of unexpected leniency may next be noticed. Elizabeth Francis of Hatfield, " spinster," who had received one year's imprisonment at Essex Summer Assizes, 1566, for bewitching a person, was again convicted of a like offence five years later, yet she was not sent to the gallows, but was sentenced as though a first offender. (Nos. 17 and 50.) Possibly the same Elizabeth was hanged in 1579 (No. 123).

A fortunate witch was Agnes Hales of Stebbing, who, in 1592, at the Essex Lent Sessions, was brought to the bar on two counts of bewitching persons to death, and before Sir Robert Clarke, baron of the Exchequer and Sir John Puckering, Lord Keeper, was found not guilty of felony and murder, but guilty of witchcraft only. This exceptional distinction reduced the sentence to one year's imprisonment and pillory (Nos. 335–6).

The treatment of Mercy Hill of Barley, was equally lenient. Arraigned at the Hertford Summer Assizes, 1601, on a double charge of murdering by witchcraft. before Gawdy, F., and

Daniel, W., she was found not guilty of the murders, but guilty of the trespass, and had judgment according to the statute, presumably one year's imprisonment and pillory (Nos. 442–3).

Lesser punishments than those prescribed by statute were given occasionally to wizards and witches, for instance Robert Browning of Aldham, at the Essex Lent Sessions, 1598, was sentenced by Justices Gawdy and Owen to be put on the pillory for the capital crime of abetting the conjuration of evil spirits (No. 417).

Another case, before that " most reverend, prudent, learned, and temperate " judge Sir Robert Houghton, and Sir Henry Montague, afterwards chief justice of the King's Bench, at the Hertford Lent Assizes, 1614, was that of Lyon Gleane, who, " suspected for a conjurer " was to be set in the stocks and whipped (No. 524).

The sentence of whipping man or woman was entered on the delivery rolls as follows :—

> He (or she) must be stripped naked from the middle upward and be whipped at the cart's tail until his (or her) body be bloody and then be delivered.

A shorter form is :—

> He (or she) must be openly whipped on his (or her) back on the next market day.

A rarer punishment was that received by Robert Garnett (No. 594) who was committed for " putting his trust in witches and conversing with them to the great dishonour of God ". At the Essex gaol delivery, Summer, 1639, before Sir Richard Weston, baron of the Exchequer, and Edmund Reeve, judge of the Common Pleas, he was ordered to be set at work in the house of correction for one week and then delivered. In another case at the Somerset Summer Assizes, 1680, held at Wells, Anne Rawlins found *not* guilty of bewitching Grace Atkins was nevertheless to be confined in the house of correction until the next sessions.[1]

[1] Assizes 23/2.

The flimsy reason for the imprisonment of acquitted witches is illustrated by an instance recorded by the Hon. Roger North. Sir James Long, before the trial of a witch at Salisbury, complained privately to Justice North that if she escaped, " his estate would not be worth anything ; for all the people would go away." The woman was acquitted, but the Judge, " to save the poor gentleman's estate," ordered her to be kept in gaol, the Town to pay her 2s. 6d. per week. At the next Assizes Sir James asked his Lordship to let her return to the Town, because they could keep her for 1s. 6d. there ! [1]

Possibly on some rare occasions the imprisoned witch received more consideration than the law designed. In one case an Elizabethan gaoler of most unusual enlightenment certainly gave favoured treatment to his prisoner, as is evidenced by a presentment which is not without a touch of humour.

Presentments presented to the greate Enqueste on the behalf of our Sou'eryne lady the quene by me Richard Wickes vycker of Seynt Dunstans near Cant. and [*churchwardens, constables, sidesmen, etc., named*] agaynst Leon'd Norgrave keper of the gayle [Canterbury Castle] the xijth day of July in the xijth yere of the Reigne of our Sou'eigne lady quene Elizabethe [1570].

Fyrst the seid leon'd Norgrave sufferethe a wytche convicted by the lawes of this Realme to have hir libtie of egresse owt of p'son cont'ary to the lawes of this Realme And hathe confer'unce wt diu's psons contynually conc'nyng wytchcraft.

the said leon'd the xxx[th] day of October last past in the psens of diu's psons as . . . dyd speake these wordes . . . the Wytche dyd more good by hir phisick than Mr. *Pund*all, and Mr. Wood being pre[achers] of godes word.[2]

## Suspicion

Suspicion appears to have been as effective as conviction in confining people in prison. Two such cases occur in the records

[1] *The Life of the Rt. Hon. Francis North*, 1742, p. 130.
[2] Assizes 35/12. Kent. Norgrave was found not guilty of various charges.

for the Kent Summer Sessions for the year 1652. Thomas Goddard and Goddard Gresham " suspected of witchcraft are to remain in gaol without bail till they shall be delivered by due course of law " (Nos. 699 and 700). Agnes Hamond at Hertford, in Lent, 1613, was likewise treated (No. 522). In 1579 or earlier, Thomas Lever, a boy of 13 years of age, was committed, with his master, to the county gaol of Essex, touching matters of conjuration. Upon his mother making humble petition to the Privy Council, their Lordships, on 17 Jan., 1579–80, '' not remembering anie particuler cause why the child should be either comitted or remayne so long tyme as he hath don," ordered his release.[1] Nevertheless, on 15 July, 1580, Thomas was still in prison, as appears by a letter to the Justices in the county of Essex whereby their Lordships " do requier them at this next Assises within that countie, upon knowledg in what sorte he was to be charged for the matter he remaineth comitted, if the same be not of moment, *as it is like it is not*, to take order he be sett at libertie ".[2]

Numerous cases of delay might be collected from the records of Scotland, but the following extract from the register of the Privy Council, 7 May, 1667, will sufficiently illustrate the tardiness of justice in that country.

> The Lords, considering that Barbara Drummond " hes been detained these three years bygone prisoner as suspect guilty of witchcraft, and that notwithstanding of severall commissions that have been direct for putting her to a tryeall, yet no sentence hath proceeded thereupon, so that the said Barbara is still keeped in great misery ", do therefore ordain the magistrates of Stirling to liberate her from their tolbooth on enacting herself to compear and be tried when called thereto.[3]

[1] *Acts of the Privy Council*, xi, 370.
[2] *Ibid.*, xii, 102.
[3] *The Register of the Privy Council of Scotland*, 3rd Ser., ii, 283.

## Pardons and Escapes

It will be noticed that the general pardon of 23 Eliz. excepted all offences of invoking and bewitching. It is, therefore, curious to note that Agnes Waters *alias* Stevens of Godalming, committed upon suspicion of bewitching goods and cattle, and against whom a true bill was found, was pardoned by this very Act (No. 188). No verdict is recorded and possibly she may have been found " not guilty " as was Margaret Hogden, who at the Essex Assizes held at Witham in Summer, 1583, was likewise " pardoned " (No. 189). It is a singular use of the word.[1]

Having regard to the condition of the gaols, it is probable that escapes were not uncommon. A Hertford Castle gaol delivery roll records that Mary Hamont, who had been convicted of killing animals by witchcraft, and sentenced to one year's imprisonment, had escaped by negligence of the gaoler (Nos. 350–2). In another Hertford case (No. 423) it is noticed that Alice Fulwood feloniously rescued herself and withdrew from the custody of the constable before her examination by the Justices. This prisoner was evidently retaken.

## Accusations in Upper Circles

The indictments abstracted in this collection from the records of the Home Circuit name 590 accused persons, who, with the exception of four (Nos. 92, 519, 665, 750), are described as tradesmen, husbandmen, and labourers, or the wives of such. It must not, however, be supposed that black magic was practised only by the lower classes, superstition was rife from the highest circles downwards, and many noble dames consulted the wizards and astrologers, or even themselves dabbled in the forbidden arts. Necromancy, heresy, and treason were largely bound up

---

[1] Several pardons for persons condemned for witchcraft in the time of Elizabeth are mentioned in the State Papers (Domestic Series, 1595–7, pp. 400, 406). Also in the following reign, 7 May, 1611. " Grant of pardon to Wm. Bate, indicted twenty years since for practising invocation of spirits for finding treasure, the evidence being found weak, &c." (1611–1618, p. 29).

with one another, and an accusation of witchcraft or heterodoxy often served to remove a hated opponent in a political sphere. The public records name numerous great personages who were accused officially and unofficially of using sorcery to attain their desires.[1]

An extract from a fifteenth century MS. illustrates the form of penance which a noble lady suffered.

In this same yere (19 Hen. VI) [Eleanor Cobham], the duchesse of Gloucetre was arested and put in Holt, for she was suspecte of treson ; and a clerk that was longyng to here, whiche was clepyd Roger Whiche, was taken for werchynge of sorcery ayens the kyng, and he was put into the Tour ; and after, he was broght into Poules, and there he stood up on high on a scaffold ageyn Poulys crosse on a Sonday, and there he was arraied like as he schulde never the in his garnementys, and there was honged rounde aboughte hym alle hise intrumentis whiche were taken with hym, and so shewyd among all the peple ; and after, he was broughte to fore the lordys, and there he was examyned ; and after broughte to the Yeldehalle, and there he was regned aforen the lordes of the kynges counseill and to fore all the juges of this land ; and anon after, the lady of Gloucestre afornseid was mad to apere thre sondry dayes afore the kyng and all hise lordes spiruell and temperell ; and there she was examyned of diverses poyntes of wicchecraft, of the whiche she knowleched that she hadde used thorugh the counseill of the Wicche of Eye ; the whiche was brent on the even of Symond and Jude in Smythefeld.

In this yere (20 Hen. VI) my lady of Gloucestre hadde confessyd here wichecraft, as it is afornseid she was yoyned be alle the spriualte assent to penaunce ; to comen to London fro Westm' on the Moneday next suynge and londe at the Temple brigge out of here barge, and there openly barehede with a keverchef on hir hede beryng she tok a taper of wax of ij lb. in here hond, and wente so thorugh Fletstrete on here foot and hoodles unto Poules, and there she offred up here taper at the high auter ; and on the Wednesday nest suenge she com fro Westm', be barge, unto the Swan in Tempse

---

[1] An interesting example will be found in Appendix III.

strete, and there she londyd, and wente forthe on here feet thorugh Brigge strete, Groschirche strete, to the Ledenhalle, and so to Crichirche in the wyse afornseyd ; and on Fryday she londed at Quen hithe, and so forth she wente into Chepe, and so to seynt Mighell in Cornhull, in the forme afornseid ; and at iche of the tymes the mair with the schirreves and the craftes of London were redy at the places there she sholde londe ; and after, Roger the clerk afornseyd on the Satirday that is to sey the xviij day of Novembre, was brought to the Yeldehalle, with Sire John Hom prest, and William Wodham squyer, the whiche S*r*. John and William hadden there chartres at that tyme ; and the clerk was dampned, and the same day was drawe fro the Tour of London to Tiborn, and there hanged, hedyd, and quartered, and the heed sett upon London bregge ; and his oo quarter at Hereford, another at Oxenford, another at York, and the fourthe at Cambregge ; and the lady put in prison, and after sent to Chestre, there to byde whill she lyvyth.[1]

A few other notable cases may be mentioned briefly. In 1478 Jaquet, duchess of Bedford, had occasion to complain to the Privy Council that Thomas Wake squier purposing " the fynall distruccion of her persone . . . caused her to be brought in a comune noyse and disclaundre of wychecraft thorouout a grete part of this reaume, surmytting that she shuld have usid wichecraft and sorcerie ". The accuser alleged that she had made an image of lead like a man of armes to use with witchcraft and sorcery.[2]

Sir Thomas More, in his *Historie of Kyng Rycharde the Thirde*, records that the Protector accused his brother's wife, Jane Shore, of having, by sorcery and witchcraft, wasted his body, and in witness exhibited his withered arm, in the condition in which it had always been ! Nevertheless, the unfortunate lady had to do penance, suffer imprisonment, and was reduced to beggary.[3]

One of the charges against Lord Hungerford of Heytesbury,

---

[1] From *A Chronicle of London* (N. H. Nicolas), p. 128.
[2] *Parliament Rolls*, vi, 232*a, b*, 241*a*.
[3] Edited by Dr. J. R. Lumby, p. 47.

who was beheaded in 1540, was procuring people to conjure with a view to showing how long the King would live.[1]

In 1546 Henry, Lord Nevill, son of the Earl of Westmoreland, confessed to employing a magician to ensure his winning at play, a most dangerous admission as the Act was then in force.[2]

In Scotland, where religious fanaticism was even more rampant, it is not surprising that many persons of noble degree were inculpated for alleged demoniacal practices. According to Buchanan, the historian, John, Earl of Mar, accused of employing witches to end the life of King James III, his brother, was condemned by the Privy Council, and was put to death by having a vein opened (1479).[3] Hutchinson states that in 1562 Elizabeth, Countess of Lennox, and others, who had consulted wizards to determine how long the Queen would live, were condemned for treason.[4] The Countess of Huntly was accused of being a patroness and encourager of sorcerers by Knox, who himself was commonly supposed to use charms to attain his ends.[5] About 1590 Catherine Ross, Lady Foulis, was indicted for various acts of witchcraft, but was acquitted.[6] The Earl of Bothwell was accused of witchcraft and imprisoned, 2 June, 1591.[7] In the following century Lady Home of Manderston was said to have attempted to kill her husband by devilish practices.[8]

### The Last Executions in England

After the holocaust in 1645 witchcraft proceedings rapidly declined in England. The last person to have been hanged in the Home Counties appears to have been Joan Neville, who was found guilty of murder by witchcraft before that " most eminent

---

[1] *Letters and Papers of the reign of Henry VIII*, vol. xv. p. 458.
[2] *Ibid.*, vol. xxi, pt. ii, p. 198.
[3] *History of Scotland*, 1799 edit., ii, 75.
[4] *Historical Essay concerning Witchcraft*, p. 26.
[5] *The Geography of Witchcraft*, by Rev. A. M. Summers, p. 209.
[6] *The Register of the Privy Council of Scotland*, 1585–92, p. 392.
[7] Cokayne's *Peerage*.
[8] *Reg. Priv. Counc.*, 1629–30, p. xli. Chambers' *Domestic Annals*, ii, pp. 32.

EXTRACT FROM GAOL BOOK, A.D. 1684

[ face p. 43

judge " Orlando Bridgman at the Assizes held at Kingston-upon-Thames on 3 Sept., 1660.[1] If, however, the entry on the gaol delivery roll—" must be kept in gaol until delivered by due course of law "—does not indicate the death sentence then various executions which took place in 1657 are the last to be recorded for assizes of the Home Circuit. At Chester Assizes there is no doubt that Mary Baguley went to the gallows as late as 1675. (Indict ad ist p incantacoe et fascinacoe & jur dic cul ca null Judm suspendi et execut fuit.) [2]

Actually the last execution in England traced by the writer is that of Alice Molland, who was tried at the Exeter Lent Assizes in 1 Jas. II [1684] [3] before Sir Francis North, chief justice of Common Pleas and Sir Thomas Raymond, justice of the King's Bench, which eminent judges had two years previously at Exeter sentenced three women to death for bewitching persons,[4] which latter case has hitherto been looked upon as the last judicial error of this nature in England.[5]

In Scotland executions for witchcraft continued into the following century, but in Ireland the Act, never enforced, was practically a dead letter.[6]

In England cases continued to be brought into court, the last occurrence for the Home Circuit, so far as can now be traced, being in 1701 (No. 790).[7] This example is of particular interest as the informer himself got into trouble, which example probably acted in the future as a deterrent to the over-zealous witch hunter. In other parts of the country persons continued to be indicted

---

[1] Indictment No. 744.
[2] Chester 21/5, p. 145.
[3] Assizes 23/2, 20 Mar., 1 Jas. II. See Plate II.
[4] Assizes 23/2, 14 Aug., 34 Chas. II.
[5] Hutchinson, p. 41 ; Summers (*Geography*), p. 149.
[6] The last trial of which record is extant was in 1711, several women being sentenced to imprisonment and the pillory. *History of Carrickfergus*, by S. M'Skimin, p. 22. *The Dublin Penny Journal*, i, 341, 370.
[7] A full account is given in Howell's *State Trials*, xiv, 639.

until some years later.[1] In 1717 a woman and her son and daughter were arrested and committed to Leicester Assizes. An extract from the very absurd informations will be found in Appendix VII.

## The Repeal of the Statute

The Act of James I was repealed in 9 Geo. II [1736] when witchcraft ceased to be a statutory or ecclesiastical offence.

## A.D. 1736.   9 Geo. II, c. 5

An Act to repeal the Statute made in the First Year of the Reign of King James the First, intituled, An Act against Conjuration, Witchcraft, and dealing with evil and wicked Spirits, except so much thereof as repeals an Act of the Fifth Year of the Reign of Queen Elizabeth, against Conjurations, Inchantments, and Witchcrafts, and to repeal an Act passed in the Parliament of Scotland in the Ninth Parliament of Queen Mary, intituled, Anentis Witchcrafts, and for punishing such Persons as pretend to exercise or use any kind of Witchcraft, Sorcery, Inchantment, or Conjuration.

Be it enacted by the King's most Excellent Majesty, by and with the Advice and Consent of the Lords Spiritual and Temporal, and Commons, in this present Parliament assembled, and by the Authority of the same, That the Statute made in the First Year of the Reign of King James the First, intituled, An Act against Conjuration, Witchcraft, and dealing with evil and wicked Spirits, shall, from the Twentyfourth day of June next, be repealed and utterly void, and of none effect (except so much thereof as repeals the Statute made in the Fifth Year of the Reign of Queen Elizabeth) intituled, An Act against Conjurations, Inchantments, and Witchcrafts.

And be it further enacted by the Authority aforesaid, That from and after the said Twentyfourth Day of June, the Act passed in the Parliament of Scotland, in the Ninth Parliament of Queen Mary, intituled, Anentis Witchcrafts, shall be, and is hereby repealed.

And be it further enacted, That from and after the said Twentyfourth Day of June, no Prosecution, Suit, or

---

[1] On the Continent, prosecutions continued to a much later date, and during the eighteenth century numerous witches were put to death. Kurtz records that in Mexico, as late as 1877, five witches were burnt alive.

Proceeding, shall be commenced or carried on against any Person or Persons for Witchcraft, Sorcery, Inchantment, or Conjuration, or for charging another with any such Offence, in any Court whatsoever in Great Britain.

And for the more effectual preventing and punishing of any Pretences to such Arts or Powers as are before mentioned, whereby ignorant persons are frequently deluded and defrauded ; be it further enacted by the Authority aforesaid, That if any Person shall, from and after the said Twenty fourth Day of June, pretend to exercise or use any kind of Witchcraft, Sorcery, Inchantment, or Conjuration, or undertake to tell Fortunes, or pretend, from his or her Skill or Knowledge in any occult or crafty Science, to discover where or in what Manner any Goods or Chattels, supposed to have been stolen or lost, may be found, every Person, so offending, being thereof lawfully convicted on Indictment or Information in that Part of Great Britain called England, or on Indictment or Libel, in that Part of Great Britain called Scotland, shall, for every such offence, suffer Imprisonment by the Space of one whole Year without Bail or Mainprize, and once in every Quarter of the said Year, in some Market Town of the proper County, upon the Market Day, there stand openly on the Pillory by the Space of One Hour, and also shall (if the Court by which such Judgment shall be given shall think fit) be obliged to give Sureties for his or her good Behaviour, in such Sum. and for such Time, as the said Court shall judge proper, according to the Circumstances of the Offence, and in such case shall be further imprisoned until such Sureties be given.[1]

## The Courts and Jurisdiction

In England trials for felony were held in the Court of King's Bench at Westminster (Hilary, Easter. Trinity, and Michaelmas terms) ; at the Courts of Assizes (Lent and Summer, or as sometimes termed, Spring and Autumn Sessions) ; at the Courts of Quarter Sessions (first week after Michaelmas, the Epiphany, Easter, and St. Thomas Becket, 7 July) ; and at Independent Courts (often at great intervals).

With regard to the Court of Quarter Sessions, it may be noticed

[1] *Acts of Parliament,* pr. by Watkins, vol. xiii, p. 9.

that the commission before 1590 did not specifically mention witchcraft, but empowered the justices of the peace to inquire *de omnimodis feloniis*.[1] More particularly by the commission as settled in Michaelmas term, 1590, powers were conferred on the justices to inquire into and hear and determine *omnia et singula felonias, veneficia, incantationes, sortilegia, artes magicas*, etc., all and singular the felonies, witchcrafts, enchantments, sorceries, magic arts, etc., according to the laws and statutes of England and to chastise and punish the persons offending, etc., provided always, that if a case of difficulty upon the determination of any of the premises happened to arise, they should not give judgment except in the presence of one of the justices of one or other bench or one of the justices of assize.[2]

Some uncertainty exists as to when justices of the peace ceased to try capital felonies. Carter states that jurisdiction under this later commission was exercised, and sentences of death pronounced and executed accordingly, but that the powers were thereafter gradually dropped.[3] On the other hand, Hale citing the statute 1 & 2 Philip & Mary, *c.* 13, directing justices of the peace to take examinations in cases of felony and murder, and to certify them to the justices of gaol delivery, adds " in point of discretion they do forbear to determine great felonies ".

It is evident from the indictments which have now been collected that it was the practice at Quarter Sessions to certify examinations of suspected witches to the justices of gaol delivery.[4] Exceptionally, during the years 1645–6, when the assizes were suspended, the justices of the peace had a free hand. One notable case was a trial by one lord and several justices of the peace, with dire results to the unfortunate witches, the proceedings being, in fact, a veritable " bloody assize ".

---

[1] *Eirenarcha*, by William Lambard, ed. 1581, p. 39.
[2] *The Countrey Justice*, by Michael Dalton, 1682, p. 18.
[3] *A History of the English Courts*, by A. T. Carter, 1927, p. 124.
[4] Hamilton (*Quarter Sessions*, pp. 113, 220) gives cases of witches' trials, but the women were certainly condemned at assizes.

Judicial proceedings in the King's Bench and independent courts do not receive more than passing mention in these notes, which are confined to those trials which were had at the Lent and Summer Assizes (*hiemalis* or *quadragesimalis* and *estivalis* or *autumnalis* as they were termed) before the itinerant justices.

Justices of Assize generally acted by virtue of commissions of gaol delivery[1] and oyer and terminer.[2] A transcript of a Commonwealth example of the former, and consequently in English, will now be given.

## The Commission of Gaol Delivery, 1653

The Keepers of the Libty of England by authority of Parliament To Oliver St John Chiefe Justice of the Comon Bench, Peter Warburton, one of the Justices of the Comon Bench, Thomas Lee, John Lee, and Richard Lee, greeting Knowe yee that wee have constituted you fower three and two of you whereof wee will that either of you the said Oliver St John and Peter Warburton be one, Justices to deliver the Gaole of the County of Essex of the Prisoners therein being And therefore wee comand you that at a c⁹teyne day wᶜʰ yee fower three or two of you whereof wee will that either of you the said Oliver St John and Peter Warburton be one shall appoint in this behalfe yee meete at Chelmesford to deliver that Gaole doeing therein as to Justice doth appteyne according to the law and custome of England saving to vs the am⁹ciamtᵖ and other thingᵖ thereof to vs belonging ffor wee have commanded the Sheriff of the said County of Essex that at the c⁹teyne day wᶜʰ yee fower three or two of you whereof wee will that either of you the said Oliver St John and Peter Warburton be one shall make knowne to him he shall cause all the prisoners in the said Gaole with their Attachmᵗᵖ to come before you fower three or two of

---

[1] A Latin form of 1607 is given in full in *Select Statutes*, by G. W. Prothero, 1913, p. 363.

[2] In Scotland special commissions for trying and executing witches were granted. *Acts of the Parliaments of Scotland*, vi(i), 197.

you whereof wee will that either of you the said Oliver St John and Peter Warburton be one. In witness whereof wee have caused these our łres to be made patentę Witnes our selves at Westm' the two and twentieth day of June in the yeare of our Lord one thowsand six hundred fifty three.

Oyer and terminer is the largest of the five commissions by which the judges of assize sit in their several circuits, and is a more lengthy document, and has not been noticed in connection with witchcraft trials.[1]

Commissions of gaol delivery directed to the Justices for taking the assizes usually issued in January and June of each year.

The precept or writ of summons (in the name of the Commissioners) to the Sheriff to proclaim the assize and empanel the juries and others occasionally was of even date with the commission, but generally later.[2]   A Commonwealth example follows :—

### A Writ of Summons, 1653

Oliver St John one of the Justices assigned to take Assizes, Jurates & Certificates arraigned before any Justices whomsoever as well by divers writs . . . within the County of Essex. To the Sheriff . . . Greeting.

We command you that you omit not for any liberty within your county but that you cause to come before us at Chelmsford on Thursday 28 July next ensuing. All writts of Assize, Jurates & Certificates arraigned before any Justices whomsoever by divers writs . . . together with the pannells, attachments, reattachments, sumons, resumons and all other minum[to] whatsoever concerning the Assizes, Jurates, & Certificates aforesaid provided always that the attachments, reattachments, sumons & resumons thereof be made 15 days before the said Thursday . . . also all prisoners remaining in that gaole together with all their attachments, indictments and other muniments those prisoners in any way concerning and of the venues of every place where the felonies were committed whereof the said prisoners stand indicted,

---

[1] A Latin form of 1607 is given by Prothero, p 361.
[2] I have seen one writ which antedated the commission.

appealed, or arrested, as well within Liberties as without, 24 good and lawful men by whom the truth of the matter may be better be known & inquired of who have no affinity to those prisoners together with 4 selected men of those townes and places to do those things which on the behalf of the said Keepers that they shall be then and there enjoyned. And that you cause to be publicly proclaimed throughout your whole Bailiwick that all they who will prosecute against the said prisoners may be then and there to prosecute against them as shall be just. And also that you give notice to all Justices of peace, Maiors, Coroners, Stewards, Bailiffs of Liberties and hundreds within your County. And also to all and singular Chiefe Constables of every libertie and hundred within your County that they be then and there in their owne person with their rolls, records, indictments and other remembrances to doe those things which to their offices in that behalf appertain to be done. And that you have yourself and your Under-Sheriff together with your Bayliffes and other your ministers be then and there in your own persons to do those things which to you and their offices appertain to be done. And that you have then and there the names of all Justices of the Peace, Mayors, Coroners, Stewards, Jurors, Bailiffes, chief Constables and the names of them by whom you shall so cause them to come. And of them by whom and to whom you shall so give notice. And that you also then and there have this p̃cept dated at Westminster the five and twentieth day of June In the year of our Lord God 1653.

Execution of the precept was endorsed, and panel annexed.

### The Circuits

The deliveries with few exceptions took place in March and August.[1]

To facilitate the administration of justice, for several centuries prior to 1876, the counties of England had been divided into six circuits, i.e. Home, Midland, Norfolk, Northern, Oxford, and Western.

---

[1] One example of a winter session is noticed on p. 118 *post*. Howard (*The State of the Prisons*, p. 20) records that at Hull they used to have the assize but once in seven years.

The counties comprising the Home circuit were Essex, Hertford, Kent, Surrey, and Sussex.[1]

The venues of the respective assizes of this circuit were as follow :—

Essex : Braintree, Brentwood, Chelmsford, Colchester (see p. 117), or Witham.

Hertford : Hertford, Hitchin, or St. Albans.

Kent : Dartford, Maidstone, or Rochester.

Surrey : Croydon, Guildford, Kingston-on-Thames, Reigate, or Southwark.

Sussex : East Grinstead, Horsham, or Lewes.

The principal gaols were the castles of Colchester, Hertford, Canterbury, Guildford, and Lewes. The Marshalsea and Maidstone are also mentioned.

A few brief notes of the judges who condemned the witches of the Home Counties may be of interest.

## The Judges

ALTHAM, James, Kt. Serjeant, 1603. Baron of the Exchequer, 1607. Died 1617. " One of the gravest and most reverend judges of this kingdom." Bacon (*Works*, vii, 267).

ASKE, Richard. Justice of the Upper Bench, 1649. Died 1656.

BACON, Francis, Kt. Judge of the King's Bench, 1642. Died 1657.

BRIDGEMAN, Orlando, Bt. Chief Baron of the Exchequer, 1660. Chief Justice of the Common Pleas, 1660. Lord Keeper of the Great Seal, 1667. Died 1674. " Most eminent judge " (Lord Ellenborough).

CLARKE, Robert, Kt. Baron of the Exchequer, 1587. Died 1607.

COVENTRY, Thomas, Kt. Judge of the Common Pleas, 1606. Died 1606.

CROKE, John, Kt. Serjeant, 1603. Judge of the King's Bench, 1607. Died 1620.

DANIEL, William. Serjeant, 1594. Judge of the Common Pleas, 1604. Died 1610. " A vearie honest, learned, and discreat man " (Lord Burleigh).

[1] The counties comprising the other circuits are given p. 109 *post*.

DODERIDGE, John, Kt. Solicitor-General, 1604. Serjeant to the King, 1607. Judge of the King's Bench, 1612. Died 1628. " A man of great knowledge " (Croke).

GAWDY, Francis, Kt. Serjeant, 1577. Judge of the Queen's Bench, 1588. Chief Justice of the Common Pleas, 1605. Died 1606.

GAWDY, Thomas, Kt. Judge of the Queen's Bench, 1574. Died 1588. " A most reverend judge and sage of the law, of ready and profound judgment, and venerable gravity, prudence and integrity." Coke (4 Report, 54).

GERARD, Gilbert, Kt. Serjeant, 1558. Attorney-General, 1559. Master of the Rolls, 1581. Died 1593.

HALE, Matthew, Kt. Judge of the Common Pleas, 1654. Chief Baron of the Exchequer, 1660. Chief Justice of the King's Bench, 1671. Died 1676. " One of the brightest luminaries of the law."

HILL, Roger. Serjeant, 1655. Baron of the Exchequer, 1657. Judge of the Upper Bench, 1660. Died 1667.

HOBART, Henry, Bt. Chief Justice of the Common Pleas, 1613. Died 1625. " A most learned, prudent, grave and religious judge " (Croke).

HOUGHTON, Robert, Kt. Judge of the King's Bench, 1613. Died 1624.

MONSON, Robert. Judge of the Common Pleas, 1574. Died 1583.

MONTAGUE, Henry. Serjeant, 1611. Chief Justice of the King's Bench, 1616. Died 1642.

OWEN, Thomas. Serjeant, 1589. Queen's Serjeant, 1593. Judge of the Common Pleas, 1594. Died 1598.

PUCKERING, John, Kt. Serjeant, 1580. Queen's Serjeant, 1586. Lord Keeper, 1592. Died 1596.

SOUTHCOTE, John. Judge of the Queen's Bench, 1563–84. Died 1585. " A judge of high reputation."

STEELE, William. Attorney-General, 1648. Recorder of London, 1649. Chief Baron of the Exchequer, 1655. " A lawyer of ability and learning."

WALMESLEY, Thomas, Kt. Judge of the Common Pleas, 1589. Died 1612.

WARBURTON, Peter. Justice of the Common Pleas, 1649. Died 1666.

WINCH, Humphry, Kt. Serjeant, 1606. Judge of the Common Pleas, 1611. Died 1625. " A learned and religious judge " (Croke).

WRAY, Christopher, Kt. Judge of the Queen's Bench, 1572–88. Died 1592. "A most reverend judge, of profound and judicial knowledge, accompanied with a ready and singular capacity, grave and sensible elocution and continual and admirable patience " (Coke. 3 Report, 26).

## Procedure

With regard to procedure, it appears from the early legal compendiums that when a felony is done, any person who suspects another to be guilty may arrest him, and bring him to the Constable or to a Justice in order to his commitment.[1] In the absence of any note to the contrary, it is to be supposed that the suspected dabbler in sorcery was subjected to the like treatment. Incidentally, the unfortunate magicians seem to have suffered from a good deal of unofficial handling, hard usage, and vulgar curiosity. For instance, in 1661, Frances Bailey of Broxbourne, widow, deposed that Andrew Camp of the said parish—

> " dragged her out of her own house into the street over a stone that bruised her back, and when he had her in the street he pinched her and kneeled upon her breast, and when he had her so under him his wife came out and clawed her by the face and said she would claw her eyes out of her head and her tongue out of her mouth and called her a d—— w—— old witch."[2]

The " witch " of Newbury, shot by order of the military has been mentioned and a case of a woman suspected of witchcraft at Wakefield being actually killed by the populace is also recorded.[3]

Upon an information being laid, and whether or not the witch had been taken into custody it was the usual practice for the magistrate to institute an inquiry. The informers' and witnesses' depositions made on oath before the Justice were committed to writing for certification to the Justices of gaol delivery. The complainant entered into a recognizance to appear before the

---

[1] *Pleas of the Crown*, by Sir Matthew Hale, p 89 *et seq.*
[2] *Hertford County Sessions Rolls*, i, 137.
[3] *Life of Oliver Heywood*, by Rev. J. Hunter, p. 168 n.

justices at the next gaol delivery of the county and prefer a bill of indictment against the accused and give evidence before grand and petty juries. The witnesses were likewise bound over. The accused upon being apprehended by warrant or otherwise and brought before a justice of the peace also went under examination, which was certified to the next assizes. If there seemed to be just cause, the justice committed the accused to prison or bound him over to the next gaol delivery.

## Bail

By Act of Parliament 1 & 2 Philip & Mary. c. 13 [1554] justices of the peace of whom one is of the " quorum "

> " when any prisoner is brought before them for man-slaughter or felony before any bailment or mainprise shall take the examination of the said prisoner and information of them that brings him of the fact and circumstances thereof and the same or as much thereof as shall be material to prove the felony shall put in writing before they make the same bailment which said examinations together with the said bailment the said Justices shall certify at the next general gaol delivery to be holden within the limits of their commission." [1]

Sometimes the charges were raked up from past history. In 1647 Margaret Cotterell was accused of bewitching Lady Holmes fifteen years before (No. 665). No bill was found to go to trial. A Kent woman was arraigned on five counts of which four were 7, 9, 13, and 16 years old respectively (Nos. 176–180). There was no conviction. One of the three charges against Christiana Stokes, who was hanged in 1606, was that she had bewitched a man to death in 1593 (No. 479).

From an entry in the common council books of Newcastle. it may be gathered that under some jurisdictions complaint might be formulated by a body of the inhabitants. Under date 26 Mar.. 1649, appears : " The petition concerning witches was read, and ordered that thanks be returned to the petitioners,

---

[1] *Statutes of the Realm*, vol. iv, pt. i, p. 259.

and the common council will contribute their best assistance therein."[1]

Examples will now be given of an information, examination, warrant, recognizances of both prisoner and witnesses, and an order for a remand. Copies of depositions will be found among the appendices.

### An Information,[2] 1647

The Information of Gillion Salter of Stretham taken upon oth before Thos. Castell Esqr. the 30th day of May, 1647.

Whoe saith that abort 7 yeares since that hir daughter Marie Salter the elder and Marie Salter the yonger daughter to Tho. Salter weare much tormented and evell handled in there bodyes Marie Salter being taken lame and had great tormenting fittes and Marie the daughter of the said Marie was so grevusly handled that when hir fitt came upon hir this Informant had much adoe to hold the said Marie in hir armes shee beinge but an yeare and a quarter old and that in the extremitie of the said Marie's ffitt was so violent upon hir that the mouth of the said child would be drawen to the eare in such a fearefull manner that it did affright the beholders to see and this miserie the said Marie did lie in for the space of a quarter of a yeare and so died w[ch] this Inform[t] doth verilie beleave was the act of Dorothy Ellis.

GILLION     X     SALTER.

Hir marke.

### An Examination,[2] 1647

The examination of Dorithy Ellis taken before Tho. Castell Esqr. the 30th day of May 1647.

Whoe saith that about thirtie yeares since shee being much troubled in her minde there appeared unto hir the Devell in the liknes of a great catt and speak unto this ex[t] and demanded of hir hir blood w[ch] she gave hime after which the spirit in the liknes of a catt suck upon the body of this ex[t] and the first thing that this ex[t] commanded her spirit to doe was to

---

[1] *Local Records*, by John Sykes, p. 103.
[2] I found no information or examination relating to an accusation of witchcraft for the Home Circuit so give examples from the records of Assizes of the Isle of Ely taken from *Ely Episcopal Records*, by A. Gibbons, F.S.A., pp. 112-13.

goe and be witch 4 of the cattell of Tho. Hitch all wh^ch cattell presently died and further this ex^t confesseth that she sent hir catt spirit to bewitch and take away the life of Marie the daughter of Tho. Salter of Stretham which spirit forthwith kild the child of the said Marie and also this ex^t confesseth she commanded hir spirit to lame the mother of the said child old Marie Salter which was done accordingly and that she commanded hir spirit to goe and be witch and lame John Gotobed because he cald this ex^t old witch and flung stones att this ex^t all w^ch command was performed by hir spirit and the said Gotobed lamed.

DORETHY      X      ELLIS.

hir marke.

Other examples of depositions will be found in Appendices VI and VII. A good selection of depositions has been printed in *A collection of Rare and Curious Tracts relating to Witchcraft*, printed by J. R. Smith, 1838 ; *The Witches of Huntingdon*, by John Davenport, 1646 *A true and exact Relation of the severall Informations* . . . by H. F., 1645.

## A Warrant,[1] 1701

To the Constables of Stanes, and either of them.

Whereas complaint hath been made, and information been given to me by G. P., of St Albans, in the County of Hertford, Physician, that John Ellis, jun., of Stanes, in the County of Middlesex, hath abused, cheated, and defrauded the said G. P. by borrowing money of him, and sending for him to London, and severall times to Stanes, uppon pretence of doing many wicked and abominable things in Negromancy and Magick and Conjuration, by assistance of an infernall Spiritt familiar to the said Ellis, which he calls Delandibus, which is death both by the law of God and man. which he the said Ellis affirms, he hath bound himselfe for terme of years to perform these abominable, wicked and treasonable actions against God and man. By which allsoe farther appears, by two notes [2] under the said Ellis's hand, with a wittness to one

---

[1] Printed in the *Antiquarian Repertory*, ii. p. 317.

[2] *Ibid.*, pp. 316, 317. The name Delandibus is said in the original to have been written with blood.

of them, wherein he confesses and acknowledges the same abominable actions with his infernal spiritt Delandibus, and binds himselfe in both them notes, uppon pain of eternall damnation, by all the powers of heaven and hell, Lucifer, Sathan and Belzebub, to whome he had bound himselfe by Delandibus, to do all them wicked, abominable and treasonable things to God and man, and to give himselfe to be caryed immediately into hell with Delandibus, there to remain for ever and ever. Witness his hand, in the presence of Richard Powell. These are therefore in his Majesty's name to charge you, and command you immediately uppon sight hereof, forthwith to bring the body of the said John Ellis before me, to be prosecuted according to law, &c. Hereof fail not at your peril. Dated 1st Dec., 1701, and in the 13th year of the reign of our Sovereign Lord William the Third, &c.

### Recognizance of a Suspected Witch, 1578 [1]

Essex. Memorandū q̃d octavo die Julij Anno Regni Regine nūc vicessimo Jane Buckstone de Westham in dicõ cõm vidua et Martinis Bruster de eadem smithe et Thomas Boothe de eadem yeoman venerunt coram me Henrico Archer vno Justiciarioru dicẽ d̃ne Regine ad pacem in dicõ cõm conservand̃ Assignat̃ et cognoverunt se debere dicẽ d̃ne Regine trigint̃ libras legalis monete Anglie viz p⁹dict J vigint̃ libras et p⁹dict̃ Martinus et Thomas quilt eorū quinq; libras de bonis et cattallis terris et tentis ad vsū dict̃ d̃ne Regine levand̃ sub conditione sequent̃ viȝ.

The condition of this recognysance is suche that if the above Bownden Jane Buckstone doe psonally apeare at the next Assises to be houlden within the said county and then and there doe answer vnto all suche Articles Matterȩ and thingȩ as then and there shalbe obiected agaynste her on the pte and behalf of oʳ saide souⁱ aigne lady the Quene for witchcrafte or suche like That then this p⁹sent Recognysance to be voyde and of none effect or ells it to stand and remayne in full power strength and vertue.

Jane Buckstone.                    Corā me Henrico Archer.
     compuit.

---

[1] Assizes 35/19, Essex file.

**Recognizance of a Witness,[1] 1578**

viij° die Julij a° 1578.

Essex. Memorandū q̃d die et Anno supradicī̃ Ricᷓus Bowland de White Chappell in com̃ Middlesexie gener̃ et Wit̃s Buck Jn̄oes Warde senior et Thomas Wilkinsone de Westham in dic̃o com̃ Essex yeoman venerunt coram me Henrico Archer vno Justiciarior̄u dic̃e d̃ne Regine ad pacem in dic̃o com̃ conservand̃ Assignat̃ et cognoverunt se debere dic̃e d̃ne Regine quilt̃ eor̄u quinq₃ libras de bonis et cattallis terris et tentis suis ad vs̄u dic̃e Đne Regine levand̃ sub conditione sequenti vi₃.

The condition of this recognysance is suche that if the above Bownden Richard Bow[land] Wiłłm Buck and Jhon Warde do psonally apeare before the Quenes Ma^ties Justicᵽ at the next Assises to be houlden for the saide Countie of Essex and then and there doe give in evidence agaynste Jane Buckstone of Westham above saide widoe for suspected witcherye wherof she is accused And allso if the Above Bownden Thomas Wilkinson and luce his wief doe in like maner apeare at the nexte Assises to be houlden for the saide countie and then and there doe give in evidence agaynste the saide Jane Buckstone touchinge witchery wherof she is vehemently suspected and apeached and there to be tried for the same That then this pᷧsent Recognysance to be void and of none effect or ells it to stand in full power strenght & vertue.

Compuit vᷧsus Janam Buckston.[2] Coram me Henrico Archer.

**An Order for a Remand, 1656**

Cheshire. At the Sessions held att Chester the last day of March, 1656. Order delivered to the Deputy Gaoler to bring to the Quarter Sessions.

It is ordered that Thomas Stanley Esqr., Thomas Brereton Esqr., Edward Hyde Esqr., and Henry Bradshawe Esqr., Justices of the peace of this County or any two or more of them

---

[1] Assizes 35/19, Essex file.
[2] Apparently same hand as above.

doe call before them such of the witnesses formerly examined ag^t Ellen Beech and Anne Osboston (who stand indicted of witch-craft at this p^rsent sessions) as they shall thinke fitt and all such other psons as they shall conceave can most pbably make further discoveryes of the truth of the severall matters layd vnto their charge oɪ anie other of like nature. And for the finding out if possible of such other psons as are or shall be suspected to bee confederates w^th the said Ellen Beech and Anne Osboston and guilty of the like divellish practises with them oɪ of being theiɪ Ayders Abbetto^rs or Councellors. And it is alsoe ordered That the examinacons formerly taken in the cause bee alsoe sent to the said Justices together w^th a copie of this p^rsent order for their better informacons and direccons in the more effectuall pformance of this service. And that they certifie vnto this co^rte at the next Sessions and gen^9all Gaole Delivery to bee houlden for this County all such further examinacons as they shall take in this cause sending back alsoe therew^th at the said next Sessions and gen^9all gaole deliv^9ry the said examɪnacons formerly taken and herew^th now sent. And also that they bind over by Recognizance (names) and such other witnesses as they the said Justices shall thinke materiall for the clearinge of the truth of those things w^ch are charged upon the said Ellen and Anne for their p^rsonall appearance at the next Sessɪons to be holden for this County of Chester to psecute and give evidence w^ch effecte ag^t the said Ellen Bech and Anne Osboston as the same requireth. By the Corte.[1]

## Witnesses

The testimony of one single evidence was sufficient in a case of felony. It is said that Justice Winch at Leicester condemned nine women on the statement of one boy that he was bewitched by them, and would have sentenced another batch to death on the same untrustworthy testimony had not the imposture been discovered by the King. A person of the age of 14, that being the

[1] Chester 21/4. p. 346*b*.

age of discretion, was permitted by law to be a witness, but in some cases even younger children have been allowed to testify in cases of witchcraft. At Lancaster Assizes, 1612, a child of 9 years gave evidence upon oath against the witches there arraigned.[1]

The names of the evidence or witnesses which are endorsed on the indictments are no doubt, as at the present day, those who were examined or were intended to be examined by the grand jury, who brought in the *billa vera* or *ignoramus* as the case might be.

Among the abstracted indictments, a number will be noticed which have the name of but one witness endorsed, and in several cases the accused were hanged (e.g. Nos. 436, 440, 568, 617, and 684). In strong contrast is the case (No. 574) of 33 witnesses appearing for the prosecution, the prisoner being found guilty and sentenced, and afterwards reprieved.

Persons guilty but unconvicted may be evidence. One of the accused (indictment No. 607) was also a witness (No. 608). Possibly this was a case of turning king's evidence, certainly Rebecca West, spinster, does not seem to have been arraigned, and her name does not appear on the gaol delivery roll.

Judging by the recurrence of the same name on the back of the indictments it appears as if there were expert witnesses, possibly these were professional watchers or searchers of whom more will be said.

## Confessions

Confession did not always result in a true bill being returned, as example No. 683 and the corresponding gaol calendar shew. Notwithstanding that Elizabeth Haynes confessed " of her self " that she entertained imps in the likeness of kitlings the grand jury did not find the bill. [Assizes 35/93 Misc. file.] Bridget Weaver likewise, who upon her examination, acknowledged that she had cherished an imp, was found not guilty and discharged.

[1] *The Wonderful Discovery of Witches*, by T. Potts, 1613, f. 4b.

[No. 743 from Assizes 35/101, Essex file.] At the Norfolk Assizes, Summer 1645, Lydia Taylor admitted that she was a witch, but the bill was thrown out. Anna Palmer. who owned to having imps like turkey cocks, was acquitted, and Mary Becket, who confessed to a not uncommon experience even in these days, that the devil had appeared to her in the likeness of a man, was also discharged. [Appendix VI.]

One would have expected the coroners' rolls and inquisitions to be full of verdicts of death by witchcraft, but the writer has never seen any entry but felo de se, visitation of God, homicide, murder, or misfortune. Possibly as in some of the gaol calendars the word murder is used to include death by witchcraft.

## The Discovery of Witches

It was recognized by even the most confirmed believers in the prevalence of witchcraft that considerable care had to be exercised in distinguishing between natural and supernatural phenomena, which often bore a marked resemblance, consequently the examination of witches took a different form from that of other suspected felons. Michael Dalton, a Master of Chancery, in his compendium, *The Countrey Justice*, first printed in 1618, a handbook which passed through many editions and must have had an extensive vogue for over a century among justices of the peace, wrote that against witches the justices " may not always expect direct evidence, seeing all their works are the works of darkness, and no witnesses present with them to accuse them ".[1] He inserted the following observations taken out of the book of discovery of the witches that were arraigned at Lancaster in 1612.[2]

1. They have ordinarily a familiar or spirit which appeareth to them.
2. Their said familiar hath some bigg ·or place upon their body where he sucketh them.

---

[1] 1st edit., 1618, p. 243. In later editions, Dalton refers to the witches " being the most cruel. revengeful. and bloody of all the rest ", *i.e.* felons.

[2] *The Wonderful Discovery of Witches*, by T. Potts, 1613.

3. They have often pictures of clay or wax (like a man &c.) found in their house.

4. If the dead body bleed upon the witches touching it.

5. The testimony of the person hurt, upon his death.

6. The examination and confession of the children, or servants of the witch.

7. Their owne voluntary confession, which exceeds all other evidence.

Other interested persons published rules for the discovery of witches, one of the most notable examples being that of the Rev. Richard Bernard of Batcombe (Soms.), whose *Guide to Grand Jurymen* published in 1627 gives advice as to what should be done before bringing in a *billa vera* in cases of witchcraft, and how witches may be known. This work was accepted as authoritative, at any rate by Dalton, who for his fourth edition (1630) made numerous extracts, which were repeated in all editions prior to that of 1736. His notes are now reproduced as an appendix. (See p. 267.)

It is evident that in the case of suspected witches, in addition to the usual oral examination of the accused, and in the absence of confession, a bodily inspection was held to be necesssary, and it is of interest to trace the authority which ordered or permitted this search to be made. Actually no written rule or instructions can be found, but it appears that this form of inquiry was carried out by order of justices of the peace, who appointed a body of women for the work. The offensive nature of the procedure is clear from a deposition of one of these searchers. The accused having been apprehended under a warrant was evidently out on bail, as the six searchers proceeded to her house where they acquainted her with their business, and asked whether she was contented that they should search her ? As she " did not oppose it they began at her head, and so stript her naked, and in the lower part of her belly they found a thing like a teat of an inch long, they questioned her about it, and she said that she had got a strain by carrying of water which caused that excrescence. But upon narrower search, they found in her privy parts three more excrescences or teats, but smaller than the former : This Deponent further saith, that in the long teat at the end thereof was a little hole, and it appeared unto them as if it had lately been sucked, and upon the straining of it there issued out white milkie matter ".[1]

In these days such a phenomenon would probably be described as a common pustule, wart, wen, or other common growth, but two and a half centuries ago it was a link in the chain of evidence upon which the unfortunate possessor was convicted at the Lent Assizes at Bury St. Edmunds, 16 Chas. II, and sentenced to be hanged by Sir Matthew Hale, Lord Chief Baron of his Majesty's Court of Exchequer.

Another form of incriminating bodily mark was insensible flesh, the presence of which was ascertained by thrusting pins into the subject. This experiment was often carried out in public, and to the guiltless must have been not only an annoying indignity, but a very painful experience. This method of discovery was largely practised in Scotland, where it was so successful in exposing the worshippers of Satan that in 1649 the inhabitants of Newcastle-upon-Tyne decided to adopt it. A Scottish expert was engaged at a fee of 20s., payable for every woman discovered and condemned. As soon as the witch-finder arrived, " the magistrates sent their bellman through the town, ringing the bell, and crying, all people that would bring in any complaint against any woman for a witch, they should be sent for and tried by the person appointed. Thirty women were brought into the Town Hall and stript, and then openly had pins thrust into their bodies." Most of them were found guilty.

" The said reputed witch-finder acquainted Lieutenant-Colonel Hobson that he knew women, whether they were witches or no by their looks, and when the said person was searching of a personable, and good like woman, the said Colonel replyed and said, surely this woman is none, and need not be tried, but the Scotch-man said she was, for the Town

---

[1] *A Tryal of Witches at Bury St. Edmunds*, 1664, p. 16.

said she was, and therefore he would try her ; and presently in sight of all the people, laid her body naked to the waste, with her cloaths over her head, by which fright and shame, all her blood contracted into one part of her body, and then he ran a pin into her thigh, and then suddenly let her coats fall, and then demanded whether she had nothing of his in her body but did not bleed, but she being amazed replied little, then he put his hand up her coats, and pulled out the pin and set her aside as a guilty person, and child of the Devil, and fell to try others whom he made guilty."

" Lieutenant Colonel Hobson perceiving the alteration of the foresaid woman, by her blood settling in her right parts, caused that woman to be brought again, and her cloathes pulled up to her thigh, and required the Scot to run the pin into the same place, and then it gushed out of blood, and the said Scot cleared her, and said she was not a child of the Devil." [1]

In England this form of examination was not adopted to any extent officially, although in Scotland it was recognized procedure. It appears, however, that a good deal of unauthorized prodding was indulged in, fatal results being not uncommon, and in 1662 the Lords of His Majesty's Secret Council having been informed that a great many persons suspected of witchcraft had been apprehended, pricked, tortured, and abused, by persons with no warrant or authority so to do, forbade pricking or torture but by order. Several prickers were sentenced to imprisonment.[2]

A further means of discovery was the " scratching " or " blooding " of suspects. It was a firm belief held by many that a bewitched person could relieve himself of magic spells by scratching the responsible witch to the effusion of blood, consequently if a sick person recovered simultaneously with or soon after the scratching of a woman, it was popularly held to be undoubted proof that such woman was the guilty party. An

---

[1] *England's Grievance Discovered in Relation to the Coal Trade,* by Ralph Gardiner, p. 107. It is satisfactory to know that the pricker was ultimately hanged, after confessing that he had caused the death of 220 women for the gain of 20s. apiece.

[2] *Register of the Privy Council of Scotland,* 1661–4, p. 198.

illustration of the practice is provided by the following extract from an information exhibited by the king's Attorney-General against the Defendant in Rex *v.* Hathaway (see p. 265).

> " That the said Richard Hathaway . . . contriving and maliciously intending one Sarah Morduck (Indictment No. 790) who for the whole course of her life was an honest and pious woman, and not a witch, nor using witchcraft, inchantment, charm or sorcery, to bring into the danger of losing her life, 11 Feb. 12 Wm. III, at Southwark . . . did pretend and affirm, himself, by the said Sarah to be bewitched . . . and that he, by drawing blood from the said Sarah, by scratching, should be freed from the said pretended witchcraft, that the said Richard Hathaway did then & there, with force and arms, scratch the said Sarah, and did draw the blood of her the said Sarah, by scratching . . ." [1]

Scratching, like pricking, seems to have been procedure recognized by the Authorities. At Leicester in 1717 the witches were so stubborn that the constable had to be called to bring assistance of persons to hold them by force while they were being " blooded ".[2]

Another common belief was that a witch could not recite the Lord's Prayer, and it is recorded that on one occasion the test was actually made in a court of justice. At the Summer Assizes held at Taunton in 1663. Archer, J., a judge of the Common Pleas " of whose abilities time hath kept no record except in a sinister way ", ordered the experiment to be made upon an old woman named Julian Cox, whom he was trying for witchcraft. It is fair to say that his Lordship pointed out that the test was not legal evidence, and that he directed the jury accordingly. The woman in open court, tried half a dozen times, could do no better than " And lead us into temptation " or " And lead us not into no temptation ".[3]

---

[1] *A Complete Collection of State Trials,* by T. B. Howell, xiv, 640.
[2] *See* Appendix VII.
[3] *History of Witches,* by W. P., p. 10.

## Torture and Ill-Treatment

The extraction of evidence and confession by the infliction of bodily torture was practised in England up to the Commonwealth period, but there is no evidence to shew that it was ever applied to facilitate the examination of suspected female witches. Such practices were, in fact, contrary to the common law, and only lawful as an act of royal prerogative which was probably never exercised in the case of women.[1] It was otherwise with the male worker in the magic arts, although cases on record are rare. In 1620 one Peacock, a schoolmaster, was committed to the Tower and tortured, for practising sorcery upon the King.[2] In Scotland procedure was more drastic as appears by a commission given by King James VI, with the advice of the Lords of his Secret Council, for the examination of suspected and convicted witches, " the personis wilfull or refusand to declair the veritie to putt to tortour, or sic uthir punishment to use and caus be usit as may move thame to utter the treuth."[3] Under the severe bodily pains the women admitted any offence suggested to them by the examiners, but many retracted their confessions when the torture was removed.

Notwithstanding that torture was not exercised in England, it may be inferred from statements in the depositions of 1645 given in Appendix VI, that if the suspected witches did not confess freely it was customary to ill-treat them, e.g. Rebecca Morris confessed " before any violence, watching, or other threats ". The persuasion consisted in walking, starving, keeping awake, and swimming. With reference to a woman named Ratcliffe, it is said that in six days' custody she was not " walked at all ", nor kept from sleep or food. John Lowis is definitely stated to have confessed " after swimming " at Framlingham. Mary Fuller acknowledged her crime " *post pena* ".

Withholdment of food as a means of persuasion, also was

---

[1] *Reading on Torture*, by David Jardine.
[2] *Calendar of State Papers*. Dom. Ser., 1619–25, p. 125.
[3] *The Register of the Privy Council of Scotland*, 1591, p. 680.

ordered by authority, for instance, we are informed that Anne Jeffries confined in Bodmin gaol in 1645 was starved by order of a justice of the peace, who kept her in his own house " a prisoner and that without victuals " [1]

Hopkins, the witch-finder, in a pamphlet explains that in the infancy of the discovery of witches. prevention of sleep was not only thought fitting, but enjoined in Essex and Suffolk by the Magistrates, with the intention that by being kept awake, they would be the more active and quicker in calling their imps to their aid in the open view of the watchers.[2]  The Rev. John Gaule (1646) has left particulars of the method in which the starving and watching was carried out by Hopkins and his colleagues.

" Having taken the suspected witch, she is placed in the middle of a room upon a stool or table, cross-legged. or in some other uneasy posture, to which if she submits not, she is then bound with cords ; there is she watched and kept without meat or sleep for the space of 24 hours for (they say) within that time they shall see her imp come and suck.  A little hole is likewise made in the door for the imp to come in at ; and lest it might come in some less discernible shape, they that watch are taught to be ever and anon sweeping the room, and if they see any spiders or flies, to kill them.  And if they cannot kill them, then they may be sure they are her imps." [3]

The names of some of these professional watchers may be detected among the witnesses' names endorsed on the indictments (e.g. Frances Burges. Nos. 672–3. 675–6. 679. 680. 722).

About 1646 the practice of starving and watching was forbidden by Judges and Magistrates.  " Walking," adopted for the same purpose, likewise fell into disuse about the same time.

The swimming test was a survival of the ancient water ordeal, and continued in use, officially and unofficially for many years.

[1] *Remarkable Providences*, by Wm. Turner, 1697, p. 119.
[2] *The Discovery of Witches*, by Matthew Hopkins (1837 ed.), p. 5.
[3] *Select Cases of Conscience touching Witches and Witchcrafts*, by John Gaule, pp. 78, 79.

King James I, the royal demonologist, considered that a very good help in the trial of witches was " their fleeting on the water ".[1] The writer has seen no authoritative contemporary description as to how the water ordeal should be carried out, but that it was officially recognized the above reference to the case of John Lowis bears evidence, as does an extant order of the Mayor of Rye and others (7 Dec. 1645) " for Martha, the wife of Stephen Bruff, and Anne Howsell, widow, being suspected to be witches, to be tried by putting them into the water ".[2]

Sir Walter Besant, who unfortunately gives no authority, supplies the following account of the water ordeal :—

" The accused was stripped, his hands were tied crosswise to his feet, he was sprinkled with holy water ; he was permitted to kiss the cross ; a rope was tied around his waist, and at a distance of two ells from his body a knot was tied ; he was thrown into deep water ; if he sank as deep as the knot he was innocent ; if not he was guilty. The administration of the ordeal was not conducted in the bare and simple method indicated above ; it was placed in the hands of priests ; mass was said before it ; there were appropriate psalms and prayers ; the accused confessed his sins to the priest ; before the whole congregation he called upon God to prove his innocence ; he swore upon the holy relics of the church that he was innocent. The function was one of great solemnity and calculated to impress the minds of the people most deeply."[3]

This account is no doubt an accurate description of the test as carried out in medieval days, but Sir Walter Besant adds that this method was long practised in the case of witches. A contemporary reference, however, points to the swimming of witches actually having been a function of a much cruder nature. William Drage, writing in 1668, says that he saw a witch ducked at St Albans, who could not sink, " though she strove by putting

---

[1] Dæmonologie, 3rd book.
[2] Hist. MSS. Comm., xiii, pt. iv, p. 216.
[3] *Mediæval London (Ecclesiastical)*, 1906, p. 191.

her head under water, and was thrust down with poles." [1]
William Gilbert, a twentieth century writer gives the following
description :—

> " The victim was stripped naked and bound with her right
> thumb to her left toe, and her left thumb to her right toe,
> and was then cast into the pond or river. If she sank, she was
> frequently drowned ; if she swam, she was declared guilty
> without any further evidence being required, and so escaped
> drowning to be hanged or burned." [2]

No authority is cited, and notwithstanding that very absurd
evidence was often considered sufficient, it cannot be agreed that
the failure to sink *per se* was a hanging matter, rather the testing
seems to have been a popular pastime.   The following example
is from the MS. diary of one John Bufton of Coggeshall.[3]

> July 13, 1699.   The widow Comon was put into the river
> to see if she would sink, because she was suspected to be a
> witch—and she did not sink, but swim.
> And she was tryed again July 19th, and then she swam
> again, and did not sink.
> July 24, 1699.   The widow Comon was tryed a third time by
> putting her into the river, and she swam and did not sink.
> Dec. 27, 1699.   The widow Comon, that was counted a witch,
> was buried.

Twenty-five informants at Leicester Assizes in 1717
(Appendix VII) all deposed that the witches " had severally their
thumbs and great toes tied together and that they were thrown
so bound into the water, and that they swam like a cork, a piece
of paper, or an empty barrell, though they strove all they could
to sink ".

Another description by an eye-witness, but neither dated nor
documented (apparently eighteenth century, and after the repeal
of the Act), says :—

[1] *A Relation of Mary Hall*, by William Drage.   (Gerish, 1912,
p. 24.)
[2] *Witchcraft in Essex*, by W. Gilbert, p. 7.
[3] *Trans. of the Essex Arch. Soc.*, i, 117.

" The suspected witch, after having been stript of all her habiliments save her under-garment, her feet and hands confined together, and a rope tied round her waist to enable the officiating person to pull her out of the water again, if they found she was in danger of drowning, was put into a large tub, where she was received by Acers [the prosecutor], who, all being arranged, immediately shoved the tub from the side, and continued floating it until they had got to the deepest part of the pond, when he threw her into the water, and—she swam ! Although she tried all she could, and even dived down into the water like a duck, she could no more sink than a piece of cork." [1]

## Professional Witch-finders

The difficulty of detecting witches with certainty led to the employment of professional witch-finders, who were supposed to have greater experience than the local searchers and watchers. Through the machinations of these mercenary monsters large numbers of women lost their lives. Although the finders often acted unofficially, yet in a number of cases they were appointed and remunerated by authority. The order relating to the engagement of a Scottish witch-finder at Newcastle-upon-Tyne affords an illustration.

Barwick-upon-Tweed.

Att a private Guild there, holden the 30th day of July, Anno Domini 1649, before the Right Worshipful Andrew Crispe, Esq., Maior, Mr Stephen Jackson, Alderman, and the rest of the Guild-brethren. Ordered, that according to the Guild's desire, the man which tryeth the witches in Scotland shall be sent for, and satisfaction to be given him by the Towne in defraying his charges, and in coming hither, and that the town shall engage that no violence be offered him by any person within the Towne.[2]

In 1579 Samuel Cocwra, by warrant of the Privy Council, was

---

[1] *A Tryal of Witches* (Appendix), p. 27. Some occurrences 1750–1760 are recorded in the *Annual Register*. iii, 112.
[2] Guild Hall Book, 1643–51, f. 134. Printed in *History of Berwick*, by John Fuller, p. 155.

paid 7s. 6d. expenses for searching for conjurors in the counties of Salop, Worcester, and Montgomery.[1]

A notorious Scottish free-lance was James or John Balfoure in Corshous, who professed " to discover persouns guiltie of the cryme of witchecraft by remarking the devill's marke upon some part of thair persouns and bodeis and thristing of preins in the same, and upon the presumptioun of this knowledge goes athort the countrie abusing simple and ignorant people for his private gayn and commoditie ". In 1632 the Lords of the Privy Council found that his knowledge " hes onelie beene conjecturall ", and he was forbidden to exercise his art and trade.[2]

Another case, recorded under 1662, is that of Alexander Chisholm of Commer (with others including the minister) who imprisoning a number of men and women in his own house " most cruellie and barbrouslie tortured the women by waking, hanging them up by the thombes, burning the soles of their feet at the fyre, drawing of others at horse taills and binding of them with widdies about the neck and feet and carying them so alongst on horseback to prison, wherby and by other tortur one of them hath become distracted, another by cruelty is departed this lyfe, and all of them have confest whatever they were pleasit to demand of them, all which is done against his Majesty's lawes and authoritie, they being frie subjects ".[3]

In England the best known finders were Hopkins and Stearne, whose discoveries and evidence were the means of bringing many women to death in the Norfolk and Home circuits. It is probable that these gentlemen confined their operations mainly to finding the witches, certainly their names do not always appear as witnesses endorsed on the indictments.[4]

In conclusion of this account of the procedure in the discovery, trial, and punishment of witches, it may be of interest to add an

[1] *Acts of the Privy Council*, New Series, II, p. 292.
[2] *The Register of the Privy Council of Scotland*, 1632, pp. 427, 433.
[3] *Ibid.*, p. 237.          [4] See Index.

extract from a brief direction to the Jury given by Sir Matthew Hale in 1665 :—

" That there were such creatures as witches he made no doubt at all , for, first, the scriptures had affirmed so much. Secondly the wisdom of all nations had provided laws against such persons, which is an argument of their confidence of such a crime. And such hath been the judgment of this kingdome, as appears by that act of parliament which hath provided punishments proportionable to the quality of the offence. And desired them, strictly to observe their evidence ; and desired the great God of Heaven to direct their Hearts in this weighty thing they had in hand : For to condemn the innocent, and to let the guilty go free, were both an abomination to the Lord." [1]

## Records of Assizes

With regard to records of assizes, it appears that by 9 Edw. III, St. 1, c. 5, it had been enacted that Justices of Assize, Gaol Delivery, and Oyer and Terminer, should send all their records and processes determined and put in to the Exchequer at Michaelmas.[2] For a century this practice was followed, but thereafter it gradually fell into abeyance. There are consequently comparatively few records of Assizes for the fifteenth century to be found in the Public Record Office. For the reign of Henry VIII practically nothing has been preserved except for the Palatinates and Wales. From the time of Elizabeth a greater proportion of documents are extant, although the bulk has been destroyed.

Records with which we are now concerned were in the hands of the Clerks of Assize until the year 1911, when they were brought to the Chancery Lane depository.[3] These documents have since been classed according to the rearranged circuits of 1876, and records appertaining to the Home circuit will now be found

---

[1] *A Tryal of Witches,* etc., p. 20.
[2] *Statutes of the Realm,* vol. i, p. 272.
[3] For further particulars of the Records of the Clerks of Assize, see Guiseppi's *Guide to the Manuscripts preserved in the P.R.O.,* i, 240–3.

amongst those of the South-Eastern circuit, of which series they form the most valuable part.

The writer selected the Home circuit documents for his illustration of the prevalence of the witch persecution, because the records of this section are the oldest of the six ancient circuits above enumerated, and comprise the best series of Elizabethan indictments, commencing as they do in 1559, the next documents of this class in point of antiquity being those of the old Northern circuit which date back to the fourth year of James I [1607]. Some notes regarding the records of the Palatinates and Wales will be given later.

### Home Circuit Documents

The only documents of the Home circuit which are old enough to contain evidence of witchcraft proceedings are those classed as indictments (Reference, Assizes 35). These records, for the 178 years from 1559 when the records commence to 1736 when the last act against witchcraft was repealed, are contained in 176 paper bundles, besides which there are two further bundles of restored documents, and one sack of fragments. Each of these bundles contains a number of files which are usually rolled, and some of which are in an excellent state of preservation, while others are in the last stage of decay, and often crushed, crumpled, and dusty, making reference troublesome, dirty, and sometimes impracticable. At first sight it would seem that for 178 years there should be 1780 files for five counties holding two assizes a year each. Actually, up to the year 1637 there was originally one file for each assize for each county, that is to say for the 79 years (1559–1637 inclusive) there should be 790 files. For the year 1638 and onwards, it appears that a supplementary or relief file was made up for each circuit and comprising the documents of lesser importance relating to all the five counties, so that the number of files for the Home circuit for a year became 12, and therefore for the years 1638 to 1736, there should be 1188 files, making 1978 in all, being the records for 1780 assizes. Actually, at the time of the writer's search, there were fit for production 1600 files, of which 97 related to counties not formerly in the Home circuit. Of the remaining 1503, 130 were supplementary for mixed counties, leaving 1373, being the indictments for 1373 assizes. For the year 1643 there was no bundle and for the year 1707 no files for the five counties. Years in which more than half the files are wanting are 1561–2–3–6, 1574, 1604, 1622, 1637, 1646, 1656, 1660, 1668, 1710, and 1728–9. Practically all of the 1600 files were looked through, somewhat rapidly it must be admitted. A few, such as that for the Kent Summer Sessions, 1611, and Summer Sessions, 1711, owing to the membranes being stuck together, had perforce to be left untouched. Eighteenth century documents were in very much the worst condition and the figures now given must be taken as an approximation only, very careful examination and rearrangement would be necessary before an exact count could be made. Some of the files have become divided, others again have become mere skeletons, and a considerable number are in the wrong bundles or wrongly labelled.

There were then, records of about 1373 of the 1780 assizes, a proportion of about 77 *per centum* made up as follows :—

| Reigns | | No of files. | Average No. of files per year |
|---|---|---|---|
| Elizabeth | 1559–1602 | 317 | 7·20 |
| James I | 1603–1624 | 160 | 7·27 |
| Charles I | 1625–1648 | 166 | 6·90 |
| Commonwealth | 1649–1659 | 90 | 8·18 |
| Charles II | 1660–1684 | 192 | 7·68 |
| James II | 1685–1688 | 34 | 8·50 |
| Wm. and Mary | 1689–1701 | 131 | 10·07 |
| Anne | 1702–1713 | 98 | 8·16 |
| George I | 1714–1726 | 100 | 7·69 |
| George II | 1727–1736 | 85 | 8·50 |

These files, in addition to indictments, contain presentments, and inquisitions of similar nature transmitted from the Quarter Sessions ; also the commissions of gaol delivery, and oyer and terminer, together with the justices' precepts or writs of venire facias to the Sheriff, with returns endorsed, writs of capias with returns (after 1610), informations and examinations, prisoners' and witnesses' recognizances, lists of those bound to appear at assizes, such as justices of the peace, coroners, seneschals of liberties, mayors, bailiffs of liberties and hundreds, constables of the hundreds ; gaol calendars, jury panels, gaol delivery rolls, petitions to the justices, affidavits of service, coroner's inquests on prisoners and others, bailiff's receipts for prisoners, certificates of character, recusancy, ill-health, etc., inventories of felon's goods, and other miscellaneous matter.

The supplementary files, referred to above, contain little of the great felonies except bills not found, and are largely made up of presentments for nuisances, unlawful games, unlicensed ale-houses, drunkenness, amending of roads, forestalling, abuses, offences, misdemeanours, etc., the whole file frequently wrapped up in an Essex gaol delivery roll.

The documents forming each file or roll were in most cases originally held together by a file of parchment or twine passing through the left hand top corners, any surplus being used to retain the file in rolled form by wrapping round the outside and fastening. Sometimes the files were bound or fastened in book form, and more rarely the membranes are sewn edge to edge, forming a continuous roll. The largest documents such as gaol delivery rolls or lists of officials were placed to the outside to form a covering for the lesser ones when rolled up. Owing to the rotting of file or binding the documents are now often detached and misplaced.

One file may have as many as 100 indictments, possibly in the whole series there may be 50,000 of these documents. Presentments are few.

### Presentments and Indictments

The little difference between a presentment and an indictment is given by William Lambard (*Eirenarcha*, 1614, pp. 485–6), who has it that a presentment is a " mere denunciation of the Jurors themselves, or of some other officer . . . without any other information : and an indictment is the verdict of the Jurors grounded upon the accusation of a third person ; so that a presentment is but a declaration of the Jurors (or Officers) without any bill offered before : and an indictment is their finding of a bill of accusation to be true." A presentment might, however, be used as an indictment.[1]

The presentment is usually written in English upon paper : the indictment is in Latin engrossed upon parchment which varies in length from 9 in. to 15 in., and in depth from 6 in. to 3 in., the most usual size being about 9 in. by 3 in.[2]

In the case of a person accused by one complainant on several counts of similar nature, a like number of bills might be drafted as Nos. 533–536, but more often one indictment would have been made to serve, in fact one document sometimes comprised the complaints of several prosecutors (No. 201). In the case of a man and his goods being both injured by witchcraft it was usual to draw two bills (as Nos. 312–13), but occasionally several complaints of different nature are included in one indictment (Nos. 56, 197). As at the present day, one document may serve for two persons on a joint charge (104–5), and occasionally two or more indictments are entered on one membrane of larger size, but these relate to prosecutions transmitted from the Quarter Sessions (89–91, 234–6).

During the interregnum (actually 1651–9) bills of indictment, in common with other legal documents, were written in English. In 1731 in accordance with the Act of 4 Geo. II, c. 26, English was permanently adopted.

A presentment or indictment for witchcraft ought to contain the following information : County ; Name, surname, address, and description of the party indicted : The time when and place where the offence was alleged to have been committed ; The name. surname, address, and description of the person offended

---

[1] An entry in Chester assizes gaol book refers to four papers of presentments which were made into indictments. Chester 21/3, p. 231.

[2] North Country bills of indictment are usually larger, 12 in. by 8 in. being the common size, conforming nearly to modern practice.

or on whom the offence was committed (in the case of infants,[1] parentage and age). Alternatively, the kind, colour, value, and ownership of the thing upon which the offence was committed. The nature of the offence.

Additional and unnecessary matter is occasionally found. Sometimes the statement of the offence is *vi et armis. baculis, cultellis*, etc., following the more general formula of a bill for assault or murder, without adding anything to the effect. (Examples Nos. 132, 223, 224, 500.) By 37 Hen. VIII, c. 8, it had been enacted that an indictment or inquisition for felony lacking the words *vi et armis videlicet cum baculis, cultellis*, etc., should be taken, deemed, and adjudged, to all intents, constructions, and purposes as good and effectual in the law as the same inquisition and indictments having the said words, etc.

Occasionally an indictment for witchcraft particularly mentions an assault made (Examples 223 and 407).

A longer form of indictment recited part of the Act of Parliament of 12 Jan. 5 Eliz. (Examples Nos. 48, 58), but this recital was soon dropped as it was found safer and surer to draw the bill with the conclusion " against the form of the Statute in such case made and provided ". Indictments of the Northern circuit were the longest, citing the Act more fully.

Inquisitions from the Quarter Sessions, giving names of justices and jury, etc., although not endorsed with the finding of the grand jury seem to have served the purpose of indictments (Examples 191, 513), but in one case there are filed the inquisition as well as an endorsed indictment in the usual form, both in the same handwriting (No. 67), which may indicate that duplicates originally were made.

Occasionally the names of imps or familiars were specified (see Nos. 196, 511, 604, etc.).

Indictments are undated except internally in the rare cases where a person languished " until the day of taking this inquisition, namely . . ." (Example No. 204).

---

[1] The age of an adult is given Nos. 686 and 689.

Clerical omissions in these documents were frequent, but usually overlooked. The address and description of persons offended, the age of infants, and colour and value of cattle were often wanting. Lambard, writing in 1581, says that by various statutes " it was enacted that the day year and place in which the offence was committed must be specified ",[1] nevertheless we find that this requisite information is often omitted without invalidating the indictment. Examples Nos. 341 and 357 omit the name of the place, and No. 364 does not mention the venue either of crime or death.

Dates are also sometimes omitted (Example No. 500), and in No. 707 they are contradictory.

Certainty in the bills evidently not being a strong point, it is the more surprising to find that No. 122 was held to be insufficient, and No. 513 vacated because it was not sound in law.

A selection of forms of indictments (Latin and English) with translations and explanations will now be given.

## Sixteen examples of Indictments

INDICTMENT NO. 1.  CHELMSFORD SUMMER SESSIONS, 2 Eliz.
(1560)

Essex. Jur ꝑsent pro dna Regina q̃d Joħes Samond de Danberie in com̃ ꝑd Berebruer als dict Joħes Smythe est com̃is incantator ac fascinator tam hominū qua animaliū Et q̃d idem Joħes deū ꝑ occulis non ħens sed instigacõe diabolica motus et seductus p artem incantacõis et fascinaciõis diabolicā xxviijº die Maij anno regni dne Elizabeth dei grac Anglie ffranc et Hiħnie Regine fidei def &c. primo ac diuꝰcis diebჳ et vicibჳ tam antea quā postea apd Danberie ꝑd ex malicia sua ꝑcogitat quosdā Joħem (sic) Graunte et Brigittā Pecocke fascinauit et incantauit p q̃d dicta Brigitta ex incantacõe et fascinacõe ꝑd a ꝑd xxviijº die Maij anno sup'dic vsqჳ xxix diem Augusti prox sequent languebat ad quem diem eadem Brigitta ex incantacõe et fascinacõe ꝑd apd Danburie ꝑd obijt. Et dict

―――――――――
[1] Eirenarcha. 1581. p. 389. I cannot trace these statutes.

Antinus Graunte ex incantacõe et fascinacõe p̃d a p̃d xxviij°
die Maij annı sup'dic̃ vsq̄ xxviij° diem Maij prox̃ sequen̄t
languebat ad quem diem p̃dc̃us Antonius ex incantaciõe et
fascinacõe p̃d apd Danburye p̃d obijt.  Et sic Jurat̃ p̃d dicunt
q̃d p̃dc̃us Joħes p incantacõem et fascinacõem p̃d die anno
et loco p̃d p̃fat̄ Brigittā et Antoniū felonice interfecit et
murderauit contra pacē dc̃e d̃ne Regine coronā et digniı̃t suas, &c.

*Translation.*

Essex.  The Jurors for our lady the Queen do present that
John Samond of Danbury in the county aforesaid, beer-brewer,
otherwise called John Smythe, is a common enchanter and witch
as well of men as beasts.  And that the said John, not having
God before his eyes, but being moved and seduced by the
instigation of the devil, by the devilish arts of enchantment and
witchcraft, on 28 May, 1 Eliz. and diverse days and places as
well before as afterwards, at Danbury aforesaid, of his malice
aforethought, a certain John (*sic*) Graunte and Brigit Pecocke
did bewitch and enchant, by reason of which the said Brigit of
the enchantment and witchcraft aforesaid, from the said 28 May
in the year abovesaid until 29 August next following did languish,
on which day the said Brigit of the enchantment and witchcraft
aforesaid at Danbury aforesaid died.  And the said Antony
Grant of the enchantment and witchcraft aforesaid from the
28 May in the year above said until the 28 May next following did
languish, on which day the said Antony of the enchantment and
witchcraft aforesaid at Danbury aforesaid died.  And so the
Jurors aforesaid say that the aforesaid John by enchantment
and witchcraft aforesaid, the day, year, and place aforesaid,
feloniously did kill and murder the said Brigit and Antony against
the peace of the said lady the Queen, her crown and dignity, etc.

INDICTMENT No. 24.  MAIDSTONE SUMMER SESSIONS, 9 Eliz.
(1567)

Kanc.  Jur̄ p̃sen̄t p d̃na Regina q̃d Agnes Bennett nup de
Boughton Mounchelsey in com̃ p̃dc̃o vidua vicesimo secundo

die ffebruarij Anno regni d̄ne ñre Elizabeth dei grã Angł ffranc̃ & hibñ Regine fidei defens̃ &c octavo apud Boughton Mounchelsey p̃dc̃am in com̃ p̃dc̃o ex diabolica instigasione instigata deū pre oculis suis non h̃ens quendam Joh̃em Lyttelhare filiū Joh̃is Lyttelhare de Boughton Mounchelsey p̃dc̃a in com̃ p̃dc̃o fremason incantacone & venifica sua diabolice spoliauit & distruxit racione quoჳ dc̃a Agnes Bennett adtunc & ibm p̃d Joh*m* Lyttelhare incantacoionib; & venificis p̃dcis apud Boughton Mounchelsey p̃dc̃am felonice murderauit & int⁹fecit cont' pacem dc̃e d̄ne Regine nunc coronam & dignitatem suas & cont' formam statuti in hac pte edit̃ & puis &c.

*Translation.*

Kent. The Jurors for our lady the Queen do present that Agnes Bennett, late of Boughton Monchelsea in the county aforesaid, widow, on 22 Feb., 8 Eliz., at Boughton Monchelsea aforesaid, in the county aforesaid, not having God before her eyes, and incited by the instigation of the Devil, a certain John Lyttelhare, son of John Lyttelhare of Boughton Monchelsea aforesaid, in the county aforesaid, freemason, by her enchantment and potion devilishly did despoil and destroy, by reason of which the said Agnes Bennett then and there the aforesaid John Lyttelhare by the enchantments and potions aforesaid at Boughton Monchelsea aforesaid, feloniously did murder and kill against the peace of the said lady the now Queen, her crown and dignity, and against the form of the statute in this case made and provided, etc.

INDICTMENT No. 56. CHELMSFORD Summer SESSIONS, 14 Eliz.
(1572)

Ess̃ Inquiratʳ p d̄na Regine si Joh̃es Smyth ał Sawmon de Danberie in com̃ p̃dc̃o berebrewer & Johanna vx̃ eius vicesimo die Julij anno regni d̄ne ñre Elizabeth dei grã Angł ffranc̃ & hib̃n Regina fidei defensoris &c duodecimo dei timorem p̃oculis non habens sed instigacone diabolica seducta quasdam malas & diabolicas artes anglice voc̃ witchcraftƴ inchantem'ƴ charmes

& sorceries nequit' diabolice apud danberie p̃d in cõm p̃d die & anno sup̃dict̃ vsa fuit & exercivit racone quaȝ quidam Edwardus Robynson de danberie p̃d sawier de corpore suo mutulat̃ fuit & adhuc est et in ãlijs bonis & cattallis suis multiplicit' lesus & deteriorat̃ existit cont' pacem dce dne Regine &c ac cont' formam statuti in hac pte edit̃ & p̃vic̃ &c.

*Translation.*

Essex.  Be it enquired for our lady the Queen if John Smith otherwise Sawmon of Danbury in the county aforesaid, beer-brewer, and Joan, his wife, on 20 July, 12 Eliz., not having the fear of God before their eyes, but seduced by the instigation of the Devil, certain evil and devilish arts called witchcrafts, enchantments, charms, and sorceries, at Danbury aforesaid in the county aforesaid, the day and year abovesaid, wickedly and devilishly did employ and exercise by reason of which a certain Edward Robynson of Danbury aforesaid, sawyer, in his body was lamed and yet is, and in his beasts, goods and chattels in manifold ways is hurt and worsened, against the peace of the said lady the Queen, etc., and against the form of the statute in this case made and provided, etc.

### INDICTMENT No. 66.  HERTFORD LENT SESSIONS, 15 Eliz. (1573)

Hertf  Juratores p̃ dna Regina p̃ntant q̃d Thomas Heather nup de Hoddesden in cõm p̃dc̃a yoman existeñ cõis coniurator et invocator malorum spiritum deum p̃oculis suis non h̃ens sed instigac̃one diabolica seductus primo die Januarij Anno regni dne Elizabethe dei gr̃a Anglie frauncie et hib̃nie Regine fidei defensoris &c quinto decimo apud Hoddesden p̃dc̃am in quadam silua ib̃m maliciose diabolice et felonice vsus est quadam coniurac̃one et invocac̃one malorum spirituum ea intenc̃one ad lucrand̃ diu⁹sis magnas pecuniam sumas contra formam statuti in huiusmodi casu nup edit & p̃uis et in malum exemplum omñ alioru̅ in consili casu delinquenc̃ et contra pacem dc̃e dne Regine nunc coram & dignitatem suas &c.

⅔ Actual Size

A BILL OF INDICTMENT. A.D. 1579

(See No. 119, p. 137)

[face p. 80

*Translation.*

Hertford. The Jurors for our lady the Queen do present that Thomas Heather, late of Hoddesdon in the county aforesaid, yeoman, being a common conjuror and invoker of evil spirits, not having God before his eyes, but seduced by the instigation of the Devil, on 1 Jan., 15 Eliz., at Hoddesdon aforesaid, in a certain wood there maliciously, devilishly and feloniously did employ certain conjuration and invocation of evil spirits with the intent of gaining diverse great sums of money against the form of the statute in this case lately made and provided, and in bad example of all others in like case offending and against the peace of the said lady the now Queen, her crown and dignity, etc.

INDICTMENT No. 122. CHELMSFORD LENT SESSIONS. 21 Eliz. (1579)

Essex. Inquisicio capta apud Branktrey in cõm p̃dc̃o die Jovis prox̃ post festū sc̃i Michis Archi existeñ sc̃do die Octobris Anno regni d̃ne Elizabeth dei grã Anglie, *etc.*, xxº coram Robto Byche milite *and 8 others named* custod pace d̃ne Regine audiend & terminand assigñ p sacr̃m Johis Sandell *and 27 others named* extitit psentat pro D̃na R̃ne q̃d Margeria Stanton de Wymbyshe in cõm Essex spinster existens cõis incantatrix et fascinatrix t'm homiñ q'm bestiaȝ et aliaȝ rerū et exercens diabolicam et nequissimam artem fascinac̃ et incantac̃ deū p̃oculis suis non hens sed diabolica instigacõe seduct̃ vicesimo die Augusti anno regni d̃ne Elizabeth, *etc.*, xxº apud Wymbyshe p̃d in cõm p̃d vnū spadonem coloris white p̃cij triū libraȝ et vnam vaccam p̃cij quadraginta solidoȝ ex malicia sua p̃cogitat̃ ad tunc et ibm nequissime fascinauit et incantauit de quaquidem fascinac̃oe et incantac̃oe p̃d p̃dict̃ spado et vacca languebant a p̃dc̃o xxº die Augusti vsq, xxiiijto diem Augusti tunc px̃ sequeñ quoquidem xxiiijto die Augusti anno supradc̃o p̃d spado et vacca obier̃ Et sic jur̃ p̃d dic̃ sup sacr̃m suū q̃d p̃dc̃a Margeria Stanton p̃d spadonem & vacca die et anno p̃d apud Wymbyshe p̃d vi et ar p̃d interfecit contra pacem dc̃e d̃ne R̃ne nūc coroñ et dignitatem suas.

*Translation.*

Essex. Inquisition taken at Braintree in the county aforesaid, on Thursday next after the feast of St Michael the Archangel, being 2 Oct., 20 Eliz., before, etc., by the oaths of, etc., it is presented for our lady the Queen that Margery Stanton of Wimbish in the county of Essex, spinster. being a common enchantress and witch, as well of men as beasts and other things, not having God before her eyes, but seduced by the instigation of the Devil, and exercising the devilish and wicked art of witchcraft and enchantment, on 20 Aug., 20 Eliz., at Wimbish aforesaid in the county aforesaid. one gelding of a white colour valued at 3*l*., and one cow valued at 40*s*. of her malice aforethought then and there wickedly did bewitch and enchant, by reason of which certain witchcraft and enchantment aforesaid, the aforesaid gelding and cow did languish, from the said 20 Aug. until 24 Aug. then next following, on which 24 Aug. in the year abovesaid the aforesaid gelding and cow died. And so the Jurors aforesaid upon their oaths say that the aforesaid Margery Stanton the aforesaid gelding and cow the day and year aforesaid at Wimbish aforesaid, with force and arms, did kill, against the peace of the said lady the now Queen, her crown and dignity, etc.

INDICTMENT No. 132. HORSHAM SUMMER SESSIONS, 21 Eliz.
(1579)

Essex   Jurator p dna Regina p̃ntant quod Allicia Stedmā vx̃ Joħis Stedman de Stedham in cõm p̃d wodbrooker existens cõis ffascinatrix & incantatrix deū p̃occulis suis non habens sed instigacõne diabolica seducta ex[malicia] sua p̃cogitata p̃mo die mensis ffebruarij Anno Regni dne ñre Elizabethe dei grã Anglie ffranc̃ et Hibernie Regine fidei defens' &c. vicesimo primo vi et armis &c. p incantacõnes et fascinacõnes suas apud Stedham p̃d duas vaccas cuiusdam Wiłłm Spuirio' ad valenc̃ iiij ti vnū juvencum ip̃ius Wiłłmi ad valenc̃ xiij. s̃. iiij. d̃. vnā aliam vaccam ip̃ius Wiłłm ad vał xl. s̃. nequiter et diabolice incantauit et fascinauit racone quarū quidem fascinaconū et incantaconū p̃d cattall p̃d die Anno et loco p̃d parierunt contra formā statᵗⁱ in huĩodi casu nup edito et pviss ac contra pac̃ d̃ce d̃ne Regine Corona et digñ suas.

*Translation.*

Essex. The Jurors for our lady the Queen do present that Alice Stedman, wife of John Stedman of Stedham, in the county aforesaid, woodbroker, being a common witch and enchantress, not having God before her eyes, but seduced by the instigation of the Devil, of her [malice] aforethought, on 1 Feb., 21 Eliz., with force and arms, etc., by her enchantments and witchcrafts at Stedham aforesaid, 2 cows of a certain William Spurior, valued at 4*l.*, 1 steer of the said William valued at 13*s.* 4*d.*, one other cow of the said William, valued at 40*s.*, wickedly and devilishly did enchant and bewitch, by reason of which certain witchcrafts and enchantments aforesaid, the cows aforesaid, the day, year, and place aforesaid, did calve, against the form of the statute in this case lately made and provided, and against the peace of the said lady the Queen, her crown and dignity.

INDICTMENT No. 196. WITHAM SUMMER SESSIONS, 25 Eliz. (1583)

Essex Juratores pro d̃na Regina p̃sentant q̃d Margeria Barnes nup de pochia sc̃i Osythes in com̃ p̃d spynster primo die mens' Julij anno regni d̃ne Elizab̃ dei gra, *etc.*, xxvᵗᵒ in possessione s's habuit gub̃navit et manutenuit tres lez Imps als vocat̃ sperytt℮ nuncupat̃ siue vocat̃ per nomen vel nomina Pygine similis a mole Russoll similis le gray catt et at voc̃ Dunsott similis le dundogge ea intenc̃one vt fascinauit et incantauit tam homũ q'm bestiaȝ et aliaȝ rerũ ad graue dampnũ cunctu populu dc̃e d̃ne Rⁿᵉ Elizabeth. Et contra pacem et coronā s's Et contra formā statuti in huiusmodi casu inde edit̃ et proviss.

*Translation.*

Essex. The Jurors for our lady the Queen do present that Margery Barnes, late of the parish of St Osyth in the county

aforesaid, spinster, on 1 July, 25 Eliz., in her possession did
entertain, govern and maintain three imps otherwise called
spirits named or called by the name or names : Pygine, resembling
a mole ; Russoll resembling a grey cat ; and the other called
Dunsott resembling a dun dog with intent that she might
enchant and bewitch as well men as beasts and other things, to
the grievous damage of the entire people of the said lady the
Queen Elizabeth. And against the peace and her crown. And
against the form of the statute in this case made and provided.

INDICTMENT No. 223. WITHAM SUMMER SESSIONS, 26 Eliz.
(1584)

Essex Jur̃ p d̃na Regina p̃sentant q̃d Elizabeth Morsby de
Chesterford magñ in com̃ p̃d spinster deum p oculis suis non
t̃iens sed instigac̃one diabolica seduc̃ ex malitia sua p̃cogitata
vicesimo quarto die Junij anno regni d̃ne Elizabeth dei grã, *etc.*,
vicesimo quarto vi et armis &c. apud Magna Chesterford in
quand'm Agnetem Wynterflud in pac̃ dei et dc̃e d̃ne Regine
insultũ fecit et ip̃am Agnetem Wynterfludd ad tunc & ib̃m
feloñ et nequissime fascinauit et incantauit racone quar' quidem
fascinac̃onis et incantac̃onis p̃d p̃fat Agnes Wynterflud apud
Chesterford p̃d a p̃dc̃o vicesimo quart̃ die Junij anno vicesimo
quarto sup'dco vsq̧ vicesimũ quartũ diem Decembr anno
vicesimo quint̃ dc̃e d̃ne Regine languebat quo quidem vicesimo
quarto die Decembr anno regni dc̃i d̃ne Regine nunc xxvᵗᵒ
sup'dco de incãtac̃one & fascinac̃one p̃d Agnes Wynterflud
apud Chesterford p̃d obijt. Et sic jur̃ p̃d dicunt sup sacr*uu*
s*uu* q̃d p̃d Elizabeth Morsby p̃d Agnetem Wynterfludd apud
Chesterford p̃d vicesimo quarto die Decembr anno xxvᵒ sup'dco
ex malitia sua p̃cogit̃ feloñ et nequissime incantauit interfecit
et murderauit contra pacem &c. contraq̧ formam statut̃ in
huioi casu nup edit̃ et p̃viss.

*Translation.*

Essex. The Jurors for our lady the Queen do present that
Elizabeth Morsby of Great Chesterford in the county aforesaid,

spinster, not having God before her eyes, but seduced by the instigation of the Devil, of her malice aforethought, on 24 June, 24 Eliz., with force and arms, at Great Chesterford. on a certain Agnes Wynterflud, in the peace of God and the said lady the Queen, did make an assault, and the said Agnes Wynterfludd then and there feloniously and wickedly did bewitch and enchant by reason of which certain witchcraft and enchantment aforesaid the said Agnes Wynterflud at Chesterford aforesaid, from the aforesaid 24 June in the twenty fourth year abovesaid until 24 Dec. in the twenty fifth year of the said lady the Queen, did languish, upon which certain 24 Dec. abovesaid, of the enchantment and witchcraft aforesaid Agnes Wynterflud at Chesterford aforesaid died. And so the Jurors aforesaid say upon their oaths that the aforesaid Elizabeth Morsby, the aforesaid Agnes Wynterfludd at Chesterford aforesaid, on 24 Dec., in the twenty fifth year abovesaid of her malice aforethought, feloniously and wickedly did enchant, kill and murder, against the peace, etc., and against the form of the statute in this case lately made and provided.

INDICTMENT No 224. WITHAM SUMMER SESSIONS, 26 Eliz.
(1584)

Essex   Jurator p⁹sentant p dna Regina quod Edmundus Mansell nup de ffingerighoo in com p̃dc̃o yeoman ałs dc̃us Edmundus Mansell nup de ffeeringe in com̃ p̃dc̃o clarke vi et armis deum pre oculis non ħens sed diabolica instigaca seductus et instigat̃ decimo die m⁹tij anno regni dne Elizabeth dei grã, *etc.*, vicesimo sexto apud Wyvenhoo in com̃ p̃dc̃i vsus est et exercebat magicia et incantac̃oem p qua quidem magicia et incantac̃oem vnũ horreũ ad valenc̃ Triginta libraȝ vnũ stabuł ad valenc̃ decem libraȝ cuiusdam Edw̃i Burgesse in Wyvenhoo p̃dc̃a in com̃ p̃dc̃o vna carectata feni ad valenc̃ viginti solid' vnus currus cũ apparata . . . ad valenc̃ Triũ libraȝ vna cella cũ apparatũ ad valenc̃ decem solid̃ ac diu⁹s'vtencił domostical ad valenc̃ quinᵹ libraȝ de bonis et cattałł ipius Edw̃i apud

Wyvenhoo p̃dc̃am igni et flamma ad tunc et ib̃m accend' de veneî et eodem igne et incendio ex magicia et incantac̃one dc̃is p̃dict̃ horreũ stabulũ ac bona et cattatt p̃dc̃a adtunc et ib̃m penitus arsa devastaî et consumpt̃ fueî contra pacem dc̃e d̃ne R̃ñe corona et dignitatem suas et contra forma diuᵒs' statutoî in itt casu edit̃ et pviss &c.

*Translation.*

The Jurors for our lady the Queen do present that Edmund Mansell, late of Feering in the county aforesaid, yeoman, otherwise called Edmund Mansell, late of Feering in the county aforesaid, clerk, with force and arms, not having God before his eyes, but seduced and urged by the instigation of the Devil, on 10 Mar., 26 Eliz., at Wyvenhoe in the county aforesaid did employ and exercise magic and enchantment by which certain magic and enchantment a barn valued at 30*l.*, a stable valued at 10*l.*, of a certain Edward Burgesse in Wyvenhoe aforesaid in the county aforesaid, a cartload of hay valued at 20*s.*, a cart with harness valued at 3*l.*, a stall with fittings valued at 10*s.*, and diverse domestic utensils valued at 5*l.*, of the goods and chattels of the said Edmund at Wyvenhoe aforesaid with fire and flame then and there became kindled and by the fire and flame of the said magic and enchantment aforesaid, the barn, stable, and goods and chattels aforesaid, then and there from within were burned, wasted, and consumed, against the peace of the said lady the Queen, her crown and dignity, and against the form of diverse statutes in this case made and provided.

INDICTMENT No. 244. CHELMSFORD LENT SESSIONS, 29 Eliz. (1587)

Essex Juî p d̃na Rⁿᵃ p̃sentant Johanna Preston de pua Sampford in com̃ p̃d spinster xxᵒ die August anno regni d̃ne Elizabethe dei grā, *etc.*, vicessimo octauo existens cõis fascinatrix & incantatrix tam hom*iu* qua bestiaʒ et aliaʒ rerũ apud puam Sampford p̃d quandam Margaretam Hankyn diabolice & nequissime fascinauit & incantauit contra pacem dne Rⁿ

nunc coroñ & dignitat̃ suis & contra forma statut̃ in huiũõi casu
nup̃ edit̃ & prouiss.

*Translation.*

Essex. The Jurors for our lady the Queen do present that Joan
Preston of Little Sampford in the county aforesaid, spinster
on 20 Aug., 28 Eliz., being a common witch and enchantress,
as well of men as beasts and other things, at Little Sampford
aforesaid, a certain Margaret Hankyn devilishly and wickedly
did bewitch and enchant, against the peace of the lady the
now Queen, her crown and dignity, and against the form of the
statute in this case lately made and provided.

INDICTMENT No. 500.  CHELMSFORD LENT SESSIONS, 7 Jas. I
(1610)

Essex Juratores pro Rege p̃sentant q̃d Katerina Lawrett
nup̃ de Colne Wake in com̃ Essex p̃dc̃o spinster deum pre occulis
suis non habens sed instigac̃one diabolica seducta existeñ cõis
fascinatrix et incantatrix vi et armis, &c, apud Colne Wake,
p̃dc̃am in com̃ p̃dc̃o quasdam malas et diabolicas artes vocat̃
witchcraft℮ inchantment℮ charmes & sorceryes nequiter et
diabolice vsa fuit practicauit et exercuit et vnũ equũ p̃cij decem
librarum de bonis et catallis cuiusdam ffrancisci Plaite adhunc
et it̃m fascinauit et incantauit racone quarum quidem
fascinacõnis et incantacõnis equus p̃dc̃us perijt et ad mortem
suam devenit ad grave dampũ p̃dc̃i ffrancisci Plaile. Et sic
p̃dc̃a Katerina Lawrett equũ p̃dc̃ũ p̃ fascinac̃ones et
incantac̃ones p̃d modo et forma p̃d occidit contra pacem dc̃i
d̃ni Regis nunc coroñ et dignitat̃ suas ac contra formam statut̃
huiõi casu edit̃ et proviss.

*Translation.*

The Jurors for the King do present that Katherine Lawrett,
late of Colne Wake in the county of Essex aforesaid, spinster,
not having God before her eyes, but seduced by the instigation
of the Devil, being a common witch and enchantress, with force

and arms, etc., at Colne Wake aforesaid in the county aforesaid, certain evil and devilish arts called witchcrafts, enchantments, charms, and sorceries wickedly and devilishly did employ, practise and exercise, and one horse valued at 10*l.* of the goods and chattels of a certain Francis Plaite then and there did bewitch and enchant, by reason of which certain witchcrafts and enchantments the aforesaid horse did perish and come to its death, to the grievous damage of the aforesaid Francis Plaile. And so [the Jurors say that] the aforesaid Katherine Lawrett, by the witchcrafts and enchantments aforesaid, in manner and form aforesaid, did kill the aforesaid horse, against the peace of the said lord the now King, his crown and dignity, and against the form of the statute in this case made and provided.

INDICTMENT No. 513.    MAIDSTONE LENT SESSIONS, 8 Jas. I
(1611)

Kanĉ Inquisicô capta ad gen⁹alem Sessionem pacis coṁ p̃dc̃i tenĩ apud Castrum Cantuaȓ in coṁ p̃dc̃o die Martis p̃x post festum Ep̃hie d̃ni Anno Regni d̃ni ñri Jacobi dei grã, etc., octavo coram [*Two justices of the peace named*] justiĉ d̃ni Regis ad pacem in coṁ p̃dc̃o conƒvand necnon ad diu⁹sã felonias t⁹nsgȓ & alia malefca in eodem coṁ ppetraĩ audiend & terminand assigñ p sacȓm [15 *names*] p̱boꝫ & leḡliũ hominñ de coṁ p̃dc̃o. Q'm diĉ sup sacȓm suũ. Et p̱ d̃no Rege p̃sentanĩ q̃d Sibilla fferrys de St. Lawrence in coṁ p̃dc̃o vidua primo die Martij Anno Regni d̃ni ñri Jacobi dei grã, etc., septimo ac diu⁹sis alijs diebꝫ & vicibꝫ tam antea q'm postea deum pre oculis suis non h̃ens sed instigacône diabolica seducĩ quasdam malas diabolicas artes Anglice voĉ witchcraftes inchantmentꝑ charmes and sorceries nequiter diabolice & felonice apud St. Lawrence p̃dc̃am in coṁ p̃dc̃o ex malitia p̃cogitata vsa fuit practizauit & exerciuit in & sup quandam Janam Nortcliffe Vxem Joh̃is Nortcliffe p'textu cuius p̃dc̃a Jana a p̃dc̃o primo die Martij Anno sup'dco vsq̱ primũ diem Junij tunc p̃x sequeñ languebat & multipliciter peioraĩ & deterioraȓ existiĩ Ad g've dampnũ ip̃oꝫ Joh̃is & Jane contra pacem dñi Regis nunc et contra formam statuī inde pviſ.

*In margin.* Vacat quia non valet in lege virtute statuti inde nup ediī.

*Translation.*

Inquisition taken at General Sessions of the Peace for the county aforesaid, holden at Canterbury Castle in the county aforesaid, on Tuesday next after the feast of the Epiphany of our Lord, 8 Jas. I, before, etc., by the oaths of, etc., Who say upon their oaths And for the lord the King do present that Sibil Ferrys of St Lawrence in the county aforesaid, widow, on 1 Mar., 7 Jas. I, and diverse other days and places as well before as afterwards, not having God before her eyes, but seduced by the instigation of the Devil, certain evil and devilish arts called witchcrafts, enchantments, charms, and sorceries, wickedly, devilishly and feloniously at St Lawrence aforesaid in the county aforesaid, of her malice aforethought, did employ, practise and exercise in and upon a certain Jane Nortcliffe, wife of John Nortcliffe, by colour of which the aforesaid Jane from the aforesaid 1 Mar. in the year abovesaid until 1 June then next following did languish and in manifold ways became worsened and poorer to the grievous damage of the said John and Jane [and] against the peace of the lord the now King, and against the form of the statute therein provided.

### INDICTMENT No. 518. CHELMSFORD LENT SESSIONS, 10 Jas. I (1612)

Essex Juratores pro dño Rege psentant q̃d Roɓtus Parker nup de Toppesfeild in com̃ pdco gen⁹osus quinto die Novembris annis regni dñi ñri Jacobi, etc., decimo et Scotie quadragesimo sexto apud Toppesfeild pd in com̃ pdc̃o suscepit sup se anglice did take vppon him p malas et diabolicas artes voc̃ charmes and sorceryes ledere et distruere anglice to hurt and distroye quendam Thomam Browne sen⁹ in corpore suo contra pacem dc̃i dñi

Regis nunc coroñ et dignitaſ suas ac contra formam statuſ in huiõi casu nup ediſ et proviss.

*Translation.*

Essex. The Jurors for the lord the King do present that Robert Parker, late of Toppesfield in the county aforesaid, gentleman, on 5 Nov., 10 Jas. I, at Toppesfield aforesaid in the county aforesaid, did take upon himself by evil and devilish arts called charms and sorceries to hurt and destroy a certain Thomas Browne, the elder, in his body, against the peace of the said lord the now King, his crown and dignity, and against the form of the statute in this case lately made and provided.

INDICTMENT No. 538. CHELMSFORD SUMMER SESSIONS, 14 Jas I (1616)

Essex  Juratores pro dno Rege ꝑsentant q̃d Susanna Barker nup de Vpminster in com̃ ꝑdc̃o spinster vx̃ Henrici Barker existens cõis fascinatrix et incantatrix deum pre oculis suis non ħens sed instigac̃one diabolica seducſ vicesimo octavo die Septembris Anno Regni dni ñri Jacobi dei grã Angł ffranc̃ et hibnie Regis fidei defensſ &c., tercio decimo et Scocie quadrigesimo nono apud Vpminster ꝑd in com̃ ꝑd felonice suscepit anglice did take vpp vnam calvam anglice a scull extra quoddam sepulchrum anglice a grave in cemitꝰio eccłie parochiał de Vpminster ꝑd existeñ pars corporis cuiusdam hõis morſ ibm nup sepelit ea intenc̃one ad vtend eadem calva in quibusdam malis et diabolicis artibꝫ anglice witchcraftſ charmes & sorceries videłt ea intenc̃one ad fastinand et incantand quandam Mariam Stevens cont' formam statuſ in huiõd casu nup ediſ & puiss ac cont' pacem dc̃i dni Regis nunc coroñ et dignitatem suas.

*Translation.*

Essex. The Jurors for the lord the King do present that Susan Barker, late of Upminster in the county aforesaid, spinster, wife of Henry Barker, being a common witch and enchantress, not having God before her eyes, but seduced by the instigation of the

Devil, on 28 Sept., 13 Jas. I, at Upminster aforesaid in the county aforesaid, feloniously did take up a skull out of a certain grave in the burying ground of the parish church of Upminster aforesaid being part of the body of a certain deceased man lately buried there, with intent to use the said skull in certain evil and devilish arts, namely witchcrafts, charms, and sorceries with intent to bewitch and enchant a certain Mary Stevens, against the form of the statute in this case lately made and provided, and against the peace of the said lord the now King, his crown and dignity.

### INDICTMENT No. 679. CHELMSFORD LENT SESSIONS. 1650–1

Essex  Juȓ p custodi libtaȓ Angȴ authoritaȓ Parliament sup Sacȓm suū psentant q̃d Johanna Wayte nup de Barneston magñ in com̃ Essex pred spinster aȴs dc̃a Johanna Wayte vx̃ Robti Wayte nup de Barneston magñ pred in com̃ pred laborer existens cõis ffascinatrix & incantratrix deum pre oculis suis non ħens sed instigac̃one diabolica moȓ & seducȓ vicesimo nono die Augusti Anno dñi miȴȴimo sexcentisimo quinquagesimo apud Audlyend in com̃ pred felonice in Societaȓ sua admisit negotiata est & fovit angce did enterteyne imploy & feede quendm malū & nephand spiritū in silitudine cuiusdam volatiȴ angce vocaȓ a butterfly ea intenc̃one & ppoit vt eadem Johanna Wayte ope & auxilio pd mali & nephand Spiritus quasdam malas & diabolicas artes viȝt iascina angce voc̃ witchcrafts incantacones angce vocat Inchantmts pcantacones angce vocat charmes & sortilegia angce vocat Sorceryes vteret' practicaret & exerceret contra formā Statuȓ huiõi casu ediȓ & pviȿ nec non contra pacem publicā, &c.

### INDICTMENT No. 727. MAIDSTONE LENT SESSIONS. 1656–7

Kent.  The Juro' for the Lord Protecto' of the Comonwealth of England, Scotland, and Ireland &c., vppon their oathes doe psent that Mary Allen the younger late of Gowdherst in the said County of Kent Spinster being a Comon Witch & Inchantrix not haveing God before her eyes butt being moved & seduced by thinstigacõn of the devill the Thirtith day of November in the yeare of o$^9$ Lord One Thousand six hundred ffifty & six att Gowdherst aforesaid in the County aforesaid feloniouslv did feed employ & entertaine a certaine evill & wicket spiritt in the like-nesse of a blacke dogg w$^{th}$ intent & purpose that shee the said Mary Allen the younger by the helpe & aid of the said evill & wicked spirit certaine evill & devillish Arts called Witchcrafts Inchantm$^{ts}$ Charmes & Sorceries might vse practise & exercise Against the forme of the Statute in this Case made & provided And against the publicke Peace, &c.

## Notes on the Indictments

These sixteen examples cover practically all the forms used. In each one, the county, name, address, and description of accused (or her husband) is given. One example omits the name of the place where the witchcraft was committed (No. 196), and one fails to give the day and year (No. 500). The name, address, and description of Complainant are all omitted in No. 122, and the address and description are left out in eight cases out of eleven where an injured party is named. The value of goods is omitted in one case out of three, and the colour of cattle once in the two examples given.

No. 1. Exemplifies the usual form of indictment in the case of a person bewitched, languishing and dying. Two counts are embodied in the one document.

No. 24. This is an accusation of murder by *incantacionibus et veneficis*. A word not often used and may here mean poison. See p. 4. In the gaol calendar for Hertford Summer Sessions, 1603, *veneficium* is equivalent to witchcraft or sorcery.

No. 56. A form commencing " Inquiratur pro domina Regine si " instead of " Juratores pro domina Regina presentant ".

No. 66. The nature of the felony in this case is conjuring and invoking evil spirits with the intention of gaining divers great sums of money.

No. 122. Is an insufficient indictment, probably because the name of complainant is omitted. From a contemporary pamphlet (*A detection of damnable driftes*) it appears that the accused Margery Staunton was indicted on another charge, but was released because no manslaughter was objected against her.

No. 132. A form relating to bewitching of cattle. No colour of the beasts is given.

No. 196. This indictment describes the imps, giving their names.

No. 223. Follows the form of an indictment for assault introducing the words " insultum fecit ". A similar example is 407.

No. 224. An example of an accusation of arson by witchcraft.

No. 244. A very short form but sufficient.

No. 500. No date of the crime is given, but accused was found guilty. Possibly the sentence here recorded is merely a copy of that entered in on No. 499.

No. 513. This bill appears to be in order, but a marginal entry records that it was vacated because it was not valid in law by virtue of the statute therein lately made.

No. 518. Another short form but effective.

No. 538. An accusation of disinterring a skull for the purposes of witchcraft.

No. 679. A Latin form of the Commonwealth period, illustrating the trivial nature of some of the charges. The grand jury did not find the bill.

No. 727. An English form of the Commonwealth period which will serve as a translation of the previous example.

## Endorsements and Annotations

Indictments were endorsed by the grand jury either " *billa vera* " or " *ignoramus* ".[1] *Billa vera* indicates that a true bill is found, *ignoramus* that it is ignored or thrown out. During the Interregnum and the later English period the endorsements read " we find this bill " or " we find noe bill ". Generally speaking

---

[1] In Newcastle indictments, temp. 12 Chas. II, " billa vera " may be found on face. (Assizes 44/8.)

indictments endorsed *ignoramus* or " we find noe bill " have not been preserved, but from those that have not been destroyed it is evident that the practice was either to erase or score out by pen the accused's name or to deface the indictments with a pen scrawl or one or more crosses.  In the Palatinate of Lancaster the thrown-out bills were slashed across by knife cuts.  About 1565 the modern practice of entering the names of witnesses on the back began, and after 1596 it became the regular method to so record them and the practice has continued to the present day. In rare cases the names of the jury were endorsed ; possibly because they were of divided opinion (Nos. 123, 273).  A rare example with witnesses' names on face is No. 468.  When a number of indictments are entered on one membrane they were not endorsed.

On the face of any indictment endorsed " billa vera " or " we find this to be a true bill " will be found a brief memorandum of the plea, verdict, and sentence.[1]  This may be entered over the name of the accused, or on the top, left hand or bottom margins of the document.[2]  These notes are carelessly and hurriedly entered by different hands, and are much contracted and often difficult to decipher, yet they are of great importance.  In the following pages these entries have been printed as nearly as possible in their original form.

The following list of explanations will form a key to the contracted annotations.

ad largū.  At large, usually written *non est in prisona*.

ad p͠x, (*ad proximam assisam*).  At the next assizes or gaol delivery.

b, b re (*breve*).  Writ.

baŧŧ (ballium).  Bail.

billa vera.  We find this to be a true bill.

ca, ca nuŧŧ (*catalla nulla*) . . . has no goods, chattels, lands, nor tenements for forfeiture.  A stereotyped form of return

[1] These are sometimes found on the jury panels.
[2] In one case the sentence was both below and above.

by the jury, and sometimes contradictorily accompanied by the Coroner's inventory and valuation of the convicted person's goods (Ex. 35/45 Herts). No case of a witch having any goods certified has been noticed. In Chester records the entry is sometimes, ca n¹ tr neq, ten.

cogn, cogn ind, cogn offens. Acknowledged, confessed, charge or offence (*cognosco*).

com, comissus. Committed to prison (*committo*).

compar, compent. Compear or appear (*compareo*).

cul, cull, cul mᵒ, cul modo. Guilty now. After 1596 *non culpabilis* gave way to Qˢ Qᵃ, etc., occasionally non cul Qᵃ.

dd. Discharged paying . . . fees.

deliberati p pclamac̃. They are discharged by proclamation.

exoñ (*exoneratur*). . . . acquitted by the court.

fac̃ est warrañ. A warrant is issued.

fiat pcess. Let process issue.

gñralem pdō. The general pardon.

igñ (*ignoramus*). We find this to be no true bill.

incantac̃ (*incantacio*). Enchantment or witchcraft. *Magia* and *fascinatio* are sometimes used for witchcraft. See p. 22.

ind̃ (*indictamentum*). Indictment.

io consid (*ideo consideratur*). Therefore it is considered by the court.

io rep̃. Therefore . . . reprieved or reprisoned.

irro. Enrolled (*irrotulo*).

judic, judm, judic mᵒ, judm modo, judic reddit, judic mᵒ reddit, are all forms which are sometimes written more fully : *judicium secundum formam statuti*, i.e. . . . judgment according to the form of the statute [in this case made and provided]. Sometimes as in No. 350, the nature of the judgment is definitely expressed. *scilicet stare super pilloriam quatuor temporibus anni*, but as a general rule this entry indicated hanging. From 1596 onwards judm gave place to the more certain Sˢ, as non cul did to Qˢ, and occasionally it was entered as judm Sˢ or judicm qd Sˢ. In the English period of the Commonwealth sometimes rendered " judgment of death ".

jur'. Sworn (*juro*).

jur'm prie (*juratam patriae*). A jury of the country.

mand' (*mandatum*). Commitment order.

n, nc, ncr, n*c*r, n*c* r, nc r, n*cr*, nec, nec re. Neither did . . . flee, nor fled, nor fly. Indictment No. 462 has *nc recessit*, and No. 757 has *ne se retrax*. A contraction used in the records of the Oxford circuit was *nec r* becoming *nec retr*, temp. George I. In the Northern circuit (Chas. I) *nec re* was extended to *nec re se*, and the Western circuit clerks from 1695 onwards made *nec re* into *nec fugit*.

nō cul, non cull. See cul.

nō est in p⁹sona. See ad largum.

pd', pdon, pdonat' (*pardonatur*) . . . pardoned or acquitted.

pilor (*pilloria, pillorium*). Pillory.

plit preg, plitat preg (*prægnans*). She pleaded pregnancy.

po se (*ponit se super patriam de bono et malo*) . . . pleads not guilty. During the Commonwealth period pu se (sometimes *puse*) meaning puts self was used. In the Cheshire records still more contracted forms *po* and *put* were current.

p⁹sa, p⁹son (*prisona*). In prison.

p anno. For one year's imprisonment with pillory.

Q, Qᵃ, Q⁹, Qˢ, qiet⁹, quietus, quieta. He or she is discharged or acquitted. The clerks often used qᵃ and qˢ regardless of gender. In Northern circuit gaol books " acquietat " was noticed.

rep, repr, repri, etc. Reprieved or reprisoned. Sometimes remanere or retornari is used. See p. 32.

S⁹, S⁹ p coll . . . hanged by the neck until . . . be dead. In Cheshire is written S₃ or Su₃. In the gaol books of the Western circuit a large asterisk entered in the margin additionally indicated the death sentence.[1] In corresponding records for the Northern circuit : suspend' per coll'.

t'ns (*transgressio*). Trespass.

[1] See Plate II.

tri . . . was tried or is to be tried (*trio*).

tri non p'gn. She was tried and found to be not pregnant.

## Gaol Calendars and Gaol Delivery Rolls

Additional information may be obtained from gaol calendars and gaol delivery rolls.

Gaol calendars, being a list of prisoners on paper or parchment, were quite commonly written in English from Jas. I onwards, but an example in that language was noticed towards the end of Elizabeth (Assizes 35/39, Essex file). These calendars give county, gaol, venue and date of assizes, the names of prisoners, place of arrest, by whom committed, and crime of which suspected. Witchcraft is, however, often merely entered as felony. Typical entries are :—

Alice presmarye capĩ apud Dunmowe p suspicõe ffelon.

Johanna Johnson comisš p Wiłłm Hamon aŕ p suspicõne de le Witchcrafte.

Rosa Chapman sent by me Thomas Ward for a witch.

Agnes Whittenbury comiss's p Philippũ Butler mił p suspicõne venefiĉ.

Gaol Delivery Rolls for the Home Circuit may be found from 1580–1603, and from 1609 onwards.[1] They are rarely written on paper,[2] and as a general rule will be found engrossed on the back of the lists of the county officials. but occasionally endorsed on a roll of indictments (e.g. Assizes 35/32 Essex file), and in one case the gaol delivery list was written in the blank spaces of a gaol calendar (e.g. Assizes 35/91 Kent file), and elsewhere on a record of some other county (e.g. Essex on a Kent document, Assizes 35/28). The delivery rolls may be found in English or Latin sometimes partly in one and partly in the other language. The early gaol delivery rolls were described by the name of the principal gaol in the county. but afterwards as the general gaol delivery for the county. For the reign of Charles I some of

---

[1] Essex is particularly fortunate in its gaol delivery rolls.

[2] An example on paper sheets occurs, temp. Chas. I. (Assizes 35/72 Kent file.)

the gaol delivery rolls have nothing but the heading, no details having been filled in. In general they give county, gaol, venue, and date of assizes, with the names of prisoners and their sentences (sometimes contradicting the entry on the indictment).

The venue of the assizes can therefore be obtained from commission, writ, or gaol delivery roll. The date of the assizes can be found on the writ or gaol delivery roll, and sometimes from a calendar of justices of the peace.

A complete example of a gaol delivery roll is given in Appendix No. I, and other partial extracts will be found on p. 242 and elsewhere. There are unfortunately no "gaol books" for the Home Circuit.

Sometimes as many as 150 persons were dealt with at a sessions. In one case 25 were sentenced to death at one assize, a slaughter which was, however, exceeded at the " Bloody Assizes " when 57 were executed for high treason at Dorchester on 3 Sept., 1685.

No useful references can be given, because neither files nor documents are numbered. The writer found bundles with wrong labels, files in wrong bundles, and a number of documents in wrong files. These will no doubt be restored to their correct places in course of time. Should any reader wish to verify any of the extracts now given, reference should be made to the P.R.O. Assize Class List (Press 9, 11a). The number of the bundle corresponding to any desired year will there be found. This should be given with the class number " Assizes 35 " on the application form. The files in the bundle must be opened, and commission, writ, or gaol delivery roll examined until the file for the required county and assize is discovered.

### Ratio of Persons Hanged to Persons Indicted

The collection of indictments which is now offered is a great advance on any list which has hitherto been made, but possibly does not represent more than half of the actual trials which took place in the Home Circuit. No information is available of the arraignments in towns judicially independent of the assizes,

# WITCHCRAFT STATISTICS FOR THE HOME CIRCUIT

| | DECADES. | ESSEX. | | | HERTFORD. | | | KENT. | | | SURREY. | | | SUSSEX. | | | TOTALS. | | |
|---|---|---|---|---|---|---|---|---|---|---|---|---|---|---|---|---|---|---|---|
| | | No. of Indictments. | No. of persons indicted. | No. of persons hanged. | No. of Indictments. | No. of persons indicted. | No. of persons hanged. | No. of Indictments. | No. of persons indicted. | No. of persons hanged. | No. of Indictments. | No. of persons indicted. | No. of persons hanged. | No. of Indictments. | No. of persons indicted. | No. of persons hanged. | No. of Indictments. | No. of persons indicted. | No. of persons hanged. |
| ELIZABETH | 1558–1567 | 15 | 13 | 2 | — | — | — | 7 | 4 | 2 | 3 | 3 | — | — | — | — | 25 | 20 | 4 |
| | 1568–1577 | 51 | 27 | 11 | 1 | 1 | — | 6 | 3 | 2 | 21 | 14 | 2 | 9 | 5 | 1 | 88 | 50 | 16 |
| | 1578–1587 | 107 | 68 | 17 | 4 | 3 | — | 12 | 7 | 1 | 20 | 11 | 1 | 4 | 3 | — | 147 | 92 | 19 |
| | 1588–1597 | 98 | 59 | 16 | 27 | 13 | 1 | 14 | 6 | 1 | 7 | 6 | — | 10 | 3 | — | 156 | 87 | 18 |
| | 1598–1607 | 39 | 20 | 10 | 21 | 12 | 4 | 11 | 5 | 2 | — | — | — | 2 | 2 | — | 73 | 39 | 16 |
| JAMES I | 1608–1617 | 37 | 22 | 4 | 13 | 11 | 2 | 2 | 2 | — | — | — | — | 3 | 1 | — | 55 | 36 | 6 |
| | 1618–1627 | 21 | 12 | 1 | 5 | 3 | — | 1 | 1 | — | — | — | — | — | — | — | 27 | 16 | 1 |
| CHARLES I | 1628–1637 | 5 | 5 | — | — | — | — | 7 | 4 | — | 2 | 2 | — | — | — | — | 14 | 11 | — |
| | 1638–1647 | 67 | 45 | 21 | 5 | 4 | 1 | 5 | 1 | — | 3 | 2 | — | — | — | — | 80 | 52 | 22 |
| COMMON-WEALTH | 1648–1657 | 16 | 12 | — | 2 | 3 | — | 41 | 36 | 8 | 5 | 7 | 1 | 3 | 2 | — | 67 | 60 | 9 |
| | 1658–1667 | 11 | 12 | — | 2 | 1 | — | 5 | 4 | — | 6 | 6 | 1 | — | — | — | 24 | 23 | 1 |
| CHARLES II | 1668–1677 | 6 | 4 | — | 1 | 1 | — | 8 | 6 | — | 1 | 1 | — | — | — | — | 16 | 12 | — |
| JAMES II | 1678–1687 | — | — | — | — | — | — | 7 | 7 | — | 2 | 1 | — | 2 | 1 | — | 11 | 9 | — |
| WILLIAM III | 1688–1697 | — | — | — | — | — | — | 5 | 4 | — | — | — | — | — | — | — | 5 | 4 | — |
| ANNE | 1698–1707 | — | — | — | — | — | — | 1 | 1 | — | 1 | 1 | — | — | — | — | 2 | 2 | — |
| GEORGE I | 1708–1717 | — | — | — | — | — | — | — | — | — | — | — | — | — | — | — | — | — | — |
| | 1718–1727 | — | — | — | — | — | — | — | — | — | — | — | — | — | — | — | — | — | — |
| GEORGE II | 1728–1736 | — | — | — | — | — | — | — | — | — | — | — | — | — | — | — | — | — | — |

| | ESSEX | HERTFORD | KENT | SURREY | SUSSEX | TOTALS |
|---|---|---|---|---|---|---|
| No. of Indictments | 473 | 81 | 132 | 71 | 33 | 790 |
| No. of persons Indicted | 299 | 52 | 91 | 54 | 17 | 513 |
| No. of persons hanged. | 82 | 8 | 16 | 5 | 1 | 112 |

In utilizing the data provided in the above table allowance must be made for the following facts :—
(i) The figures relate to indictments for 1373 assizes, being about 77 *per centum* of the original documents.
(ii) Before the reign of Charles I it was not the practice to file bills thrown out by the grand jury.
(iii) Essex has been somewhat better served in the preservation of its documents than any one of the other four counties.

and indications point to trials by order of municipal authorities as having been numerous, so that caution must therefore be exercised in utilizing the diagrams and statistics given here.

The table shews at a glance the number of bills, the number of persons indicted, and the number of persons sentenced to be hanged at the assizes held for each county of the Home Circuit during each decade from 1558 to 1736, so far as can be obtained from about 77 *per centum* of the original documents. 790 bills of indictment relate to 513 persons, of whom 112 were suspended *per collum*, consequently 78 out of every 100 persons charged escaped execution. It may be surmised that the proportion of hangings at independent courts was higher. It is of interest to work out the percentage for each decade.

| Decades ending. | Percentages. | Decades ending. | Percentages. |
|---|---|---|---|
| 1567 | 20 per cent | 1647 | 42 per cent |
| 1577 | 32 ,, | 1657 | 15 ,, |
| 1587 | 21 ,, | 1667 | 4 ,, |
| 1597 | 21 ,, | 1677 | 0 ,, |
| 1607 | 41 ,, | 1687 | 0 ,, |
| 1617 | 17 ,, | 1697 | 0 ,, |
| 1627 | 6 ,, | 1707 | 0 ,, |
| 1637 | 0 ,, | 1717 | 0 ,, |

A diagram has been prepared giving a comparative view of the rise and decline of witchcraft prosecutions at the various assizes of the Home Circuit. A glance leads to the immediate conclusion that the belief in witchcraft was much more pronounced in Essex, which county must have been seething in superstition. The Essex indictments actually outnumber those of the four counties of Herts, Kent, Surrey, and Sussex combined.

A list of witches convicted at the assizes of the Home Circuit has been compiled, together with the names of the presiding judges, and the sentences given. In a further list which forms Appendix IV, are the names of witches of whom no record appears in the P. R. O. documents, but who are mentioned in various contemporary pamphlets, etc.

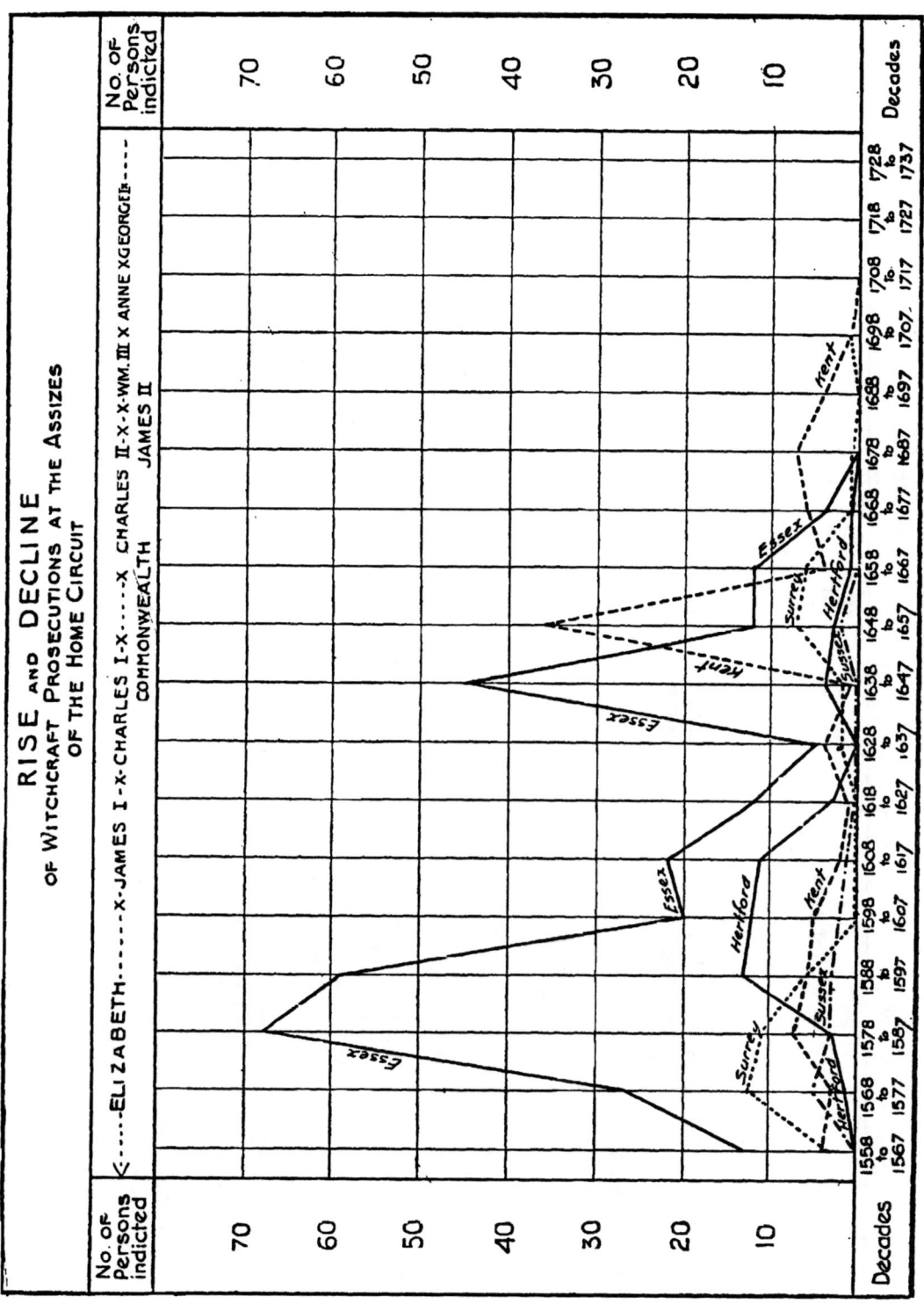

RISE and DECLINE
of Witchcraft Prosecutions at the Assizes
of the Home Circuit

<----ELIZABETH------x-JAMES I-x-CHARLES I-x-----x CHARLES II-x-x-WM.III x ANNE xGEORGEI----
COMMONWEALTH        JAMES II

# LIST OF CONVICTED WITCHES (HOME CIRCUIT)

| Nos. of Indictment. | Assize. | Prisoner's Name. | Nature of Witchcraft. | Notes. | Sentence. | Judges. |
|---|---|---|---|---|---|---|
| 3–5 | 1564 Essex Sum. | Elizabeth Lowrys | persons to d. | preg. | [Hanged] | Southcote, J., Gerard, G. |
| 7 | ,, Surr. Winter | Eden Worsley | person to d. | rep. | [1 year] | Saunders, T. |
| 11–13 | 1565 Kent Lent | Joan Byden | persons to d. &c. | | [Hanged] | Gerard, G. |
| 14 | ,, Surr. Sum. | Joan Gowse | bull to d. | | [1 year] | ,, |
| 15 | ,, ,, | Rose a Borow | person to d. | rep. | ? | ,, |
| 17 | 1566 Essex Sum. | Elizabeth Fraunces (1) | person | confessed | 1 year | ,, |
| 18 | ,, ,, | Agnes Waterhouse | person to d. | confessed | Hanged | ,, |
| 20 | 1567 Essex Lent | Alice Prestmarye | person | | [1 year] | ,, |
| 23 | ,, Sum. | Alice Atrum | horse, pig | | [1 year] | ,, |
| 24 | ,, Kent | Agnes Bennett | person to d. | | [Hanged] | ,, |
| 25 | ,, ,, | Cecilia West | person | | 1 year | ,, |
| 29–32 | 1569 Essex Lent | Alice Swallow | persons to d. &c. | | [Hanged] | Wray, C. |
| 35–37 | ,, Surr. Sum. | Jane Baldwyn | ,, ,, | rep. | [1 year] | ,, |
| 43 | 1571 Kent Sum. | Ellen Peckman | person to d. | | [Hanged] | Gawdy, T. |
| 45–48 | 1572 Essex Lent | William Skelton | persons to d. | | [Hanged] | Monson, Robt. |
| 46–48 | ,, ,, | Margery Skelton | person to d. | | [Hanged] | ,, |
| 49 | ,, ,, | Katherine Pullen | ,, ,, | | [Hanged] | ,, |
| 50 | ,, ,, | Elizabeth Francis (2) | person | | 1 year | ,, |
| 53–54 | Sussex Lent | Joan Usbarne | cattle to d. | | [1 year] | Gawdy, T. |
| 58–61 | Essex Sum | Agnes Francys | persons to d. | | [Hanged] | ,, |
| 62–64 | ,, | Agnes Steademan | persons &c. | | [1 year] | ,, |
| 66 | 1573 Herts Lent | Thomas Heather | invocation | | ? | Monson, Robt. |
| 67–69 | 1574 Essex Sum. | Alice Chaundeler | persons to d. | preg. | [Hanged] | ,, |
| 72–74 | ,, Kent Lent | Alice Daye | persons to d. &c. | | [Hanged] | ,, |
| 75–79 | ,, Essex Sum. | Cecilia Glasenberye | persons to d. | | Hanged | ,, |
| 80–81 | ,, ,, | Elizabeth Taylor | persons to d. | | Hanged | ,, |
| 82 | ,, ,, | Alice Hynckson | cattle to d. | | 1 year | ,, |
| 85–86 | ,, Kent Sum. | Alice Stanton | ,, | | [1 year] | ,, |
| 88 | 1575 Surr. Lent | Thomas Heather | invocation | preg. | Hanged | Gawdy, T. |
| 89–91 | ,, ,, | Agnes Crockford | persons to d. | | [Hanged] | ,, |

## LIST OF CONVICTED WITCHES (HOME CIRCUIT)—*Continued.*

| Nos. of Indictment | Assize. | Prisoner's Name. | Nature of Witchcraft. | Notes. | Sentence. | Judges |
|---|---|---|---|---|---|---|
| 92-94 | 1575 Suss. Lent | Margaret Cooper | persons to d. | | Hanged | Southcote, J., Gawdy, T |
| 97-99 | 1576 Essex Lent | Agnes Bromley | persons to d. &c. | | [Hanged] | ,, ,, ,, |
| 101-102 | 1576 Essex Sum. | Margery Spencer | persons to d. | | [Hanged] | ,, ,, ,, |
| 103-105 | ,, ,, | Joan Baker | ,, ,, | | [Hanged] | ,, ,, ,, |
| 104-105 | ,, ,, | Elizabeth Aylett | ,, ,, | | 1 year | ,, ,, ,, |
| 112-113 | 1577 Sussex Sum. | Alice Casselowe | cattle to d. | died | 1 year | ,, ,, ,, |
| 116 | 1578 Kent Sum. | Alice Day (1) | person &c. | | See 124 | ,, ,, ,, |
| 117 | ,, ,, | Katherine Burbage | geldings to d. &c. | | 1 year | ,, ,, ,, |
| 119 | 1579 Essex Lent | Ellen Smythe | person to d. | | [Hanged] | ,, ,, ,, |
| 120 | ,, ,, | Alce Nokes | ,, ,, | | [Hanged] | ,, ,, ,, |
| 123 | ,, ,, | Elizabeth Fraunces | ,, ,, | | [Hanged] | ,, ,, ,, |
| 124 | ,, Kent Lent | Alice Daye (2) | ,, ,, | | [Hanged] | ,, ,, ,, |
| 125 | ,, Essex Sum. | Richard Presmary | ,, ,, | | [Hanged] | ,, ,, ,, |
| 125 | ,, ,, | Joan Presmary | ,, ,, | | [Hanged] | ,, ,, ,, |
| 126-128 | ,, ,, | Elizabeth Hardinge (1) | person &c. | | [1 year] | ,, ,, ,, |
|  |  | ,, (2) | person to d. | | [Hanged] | ,, ,, ,, |
| 137 | 1580 ,, Lent | Joan Dowtie | ,, ,, | | [Hanged] | ,, ,, ,, |
| 142 | ,, Sum. | Joan Turnor | ,, ,, | | 1 year | ,, ,, ,, |
| 143-145 | 1581 ,, Lent | | unborn infant to d. | rep. | [Hanged] | ,, ,, ,, |
| 146-148 | ,, Sum | Alice Mylles | persons to d. | | [Hanged] | ,, ,, ,, |
| 155-157 | 1582 Lent | Agnes Glascock | ,, ,, | rep. | ? | ,, ,, ,, |
| 159 | ,, ,, | Cecilia Celles | person to d. | rep. | ? | ,, ,, ,, |
| 160-162 | ,, ,, | Ursula Kemp | persons to d. | | [Hanged] | ,, ,, ,, |
| 160-162 | ,, ,, | Alice Newman | ,, ,, | | ? | ,, ,, ,, |
| 165 | ,, ,, | Elizabeth Bennett | person to d. | confessed | [Hanged] | ,, ,, ,, |
| 170 | Surr. Lent | Mabel Jackson | ,, ,, | | [Hanged] | ,, ,, ,, |
| 171-173 | Essex Sum. | Agnes Bryant | various | | Hanged | ,, ,, ,, |
| 188 | Surr. Sum. | Agnes Waters | ,, ,, | pardoned | 1 year | ,, ,, ,, |
| 192 | 1583 Essex Sum. | Anne Smythe | ? | | [1 year] | Gawdy, T., Gawdy, F. |
| 193 | ,, ,, | Joan Thatcher | cattle to d. | | 1 year | ,, ,, |
| 200-201 | ,, ,, | Elizabeth Brooke | person to d. &c. | confessed | Hanged | ,, ,, |

LIST OF CONVICTED WITCHES (HOME CIRCUIT)—*Continued.*

| Nos. of Indictment. | Assize. | Prisoner's Name. | Nature of Witchcraft. | Notes. | Sentence. | Judges. |
|---|---|---|---|---|---|---|
| 204–207 | 1583 Essex Sum. | Lucy Fisher | persons to d. | | Hanged | Gawdy, T., Gawdy, F, |
| 210–211 | ,, ,, | Thomas Kynge | persons to d. &c. | | Hanged | ,, ,, |
| 212–213 | 1584 ,, ,, | Joan Colson | persons to d. | | ? | ,, ,, |
| 214–219 | ,, ,, ,, | Joan Thorocke | persons to d. &c. | | Hanged | ,, ,, |
| 220–221 | ,, ,, ,, | Margaret Lyttelberie | persons | | [1 year] | ,, ,, |
| 222–223 | ,, ,, ,, | Elizabeth Morrisbee | person to d. | | Hanged | ,, ,, |
| 224–225 | ,, ,, ,, | Edmund Mausell | arson | | ? | ,, ,, |
| 226 | ,, | Alice Bolton | hogs to d. | | [1 year] | ,, ,, |
| 234–236 | 1585 Surr. Sum. | Agnes Stevens | persons to d. | | ? | Gent, T. |
| 242–244 | 1587 Essex Lent | Joan Preston | cows to d. &c. | | 1 year | ,, ,, |
| 242 | ,, ,, ,, | Frances Preston | cows to d. | | 1 year | ,, ,, |
| 245–246 | ,, ,, ,, | Rose Clarens | animals to d. | | 1 year | ,, ,, |
| 248–249 | 1587 Herts Lent | Agnes Morris | person to d. &c. | rep. | ? | Glascock J. |
| 250, &c. | ,, Essex Sum. | John Smyth | | | Hanged | Clarke, R. |
| 270–271 | 1588 ,, ,, | Katherine Harrys | persons to d. | | Hanged | ,, ,, |
| 270–271 | ,, ,, ,, | Agnes Smythe | ,, ,, ,, | | [Hanged] | ,, ,, |
| 279 | 1589 ,, ,, | Joan Prentice | ,, ,, ,, | | Hanged | Clarke R. Puckering. J. |
| 283–284 | ,, ,, ,, | Ellen Bett | | | ? | ,, ,, |
| 285–286 | ,, ,, ,, | Margaret Cony | persons | | 1 year | ,, ,, |
| 286–287 | ,, ,, ,, | Avice Cony | person to d. | preg. | Hanged | ,, ,, |
| 288–291 | ,, ,, ,, | Joan Cony | ,, ,, | | Hanged | ,, ,, |
| 296 | 1590 Essex Lent. | Joan Uptney | persons to d. | | Hanged | ,, ,, |
| 299 | ,, ,, ,, | Anne Crabbe | person | | 1 year | ,, ,, |
| 300 | ,, ,, | Joan Mose | person to d. | | Hanged | ,, ,, |
| 301–305 | ,, ,, ,, | Alice Aylett | ,, ,, | | 1 year | ,, ,, |
| 307 | ,, ,, ,, | Alice Adcock | ,, ,, | non preg. | Hanged | ,, ,, |
| 309–313 | ,, Herts Sum. | Mary Burgis | persons &c. | | [1 year] | ,, ,, |
| 317 | ,, ,, | Ellen Browne | ? | | 1 year | ,, ,, |
| 320–324 | 1591 Essex Sum. | Ellen Graye | person to d. &c. | | [Hanged] | ,, ,, |
| 325 | ,, ,, ,, | Margaret Rooman | cattle to d. | | [1 year] | ,, ,, |
| 327–329 | ,, ,, ,, | Agnes Whilland | animals to d. | | [1 year] | ,, ,, |

LIST OF CONVICTED WITCHES (HOME CIRCUIT)—*Continued.*

| Nos. of Indictment. | Assize. | Prisoner's Name. | Nature of Witchcraft. | Notes. | Sentence. | Judges. |
|---|---|---|---|---|---|---|
| 330 | 1591 Essex Sum. | Juliana Cocke | animals to d. | | [1 year] | Clarke, R., Puckering, J. |
| 334 | ,, Sussex Sum. | Agnes Mowser | person | | 1 year | ,, ,, |
| 335–336 | 1592 Essex Lent | Agnes Hales | persons | | [1 year] | ,, ,, Walmesley, T. |
| 344 | ,, ,, Sum. | Anne Scott | person to d. | | [Hanged] | ,, ,, ,, |
| 345 | ,, ,, ,, | Audrey Mathew (1) | cattle to d. | | 1 year | ,, ,, ,, |
| 346 | ,, ,, ,, | Agnes Draper | person | | 1 year | ,, ,, ,, |
| 347–348 | ,, ,, ,, | Jane Wallys | person to d. &c. | non preg. | [Hanged] | ,, ,, ,, |
| 350–352 | ,, Herts Sum. | Mary Hamont | animals to d. | | 1 year | ,, ,, ,, |
| 353 | 1593 Essex Lent | Alice Alberte | person to ,, | | 1 year | ,, ,, Owen, T. |
| 357 | ,, ,, Sum | Agnes Haven | person to d. | | Hanged | ,, ,, ,, |
| 359–361 | ,, ,, ,, | Elizabeth Esserford | animals | | 1 year | ,, ,, ,, |
| 363–366 | ,, ,, ,, | Margaret Mynner | persons to d. | | Hanged | ,, ,, ,, |
| 368–372 | ,, Herts Sum. | Joan Garrett | mare to d. | | 1 year | ,, ,, ,, |
| 379–382 | ,, Kent Sum. | Agnes Bigg | person to d. | | Hanged | ,, ,, Drewe, E. |
| 389–390 | 1594 Essex Lent | Elizabeth Garrett | ,, ,, | | [Hanged] | ,, ,, ,, |
| 390 | ,, ,, ,, | Joan Garrett | person | | 1 year | ,, ,, ,, |
| 393 | ,, ,, ,, | Mary Belsted | animals to d. | | 1 year | ,, ,, ,, |
| 394–395 | ,, ,, ,, | Anne Harrison | persons to d | | ? | ,, ,, ,, |
| 396–397 | ,, ,, Sum. | Audrey Mathew (2) | ,, ,, | | Hanged | ,, ,, ,, |
| 398–399 | ,, ,, ,, | Bridget Hayle | mare | | 1 year | ,, ,, ,, |
| 400–402 | ,, ,, ,, | Anne Harvey | person to d. | | Hanged | ,, ,, ,, |
| 403 | 1595 ,, Lent | John Cremer | animals to d. | | 1 year | ,, ,, ,, |
| 403 | ,, ,, ,, | Grace Trower | ,, | | 1 year | ,, ,, ,, |
| 404 | 1595 Herts Lent | Alice Games | ,, ? | | 1 year | ,, ,, ,, |
| 406–408 | 1596 ,, Lent | Katherine Dewxburie | person | | 1 year | Gawdy, F., Owen, T |
| 411–413 | ,, ,, Sum. | Alice Crutch | persons to d. &c. | | Hanged | ,, ,, ,, |
| 416 | 1597 Essex Sum. | Alice Warren | person | | 1 year | ,, ,, ,, |
| 417 | 1598 ,, Lent | Robert Browning | conjuring spirits | | Pillory | ,, ,, ,, |
| 418–419 | ,, Herts Lent | Mary Taylor | person to d. &c. | | Hanged | ,, ,, Daniel, W. |
| 429–430 | 1601 Essex Sum. | Ursula Harvey | persons to d. | | Hanged | ,, ,, ,, |
| 431–433 | ,, ,, ,, | Anne Harris | person to d. | | Hanged | ,, ,, ,, |

## LIST OF CONVICTED WITCHES (HOME CIRCUIT)—Continued.

| Nos. of Indictment. | Assize. | Prisoner's Name. | Nature of Witchcraft. | Notes. | Sentence. | Judges. |
|---|---|---|---|---|---|---|
| 436 | 1601 Essex Sum. | Clemence Vale | person to d. | | Hanged | Gawdy, F., Daniel, W. |
| 437–439 | ,, ,, | Lucy Eltheridge | persons to d. | | Hanged | ,, |
| 440 | ,, ,, | Magdalen Purcas | person to d. | | Hanged | ,, |
| 442–444 | ,, Herts Sum. | Mercy Hill | persons | | [1 year] | ,, |
| 445 | 1602 Essex Lent | Anne Hyble | person to d. | | [Hanged] | ,, |
| 447–449 | ,, ,, Sum. | Elizabeth Pegge | persons &c. | | 1 year | ,, |
| 450–451 | ,, ,, | Audrey Pond | persons to d. &c. | | Hanged | ,, |
| 456–458 | 1603 ,, ,, | Margery Wilson | person to d. &c. | | Hanged | Heale, J. |
| 460–461 | ,, ,, | Joan Roath | person to d. &c. | | [Hanged] | ,, |
| 463–465 | ,, Herts Sum. | Agnes Whttenbery | persons &c. | | Hanged | ,, |
| 466–469 | ,, Kent Sum. | Anne Wynchester | persons to d | | [Hanged] | ,, |
| 473–474 | 1605 ,, ,, | Mary Mercy | person to d." | | Hanged | ,, |
| 476–477 | 1606 Herts Sum | Alice Stokes | person to d. | | Hanged | Daniel, W., Coventry, T. |
| 478–480 | ,, ,, | Christiana Stokes | persons to d | | Hanged | Altham, J., Croke, J. |
| 481–486 | 1607 Essex Lent | Blanche Worman | persons to d | | Hanged | Walmesley, T., ,, |
| 493–496 | ,, Sum. | Mary Wade | persons | preg. | ? | ,, ,, |
| 497 | ,, ,, | Alice Buske | person to d. | | Hanged | ,, ,, |
| 499–500 | 1610 ,, Lent | Katherine Lawrett | person to d. &c. | | Hanged | ,, ,, |
| 506 | ,, Herts Lent | Margery Raye | person to d. | | Hanged | Winch, H., Doderidge, J. |
| 509 | ,, ,, Sum. | Agnes Sutton | person | | [1 year] | ,, |
| 512 | 1611 Essex Lent | Richard Jonn | consulting spirits | | Hanged | ,, |
| 518 | 1613 ,, ,, | Robert Parker | intent | | [1 year] | Montagu, H., Glascock, H. |
| 521 | ,, Herts Lent | George Adowins | person to d. | | Hanged | ,, |
| 522 | ,, ,, | Agnes Hamond | ,, ,, | | ? | Houghton, R., Montague, H. |
| 524 | 1614 ,, ,, | Lyon Gleane | susp. conjuring horse to d. | | stocks | Hobart, H., Houghton, R. |
| 526–527 | 1615 ,, ,, | Anne Smith | person to d. | | [1 year] | ,, |
| 531 | 1616 ,, ,, | Anne Smith | persons to d. | | ? | Houghton, R., Crewe, R. |
| 538–541 | 1618 Essex Sum. | Susan Barker | person to d. | | Hanged | ,, [Herbert, E., Wythens, F.] |
| 545–546 | ,, ,, Lent | Mary Holt | person | | ? | Vernon, G., Hitcham, K. |
| 568 | 1626 ,, Sum. | Katherine King | persons to d. | | Hanged | |
| 574–575 | 1630 ,, ,, | Margery Brotherton | | | ? | |

## LIST OF CONVICTED WITCHES (HOME CIRCUIT)—*Continued.*

| Nos. of Indictment. | Assize. | Prisoner's Name. | Nature of Witchcraft. | Notes. | Sentence. | Judges. |
|---|---|---|---|---|---|---|
| 577–578 | 1631 Kent Sum. | Katherine Younge | person to d. | | To next sessions. | Vernon, G., Weston, J. |
| 588–589 | 1638 Essex Sum. | Jane Prentice | person | | ? | Crawley, F., Weston, R. Weston, R., Reve, E. Robert, E. of Warwick, Barrington, J. |
| 594 | 1639 ,, ,, | Robert Garnett | conversing | | 1 week | |
| 599 | 1645 ,, ,, | Helen Bretton | person to d. | | Hanged | |
| 600–601 | ,, ,, | Margery Grew | entertaining &c. | | Hanged | ,, ,, |
| 602 | ,, ,, | Anne Leach | person to d. | | Hanged | ,, ,, |
| 603–604 | ,, ,, | Elizabeth Clarke | entertaining &c. | | Hanged | ,, ,, |
| 605–606 | ,, ,, | Rebecca Jonas | persons to d. | | Hanged | ,, ,, |
| 608–609 | ,, ,, | Anne West | person to d. | | Hanged | ,, ,, |
| 610–612 | ,, ,, | Margaret Moone | persons to d. | | Hanged | ,, ,, |
| 613–614 | ,, ,, | Mary Sterling | entertaining &c. | | To next sessions | ,, ,, |
| 615–616 | ,, ,, | Anne Cate | persons to d. | | Hanged | ,, ,, |
| 617 | ,, ,, | Alice Dixon | person to d. | | Hanged | ,, ,, |
| 618–620 | ,, ,, | Mary Johnson | entertaining | | To next sessions | ,, ,, |
| 624 | ,, ,, | Mary Coppin | person to d. | | ,, | ,, ,, |
| 625 | ,, ,, | Ellen Clarke | ,, ,, | | Hanged | ,, ,, |
| 626 | ,, ,, | Sarah Bright | ,, ,, | | Hanged | ,, ,, |
| 627–628 | ,, ,, | Elizabeth Goodwin | entertaining &c. | | Hanged | ,, ,, |
| 628 | ,, ,, | Dorothy Waters | entertaining | | To next sessions. | ,, ,, |
| 630 | ,, ,, | Elizabeth Heare | ,, ,, | | Hanged | ,, ,, |
| 631–632 | ,, ,, | Mary Wiles | persons to d. | | Hanged | ,, ,, |
| 634–636 | ,, ,, | Anne Cooper | person to d. | | Hanged | ,, ,, |
| 637–638 | ,, ,, | Anne Therston | entertaining &c. | | To next sessions | ,, ,, |
| 639 | ,, ,, | Susan Cocke | ,, ,, | | ,, | ,, ,, |
| 640 | ,, ,, | Joyce Boones | ,, ,, | | **Hanged** | ,, ,, |

LIST OF CONVICTED WITCHES (HOME CIRCUIT)—*Continued.*

| Nos. of Indictment. | Assize. | Prisoner's Name. | Nature of Witchcraft. | Notes | Sentence. | Judges. |
|---|---|---|---|---|---|---|
| 641 | 1645 Essex Sum. | Margaret Landish | person | | Hanged | Robert, E. of Warwick, Barrington, J. |
| 642–644 | " | Sarah Hatyn | entertaining, &c. | | Hanged | " " |
| 645 | " | Elizabeth Harvy | entertaining | | To next sessions | " " |
| 646 | " | Mary Hockett | " | | Hanged | " " |
| 647 | " | Bridget Mayers | " | | To next sessions | " " |
| 648 | " | Susan Went | | | | |
| 664 | 1647 Herts Sum. | Elizabeth Browne | person to d. | | ? | Bacon, F., Cresheld, R. |
| 666 | 1648 Kent Sum. | Anne Radwell | | | ? | |
| 684–686 | 1652 " " | Susan Pickenden | person to d. | | Hanged | Aske, R., Warburton, P. |
| 687 | " " | Thomas Wilson | hogs, &c. | | 1 year | " " |
| 687 | " " | Jane Wilson | " | | 1 year | " " |
| 688–689 | " " | William Reynolds | sheep | | 1 year | " " |
| 693 | " " | Mary Reade | person to d. | | Hanged | " " |
| 694–696 | " " | Anne Ashby | " | | Hanged | " " |
| 694–696 | " " | Anne Martyn | " | | Hanged | " " |
| 695–696 | " " | Mildred Wright | " | | Hanged | " " |
| 695–696 | " " | Anne Wilson | " | | Hanged | " " |
| 695 | " " | Mary Browne | " | confessed | ? | " " |
| 711 | 1653 Essex Sum. | Benjamin Brand | sorcery | | 1 year | Oliver, St J., |
| 712 | " " | Mary Hurst | person | | ? | |
| 723 | 1655 Surr. Lent | Elizabeth Hatton | person to d | | Hanged | Aske, R., Steele, W |
| 727 | 1657 Kent Lent | Mary Allen, the younger | entertaining | | Hanged | Hill, R., Lee T. |
| 728 | " " | Mary Allen, the elder | entertaining | | Hanged | " " |
| 729 | " Surr. Lent | Mary Wallis | person to d. | | ? | " " |
| 730 | " Kent Sum. | Judith Sawkins | person &c. | | Hanged | Hale, M., |
| 744 | 1660 Surr. Sum. | Joan Neville | ? | | ? | Bridgeman, O., Waller, T. |
| 748 | 1663 Essex Lent | Sarah Houghton | ? | Dead | [1 year] | " Browe, S. |

Sentence of 1 year's imprisonment always carried with it four periods of 6 hours each in the pillory.

A second diagram (p. 110) giving a comparison of the number of the witchcraft prosecutions of the various circuits is not so satisfactory in its completeness as the one above, and the reader must be left to draw his own conclusions.

It may be of interest to consider briefly the position in parts of the country outside the Home Circuit. The county histories have wonderfully little to tell us of the prevalence of the witch-mania and research has to be made in contemporary records.

*Norfolk Circuit* (prior to 1876). Counties of Bedford, Buckingham, Cambridge, Huntingdon, Norfolk, and Suffolk.

Files preserved are few, and the writer found none before 1690. Four witchcraft indictments (one accused person) for Suffolk Lent Assizes, 5 Wm. & Mary came to notice. A number of Suffolk depositions are given in Appendix VI, resulting from the activities of Stearne and his colleagues.

There are probably numerous records of witchcraft trials to be obtained from the gaol delivery rolls for the Assizes for the Isle of Ely (see *Ely Episcopal Records*, p. 112).

*Midland Circuit* (prior to 1876). Counties of Derby, Leicester (up to 1863), Lincoln, Northampton (up to 1863), Nottingham, and Rutland (up to 1863).

There are no records of Assizes prior to the nineteenth century.

*Northern Circuit* (prior to 1876). Counties of Cumberland, Durham, Lancaster, Northumberland, Westmorland, and York.

Geographically so close to Scotland where the witch-mania raged, much was to be expected here, yet files for 34 assizes for the years 1607–50 yielded nothing. 160 files for the years 1651–68 gave 23 indictments charging 22 persons, of whom two were hanged in 1657. There are no documents relating to Lancaster in these bundles.

*Western Circuit* (prior to 1876). Counties of Cornwall, Devon, Dorset, Somerset, Southampton, and Wiltshire.

No early indictments are preserved, but in the gaol books (Assizes 23), for 804 sessions for the years 1670–1736 were noted

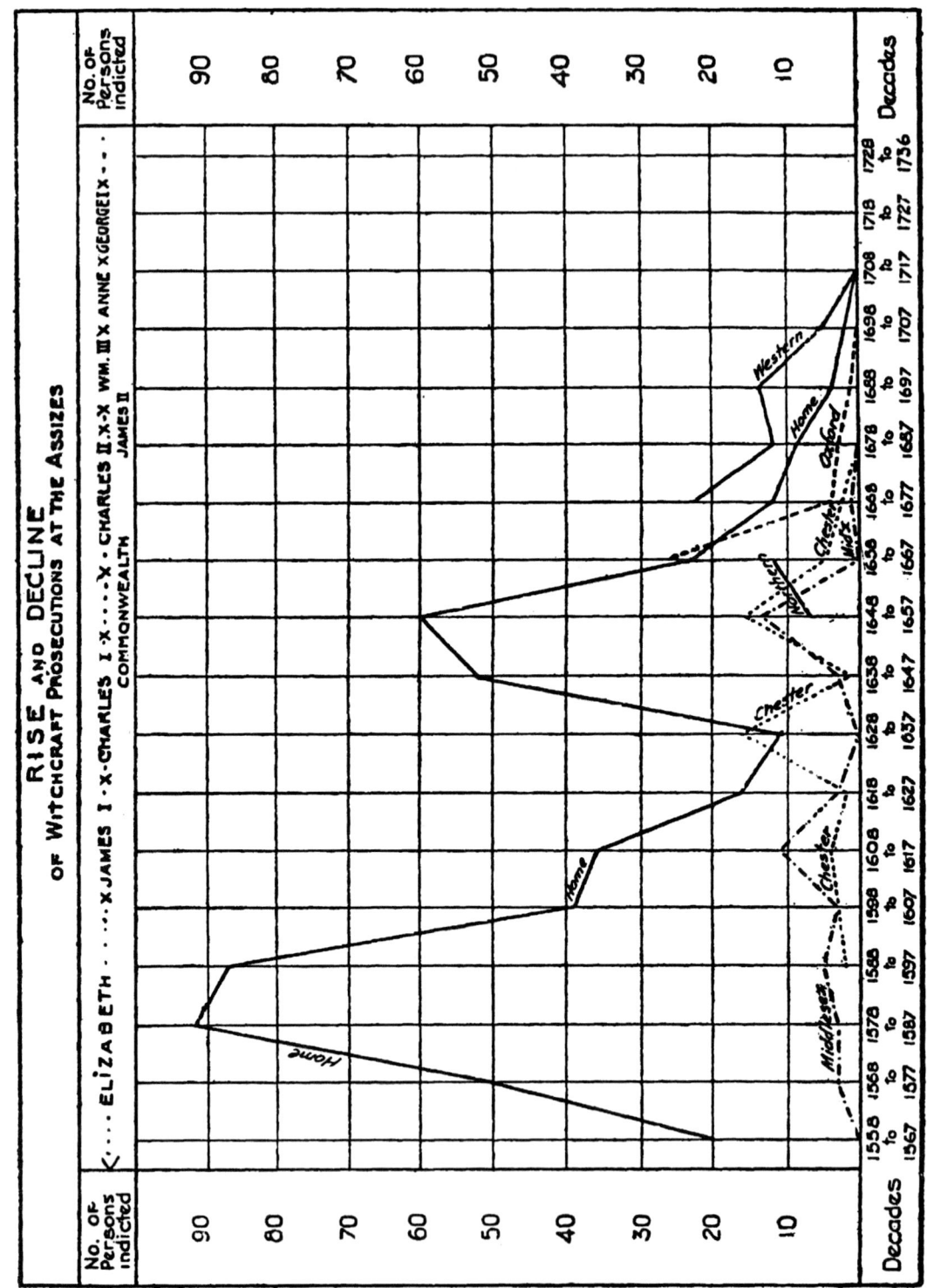

RISE and DECLINE
of Witchcraft Prosecutions at the Assizes

(···· ELIZABETH ·····x JAMES I ·x·CHARLES I x····X·CHARLES II.x·X WM. III x ANNE x GEORGE IX - - ·
COMMONWEALTH
JAMES II

69 indictments, the last of which was in 1707. Reference has been made to the few cases of execution (see p. 43).

*Oxford Circuit* (prior to 1876). Counties of Berkshire, Gloucester, Hereford, Monmouth, Oxford, Salop, Stafford, and Worcester.

Search of Crown books (Assizes 2/1–5), 1656–1716, revealed 30 persons indicted, of whom only one was found guilty.

*Middlesex.*—From information transcribed and edited by Mr. J. C. Jeaffreson (*Middlesex County Records*), a list of 78 indictments for witchcraft for the period 3 Edw. VI (1549) to 4 Jas. II (1689) can be compiled. These indictments relate to 46 persons, of whom 6 were hanged, 2 found guilty, but sentence unknown, 32 acquitted, 4 bound over, 1 not sent for trial, and one woman with the appropriate name of Dorothy Magicke had 1 year's imprisonment with the usual spells in the pillory.

*Palatinate of Chester.* In the Crown books 1560–1711, 58 indictments were noted. Of the 50 witches or " wise men " accused of witchcraft, prophesying, conjuring, sorcery, " charming and blessing ", eight went to the gallows.

*Palatinate of Lancaster.* There are very few records of the Clerk of the Crown.

*Palatinate of Durham.* Nothing relating to witchcraft was found in a few indictments for the years 1582–1719.

*Wales.* Counties of Anglesey, Brecon, Cardigan, Carmarthen, Carnarvon, Denbigh. Flint, Glamorgan, Merioneth, Montgomery, Pembroke, and Radnor. Gaol files commence as early as Henry VIII for seven of the counties, although there are not many until the time of Elizabeth A cursory examination did not reveal anything relating to witchcraft.

## Estimate of Total Executions

It is perhaps idle to attempt to estimate the number of executions for witchcraft throughout the country. Various writers have made suggestions, some of which are widely fantastical. On the Continent, where burnings were carried out wholesale, Kurtz has estimated that subsequent to the bull of Innocent VIII (1484) 300,000 witches were brought to the stake.[1] Such figures may well be true, but what is to be thought of Robert Steele's statement in *Social England*,[2] that 70,000 witches were hanged under the Act of James I. One hundredth part of such a figure would obviously be an over-estimate. One must hesitate also to accept the same writer's suggestion that in Scotland 8,000 women were burnt to death between the years 1560 and 1600. Had the slaughter during that period been anything like so great, surely some indication of it could be gathered from the Registers of the Privy Council for that period?

Basing an estimate on the results of the present search, the writer would have arrived at a much smaller figure for the entire period 1558–1736. If records of 77 *per centum* of the Home Circuit Assizes shew 112 executions, it is improbable that the total could have exceeded 150, or for the six circuits 900, and adding an equal number for the independent courts, 1,800. Such a total would be the result of allowing for 12 times the Essex activities of Hopkins, and is therefore much in excess of fact, actually the number of executions for witchcraft in England from 1542–1736 may be guessed at less than 1,000.

The period of greatest activity has also given rise to varying views. Pollock and Maitland considered the Commonwealth " as the worst days for witches in England ",[3] and Professor P. H. Browne, on the other hand, held that the Cromwellian Courts of Justice " discountenanced accusations of witchcraft ".[4] The data now collected clearly shews that for the Home Circuit, at any rate, the devil-worshippers were harassed most in the reign of Elizabeth. In the counties of Chester and Middlesex the persecution did not reach its height until a later period. Complete records for other areas unfortunately are not now extant.

Such indications as exist, point to the mania having varied

[1] *Church History*, (ed. Nicoll), ii, 197.
[2] Edited by H. D. Traill, 1903. iv. 120.
[3] See preface, *supra*.
[4] *Acts of Privy Council of Scotland*, 1661, lv.

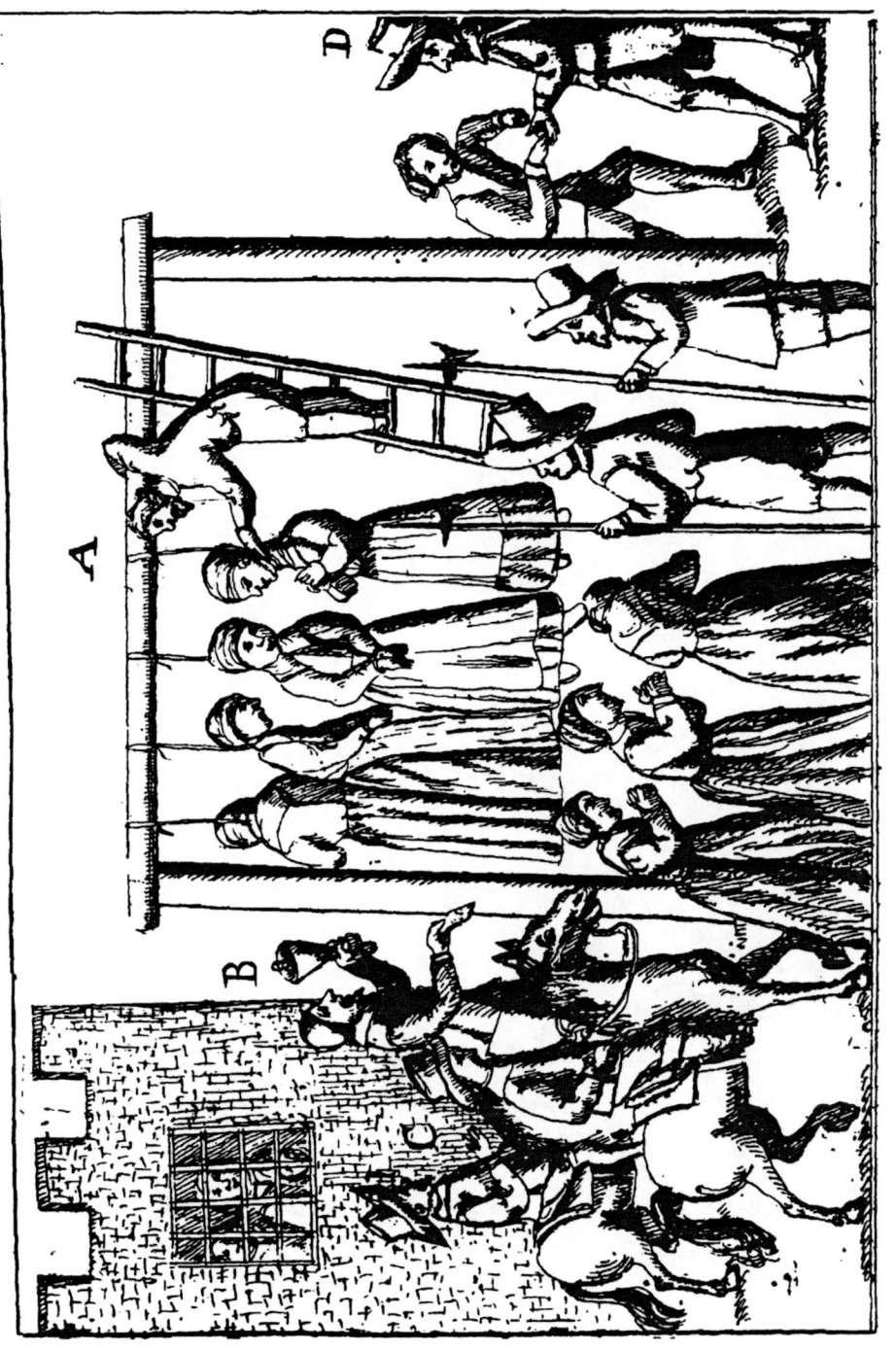

EXECUTION OF WITCHES, A.D. 1655

A. Hangman    B. Bellman    C. Two Sergeants    D. Witchfinder, taking his money

From *England's Grievance discovered in relation to the Coal-Trade*, by Ralph Gardiner

[*face p.* 112

in strength in different parts of the country, waning or waxing according to the amount of support given by local authority. Thus we notice the outbreak in Essex in 1582, in Lancashire 1633, Scotland 1643–50, East Anglia 1645, Newcastle 1649, Kent 1652. Scotland 1661, and so on. There was, in fact, no clearly defined periodic wave of witch-mania sweeping throughout the country, but rather a succession of sporadic outbursts. The underlying current of superstition always present, manifested itself unpleasantly whenever and wherever fanaticism was unusually rampant, the influence of one man often being sufficient to raise the excess of zeal to the danger point.

## Comparison of Witchcraft Belief with Modern Superstitions

It is customary for the present generation of critical writers to express amazement at the credulity and ignorance of the seventeenth century witch persecutors, yet considered impartially such gullibility and want of understanding have their counterpart in the twentieth century in the delusions of the spirit seekers, and their trusting belief in the genuineness and integrity of the numerous charlatans and tricksters, who provide them with psychic manifestations. In fact, there is much in common between the anciently popular pursuit of hunting the witch and the modern pastime of luring the ghost. In the first case opinions were largely the outcome of failure to recognize the true nature of human ailments, such as the dementia and hysteria, and body marks of the witch, and inaccurate diagnosis and complete misunderstanding of the cause of the diseases and accidents of the victims, readily explainable by doctor or veterinary surgeon, and even the man-in-the-street of the present day. In the modern parallel of superstition run riot, the extraordinary beliefs now held are the result of insufficient knowledge of such natural phenomena as telepathy, magnetism, hypnosis, and possibly other forces as yet unknown and unnamed, someday to be clearly explained by our scientists, and to be common knowledge of the man-in-the-street of the future.

In both cases the delusions of the people were and still are heightened by imposture and falsehood, conscious or unwilling, often aided by coincidental occurrence.

The old-time witch never succeeded in doing anything extraordinary or which might not have been a natural occurrence. Their victims died from diseases now easily identifiable or they suffered from recognizable bodily or mental afflictions or common accidents. Their devil's marks were never anything but common physical defects of the human being. Their imps and familiars were always well-known animals or insects existing in their natural elements, if somewhat domesticated, and their charms were common inanimate objects. There was nothing extraordinary about anything they or their victims suffered or performed, yet they gulled most of the public and in some cases deluded themselves as well.

So at the present time in our equally superstitious age the mediums, or the spirits or familiars which they summon, have never been able to accomplish any physical act outside the powers of some human being, or to attain to any mental achievement beyond the capacity of some living person. The twentieth century imp, or mascot, as it is now called, is if a living example, an animal of familiar form. As we read in a record of 1645, of men taking imps with them to the army for protection,[1] so to-day some of our regiments have pet animals recognized as mascots, and in parallel with the charms of ancient days we have a vast variety of inanimate and ridiculous talismans.

That there is as much superstition now as in the past is clear from our religious rites, our belief in mascots, our dabbling in the occult, and our attempts to receive the idle chatter of ghosts, and ascribing the manifestations of natural phenomena, coupled with legerdemain and trickery, to the restlessness of departed spirits.[2]

[1] See Appendix VI, Margery Spara', p. 309, and Ann Smith, p. 311.
[2] In village districts the old beliefs in the existence of witches may yet be found. *The Sunday Chronicle*, 9 Sept., 1928, on the

To be honest, we of the present generation can offer little adverse criticism of the witchcraft believers. In the future among a more enlightened people, with more exact scientific observation and inference and knowledge of fundamental factors, no doubt the ancient witch-mania will be classed equally with the present spiritualistic phantasmagoria and charlatancy and religious rites and miraculous mumbo-jumbo, as the products of an exceedingly ignorant, gullible and superstitious age.

authority of a Horseheath resident, relates regarding Mother Redcap, an old woman who died in 1926. " One day a black man called, produced a book, and asked her to sign her name in it. The woman signed the book, and the mysterious stranger then told her she would be the mistress of five imps who would carry out her orders. Shortly afterwards the woman was seen out accompanied by a rat, cat, a toad, a ferret, and a mouse. Everybody believed she was a witch, and many people visited her to obtain cures." Such an account might well have been taken from a seventeenth century deposition.

# ABSTRACTS OF INDICTMENTS

## Elizabeth 1558–1603

1560. Essex Summer Sessions and general gaol delivery holden at Chelmsford on 4 July, 2 Eliz. Commission dated 8 June, 2 Eliz.

1. John Samond of Danberie, beerbrewer, otherwise John Smythe, on 28 May, 1 Eliz., at D., bewitched John Graunte and Bridget Pecocke. Bridget languished until 29 Aug., when she died at D., and Antony (*sic*) Graunte until 28 May following, when he died at D. *Endorsed. Billa vera.*

Po se [no verdict].
See Nos. 55, 56, 241, 247. 250, and 253.[1]
*Full Latin transcript and English version, p. 77 supra.*

2. Joan (*Johanna* [2]) Haddon of Wytham, spinster, on 8 Feb., 2 Eliz., at W., bewitched Joan, wife of Robert Bowltell, and Thomas Emerye and others, and deceived and extorted divers sums of money. *Endorsed. Billa vera.*

Judic qd stat sup pilloria et. Po se quoad incantac non cul quo ad residu est cull puit'p Io considiar cusie (*sic*).

1564. Essex Summer Sessions and general gaol delivery holden at Colchester on 21 July, 6 Eliz. Commission dated 1 June, 6 Eliz.

3. Elizabeth Lowys of Great Waltham, spinster, wife of John L. of W., husbandman, on 15 Apr., 6 Eliz., at . . ., bewitched John Wodley of Chelmsford, who languished until 16 Apr.. following, when he died at C. *Endorsed. Billa vera.*

Po se cul ca null plit pregn.

---

[1] In Lent, 1569, John Smyth otherwise Salmon was found guilty of stealing certain rams. He escaped hanging by reading as a clerk.

[2] I have translated *Johanna* throughout, Joan, and *Jana*, Jane.

4. ——, on 25 Apr., 6 Eliz., at Chelmsford, bewitched Robert Wodley of Chelmesforde, husbandman, who languished until 1 May following, when he died at C. *Endorsed.* Billa Vera.

Po se cul ca null   plit pregn.

5. ——, on 20 Apr., 6 Eliz., at W., bewitched John Canell, son of Gregory C. of Great Waltham, yeoman, aged about 3 years. who languished until 1 May following, when he died at W. *Endorsed.* Billa vera.

Po se cul ca null   plit pregn.

6. William Rande of Great Totham, labourer, on 12 Jan., 6 Eliz., at T., bewitched to death a brown cow valued at 30s. of the goods and chattels of Robert Carnell. *Endorsed.* Billa vera.

Po se.

1564.   Surrey Winter Sessions and general gaol delivery holden at Southwark on 13 Dec., 7 Eliz. Commission dated 21 Nov., 7 Eliz.

7. Eden Worsley of Ewell, spinster, on 4 July, 6 Eliz., at E., bewitched and killed Elizabeth Dybye, daughter of Robert D. *Endorsed.* Billa vera.

Po se cul ca null   Judicm reddit.

[The gaol calendar has " rep " in margin.]

1565.   Essex Lent Sessions and general gaol delivery holden at Chelmsford on 23 Mar., 7 Eliz. Commission dated 1 Feb., 7 Eliz.

8. Anne Vale of Whyght Rodinge, widow, on 6 Oct., 6 Eliz., at W. R., bewitched to death 8 pigs valued at . . . of the goods and chattels of John Berde of W. R. *Endorsed.* Billa vera.

Po se non cul exon.

1656.   Kent Lent Sessions and general gaol delivery holden at Dartford on 2 April, 7 Eliz. Commission dated 1 Feb., 7 Eliz.

9. Alice Latter of Tunbrydge, widow, on 20 Mar., 6 Eliz., at T., bewitched Joan Harrys, daughter of Antony H. of T.,

butcher, who languished until 22 Mar. following, when she died at T. *Endorsed*. Billa vera.

Po se non cul nec re.

10. ——, on 26 Feb., 5 Eliz., at T., bewitched William Harris, son of Antony H., etc., who languished until 28 Feb. following, when he died at T. *Endorsed*. Billa vera.

Po se non cul nec re.

11. Joan Byden of Maidstone, widow, on 1 July, 6 Eliz., at M., bewitched Mary Huett. daughter of Robert H. of M., pewterer, who languished until 31 July following, when she died at M. *Endorsed*. Robert Huett. Billa vera.

Po se cul ca null.

12. ——, on 1 June, 5 Eliz., at M., bewitched to death 13 turkeycocks of the goods and chattels of Ralph Moore. *Endorsed*. Ralph Moore, John Startowte, Robert Maplesden. Billa vera.

Po se cul ca null.

13. ——, on 6 Dec., 7 Eliz., at M., bewitched Arthur Startowte, son of John S., merchant, who languished, etc. *Endorsed*. [Three witnesses named in No. 12.] Edward Hytchecook, William Kempe. Billa vera.

Po se cul.

1565. Surrey Summer Sessions and general gaol delivery holden at Croydon on 7 Aug., 7 Eliz. Commission dated 22 June, 7 Eliz.

14. Joan Gowse, wife of Roger G. of Cobham. spinster, on 1 Dec., 7 Eliz., at C., bewitched to death a bull valued at 4*l*. of James Adowne at C. *Endorsed*. Billa vera.

Po se cul    rep (*in margin*).

15. Rose a Borow of Bansted, spinster, on 22 June, 7 Eliz., at B. bewitched and killed Alice Lambert, wife of Geoffrey L. *Endorsed*. Billa vera.

Po se   cul ca null rep.

1566. Essex Summer Sessions and general gaol delivery holden at Chelmsford on 26 July, 8 Eliz. Commission dated 14 June, 8 Eliz.

16. Lora Wynchester of Hatfeld Peverell, wife of Jeromie W. of H. P., on 1 Feb., 8 Eliz., at H. P., bewitched to death . . . cows valued at 20s., 6 sheep valued at 20d. each, 4 pigs valued at 20d. each of the goods and chattels of William Higham. *Endorsed.* Billa vera.

Po se non cul.

17. Elizabeth Fraunces of Hatfelde Peverell, spinster, wife of Christopher F of H. P., on 8 Feb., 8 Eliz., at H., bewitched the infant of William Auger of H., who became decrepid. *Endorsed.* Billa vera.

Cogn indictamen Judm imp'sonamenti p vno anno integr &c. See Nos. 50, 123, also p. 317.

18. Agnes Waterhowse of Hatfelde Peverell, widow, on 1 Oct., 5 Eliz., at H. P., bewitched William Fynee of H. P., who languished until 1 Nov. following, when he died at H. P. *Endorsed.* Billa vera.

Cogn felon et murdri  Judm modo. *See* p. 319.

19. Joan Waterhouse of Hatfelde Peverell, spinster, on 17 July, 8 Eliz., at H. P., bewitched Agnes Browne of H. P., spinster, who on 21 July following became decrepid in her right leg and in her right arm. *Endorsed.* Billa vera.

Po se non cul. *See* p. 320.

1567.    Essex Lent Sessions and general gaol delivery holden at Brentwood on 6 Mar., 9 Eliz. Writ dated 28 Jan., 9 Eliz.

20.    Alice Prestmarye of Donmowe Magna, wife of John P. of D. M., spinster, on 1 Feb., 9 Eliz., at D., bewitched Edward Parker, son of Robert P., tanner, who did despair of his life. *Endorsed.* Billa vera.

Po se cul   Judm scdm formam statuti &c.

21. Joan Cocke of Kelwydon, spinster, on 1 Dec., 8 Eliz., at K., bewitched Agnes Crispe, aged 1 year, who became and yet is decrepid. *Endorsed* Billa vera.

Po se non cul.

22. Joan Osborne of Hatfeld Peverell, spinster, on 26 Dec.,

9 Eliz., at H. P., bewitched Peter Thredgold, aged 6 years, who languished until 3 Jan. following, when he died at H. P. *Endorsed. Billa vera.*

Po se non cul nec re.

1567.  Essex Summer Sessions and general gaol delivery holden at Chelmsford on 17 July, 9 Eliz. Commission dated 18 June, 9 Eliz.

23. Alice Atrū of Great Coggishall, widow, on 14 June, 9 Eliz., at C., bewitched to death a brown bay horse, valued at 4*l.*, of the goods and chattels of Thomas Richolde of C., and a white pig valued at 3*s.* 4*d.*, of the goods and chattels of Edward Gooddaye of C. *Endorsed. Billa vera.*

Po se cul de fascinatioe  Judm scdm formam statuti &c.

1567.  Kent Summer Sessions and general gaol delivery holden at Maidstone on 10 July, 9 Eliz. Commission dated 18 June, 9 Eliz.

24. Agnes Bennett of Boughton Mounchelsey, widow, on 22 Feb., 8 Eliz., at B. M., bewitched John Lyttelhare, son of John L., of B. M., freemason, who instantly died. *Endorsed. Billa vera.*

Po se cul ca null  Judic*u*.

*Full Latin transcript and English version, p. 78 supra.*

25. Cecelia West of Bethersden, spinster, on 12 Dec., 9 Eliz., at B., bewitched Martha Loppam, daughter of William L. of B., who did despair of her life. *Endorsed.* Billa vera.

Po se cul  Judic p anno p'soni et iiij$^{to}$; pilor.

1568.  Surrey Summer Sessions and general gaol delivery holden at Croydon on 9 July, 10 Eliz. Commission dated 21 June, 10 Eliz.

26. Katherine Cockes of Wandelsworthe, spinster, on 18 Mar., 10 Eliz., at Totinge Beck, bewitched Bridget Tegge, wife of Geoffrey T. of Totinge Graveney, labourer, who languished until 10 Apr. following when she died. *Endorsed.* Billa vera.

Po se non cul nec re qiet$^{9}$.

27. ——, on 5 May, 10 Eliz., at T. G., bewitched a gray horse

valued at 40s., of the goods and chattels of Guy Harman. *Endorsed.* Billa vera.

Po se no cul qiet.

28. ——, on 4 May, 9 Eliz., at T. G., bewitched a red cow valued at 20s. of the goods and chattels of Edward Sawe. *Endorsed.* Billa vera.

Po se non cul qiet.

1569.    Essex Lent Sessions and general gaol delivery holden
    at Chelmsford on 2 Mar., 11 Eliz.  Commission dated
    26 Jan., 11 Eliz.

29.    Alice Swallow of Little Baddowe, spinster, on 1 Apr. 11 Eliz., at Lit. B., bewitched Alice Basticke, wife of William B., who languished until 1 May following, when she died at Lit. B. *Endorsed.* Billa vera.

Po se cull ca null  Judm modo.

30. ——, on 2 Mar., 10 Eliz., at Lit. B., bewitched to death, Elizabeth Goores, daughter of William G. of Lit. B., yeoman. *Endorsed.* Billa vera.

Po se cull ca null  Judm modo.

31. ——, on 27 Feb., 12 Eliz., at Lit. B., bewitched to death 4 horses valued at 20 marks of the goods and chattels of John Francke. *Endorsed.* Billa vera.

Po se cull.

32. ——, on 20 June, 10 Eliz., at Lit. B., bewitched John Daggnett, of Lit. B., husbandman, who did despair of his life. *Endorsed.* Billa vera.

Po se cull.

33.  Alice Bambricke of Little Baddowe, spinster, on 9 Oct., 10 Eliz., at Lit. B., bewitched Richard Hawkes, aged 7 days, who languished until 1 Sept., 11 Eliz., when he died at Lit. B. *Endorsed.* Billa vera.

Po se non cull nec re.

1569.    Surrey Summer Sessions and general gaol delivery holden
    at Guildford on 8 July, 11 Eliz.  Commission dated
    1 June, 11 Eliz.

34. Jane Baldwyn, wife of John B. of Wymbleton, yeoman, on 20 July, 8 Eliz., bewitched Elizabeth Bonnam of W., who died at W. *Endorsed.* Billa vera.

Po se non cul nec re.

35. ——, on 12 Apr., 11 Eliz., bewitched Elena Lingarde, wife of Hugh L. of W., who died at W. *Endorsed.* Billa vera.

Po se cul ca null rep.

36. ——, on 21 Oct., 9 Eliz., bewitched Richard Hollingworth, aged 1 year, who died at W. *Endorsed.* Billa vera.

Po se cul ca null rep.

37. ——, on 20 Mar., 11 Eliz., bewitched 4 pigs valued at 3s. of the goods and chattels of William Walter, gentleman. *Endorsed.* Billa vera.

Po se non cul nec re.

1570. Surrey Lent Sessions and general gaol delivery holden at Croydon on 27 Feb., 12 Eliz. Commission dated 26 Jan., 12 Eliz.

38. Richard Marshall of Croydon, labourer, and Clemence Marshall of C., widow, on 20 Dec., 11 Eliz., at C., bewitched to death a mare valued at 30s. of the goods and chattels of William Lewen. *Endorsed.* Billa vera.

Po se non cull [both prisoners].

39. ——, ——, on 5 Jan., 12 Eliz., at C., bewitched to death 2 mares valued at 3l. of the goods and chattels of Henry Freman. *Endorsed.* Billa vera.

Po se non cull [both prisoners].

40. ——, ——, on 10 Dec., 12 Eliz., at C., bewitched to death 1 mare valued at 20s. of the goods and chattels of John Sewer. *Endorsed.* Billa vera.

Po se no cull [both prisoners].

41. ——, ——. on 10 Dec., 12 Eliz., at C., bewitched to death 1 cow valued at 20s. of the goods and chattels of John Fardinge. *Endorsed.* Billa vera.

Po se non cull [both prisoners].

1571.   Essex Summer Sessions and general gaol delivery holden
at Chelmsford on 12 July, 13 Eliz. Commission dated
[16] June, 13 Eliz.

42. Elizabeth Egles of Fifilde, wife of George E. of F.,
labourer, on 12 Apr., 13 Eliz., at F., bewitched John Stokes of
F., husbandman, who languished so that he did despair of his
life. *Endorsed.* Billa vera.

Po se non cul.

1571.   Kent Summer Sessions and general gaol delivery holden
at Maidstone on 16 July. 13 Eliz. Commission dated
16 June, 13 Eliz.

43. Ellen Peckman of Alhallowes, wife of Leurence P. of A.,
labourer, on 3 Apr., 13 Eliz., at A., bewitched Robert Nicholas,
infant son of John N. of A., labourer, who languished until
13 Apr. following, when he died at A. *Endorsed.* Billa vera.

Po se cul ca null Judm mᵒ.

1571.   Surrey *Summer* [1] Sessions and general gaol delivery
holden at Croydon on 23 July. 13 Eliz. Commission
dated 16 June, 13 Eliz.

44. Mary Bartrome of Newington, spinster, on 20 May,
13 Eliz., at St. George's, Southwark, bewitched Agnes Thompson,
widow, of St. G., who vehemently languished. *Endorsed.*
Billa vera.

Po se non cul.

1572.   Essex Lent Sessions and general gaol delivery holden
at Chelmsford on 17 Mar., 14 Eliz. Writ dated
24 Jan . . .

45. William Skelton of Little Wakeryng, labourer, on 10 July,
13 Eliz., at Lit. W., bewitched Dorothy Fuller, daughter of
John F. of Lit. W., yeoman, who languished until 30 Nov.,
14 Eliz., when she died at Lit. W. *Endorsed.* Billa vera.

Po se cul ca null Judm mᵒ.

---

[1] Some uncertainty exists, as commissions for both Jan. and
July. 13 Eliz. are on this file.

46. Margery Skelton of Little Wakeryng,[1] spinster, on 26 Sept., 13 Eliz., at Lit. W., bewitched Phyllis (*philiciam*) Pyckett, daughter of Richard P. of Lit. W., yeoman, who languished until 20 Oct. following, when she died at Lit. W. *Endorsed.* Billa vera.

Po se cul ca null Judm m°.

47. William Skelton of Little Wakeringe, labourer, and Margery Skelton of the same, spinster, wife of W. S., on 16 Nov., 10 Eliz., at Barlinge, bewitched John Churchman of B., sailor, who then and there immediately died. *Endorsed.* Billa vera.

Po se cul ca null Judm m° [both prisoners].

48. ——, ——, on 29 July, 14 Eliz., at Barling, bewitched Agnes Collen, aged 1½ yrs. and more, daughter of William C. of B., who languished and became decrepid. *Endorsed.* Billa vera.

Po se cul [both prisoners].

49. Katherine Pullen of Tollesbury, spinster, on 12 Nov., 12 Eliz., at T., bewitched Joan Dennynge, wife of John D., who then and there died. *Endorsed.* Billa vera.

Po se cul ca null Judm m°.

50. Elizabeth Francis of Hatfield, spinster, wife of Christopher F., yeoman, on 5 Mar., 14 Eliz., at H., bewitched Mary Cocke, wife of Nicholas C. of H., miller, who languished for 10 days following, etc. *Endorsed.* Billa vera.

Po se cul Judm p pillorm & imp'sonamentu corporis p vno anno integr°. See Nos. 17, 123.

1572. Surrey Lent Sessions and general gaol delivery holden at Croydon on 21 Feb., 14 Eliz.

51. Elizabeth Robinson of Wansworthe, spinster, on 29 Apr., 9 Eliz., at W., bewitched George Ashefield, infant son of Richard A. of W., yeoman, who languished until 12 May following, when he died at W. *Endorsed.* Billa vera.

---

[1] In 1566 Margery Skelton, of Little Wakering, had been suspected of sorcery and examined by Archdeacon Cole in these words. " Whether she ever used to hele any of her neighbours that were sycke or deseased, other [either] women or children, and she sayde she hathe, w^th prayinge of her prayers she hath healed vi persones [etc.]." *Precedents and Proceedings*, by W. H. Hale, p. 148.

Po se non cul nec re.

52. ——, on 28 May, 13 Eliz., at W., bewitched William Pickbone of W., labourer, who languished until 24 Jan. following. *Endorsed.* Billa vera.

Po se non cul nec.

1572.   Sussex Lent Sessions and general gaol delivery holden at East Grinstead on 25 Feb., 14 Eliz.

53. Joan Usbarne of Haylesham, spinster, wife of John U. of H., husbandman, on 10 May, 13 Eliz., at H., bewitched to death 1 bull valued at 40s. of the goods and chattels of John Browninge. *Endorsed.* Billa vera.

Po se cul judic.

54. ——, on 24 July, 13 Eliz., at H., bewitched to death 1 cow valued at 30s., of the goods and chattels of Thomas Cosen. *Endorsed.* Billa vera.

Po se cul  Judic secnd form statut.

1572.   Essex Summer Sessions and general gaol delivery holden at Chelmsford on 28 Aug., 14 Eliz.  Commission dated 6 June, 14 Eliz.

55. John Smythe otherwise Salmon of Danburye, yeoman, on 20 Jan., 14 Eliz., at D., bewitched to death 2 cows valued at 4l. of the goods and chattels of William Treasure. *Endorsed.* Billa vera.

Po se non cull.

See Nos. 1, 56, 241, 247, 250, and 253.

56. John Smythe otherwise Sawmon of D., beerbrewer, and Joan, his wife, on 20 July, 12 Eliz., at D., bewitched Edward Robynson of D., sawyer, who became lamed in his body and yet is, and in his beasts, goods, and chattels in manifold ways is hurt and worsened. *Endorsed.* Billa vera.

Po se non cull [both prisoners].

See Nos. 1, 55, 241, 247, 250, and 253.

*Full Latin transcript and English version, p. 79 supra.*

57. Joan Smythe, wife of John S., etc., spinster, on 2 Dec.,

10 Eliz., at D., bewitched Richard Pereson of D., tanner, so that he became and yet is lame. *Endorsed.* Billa vera.

Po se non cull.

58. Agnes Francys, wife of William F. of Hatfeld Peverell, weaver, on 28 Nov., 14 Eliz., at H., bewitched a sorrell horse valued at 40*s.* of the goods and chattels of William Brodebelt of H., butcher, which languished until 30 Nov., when it died at H. *Endorsed.* Billa vera.

Po se non cul.

59. ——, on 2 Nov., 11 Eliz., at H., bewitched Clemence Willmott, wife of Walter W. of H., yeoman, who languished until 4 Nov. following, when she died at H. *Endorsed.* Billa vera.

Po se non cul nec re.

60. ——, on 1 Oct., 8 Eliz., at H., bewitched Alice Wilmott, wife of Alexander W. of H., yeoman, who languished until 4 Nov. following, when she died at H. *Endorsed.* Billa vera.

Po se non cul nec re.

61. ——, on 25 Mar., 14 Eliz., at H. P., bewitched Walter Wilmotte, who languished until 1 Apr. following, when he died at H. P. *Endorsed.* Billa vera.

Po se cul ca null plitat pregn.

62. Agnes Steademan of Halsted, spinster, on 1 July, 14 Eliz., at H., bewitched Sibil Bentall, wife of Thomas B. of H., yeoman, who languished for 12 days following, etc. *Endorsed.* Billa vera.

Po se cul ca null.

63. ——, on 1 May, 14 Eliz., at H., bewitched 3 cows valued at 4*l.* of the goods and chattels of John Rome which languished for 3 days. *Endorsed.* Billa vera.

Po se cul.

64. ——, on 7 June, 14 Eliz., at H., bewitched 1 cow valued at 30*s.* of the goods and chattels of Owin Norman which languished. *Endorsed.* Billa vera.

Po se cul.

1572.    Surrey Summer Sessions and general gaol delivery holden
at Kingston-upon-Thames on 8 Sept., 14 Eliz.  Commission dated 6 June, 14 Eliz.

65. Isabella otherwise Sibell Tylley, wife of John T. of St Saviour's, Southwark, on 14 June, 14 Eliz., at S., bewitched Anne Gallaway, aged 2 yrs., daughter of Thomas G. of S., butcher, who languished until 21 Aug. following, when she died at S. *Endorsed.* Billa vera.

Po se non cul nec re.

1573.    Hertford Lent Sessions and general gaol delivery holden
at Hertford on . . . Commission dated 28 Jan., 15 Eliz.

66. Thomas Heather of Hoddesden, yeoman, on 1 Jan., 15 Eliz., at H., in a wood invoked evil spirits with the intention of gaining divers great sums of money. *Endorsed.* Billa vera.

Po se cul ca null  Judic reddit' pd' postea p. pd dis [*illegible*] rep'.

*Full Latin transcript and English version, p. 80 supra.*

1574.    Essex Lent Sessions and general gaol delivery holden
at Chelmsford on 17 Mar., 16 Eliz.  Commission dated 23 Jan., 16 Eliz.

67. Alice Chaundeler of Maldon, spinster, 3 July, 15 Eliz., at M., bewitched Mary Cowper, aged 8 yrs., daughter of Francis C. of M., fletcher, who then and there died. *Endorsed.* Billa vera.[1]
Po se cul ca null  Judic.

68. ——, on 7 Apr., 15 Eliz., at M., bewitched Robert Briscooe of M., weaver, who then and there died. *Endorsed.* Billa vera.
Po se cul ca null  Judic.

69. ——, on 3 Feb., 15 Eliz., at M., bewitched  Robert Brisco of M., weaver, aged 30 yrs., George Brisco, aged 2 yrs., and Prudence Brisco, aged 5 yrs., daughter of said Robert B., who died at M. *Endorsed.* Billa vera.

Po se cul ca null  Judic m° reddit.

[1] A damaged inquisition dated 6 July, 15 Eliz., taken at Maldon in General Sessions holden at the Motehall is also filed.

70. Joan Stubbinge of Ryddeswell, spinster, on 31 Aug., 14 Eliz., at R., bewitched Marion Cootes, aged 1½ yrs., daughter of Thomas C., who languished for 10 days. *Endorsed.* Billa vera.

Po se non cul.

71. ——, on 8 Sept., 13 Eliz., at R., bewitched Henry Melser, who languished for 7 days. *Endorsed.* Billa vera.

Po se non cull.

1574. Kent Lent Sessions and general gaol delivery holden at Dartford on 4 Mar., 16 Eliz. Commission dated 23 Jan., 16 Eliz.

72. Alice Daye, wife of Thomas Daye of Boxley, tanner, on 12 Jan., 15 Eliz., at B., bewitched Isabella Chylde, daughter of Thomas C. of B., who languished until 16 Feb. following, when she died at B. *Endorsed.* Billa vera.

Po se cul ca null   Rep p pg.   See Nos. 116, 124.

73. ——, on 13 June, 15 Eliz., at B., bewitched Alice Goodwyne of Boxley, who languished until 13 July following, when she died at B. *Endorsed.* Billa vera.

Po se cul ca null   Rep.

74. ——, on 30 June, 15 Eliz., at B., bewitched Thomas Chylde of B., husbandman, who languished until 3 July following, when he died at B. *Endorsed.* Billa vera.

Po se cul ca null   Rep' p p'g.

1574. Essex Summer Sessions and general gaol delivery holden at Brentwood on 19 July, 16 Eliz.[1] Commission dated 12 June, 16 Eliz [1]

75. Cecilia Glasenberye,[1] wife of Thomas G. of Barkyng, on 2 Oct., 14 Eliz., at B., bewitched John Fyssher of B., tanner, who languished until 1 Nov. following, when he died at B. *Endorsed.* Billa vera.

Po se cul ca null   Judic.

[1] The Examination and Confession of a notorious Witch named Mother Arnold, alias Whitecote. alias Glastonbury. at the Assise of Burntwood in July, 1574 ; who was hanged for Witchcraft at Barking. 1575. Mentioned by Lowndes (*Bibliographers' Manual*, p. 1967).

76. ——, on 13 Oct., 15 Eliz., at B., bewitched Giles Graye of B., glover, who languished until 1 Nov. following, when he died at B. *Endorsed.* Billa vera.

Po se cul ca null    Judic.

77. ——, on 20 Oct., 13 Eliz., at B., bewitched a gray gelding valued at 4*l.* of the goods and chattels of Roger Fyssher of B., yeoman, which within 4 days died. *Endorsed.* Billa vera.

Po se cul ca null    Judic.

78. ——, on 20 Aug., 14 Eliz., at B., bewitched William Gyllett, son of William G., yeoman, who languished until 10 Sept. following, when he died at B. *Endorsed.* Billa vera.

Po se cul ca null    Judic.

79. ——, on 6 June, 16 Eliz., at B., bewitched William Newman of Stratforde, yeoman, who languished until 20 June following so that he lost the use of his members. *Endorsed.* Billa vera.

Po se cul    Judic.

80. Elizabeth Taylor, wife of John T. of Thaxstede, labourer, on 10 Apr., 15 Eliz., at T., bewitched Alice Holmes, daughter of William H. of London, basket-maker, who languished until 14 Apr., following, when she died at T. *Endorsed.* Billa vera.

Po se cul ca null    Judic.

81. ——, on 10 Oct., 14 Eliz., at T., bewitched Agnes Townesend, daughter of William T. of T., carpenter, who languished until 20 May following, when she died at T. *Endorsed.* Billa vera.

Po se cul ca null    Judic.

82. Alice Hynckson of Thaxstede, widow, on 20 Jan., 14 Eliz., at T., bewitched 3 cows valued at 4*l.* and 7 ewes valued at 20*s.* of the goods and chattels of James Jarvys of T., husbandman, which within 4 days died. *Endorsed.* Billa vera.

Po se cull Judc p̃sone p a° et quater pillorie &c.

83. Agnes Dix, wife of John D. of Waterbelcham, labourer, on 1 May, 16 Eliz., at W., bewitched Richard Hayward, who languished for 14 days following. *Endorsed.* Billa vera.

Po se non cul nec re.

84. ——, on 20 Jan., 16 Eliz., at W., bewitched Elizabeth Potter, wife of John P. of W., who languished until 30 Jan. following, when she died at W. *Endorsed.* Billa vera.

Po se non cul nec re.

### Gaol Delivery Roll

Elizabeth Taylor  
Cecilia Glassenbury al Arnold } Cul modo et Judicm qd S⁹.

Alicia Hynckeford cul modo p ffascinatioe et adiudicatur p'sone p anno a quater pillore put in Statuto.

Agnes Dyxe  Quiet' . . . modo.

1574.  Kent Summer Sessions and general gaol delivery holden at Maidstone on 15 July, 16 Eliz. Commission dated 12 June, 16 Eliz.

85. Alice Stanton, wife of Robert S. of Northflete, yeoman, on 21 Dec., 12 Eliz., at N., bewitched William Allyn, who languished until 1 Feb. following, when he died at N. *Endorsed.* Billa vera.

Po se non cul nec re.

86. ——, on 30 Apr., 16 Eliz., at N., bewitched to death 1 heifer valued at 20s., and 1 sow and 10 pigs valued at 10s. of John Goodwyne. *Endorsed.* Billa vera.

Po se cul *ca*[1]  Judicat scnd form statuti.

1575.  Surrey Lent Sessions and general gaol delivery holden at Croydon on 21 Feb., 17 Eliz. Commission dated 27 Jan., 17 Eliz.

87. Marion Constable, wife of John C. of Dorking, on 24 Dec., 17 Eliz., at D., bewitched to death 2 pigs valued at 6s. 8d. of the goods and chattels of Christopher *Pown*yngfoulde of D. *Endorsed.* Billa vera.

Po se non cull.

88. Thomas Heather[2] of Battersey, labourer, William Williamson of the same, labourer, Richard Pope of the same, labourer, and Thomas Twyford of the same, labourer, on 31 Jan.,

---

[1] Deleted or smudged.  
[2] Can this be the Thomas Heather of No. 66 ?

17 Eliz., at B., conjured and invoked evil spirits with the intention of gaining divers great sums of money. *Endorsed.* Billa vera.

Above the name of Thomas Heather, nō est in p'sona.

At foot of document : William Wylliamson, po se non cul r nec re.

Richard Pope, po se non cul nec re.

Thomas Twyford, po se non cul nec re.

Thomas Heather, po se cul ca null Judm. tri ffebr xixº irro.

*Remitted from the General Sessions of the Peace holden at Kingston-upon-Thames on 5 Oct., 16 Eliz. [1574].*

89. Agnes Crockford of Chertsey, spinster, on 7 July, 16 Eliz., at C., bewitched John Arthur, aged 6 yrs., son of Richard A., husbandman, who languished until 17 July following, when he died at C.

Po se cul ca null   Pregn vt di . . . irro.

90. ——, on 20 Dec., 16 Eliz., at C., bewitched Thomas Croft aged 1¼ yr., son of John C., husbandman, who languished until 31 Dec. following, when he died at C.

Cul ca null   irro.

91. ——, on 1 Mar., 15 Eliz., at C., bewitched . . Tucker, wife of . . . T. of C., miller.

Po se cul.

1575.   Sussex Lent Sessions and general gaol delivery holden at East Grinstead on 18 Feb., 17 Eliz. Commission wanting.

92. Margaret Cooper, wife of William C., of Kerdeforde, surgeon, on 1 Apr., 16 Eliz., at K., bewitched Henry Stoner, who languished until 20 Apr. following, when he died at K. *Endorsed.* Billa vera.

Po se cul ca null   Judm modo.

93. ——, on 1 Sept., 14 Eliz., at K., bewitched William Fowler, who languished until 4 Sept. following, when he died at K. *Endorsed.* Billa vera.

Po se cul ca null   Judm modo.

94. ——, on 1 June, 16 Eliz., at K., bewitched Elizabeth Fowler, wife of Thomas F., who languished until 20 June following, when she died at K. *Endorsed.* Billa vera.

Po se cul ca null   Judm modo.

1576.   Essex Lent Sessions and general gaol delivery holden at Brentwood on 19 Mar., 18 Eliz. Commission dated 1 Feb., 18 Eliz.

95. Margery Pavett, wife of Henry P. of High Rodinge, husbandman, on 31 July, 15 Eliz., at H. R., bewitched Margaret Gudgin, who languished until 1 May following, when she died at H. R. *Endorsed.* Billa vera.

Po se non cul nec re.

96. Margery Pavett of High Rodinge. spinster, on 1 Mar., 16 Eliz., at H. R., bewitched Elizabeth Burton, who languished until 21 Mar., following, when she died at H. R. *Endorsed.* Billa vera.

Po se non cul.

97. Agnes Bromley of Hatfeld Peverell, spinster, on 20 Feb., 16 Eliz., at H. P., bewitched John Baker of H. P., labourer, who languished until 17 Sept., 17 Eliz., when he died at H. P. *Endorsed.* Billa vera.

Po se cul ca null   Judic.

98 ——, on 13 June, 17 Eliz., at H. P., bewitched to death a pig valued at 8s., and on 6 July, 17 Eliz., 2 other pigs valued at 6s. of the goods and chattels of Thomas Smythe of H. P., husbandman. *Endorsed.* Billa vera.

Po se non cull.

99. ——, on 26 Sept., 17 Eliz., at H. P., bewitched to death 2 "*juvenc*' voc' wenn ewes "[1] valued at 26s. 8d., 1 sow valued at 10s., and 3 pigs valued at 6s. each of the goods and chattels of Nicholas Whale of H. P. *Endorsed.* Billa vera.

Po se non cul.

100. Margaret Saunder of Raynham, spinster, on the 14 July,

[1] *Juvenca* is usually translated heifer and *juvencus*, steer.

17 Eliz., at R., bewitched John Wynter, son of Christopher W. of R., mariner, who languished until 19 July following, when he died at R. *Endorsed.* Billa vera.

Po se non cul nec re.

1576.    Essex Summer Sessions and general gaol delivery holden at Chelmsford on 30 July, 18 Eliz. Commission dated 22 June, 18 Eliz.

101. Margery Spencer of Hawsted, spinster, on 12 Jan., 18 Eliz., at H., bewitched Mary Foxe of H., spinster, who languished until 30 May following, when she died at H. *Endorsed.* Billa vera.

Po se cul ca nul   Judm.

102. ——, on 12 Jan., 18 Eliz., at H., bewitched Alice Ambrose, aged 1½ yr., daughter of James A., of H., who languished until 1 Mar. following, when she died at H. *Endorsed.* Billa vera.

Po se cul ca null   Judm.

103. Joan Baker, otherwise Johnson of Brentwoodde, spinster, on 20 Nov., 11 Eliz., at B., bewitched Mary Noke, wife of Richard N. of B., glover, who languished until 18 Aug. following, when she died at B. *Endorsed.* Billa vera.

[*No plea.*] Cul ca null   Judm.

104. ——, and Elizabeth Aylett of B., spinster, on 14 July, 18 Eliz., at B., bewitched Anne Noke, daughter of Richard N. of B., glover, who languished until the day of taking this inquisition, viz. the last day of July. *Endorsed.* Billa vera.

Joan Baker.  Po se cul ca null.

Elizabeth Aylett.  Po se cul   Judic qd reto . . . inet' ꝑson ꝑ aᵒ et quater pillorie in aᵒ ꝑ vj horas et qᵒlibit tempor confitentȝ offens.

105. ——, ——, on 1 June, 18 Eliz., at B., bewitched John Welles, aged 10 yrs., who then and there immediately died. *Endorsed.* Billa vera.

[*Margin destroyed.*] cul.

*Inquisition taken at Chelmsford on 3 May, 18 Eliz.*

106. Agnes Berden of Elsnam, spinster, on 15 Apr. . . . at E.. bewitched Thomas Barlet, *generosus*, aged 1½ yr., who languished so that he did despair of his life. *No endorsement.*

Po se non cull.

1577. Essex Lent Sessions and general gaol delivery holden at Chelmsford on 27 Feb., 19 Eliz. Commission dated 26 Jan., 19 Eliz.

*Remitted from the General Sessions of the Peace holden at Chelmsford, 4 Oct., 18 Eliz. [1576].*

107. Robert (*incertans est*) Chambers of Westham on 30 Nov., 19 Eliz., at W., in the house of Charles Bonifant invoked an evil spirit with the intention of gaining divers great sums of money. Richard Ball of W., husbandman, and Thomas Foster of the same, husbandman, were present and abetted John [*sic*] Chambers. *Endorsed.* Billa vera.

Po se non cul nec re (Ball and Foster).

108. Agnes Sawen of Stock, spinster, on 20 Sept., 16 Eliz., at S., bewitched Christopher Veele, son of Roger V. of S., husbandman, so that he became lame, etc. *Endorsed.* Billa vera.

Po se non cul nec re.

1577. Surrey Summer Sessions and general gaol delivery holden at Croydon on 11 July, 19 Eliz. Commission dated 8 June, 19 Eliz.

109. Bridget Hitchecocke of Bisley, spinster, on 15 June, 15 Eliz., at Horsell, bewitched to death 1 mare valued at 46s. 8d. of the goods and chattels of John Mellist ; on 25 Aug., 15 Eliz., 1 cow valued at 46s. 8d. of J. M. ; on 26 May, 19 Eliz., 1 horse valued at 20s. of J. M. ; *Endorsed.* Billa vera.

Po se non cul.

1577. Sussex Summer Sessions and general gaol delivery holden at Horsham on 8 July, 19 Eliz. Commission dated 8 June, 19 Eliz.

110. Margery Barrowe of Chayley, spinster, on 12 Apr., 19 Eliz., at C., bewitched Isabella Marten, wife of John M., who

languished until the day of taking this inquisition, viz. 8 July. *Endorsed*. Billa vera.

Non *sut* in p̃son.  fiat p̃cess  fact est warran.

111. Juliana Curtis of Crawley, spinster, on 20 Dec., 19 Eliz., at C., bewitched Dionisia Snell, who languished until 31 May following. *Endorsed*. Billa vera.

fiat p̃cess  trı ffeb xx°  fact est warran  trı marcij anno xx° dne Elizabeth.

Po se non cull nec re.

112. Alice Casselowe of Mayfilde, spinster, on 6 June, 19 Eliz., at M., bewitched to death 1 ox valued at 4*l.* of the goods and chattels of Magin Fowle, gentleman. *Endorsed*.   Billa vera.

Po se cul  Judic p̃sa p a° et iiij' pillorie.  mortua *est* in p̃sa.

113. ———, on 1 June, 18 Eliz., at M., bewitched to death 2 pigs valued at 10*s.*, of the goods and chattels of Richard Roose. *Endorsed*. Billa vera

Memoranda as No. 112.   She died in prison as appears by Coroner's inquisition taken in Easter term, 19 Eliz.

1578.   Essex Summer Sessions and general gaol delivery holden at Brentwood on 14 July, 20 Eliz.  Commission dated 30 May, 20 Eliz.

114. Joan Prestmary of Great Dunmowe, spinster, on 1 Mar., 20 Eliz., at G. D., bewitched to death 3 heifers and 2 cows valued at 5*l.* of the goods and chattels of Nicholas Whale. *Endorsed*. Billa vera.

Po se non cul.

115. Jane Buxstone of Stratford Langthorne, spinster, on 20 Dec., 20 Eliz. [1577], at S. L., bewitched to death 14 pigs of John Warde. *Endorsed*. Billa vera.

Po se non cul nec re.

See introduction, p. 56.

1578.   Kent Summer Sessions and general gaol delivery holden at Maidstone on 10 July, 20 Eliz.  Commission dated 30 May, 20 Eliz.

116. Alice Daye of Boxley, spinster, on 25 Aug., 19 Eliz., at Maydestone, bewitched John Collyns of M., who languished until 12 July following and yet does languish, etc.   Also on 19 Apr., 20 Eliz., at B., bewitched to death 2 heifers of Francis Waynewright valued at 3*l*. *Endorsed*. Billa vera.

Po se cul. [Sentence is entered on No. 124.]
See Nos. 72, 124.

117. Katherine Burbage of All Saints', Hoo, spinster, on 25 Sept., 19 Eliz., at All S., bewitched to death 2 geldings of John Renwell valued at 6*l*.   Also on 19 Apr., 20 Eliz., at All S., bewitched to death 1 pig valued at 6*s*. 8*d*., of Thomas Bull. *Endorsed*. Billa vera.

Po se cull   Judic scdm statuti viz. prisona p a° et iiij' pillorie.

1579.   Essex Lent Sessions and general gaol delivery holden at Chelmsford on 26 Mar., 21 Eliz. Commission dated 27 Jan., 21 Eliz.[1]

118. Margaret Rogers of Stratford Langthorne, spinster, on 22 Jan., 21 Eliz., at S. L., bewitched Joan Warlowe, who languished until 31 Jan. following, when she died at S. L. *Endorsed*. Billa vera.

Po se non cul nec re.  See No. 149.

119. Ellen Smythe of Maldon, spinster, on 7 Mar., 21 Eliz., at M., bewitched Susan Webbe, aged about 4 yrs., who languished until 8 Mar. following, when she died at M.  *Endorsed*.  Billa vera.

Po se cul ca null.  Judm.

120. Alice Nokes of Lamborne, spinster, on 1 Dec., 18 Eliz., at L., bewitched Elizabeth Barfott, who instantly died. *Endorsed*. Billa vera.

Po se cul ca null  Judm.

*Inquisition taken at Branktrey on 2 Apr., 20 Eliz.* [1578].

121. Margaret Ga*nn*e of Borley, spinster, otherwise Margaret Welles and Joan Norfolke of B., spinster, on 1 Mar., 20 Eliz.,

[1] A Detection of damnable driftes, practised by three Witches arraigned at Chalmsforde in Essex . . . which were executed in Aprill 1579. *Collection of Tracts*, printed by J. R. Smith, 1838.

at B., bewitched John Furmyn, who languished until 1 May following, when he died at B. *No endorsement.*

Po se non cul nec re.  Joan Norfolk po se non . . .

Bound in 10*l.* a pece to *give* evidence at this daie ageynst the above-named Margaret Ga*nn*e.  John Bragge, Alice Fyrmyn, William Fyrmyn.

See Nos. 129, 130, 131.

*Inquisition taken at Branktrey on 2 Oct., 20 Eliz.* [1578].

122. Margery Stanton of Wymbyshe, spinster, on 20 Aug., 20 Eliz., at W., bewitched 1 white gelding valued at 3*l.* and 1 cow valued at 40*s.*, which languished until 24 Aug., following, when they died.

Indictamen insufficien est.

*Full Latin transcript. and English version, pp. 81–2 supra.*

*Remitted from the General Sessions of the Peace holden at Chelmsford, 8 Jan., 21 Eliz.* [1579].

123. Elizabeth Fraunces of Hatfield Peverell, spinster, on 26 June, 20 Eliz., at H. P., bewitched Alice Poole, wife of Richard P. of H. P., spinster, who languished until 1 Nov. following, when she died at H. P. *Endorsed.* Twenty-one names of jurors before whom the inquisition was taken.

Po se cul ca null Judm.  See Nos. 17. 50.

1579.    Kent Lent Sessions and general gaol delivery holden at Rochester, 12 Mar., 21 Eliz.  Commission dated 27 Jan., 21 Eliz.

124. Alice Daye of Boxley, spinster, on 20 June, 20 Eliz., at B., bewitched John Collyns of B., yeoman, who languished until 24 July following, when he died at B. *Endorsed.* Billa vera.

Po se cul ca null Judic.  See Nos. 72, 116.

1579.    Essex Summer Sessions and general gaol delivery holden at Chelmsford on 6 Aug., 21 Eliz.  Commission dated 19 June, 21 Eliz.

125. Richard Presmary of Great Dunmowe, tailor, and Joan, his wife, spinster, on 10 Jan., 21 Eliz., at D., bewitched Gabriel

Smythe of D., bricklayer, who languished until 17 July following, when he died at D. *Endorsed.* Billa vera.

Po se cul ca null Judm. [both prisoners].

126. Elizabeth Hardinge of Barkinge, spinster, on 6 Feb., 21 Eliz., at B., bewitched Ciscilia Myles aged 3 yrs., who languished until 23 Mar. following, when she died at B. *Endorsed.* Billa vera.

Po se non cul nec re. See No. 137.

127. ———, on 1 Nov., 21 Eliz., at B , bewitched to death 12 "pullos vocat coltes" valued at 30*l.* of the goods and chattels of Nicholas Towler. *Endorsed.* Billa vera.

Po se cul Judm secundu formam statuti.

128. ———, on 1 Aug., 20 Eliz., at B., bewitched Ellen Goode, wife of John G., who did despair of her life. *Endorsed.* Billa vera.

Po se cul Judm scdum formam statuti.

129. Joan Norfolke of Borley, spinster. on 28 Aug.. 20 Eliz., at Foxeyerthe, bewitched Henry Kent of F., who for 3 days was greatly troubled in divers parts of his body. *Endorsed.* Billa vera.

Po se non cul. See Nos. 121. 130.

130. ———, on 12 Dec., 18 Eliz., at B., bewitched to death 1 grey gelding valued at 3*l.* of the goods and chattels of John Bragg of B., yeoman. *Endorsed.* Billa vera.

Po se non cull. See Nos. 121, 129.

131. Margaret Welles of B., spinster, otherwise Margaret Gan, on 15 Apr., 21 Eliz., at Foxeyerthe, bewitched to death 5 store-pigs valued at 10*s.* of the goods and chattels of Henry Kent of F. *Endorsed.* Billa vera.

Po se non cull. See No. 121.

1579. Sussex Summer Sessions and general gaol delivery holden at Horsham on 27 July, 21 Eliz. Commission dated 19 June, 21 Eliz.

132 Alice Stedman, wife of John S. of Stedham, "wod-brooker," on 1 Feb., 21 Eliz., at S., bewitched 2 cows of William

Sp*u*irior valued at 4*l.* ; 1 steer of W. S. valued at 13*s.* 4*d.* ;
1 other cow of W. S. valued at 40*s.*, which cattle did calve.
*Endorsed.* Billa vera.

Po se non cul.

*Full Latin transcript and English version, p. 83 supra.*

1580.   Essex Lent Sessions and general gaol delivery holden
at Brentwood on 10 Mar., 22 Eliz. Commission dated
26 Jan., 22 Eliz.

133. John Symonde of Shenfeild, labourer, on 31 Aug.,
21 Eliz., at S., bewitched Anne Fowell, who languished until
3 Dec., 22 Eliz., when she died at S. *Endorsed.* Billa vera.

Po se non cul nec re.

134. ——, on 7 Nov., 21 Eliz., at S., bewitched Joan Smythe,
wife of Christopher S., who languished until 3 Jan. following,
when she died at S. *Endorsed.* Billa vera.

Po se non cul nec re.

135. ——, on 4 Aug., 19 Eliz., at Brentwood, bewitched
Robert Palmer of B., labourer, who languished until 1 Nov.
following, when he died at B. *Endorsed.* Billa vera.

Po se non cul nec re.

136. Agnes Mylles of Dedham, spinster, on 22 Mar., 21 Eliz.,
at D., bewitched 2 cows and 2 calves of the goods and chattels
of John Perpoyne, of which 1 calf valued at 4*s.* on the 27 Mar.
following died. *Endorsed.* Billa vera.

Po se non cull.

137. Elizabeth Hardinge of Barkynge, spinster, on 3 Feb.,
21 Eliz., bewitched Cecilia Miles, aged 3 yrs., daughter of William
M. of B., who languished until 20 Mar. following, when she died.
*Endorsed.* Billa vera.

Po se cul ca null  Judm.  Non est in p'son apud Colcestr. tri
Julij xxij°. See No. 126.

1580.   Herts Lent Sessions and general gaol delivery holden at
Hertford on 14 Mar., 22 Eliz.  Commission dated
26 Jan., 22 Eliz.

138. Joan Danne of Hytchen, spinster, on 1 Nov., 21 Eliz., at H., bewitched John Sympson of H., yeoman. who languished until 31 Jan. following. *Endorsed*. Billa vera.

Po se non cul.

1580. Sussex Lent Sessions and general gaol delivery holden at East Grinstead on 7 Mar., 22 Eliz. Commission dated 26 Jan., 22 Eliz.

139. Ursula Welfare of Alfriston, spinster, on 1 June, 21 Eliz., at A., bewitched to death 1 sow valued at 3s. 4d., and 8 chickens and 2 hens valued at 3s. of the goods and chattels of John Blunt. *Endorsed*. Billa vera.

Po se non cul n.

140. ——, on 1 Feb., 21 Eliz., at Berwyck, bewitched to death 2 oxen valued at 6l. of William Suzan. *Endorsed*. Billa vera.

Po se non cull.

1580. Essex Summer Sessions and general gaol delivery holden at Chelmsford on 25 July, 22 Eliz. Commission dated 7 June, 22 Eliz.

141. Rose Pye of Canneydon. spinster, on 30 June, 17 Eliz., at C., bewitched John Snow, aged 1 yr., daughter of Richard S. of C., who languished until 20 Aug. following, when she died at C. *Endorsed*. Billa vera.

Po se non cul nec re.

142. Joan Dowtie of Brykelsey, spinster, on 12 Mar., 22 Eliz., at B., bewitched Rose Cooke who languished until 16 Apr. following, when she died at B. *Endorsed*. Billa vera.

Po se cul ca null Judm.

1581. Essex Lent Sessions and general gaol delivery holden at Brentwood on 13 Mar., 23 Eliz. Commission dated 24 Jan., 23 Eliz.

143. Joan Turnor of Stysted, spinster, on 1 July, 21 Eliz., at S., bewitched Anne Feast, wife of Richard F., who did despair of her life. *Endorsed*. Billa vera.

Po se cul Judic.

144. ——, on 1 May, 22 Eliz., at S., bewitched George Sparrowe, aged 7 yrs., who languished for half a year. *Endorsed.* Billa vera.

Po se cul    Judic.

145. ——, on 8 Jan., 22 Eliz., at S., bewitched Ellen Sparrowe, wife of John S., and infant unborn, who then and there died. And so the Jurors say . . . that Joan Turner, the aforesaid Ellen Sparrowe . . . maliciously and devilishly did bewitch and enchant and the quick child of which the aforesaid Ellen was then pregnant by reason of those enchantments and witchcrafts did deprive of life, against the form of the statute, etc. *Endorsed.* Billa vera.

Po se cul    Judic.

**1581.** Essex Summer Sessions and general gaol delivery holden at Braintree on 17 July, 23 Eliz. Commission wanting.

146. Alice Mylles of Bryckelsea, spinster, wife of Richard M. of B., on 20 May, 21 Eliz., at B., bewitched Susanna Thymble, aged $\frac{3}{4}$ yr., daughter of Henry T., who languished until 20 July following, when she died at B. *Endorsed.* Billa vera.

Po se cul ca null  Judm.

147. ——, on 8 Mar., 33 Eliz., at B., bewitched John Eyer, aged 11 yrs., who languished until 9 Mar. following, when he died at B. *Endorsed.* Billa vera.

Po se cul ca null  Judm.

148. ——, on 12 Oct., 22 Eliz., at B., bewitched Margaret Camberlen, who languished until 18 July following, when she died at B. *Endorsed.* Billa vera.

Po se cul ca null  Judm.

149. Margaret Rogers of Stratforde Langethorne, spinster, on 17 May, 23 Eliz., at S., bewitched Dorothy Warlowe, aged 8 yrs., daughter of Gregory W., who languished until 29 June following, when she died at S. *Endorsed.* Billa vera.

Po se non cul nec re. See No. 118.

150. Benneta (elsewhere Benedicta) Buxton of Stratford Langthorne, spinster, on 1 Nov., 22 Eliz., at S., bewitched Thomas

Hamond, who languished until 1 Dec. following at Chinckeforde.
*Endorsed.* Billa vera.

Po se non cul nec re.

### *Gaol Delivery Roll*

Johanna Turner cul ad vltiam p fascinacone & rep' p anno.

1581.　Surrey Lent Sessions and general gaol delivery holden at Croydon on 6 Mar., 23 Eliz. Commission dated 26 Jan., 23 Eliz.

151. Joan Warter of Southwark otherwise Joan Chatterton, spinster, on 1 June, 22 Eliz, at S., bewitched Edward Peter, aged 20 wks., who then and there died. *Endorsed.* Billa vera.

Po se non cul nec re.

1581.　Kent Summer Sessions and general gaol delivery holden at Rochester on 3 July, 23 Eliz. Commission wanting.

152. Margaret Symons, wife of John S. of Brencheley, spinster, on 20 Apr., 21 Eliz., at B., bewitched Agnes Champe, wife of James C. of B., who languished until 24 Aug. following, when she died at B. *Endorsed.* Billa vera.

Po se non cul nec re.

153. ——, on 8 Oct., 22 Eliz., at B., bewitched Stephen Farrawe, aged 14 yrs., son of John F., who languished until 20 Dec. following at B. *Endorsed.* Billa vera.

Po se non cul.

154. Agnes Maye, wife of Thomas M. of Gillingeham, labourer, on 1 Apr., 23 Eliz., at Chakham, bewitched Elizabeth Bennes, wife of James B., who languished until 30 June following. *Endorsed.* Billa vera.

Po se non cul nec re.

Indictment No. 153 is in duplicate.

1582.　Essex Lent Sessions and general gaol delivery holden at Chelmsford on 22 Mar., 24 Eliz. Writ dated 24 Jan., 24 Eliz.[1]

[1] A True and just Recorde of the Information, Examination, and Confessions of all the Witches taken at St Oses in the countie of Essex ; wherefore some were executed, and other some entreated accordingly to the determination of Lawe. . . . Written orderly, as the cases were tryed by evidence, by W. W. 1582.

*Gaol Calendar* [1]

Wiches :  Alice Huntt
Agnes Hearde
Alice Mansfeld
Elizabeth Ewstace [2]
Margaret Grewell
Agnes Glascock
Johan Pechye [2]
Alice Newman
Elizabeth Bennett
Ursula Kentt als Graye

155. Agnes Glascock of St Osithes, spinster, on 26 Dec., 24 Eliz., at St O., bewitched Martha Stevens, daughter of Michael S., who languished until 1 Feb. following, when she died at St O. *Endorsed.* Billa vera.

Po se cul ca null Reꝑ.

156. ——, on 20 Feb., 24 Eliz., at St O., bewitched Abraham Hedg, who languished until 1 Mar. following, when he died at St O. *Endorsed.* Billa vera.

Po se cul ca null Reꝑ.

157. ——, on 1 Mar., 22 Eliz., at St O., bewitched Charity Page, daughter of William P., who languished until 8 May following, when she died at St O. *Endorsed.* Billa vera.

Po se cul ca null Reꝑ.

158. Margaret Grevell of Thorpe. spinster, on 20 Apr., 19 Eliz., at T., bewitched Robert Cheston, who languished until 20 Nov. following, when he died at T. *Endorsed.* Billa vera.

Po se non cul nec re.

159. Cecilia Celles, wife of Henry C. of Lit. Clapton, on 4 June, 22 Eliz., at Grt. Clapton, bewitched John Death, son of Thomas D.. who languished until 4 p.m. the same day, when he died at C. *Endorsed.* Billa vera.

Po se cul ca null reꝑ.

160. Ursula Kempe of St Osythes, spinster, otherwise Ursula

[1] The calendar omits Cecilia Celles.    [2] No indictment.

Grey, and Alice Newman of the same, spinster, on 12 Feb., 24 Eliz., at St O., bewitched Elizabeth Letherdall, daughter of Richard L., who languished until 26 Feb. following, when she died at St O. *Endorsed.* Billa vera.

[Kempe] Po se cul ca null Judic. [Newman] Po se cul ca null Rep.

161. ——, ——, on 30 Nov., 23 Eliz., at St O., bewitched Edna (*Edenem*) Stratton, wife of John S., who languished until 14 Feb., 24 Eliz., when he died at St O. *Endorsed.* Billa vera.

Annotations as indictment No. 160.

162. ——, ——, on 3 Oct., 23 Eliz., at St O., bewitched Joan Thorlowe, daughter of John T., who languished until 6 Oct. following, when she died at St O. *Endorsed.* Billa vera.

Annotations as indictment No. 160.

163. Alice Hunt, wife of William H. of St O., mason, on 4 Nov., 23 Eliz., at St O., bewitched Rebecca Durrant, daughter of Henry D., who languished until 24 Nov. following, when she died at St O. *Endorsed.* Billa vera.

Po se non cul nec re.

164. ——, on 1 Jan., 24 Eliz., at St O., bewitched to death 6 cows valued at 10*l.*, of the goods and chattels of William Hayward. *Endorsed.* Billa vera.

Po se non cul nec re.

165. Elizabeth Bennett, wife of John B. of St O., on 1 Aug., 23 Eliz., at St O., bewitched William Byett and Joan, his wife, who languished until 10 Feb. following, when they died at St O. *Endorsed.* Billa vera.

Cogn ffelon. Judic.

166. Cislia Silles, wife of Henry S. of Clacton, labourer, and Alice Manfeld of Thorpe, spinster, on 1 Sept., 24 Eliz., at C., burnt a corn-house with grain, valued at 100 marks of the goods and chattels of Richard Rose at C.[1] *Endorsed.* Billa vera.

[1] There is nothing to show that this indictment related to a charge of witchcraft except that Mansfield is entered in the list of witches given in the gaol calendar. Celles or Silles is omitted entirely in the same document.

Po se non cul nec re [both prisoners].

167. Agnes Heard of Lit. Okely, spinster, on 1 Jan., 24 Eliz.,
at O., bewitched to death 1 cow, 10 sheep, and 10 lambs,
valuec at 4*l*., of the goods and chattels of John Wade. *Endorsed.*
Billa vera.

Po se non cul.

*Gaol Delivery Roll*

Elizabeth Bennett  
Ursula Kempe  } cul modo iudicati & su⁹ p collum

Alicia Newman  
Cecilia Selle  
Agnes Glascocke } cul modo & rep̃.

Alicia Hunt  
Alicia Mansfild  
Margareta Grevell  
Agnes Herdes } Quieti modo omes et deliberati.

168. Elizabeth Ewstace  
169. Johanna Pechye } comissi prisone p suspic̃one diusa₹  
felon̄ et quia sup inquisic̃one de  
eis h̄ita nihil mali comptom fuit  
v⁹sus eo₹ aliquem dignū vlt⁹iori  
imp^isonamento Io quilibt eo₹  
delibat' modo p pclamacoem.

Johanna Turner p fascinacone Judm & rep̃ p anno.
[Joan Robinson and Margery Sammon are not mentioned.]

1582.    Surrey Lent Sessions and general gaol delivery holden
at Croydon on 15 Mar., 24 Eliz. Commission dated
23 Jan., 24 Eliz.

170. Mabel Jackson, wife of Randall J. of London, labourer,
on 14 Aug., 23 Eliz., at Southwark, bewitched Jane Pynckney,
wife of Robert P. of Southwark, joiner, who languished until
5 Feb., 24 Eliz., when he died at S. *Endorsed.* Billa vera.

Po se cul ca null   Judic.

1582.    Essex Summer Sessions and general gaol delivery holden
at Chelmsford on 2 Aug., 24 Eliz. Commission dated
16 June, 24 Eliz.

171. Agnes Bryant of Great Bursted, spinster, on 20 Oct., 22 Eliz., at Billerica, bewitched 20 brewings of beer of Gabriel Bec, so that they " wolde not worke and sporge ", i.e. ferment,[1] and he lost the brewings. *Endorsed.* Billa vera.

Po se cul ca null.

172. ——, on 20 Mar., 24 Eliz., at Gt. Bursted, bewitched to death 1 gelding of John Atkynsonne. *Endorsed.* Billa vera.

Po se no cull.

173. ——, on 23 Apr., 24 Eliz., at Bursted, bewitched Daniel Fynche, who languished until 5 May, 24 Eliz., when he died at B. *Endorsed.* Billa vera.

Po se cul ca null Judic.

174. Anne Swallowe of Chich St Osyth, spinster, otherwise Anne Eswell on 30 Apr., 24 Eliz., at St O., bewitched John Byrde, who languished until 14 May following, when he died at St O. *Endorsed.* Billa vera.

Po se non cul nec re.

*Gaol Delivery Roll*

Agnes Bryan    cul modo iudicat' et S⁹ p coll.

1582.   Herts Summer Sessions and general gaol delivery holden at St Albans on 30 July, 24 Eliz. Writ dated 16 June, 24 Eliz.

175. Margaret Bonner, wife of James B. of Flampsted, labourer, on 8 Apr., 24 Eliz., at F., bewitched John Skelton of F., who languished until 10 Apr., following, when he died at Watforde. *Endorsed.* Billa vera.

Po se non cul nec re.

1582.   Kent Summer [2] Sessions and general gaol delivery.

176. Elizabeth Jhonson of Kemsinge, spinster, on 1 Aug., 11 Eliz., at K., bewitched Joan Ponde of K., who languished until 20 Sept. following, when she died at K. *Endorsed.* Billa vera.

Po se non cul nec re.

[1] Sporge was probably written for sponge.
[2] There are no dated documents on the file. The latest date of the crime in any one of the indictments is July, 24 Eliz.

177. ——, on 11 Apr., 17 Eliz., at K., bewitched Joan a Court otherwise Gardner of K., who languished until 14 March following, when she died at K. *Endorsed.* Billa vera.

Po se non cul nec re.

178. ——, on 15 Mar., 8 Eliz., at K., bewitched Elizabeth Fremlynge, wife of William F. of K., who languished until 1 Apr. following, when she gave birth to a dead infant at K. *Endorsed.* Billa vera.

Po se non cul nec re.

179. ——, on 1 Dec., 24 Eliz., at K., bewitched Clement Johnson, aged 7 yrs., who languished until 5 Mar. following, when he died at K. *Endorsed.* Billa vera.

Po se non cul nec re.

180. ——, on 16 Mar., 15 Eliz., at Kingsdowne, bewitched Dorothy Miller, wife of Gilbert M. of K., who languished until 24 Sept. following, when she died at K. *Endorsed.* Billa vera.

Po se non cul nec re.

1582. Surrey Summer Sessions and general gaol delivery holden at Kingston-upon-Thames on 26 July, 24 Eliz. Commission dated 16 June, 24 Eliz.

181. Joan Marlow of Egham, spinster, on 1 Dec., 23 Eliz., bewitched William Haydon, who languished until 10 Mar. following, when he died at E. *Endorsed.* Billa vera.

Non est in psona.

*The next seven indictments were found rolled up with a file for* 1585, *but possibly belong here.*

182. Elizabeth Coxe of Godalming, spinster, and Joan Coxe, her daughter, on 10 Sept., 23 Eliz., at G., bewitched John Wilson, otherwise Brombricke of G., tailor, who languished until 10 Dec. following, when he died at G. *Endorsed.* Billa vera.

Po se non cul nec re [both prisoners].

183. ——, ——, on 10 July, 21 Eliz., at G., bewitched William Smith of G., who languished until 1 Dec., 22 Eliz., when he died at G. *Endorsed.* Billa vera.

Po se non cul nec re [both prisoners].

184. Elizabeth Coxe of G., spinster, on 1 Sept., 23 Eliz., at G., bewitched Nicholas Peytowe of G., who languished until 1 June, 23 Eliz., when he died at G. *Endorsed.* Billa vera.

Po se non cul nec re.

185. ——, on 1 May, 22 Eliz., at G., bewitched Ralph Bastowe, labourer, who languished until 22 May following, when he died at G. *Endorsed.* Billa vera.

Po se non cul nec re.

186. Julia Payge of Godalming, spinster, on 4 Nov., 23 Eliz., at G., bewitched John Breden, aged 5 weeks, son of Stephen B. of G., yeoman, who languished until 8 Nov., when he died at G. *Endorsed.* Billa vera.

Po se non cul nec re.

187. Elizabeth Cowper of Shalford, spinster, on 20 Dec., 24 Eliz., at S., bewitched Joan Lambert, wife of Nicholas L., who became lame. *Endorsed.* Billa vera.

Po se non cul.

188. Agnes Waters of Godalming, spinster, otherwise Agnes Stevens, [*no date or place*] bewitched " a hide fatt " valued at 4*l.* of the goods and chattels of Thomas Allen of G. Also on 1 May, 14 Eliz., at G., 10 bullocks valued at 13*l.* of the goods and chattels of Robert Bocher of G. *Endorsed.* Billa vera.

Po se   pdon p gnralem pdo de aᵒ xxiij de Eliz.

1583.   Essex Summer Sessions and general gaol delivery holden at Witham on 29 July, 25 Eliz.  Commission dated 1 June, 25 Eliz.

189. Margaret Hogden of Stebinge, spinster, on 1 Sept., 16 Eliz., at S., bewitched Mary, daughter of John Haywarde, husbandman, who languished until 30 July, 25 Eliz. *Endorsed.* Billa vera.

Po se no cull  pdn . . . xxiij.

190. ——, on 1 July, 24 Eliz., at S., bewitched Elizabeth Robynsone, widow, who languished until 11 June following, when she died at S. *Endorsed.* Billa vera.

Po se non cul nec re.

*Inquisition taken at Chelmsford at General Sessions of the Peace on* 11 *Apr.,* 25 *Eliz.*

191. Margaret Hogdine of Stebbinge, spinster, on 25 Feb., 24 Eliz., at S., bewitched Margaret Hull, wife of John H., who languished until 21 Jan. following, when she died at S. *No endorsement.*

Po se non cul nec re.

### Gaol Delivery Roll

Margareta Hogden quieti modo & delibati.

Cul de antiquo.

192. Anna Smythe  cul ad vltum p fascinacone reʒ  ꝑ anno.

1584.    Essex Lent Sessions and general gaol delivery holden at Chelmsford on 2 Mar., 26 Eliz.   Writ dated 25 Jan., 26 Eliz.

193. Joan Thatcher of Lawford, spinster, otherwise Pfemia Thatcher, on 29 Apr., 25 Eliz., at Bromeley, bewitched to death 3 cows valued at 6*l.*, 10 sheep valued at 5 marks, 1 pig valued at 6*s.* 8*d* of the goods and chattels of John Dix. *Endorsed.* Billa vera.

Po se cul ca null.

194. ——, on 1 June, 25 Eliz., at L., bewitched to death 1 ox (*boviculum*) valued at 40*s.*, 1 cow valued at 40*s.*, 14 sheep valued at 51*s.*, 1 sow valued at 13*s.*, and 1 pig valued at 4*s.*, of the goods and chattels of Christopher Hansteede of L. *Endorsed.* Billa vera.

Po se cul ca null.

195. ——, on 25 Oct., 25 Eliz., at Bromley, bewitched to death 1 horse valued at 30*s.*, 1 cow valued at 4 marks, 1 pig valued at 3*s.* 4*d.*, of the goods and chattels of Nicholas Frende. *Endorsed.* Billa vera.

Po se cul ca null  Judm scdm formam statuti.

196. Margery Barnes of St Osythes, spinster, on 1 July, 25 Eliz., governed and maintained " tres leʒ Imps " otherwise called " speryttes ", one called Pygine, in likeness like a mole, Russoll in the likeness of " le gray Catt ", and another called Dunsott in the likeness of " le dundogge " to the great damage of the public. *Endorsed.* Billa vera.

*Full Latin transcript and English version, p. 83 supra.* See No. 202.

197 Agnes Byllinge of Northokenden, spinster, on 23 June. 25 Eliz., at N., bewitched 2 pigs of the goods and chattels of Humfrey Frith of N., yeoman, which died on 27 June at N. On 20 Aug., 25 Eliz., at N., bewitched 1 heifer of said Humfrey, which died on 24 Aug. at N. On 21 Aug., 25 Eliz., at N., bewitched the said Humfrey, who languished until 28 Aug. following. *Endorsed.* Billa vera.

Po se non cul nec re.

198. ——, on 3 Oct., 25 Eliz., at N., bewitched Judith Foster, wife of John F., gentleman, who languished until 22 Oct. following *Endorsed.* Billa vera.

Po se non cul nec re.

199. ——, on 26 Nov., 25 Eliz., at N., bewitched 3 sheep of the goods and chattels of Peter Hodgeson of N., labourer, which died 28 Nov. following. *Endorsed.* Billa vera.

Po se non cul nec re.

200. Elizabeth Brooke of Great Leighes, spinster, on 1 June, 20 Eliz., at L., bewitched Margaret, wife of John Cleveland, who languished until 10 June following, when she died at L. *Endorsed.* Billa vera.

Po se cul ca null. Judm.

201. ——, on 1 Oct., 20 Eliz., at Gt. L., bewitched 6 cows and 6 horses and mares valued at . . . of the goods and chattels of James Holmested, and 1 cow, 5 heifers (*juvenc*) and 4 hogs valued at 10*l.* of the goods and chattels of James Spylman, and 2 cows and 2 horses valued at 5*l.* of the goods of Thomas Cornyshe, and . . sows valued at 40*s.* of the goods and chattels of George Fytche of L. *Endorsed* Billa vera.

Cogn offens Judm.

202. Joan Dale of Chich St Osyth, spinster, and Margery Barnes of the same, spinster, on 10 July, 25 Eliz., at St O., bewitched John Lanne, who languished until 20 Oct., when he died at St O. *Endorsed.* Billa vera.

Po se mortua in p̃sona. Po se non cul nec re. See No. 196.

203. Agnes Duke of Hatfelde Peverell, spinster, on 7 Feb., 26 Eliz., at H. P., bewitched John Byrd of H., husbandman, who languished until 3 Feb. following, when he died at H. *Endorsed.* Billa vera.

Po se non cul nec re.

204. Lucy Fyssher of Feringe, spinster, on 24 Aug., 23 Eliz., at F., bewitched John Dayes of F., who languished until the day of taking this inquisition, viz., 1 Mar., 26 Eliz. *Endorsed.* Billa vera.

Po se cul ca null Judm.

205. ———, on 24 Sept., 25 Eliz., at F., bewitched Henry Toyse of Broxsted, miller, who languished until 18 Dec. following, when he died at F. *Endorsed.* Billa vera.

Po se cul ca null Judm.

206. ———, on 20 Sept., 23 Eliz., at F , bewitched John Wrighte, the elder, of F., who languished until 24 Nov. following, when he died at F. *Endorsed.* Billa vera.

Po se cul ca null. Judm.

207. ———, on 1 Feb., 26 Eliz., at F., bewitched John Ballerd of F., who languished until 14 Feb. following, when he died at F. *Endorsed.* Billa vera.

Po se cul ca null Judm.

208. Joan Cocke of Hatfeld Peverell, spinster, on 30 Apr., 23 Eliz., at H. P., bewitched Anne, daughter of Richard Wilson of Purligh, smith, who languished until 23 May following, when she died at H. *Endorsed.* Billa vera.

Po se non cul nec re.

209. ———, on 11 Oct., 25 Eliz., at H. P., bewitched Katherine Benson, wife of John Benson, of H., labourer, who languished until 3 Jan. following, when she died at H. *Endorsed.* Billa vera.

Po se non cul nec re.

210. Thomas Kynge of South Hammyngefeild, tailor, on 6 Sept., 25 Eliz., at S. H., bewitched to death 1 horse valued at 33s. 4d. and 1 cow valued at 26s. 8d. and 3 swine valued at 25s. of the goods and chattels of Henry Abell. *Endorsed.* Billa vera.

211. ———, on 7 Feb., 26 Eliz., at S. H., bewitched John Marten

at S. H., who languished until 21 Feb. following, when he died at S. H. *Endorsed*. Billa vera.

Po se cul ca null   Judm.

*Gaol Delivery Roll*

Elizabeth Brooke⎫
Thomas Kynge   ⎬cul modo judicati & S⁹ p coll quousq̨ &c.
Lucia  Fysher ⎭

Johanna Dyxe⎫
  als Thatche⎬cul modo p fascinacone reꝓ p anno.

Agnes Duke     ⎫
Margeria Barnes⎬quieti modo & deliberati.
Agnes Billinge ⎪
Joan Cocke     ⎭

1584.   Essex Summer Sessions and general gaol delivery holden at Witham on 27 July, 26 Eliz.   Commission dated 29 June, 26 Eliz.

212. Joan Colson of Est Mersey, spinster, on 11 Jan., 23 Eliz., at E. M., bewitched John Wager, son of Richard W., who languished until 10 Mar. following, when he died at E. M. *Endorsed*. Billa vera.

Po se cul ca null   Reꝓ.

213. ——, on 30 June, 25 Eliz., at E. M., bewitched Richard Kennett, son of Richard K., who languished until 20 Aug. following, when he died at E. M.   *Endorsed*.   Billa vera.

Po se cul ca null   Reꝓ.

214. Joan Thorocke of Burneham, spinster, on 1 Aug., 25 Eliz., at B., bewitched to death 4 hogs valued at 40s. of the goods and chattels of John Lawe. *Endorsed*. Billa vera.

Po se non cul nec re.

215. ——, on 20 Oct., 25 Eliz., at B., bewitched Thomas Owgham, son of Thomas O. of B., who languished until 22 Dec. following, when he died at B.   *Endorsed*.   Billa vera.

Po se cull ca null   Judm.

216. ——, on 1 July, 24 Eliz., at B., bewitched to death a gelding of a " ronded " colour, 1 grey horse, and 1 iron-grey

mare valued at 15*l.* of the goods and chattels of William Leper. *Endorsed.* Billa vera.

Po se non cul nec re.

217. ——, on 20 Jan., 26 Eliz., at B., bewitched to death 2 cows valued at 4*l.* of the goods and chattels of John Gybbons. *Endorsed.* Billa vera.

Po se non cul nec re.

218. ——, on 20 Dec., 21 Eliz., at B., bewitched Jasper Leper, son of William L. of B., who languished until the last day of Feb. following, when he died at B. *Endorsed.* Billa vera.

Po se cul ca null   Judm.

219. ——, on 8 Dec., 26 Eliz., at B., bewitched Mary Bowels, wife of Isaac B., who languished until 10 Feb., 26 Eliz. following, when she died at B. *Endorsed.* Billa vera.

Po se cul ca null   Judm.

220. Margaret Lyttelberie of Bradwell, spinster, on 20 Dec., Eliz., at B., bewitched Elizabeth Motte, wife of John M. of B., who languished until 10 Feb. following at B. *Endorsed.* Billa vera.

Po se cul ca null   Judm scdm formam statuti.

221. ——, on 8 Feb., 26 Eliz., at B., bewitched Josiah Osborne, son of Josiah O., of B., who languished until 6 June following at B. *Endorsed.* Billa vera.

Po se cul   Judm scdm formam statuti.

222. Elizabeth Morrisbee (Morsby) of Great Chesterford, spinster, on 26 June, 25 Eliz., at Grt. C., bewitched Jane Rowland, daughter of Thomas R. of Grt. C., husbandman, who languished until 1 Aug. following at Grt. C. *Endorsed.* Billa vera.

Po se cul ca null   Judm

223. ——, on 24 June, 24 Eliz., at Grt. C., bewitched Agnes Wynterflud, who languished until 24 Dec., 25 Eliz., when she died at Grt. C. *Endorsed.* Billa vera.

Po se cul ca null   Judm.

*Full Latin transcript and English version, p. 84 supra.*

224. Edmund Mansell of Fingerighoo, yeoman, otherwise of Feeringe, clerk, on 10 Mar., 26 Eliz., at Wyvenhoo, by magic

art burnt a barn, stable, and goods of Edward Burgess of Wyvenhoo. *Endorsed*. Billa vera.

Po se cul Rep.

*Full Latin transcript and English version, p. 85 supra.*

225. ——, on 10 Sept., 23 Eliz., at W., bewitched Edward Burgess, who languished for 2½ yrs. so that of his life he did despair. *Endorsed.* Billa vera.

Po se non cul nec re.

226. Alice Bolton of Chich St Osyth, spinster, and Elizabeth Lumney of the same, spinster, on 20 Nov., 26 Eliz., at St O., bewitched to death 6 hogs valued at 40s. of the goods and chattels of Isaac Grene. *Endorsed*. Billa vera.

Alicia Bolton  Po se cul  Judm scdm Statut.

[Elizabeth Lumney]  Po se non cul.

227. Elizabeth Lumley [*deleted*] and Alice Bolton, on 28 Mar., 25 Eliz., bewitched Grisel Greene, wife of Isaac G. of St O., yeoman, who languished until 31 May, 26 Eliz., when she died at St O. *Endorsed*. Billa vera ꝑ Bolton. Ignoramus ꝑ Elizabethe Lumley.

Po se non cul nec re.

### Gaol Delivery Roll

Elizabeth Morrisbe ⎫
Johanna Thurrocke ⎬ cul modo judicati & Sᵒ.

Joħes Colson cul modo & repᵈ sine judicio.

Eđus Mansell cul modo ꝑ fascinacone & repᵈ sine judicio.

Alicia Bolton ⎫ cul modo ꝑ fascinacone & judicati scdm
Margareta litlebury ⎬ formam st.

Elizabeth Lumey non cul modo et exonerat'.

1585.  Essex Lent Sessions and general gaol delivery holden at Chelmsford on 8 Mar., 27 Eliz. Writ dated 1 Feb., 27 Eliz.

228. Lettice (*Letucia*) Tybbold of Maplested, spinster, on 24 Jan., 27 Eliz., at M., bewitched Margery Sampson, wife of William S. of M., labourer, who languished until 8 Mar. following at M. *Endorsed*. Billa vera.

Po se non cul.

229. ——, on 20 Oct., 22 Eliz., at M., bewitched to death 7 heifers of the goods and chattels of Nicholas Martyn of M. *Endorsed.* Billa vera.

Po se non cul.

230. ——, on 4 Nov., 22 Eliz., at M., bewitched Margery Martyn, daughter of Nicholas M. of M., who languished until 8 Mar., 27 Eliz. *Endorsed.* Billa vera.

Po se non cul.

231. Alice Dragge, wife of Robert D., of Finchinfeilde, tailor, on 20 Nov., 27 Eliz., bewitched James Harrington and Richard Daken, son of William D., who yet languish at F. Also bewitched to death 2 hogs of the goods and chattels of John Tailor of F. *Endorsed.* Billa vera.

Non est in p̃sona.

232. Agnes Thurrock of Burnham, spinster, on 12 Aug., 26 Eliz., at B., bewitched John Lawe of B., husbandman, who languished in great danger of death until 10 Sept. following. *Endorsed.* Billa vera.

Po se non cul nec re.

233. ——, on 20 Jan., 26 Eliz., at B., bewitched Mary Bowles, wife of Isaac B. of B., mariner, who languished until 11 Feb. following, when she died at B. *Endorsed.* Billa vera.

Po se non cul nec re.

1585.    Surrey Summer Sessions and general gaol delivery holden at Croydon 12 July, 27 Eliz.    Commission dated 28 June, 27 Eliz.

*Remitted from the General Sessions of the Peace holden at Guildford on 29 June, 27 Eliz.*

234. Agnes Stevens of Godalmyng, spinster, or 29 . . . 25 Eliz., at G., bewitched Margaret Roker, aged 6 yrs., daughter of Alice R. of G., spinster, who languished until 20 Jan. following, when she died at G. *No endorsement.*

Po se cul ca null rep̃ post   Judm.

235. ——, on 21 June, 25 Eliz., at G., bewitched Richard

Charman of G., who languished until 30 July following, when he died at G. *No endorsement.*

Po se cul ca null rep̅ post   Judm.

236. ——, on 26 June, 25 Eliz., at G., bewitched Katherine Hamond of G., spinster, who languished until 29 Mar. following, when she died at G. *No endorsement*

Po se cul ca null rep̅ post   Judm.

*Gaol Delivery Roll*

Agnes Stevens cul modo judicat' & rep̅.

1586.   Essex Lent Sessions and general gaol delivery holden at Chelmsford on 3 Mar., 28 Eliz.  Writ dated 28 Jan., 28 Eliz.

237. Anne Joyce, wife of John J., of Stanforde Ryvers, labourer, on 20 Apr., 27 Eliz., at S. R., bewitched to death 6 sheep and 6 lambs of the goods and chattels of John Fullur at S.R. And on 28 June, 27 Eliz., at S. R., bewitched to death 2 cows of the goods and chattels of J. F. *Endorsed.* Billa vera.

Po se non cull.

238. ——, on 1 Apr., 26 Eliz., at S. R., bewitched to death 9 hogs and 1 cow of the goods and chattels of John Herd.  And on 4 Apr., at S. R., 1 mare of John Hare which languished. *Endorsed.* Billa vera.

Po se non cull.

239. ——, on 20 Dec., 28 Eliz., at S. R., bewitched Elizabeth Elles, who languished for 7 days. *Endorsed.* Billa vera.

Po se non cul.

1586.   Kent Lent Sessions and general gaol delivery holden at Rochester on 20 Feb., 28 Eliz.  Writ dated 28 Jan., 28 Eliz.

240. Elizabeth Hilbie, wife of Clement H., of Watringburie, on 4 Feb., 27 Eliz., at W., bewitched James Collison, aged 4 yrs., son of John C. of W., glover, who languished until 24 Feb., 27 Eliz., when he died at W. *Endorsed.* Billa vera.

Po se non cul nec re.

1587.   Essex Lent Sessions and general gaol delivery holden at Chelmsford on 13 Mar., 29 Eliz.  Writ dated 26 Jan., 29 Eliz.

241.  John  Smyth  of  Danbery,  otherwise  John  Salmon,  on 6  Nov.,  28 Eliz.,  at  Stowe  Marish,  bewitched  Rose  Larkyn  who languished  until  11  Nov.,  when  she  died  at  Stowe  Marish. *Endorsed.*  Billa vera.

Po se non cul nec re.

See Nos. 1, 55, 56, 247, 250, 253.

242.  Joan  Preston  of  Little  Sampford,  spinster,  and  Frances Preston  of  the  same,  spinster,  on  24  Apr.,  28 Eliz.,  at  Lit. S., bewitched  to  death  2 cows  valued  at  4*l.*  of  the  goods  and  chattels of George Wynterfludd.  *Endorsed.*  Billa vera.

Joan Preston.  Po se cul rep̃ p anno.  Frances Preston.  Po se cul p anno.

243.  Joan  Preston,  on  31  May,  28 Eliz.,  at  Lit. S.,  bewitched 2  sows  valued  at  20*s.*  of  the  goods  and  chattels  of  Thomas Muskall.  *Endosed.*  Billa vera.

Po se cul rep̃ p anno.

244.  ——,  on  20  Aug.,  28 Eliz.,  at  Lit. S.,  bewitched  Margaret Hankyn.  *Endorsed.*  Billa vera.

Po se cul rep̃ in p̃son p anno.

*Full Latin transcript and English version,  p. 86 supra.*

245.  Rose  Clarens  of  Great  Sampford,  spinster,  on  31  Mar., 24 Eliz.,  at  Grt. S.,  bewitched  to  death  2 sows  of  the  goods  and chattels  of  Richard Baker.  *Endorsed.*  Billa vera.

Po se cul rep̃ p anno.

246.  ——,  on  31  May,  27 Eliz.,  at  Grt. S.,  bewitched  to  death 1  horse,  1  cow,  and  1 hog  valued  at  4*l.*  of  the  goods  and  chattels of Thomas Onyon.  *Endorsed.*  Billa vera.

Po se cul rep̃ p anno.

*Remitted  from  the  General  Sessions  of  the  Peace  holden  at Chelmsford on 12 Jan., 29 Eliz.*

247.  John  Smyth  otherwise  Salmon  of  Danburye,  labourer,  on 3  Feb.,  28 Eliz.,  at  Stowe,  bewitched  to  death  8 cows,  6 calves, 3 hogs, 7 sheep, of . . . Symon.  *No endorsement.*

Po se non cul.

See Nos. 1, 55, 56, 241, 250, 253.

1587.   Hertford Lent Sessions and general gaol delivery holden
at Hertford on 10 Mar., 29 Eliz.   Commission dated
23 Jan., 29 Eliz.

248. Agnes Morris of Stevenage, spinster, on 1 July, 24 Eliz.,
at S., bewitched Richard Jenkinson, who languished until 1 May
following, when he died at S. *Endorsed.* Billa vera.

Po se cul ca null   Judm.

249. ——, on 24 June, 28 Eliz., at S., bewitched 1 cow valued
at 30s., of the goods and chattels of John Clark. *Endorsed.*
Billa vera.

Po se cul.


*Gaol Delivery Roll*

Agnes Morris, cul modo rep̃ post   Judm " Weake evidence ".

1587.   Essex Summer Sessions and general gaol delivery holden
at Chelmsford on 24 July, 29 Eliz. Writ dated 20 June,
29 Eliz.

250. John Smyth of Danbery, husbandman, otherwise John
Salmon, on 13 May, 29 Eliz., at D., bewitched Henry Hone,
who languished until 5 Apr. following, when he died at D.
*Endorsed.* Billa vera.

Po se cul ca null   Judm.

See Nos. 1, 55, 56, 241, 247, 253.

251. Joan Gibson of Messing, spinster, on 20 May, 29 Eliz.,
at Inworth, bewitched a windmill of George Clarke. *Endorsed.*
Billa vera.

Po se non cul nec re.

252. Alice Bust, wife of John B. of Alphamstone, husbandman,
about 6 years past and afterwards, bewitched to death 3 hogs
and 1 mare valued at 4l. of the goods and chattels of William
Hoy. *Endorsed.* Billa vera.

Po se non cull.

*Remitted from the General Sessions of the Peace holden at Chelmsford on 6 July, 29 Eliz. [1587].*

253. John Smyth, etc., on 21 Mar., 29 Eliz., at Stowemaryes bewitched to death 1 cow of the goods and chattels of Francis Symon of S., husbandman. *No endorsement.*

Po se cul (*illegible*).

See 1, 55, 56, 241, 247, 250.

*Gaol Delivery Roll.* Cul modo judicat' & s⁹ p coll.

1587. Surrey [Summer] Sessions and general gaol delivery holden at . . . [July 29 Eliz.]. [Commission dated 19 June, 29 Eliz.]

254. Elizabeth Watson, wife of John W. of Sowthwarke, yeoman, on 31 Mar., 29 Eliz., at S., bewitched John, son of Soward Hanson, who languished until 31 May, 29 Eliz., when he died at S. *Endorsed.* Billa vera.

Po se non cul nec re.

255. ——, on 5 Aug., 28 Eliz., at S., bewitched Thomas, son of Thomas Looman of S., who languished until 4 Jan., 29 Eliz., when he died at S. *Endorsed.* Billa vera.

Po se non cul nec re.

256. ——, on 8 June, 26 Eliz., at S., bewitched Agnes Crockelbone, who languished until 2 Nov. following, when she died at S. *Endorsed.* Billa vera.

Po se non cul nec re.

257. ——, on last day of Feb., 23 Eliz., at S., bewitched Robert Saunders. *Endorsed.* Billa vera.

Po se non cul.

258. Clement Sownde of Leigh, spinster, on 16 Apr., 29 Eliz., at L., bewitched 1 cow and 1 calf of the goods and chattels of Thomas Carrington. *Endorsed.* Billa vera.

Po se non cull.

259. ——, on 16 Apr., 27 Eliz., at L., bewitched Richard Sompner, who languished until 22 Apr. following, when he died at L. *Endorsed.* Billa vera.

Po se non cul nec re.

260. ——, on 1 June, 29 Eliz., at L., bewitched Henry Elsey, who languished until 14 June following, when he died at L. *Endorsed.* Billa vera.

Po se non cul nec re.

1588. Essex Lent Sessions and general gaol delivery holden at Chelmsford on 4 Mar., 30 Eliz. Commission dated 23 Jan., 30 Eliz.

261. Elizabeth Harris of Wytham, spinster, on 18 Nov., 30 Eliz., at W., bewitched Gilder Wayland, son of Thomas W., who languished until 29 Nov. following, when he died at W. *Endorsed.* Billa vera.

Po se non cul nec re.

262. ——. on 1 Dec., 30 Eliz., at W.. bewitched Ursula Netherstreat, who languished until 7 Dec. following, when she died at W. *Endorsed.* Billa vera.

Po se non cul nec re.

263. Margaret Harrison, wife of William H. of Harkwell, labourer, on 4 Dec., 22 Eliz., at H., bewitched 1 cow, 1 calf, and 1 sheep of the goods and chattels of Joan Derifall, widow. *Endorsed.* Billa vera.

Po se non cul.

264. ——, on 20 Mar., 28 Eliz., at H., bewitched 3 hogs, 3 pigs, 2 calves, and 1 mare of the goods and chattels of John Ingland. *Endorsed.* Billa vera.

Po se non cul.

265. ——, on 1 Mar., 27 Eliz., at H., bewitched 2 hogs of the goods and chattels of Robert London. *Endorsed.* Billa vera.

Po se non cul.

266. ——, on 2 Sept., 28 Eliz., at H., bewitched Abigail Clarke, daughter of Florence C., widow, who languished until 16 Sept. following, when she died at H. *Endorsed.* Billa vera.

Po se non cul nec re.

267. William Bennet of Finchinfeld, yeoman, and Edward Mason of Berdefeld, yeoman, on 4 July. 29 Eliz., at Shawford, invoked an evil spirit with the intention of gaining divers great sums of money. *Endorsed.* Billa vera.

M

Non sunt in p̃sona   b p compent . . . ad px.

Po se non cul [both prisoners].

268. William Benett of F., yeoman, on 7 Jan., 29 Eliz., at Halsted, and other days and places invoked evil spirits to gain great sums of money by which enchantments he deceived and defrauded divers subjects of the king at H. *Endorsed*. Billa vera.

Non est in p̃sona   b re p compar . . . ad px. tri July xxxº. Non cull.

1588.   Essex Summer Sessions and general gaol delivery holden at Braintree on 15 July, 30 Eliz.  Commission dated 7 June, 30 Eliz.

269. Joan Pakeman of Great Ocle, spinster, on 13 May, 30 Eliz., at Grt. O., bewitched John Bleake, who languished until 31 May following, when he died at Grt. O. *Endorsed*. Billa vera.

Po se non cul nec re.

270. Katherine Harrys of Henyngham Syble, spinster, and Agnes Smythe of the same, spinster, otherwise Agnes Lawsell on 20 Aug., 27 Eliz., at H. S., bewitched George Glascock who then and there died. *Endorsed*. Billa vera.

Po se cul ca null   Judm [both prisoners].

271. ——, ——, on 20 Oct., 29 Eliz., at H. S., bewitched Giles Bridge, aged 3 months, who then and there died.

Po se cul ca null Judm [both prisoners].

*Gaol Delivery Roll.*

Kat⁹ina Harris cul modo judicat' et S⁹ p coĪt.

1589.   Essex Lent Sessions and general gaol delivery holden at Chelmsford on 6 Mar., 31 Eliz. [Commission dated 5 Feb., 31 Eliz.]

272. John Hoare otherwise Jenny of Hatfeld Peverill, glover, and Agnes Duke of H. P., spinster, on 10 Nov., 31 Eliz., bewitched Joan Hawkins, who languished until 10 Mar. following and yet does. *Endorsed*. Billa vera p Agnet' Duke. Ignoramus p Hoare als Jennye.

Po se non cul.

1589. Kent Lent Sessions and general gaol delivery holden at Rochester on 20 Feb., 31 Eliz. Commission dated 5 Feb., 31 Eliz.

273. Alice Fuller of Itham, spinster, on 20 June, 29 Eliz., at I., bewitched Mabel Petley, daughter of William P., who languished until 1 Sept. following, when she died at Itham. *Endorsed* Billa vera. By the judgment of these men whose names are heare underwritten (12 names). Ignoramus. To the judgement of the rest.

Non est in p̃sona  Tri July 31. Po se non cul nec re.

1589. Sussex Lent Sessions and general gaol delivery holden at East Grinstead on 3 Mar., 31 Eliz. Commission dated 5 Feb., 31 Eliz.

274. Edward Roydon of Haylesham, glover, on 16 June, 31 Eliz., at H., bewitched to death 1 cow of the goods and chattels of John Rolf. *Endorsed*. Billa vera.

Po se non cul.

275. ——, on 1 July, 29 Eliz., at Pemsey, bewitched Richard Almon at P., who languished until 29 Sept. following and lost the use of his right arm. *Endorsed*. Billa vera.

Po se non cul.

276. ——, on 29 Sept., 29 Eliz., at Aylesham, bewitched Nicholas Foster, who languished until 1 Aug., 30 Eliz. *Endorsed*. Billa vera.

Po se non cul.

277. ——, on 20 June, 30 Eliz., at Haylesham, bewitched to death 1 mare valued at 6*l*. of the goods and chattels of Abraham Kenchely. *Endorsed*. Billa vera.

Po se non cul.

278. ——, on 4 May, 27 Eliz., at H., bewitched to death Edward Furner. *Endorsed*. Billa vera.

Po se non cul nec re.

1589. Essex Summer Sessions and general gaol delivery holden at Chelmsford on 3 July, 31 Eliz.[1] [Commission dated 2 June, 31 Eliz.]

[1] The apprehension and confession of three notorious Witches arraigned and by Justice condemnede in the Countye of Essex the 5 day of Julye last past. 1589.

279. Joan Prentice of Sybill Heningham, spinster, on 10 Feb., 31 Eliz., at S. H., bewitched Sara Glascock, aged 2 yrs., who languished until 28 Mar. following, when she died at S. H. *Endorsed.* Billa vera.

Po se cull ca null   Judm.

280. Richard Dunne of Waltham Holy Cross, labourer, and Agnes Dunne of the same, spinster, on 12 Feb., 29 Eliz., at W., bewitched 1 gelding valued at 40s. of the goods and chattels of Thomas Warren. *Endorsed.* Billa vera.

Po se non cull [both prisoners].

281. ——, ——, on 1 July, 29 Eliz., at W., bewitched Henry Ludd, who languished at W. *Endorsed.* Billa vera.

Po se non cull [both prisoners].

282. ——, ——, on 1 Oct., 30 Eliz., at W., bewitched Simon Beck, who languished at W. *Endorsed.* Billa vera.

Po se nō cull [both prisoners].

283. Ellen Bett, wife of John B. of Much Waltham, spinster, on 20 Oct., 27 Eliz., at W., bewitched Margery Bankerson, wife of William B., who languished until 20 Sept., 28 Eliz., when she died at W. *Endorsed.* Billa vera.

Po se cul ca null reꝑ sine Judico.

284. ——, on 20 May, 30 Eliz., at W., bewitched Anne Manninge, who languished until 29 Nov., 31 Eliz., when she died at W. *Endorsed.* Billa vera.

Po se cul ca null reꝑ sine Judico.

285. Margaret Cony of Stysted, spinster, on the last day of Feb., 30 Eliz., at S., bewitched John Gwian, who then and there was totally deprived of his eyesight. *Endorsed.* Billa vera.

Po se cul   Judm scdm formam statuti &c.

286. ——, and Avice Cony of S., spinster, on 10 Mar., 30 Eliz., at S., bewitched Jeremiah Browne, who languished until the taking of this inquisition, troubled in his left leg. *Endorsed.* Billa vera.

Po se cul   Judm scdm formam statuti. Avicia Cony po se cul.

287. Avice Cony of S., spinster, on 1 Aug., 25 Eliz., at S., bewitched Richard Franck, son of William F., who died at S. *Endorsed.* Billa vera.

Po se cul ca null rep͛ p' . . .

288. Joan Cony of S., spinster, on 20 Apr., 21 Eliz., at S., bewitched Joan Danishe, who languished, until the taking of this inquisition, troubled in her right leg. *Endorsed*. Billa vera.

Po se cul.

289. ——, on 3 Feb., 31 Eliz., at S., bewitched Barnard Gryffyn, who languished. *Endorsed*. Billa vera.

Po se cul.

290. ——, on 1 June, 25 Eliz., at S., bewitched Elizabeth Sparow, who languished in the whole of her body. *Endorsed*. Billa vera.

Po se cul.

291. ——, on 10 Feb., 31 Eliz., at S., bewitched Elizabeth Fynch. wife of Henry F., who languished until 17 Feb. following, when she died at S. *Endorsed*. Billa vera.

Po se cul ca null.

292. Joan Dering of Thaydon Garnons, spinster, on 20 Dec., 31 Eliz., at T. G., bewitched Alice Odell, who languished until the taking of this inquisition and yet does. *Endorsed*. Billa vera.

Po se non cul.

293. ——, on 30 Nov., 31 Eliz., at T. G., bewitched Stephen Clerke and certain of his pails of milk so that his servants could not make cheese. *Endorsed*. Billa vera.

Po se non cull.

294. ——, on 23 July, 31 Eliz., at T. G., bewitched James Bennet, son of John B., of T. G., who languished and yet does. *Endorsed*. Billa vera.

Po se non cull.

295. Margaret Newman of Great Bentley, spinster. on 10 Feb., 31 Eliz., at Grt. B., bewitched Susan Davie, who languished until 16 Mar. following, when she died at B. *Endorsed*. Billa vera.

Nō est in p͛sona " bayled ".

296. Joan Uptney of Dagensham. spinster, on 20 Nov., 31 Eliz., at D., bewitched Alice Foster, who languished until 14 Apr. following, when she died at D. *Endorsed*. Billa vera.

Po se cul ca null Judm.

297. ——, on 27 Mar., 30 Eliz., at D., bewitched Joan Harwood, who languished until 24 Aug. following, when she died at D. *Endorsed.* Billa vera.

Po se cul ca null Judm.

*Gaol Delivery Roll*

Johanna Upney
Johanna Prentis } cul m° omes judicati et S⁹ p colł.
Johanna Cuney

Margareta Cuney { cul m° ꝑ incantacone et rep̃ in ꝑsona ꝑ anno et iiij pilloriam scdm formam statuti &c.

Avicia Cuney cul m° ꝑ murdro et tri pgn m° et rep̃.

1589. Surrey Summer Sessions and general gaol delivery holden at Southwark on 30 June, 31 Eliz. Commission dated 2 June, 31 Eliz.

*Remitted from the General Sessions of the Peace holden at Guildford on Tuesday next after the feast of St Peter the Apostle,* 30 *Eliz.* [29 *June*, 1588].

298. Sibil Preston of Effingham, spinster, on 31 Aug., 29 Eliz., at E., bewitched to death 1 mare valued at 40*s*. of the goods and chattels of Bartholomew Humphrey of E., and 1 horse valued at 50*s*. of the goods and chattels of Richard Atlee of E. *Endorsed.* Billa vera.

Po se non cul.

*Gaol Delivery Roll*

Sibilla Preston and others } quieti m° omnes et delibati.

1590. Essex Lent Sessions and general gaol delivery holden at Chelmsford on 19 Feb., 32 Eliz. Commission dated 23 Jan., 32 Eliz.

299. Anne Crabbe of Colne Engayne, spinster, on 24 July, 31 Eliz., at C. E., bewitched Ellen Lessingwell so that her right thigh " did rot off ". *Endorsed.* Billa vera.

Po se cul Judm scdm formam statuti.

300. Joan Mose of Lucton, spinster, and Agnes Mose of the same, spinster, on 28 Jan., 32 Eliz., at L., bewitched Richard Stace, son of Thomas S., who died at L. *Endorsed.* Billa vera.

Joan Moose po se cul ca null Judm.

*Above the name of Agnes " mortua ".*

### Gaol Delivery Roll

Johanna Mosse cul modo judicati & S$^9$ p coŧŧ.

*Inquisition taken at Chelmsford at the General Sessions of the Peace with gaol delivery holden on 8 Jan., 32 Eliz., before Robert Clarke, Baron of the Exchequer, etc.*

301. Alice Aylett, wife of Thomas A. of Braynktrey, shoe-maker, on 6 Mar., 22 Eliz., at B., bewitched Susanna Parman, aged about 6 yrs., who languished until 26 Apr., 25 Eliz., when she died at B. *No endorsement.*

Po se cul (*sic*) cul nec re.

302. ——, on 20 July, 26 Eliz., at B., bewitched Simon Huckerbye, who languished until 1 Aug., 28 Eliz., when he died at B. *No endorsement.*

Po se non cul nec re.

303. ——, on 10 Aug., 31 Eliz., at B., bewitched Margery Egles, daughter of Thomas E., who languished until 1 Nov. following at B. *No endorsement.*

Po se non cul nec re.

304. ——, on 1 Aug., 31 Eliz., at B., bewitched Rachel Skynner, daughter of William S., who languished until 10 Nov. following at B. *No endorsement.*

Po se cul  Judm scdm formam statuti.

305. ——, on 25 Nov., 31 Eliz., at B., bewitched Henry Joye, who languished until 1 Dec. following at B. *No endorsement.*

Po se cul  Judm scdm formam statuti.

306. Agnes Whitland of Dagenham, spinster, on 13 July, 31 Eliz., at D., bewitched William Greene, infant, of D., who languished until 29 July following, when he died at D. *No endorsement.*

Po se non cul nec re.

Indictments Nos. 301–6 are on one membrane upon which is endorsed the gaol delivery roll.

Alicia Aylett⎫
Anna Crabbe⎭ cul p incantacone et rep̃ p anno in p̃sona

Cuł de antiquo.

307. Alicia Adcock cuł adtunc p murdro p incantacõem tri non p̃gn Julij . . .

Ellena Bettes cul July xxxj° p murdro p incantacõem rep̃ sine Judico

Alicia Cumey cul July xxxj° p murdro p incantacõem tri adtunc p̃gn.

Margareta Cunney cul ad tunc p̃ fascinacone rep̃ p anno.

1590.   Essex Summer Sessions and general gaol delivery holden at Chelmsford on 20 July, 32 Eliz.  Commission dated 19 June, 32 Eliz.

308. Margaret Snell of Thaxsted, spinster, on 1 June, 31 Eliz., at Broxted, bewitched Rose Biatt, who languished until 7 June, 32 Eliz., when she died at B. *Endorsed.*  Billa vera.

Po se non cul nec re.

*Gaol Delivery Roll*

Margareta Snell⎫
  and others  ⎭ quieti modo omes et delibati.

Cul de antiquo.

Ellena Bettes cul July xxxj° p murdro p incantaconem rep̃ sine Judico

Anne Crabbe cul m⁹tij xxxij p incantacoe rep̃ in p̃sona p anno
Avicia Aylett cul m⁹tij xxxij p incantacone rep̃ p anno.

Alicia Adcock ⎫
Avicia Conney⎭ cul de antiquo Judicati modo et S⁹ p coħ.

1590.   Hertford Summer Sessions and general gaol delivery holden at St Albans on 31 July, 32 Eliz.  Commission dated 19 June, 32 Eliz.

309. Mary Burgis of Bemoy, spinster, on 20 Dec., 32 Eliz., at Hertford, bewitched William Noble, son of Thomas N., who languished until 22 Dec. following, when he died at H. *Endorsed.* Billa vera.

Po se non cul nec re.

310. ——, on 7 Oct., 31 Eliz., at H., bewitched Elizabeth Noble, daughter of Thomas N., who languished until 20 Nov. following, when she died at H. *Endorsed.* Billa vera.

Po se non cul nec re.

311. ——, on 6 Oct., 31 Eliz., at Bemoye, bewitched Susan Hill, daughter of John H., who languished until 25 Nov. following, when she died at B. *Endorsed.* Billa vera.

Po se non cul nec re.

312. ——, on 20 Sept., 28 Eliz., at B., bewitched to death 1 brown horse valued at 5*l*. of the goods and chattels of George Grave. *Endorsed.* Billa vera.

Po se cul. Judm scdm formam statuti.

313. ——, on 4 Apr., 32 Eliz., at Stapleford, bewitched George Grave, who languished for a long time crippled in his right arm. *Endorsed.* Billa vera.

Po se cul. Judm scdm formam statuti.

314. Thomas King of Barkwaye, labourer, on 30 June, 31 Eliz., at B., bewitched James Moyses, who for a long time was lamed in his left leg. *Endorsed.* Billa vera.

Po se non cul nec re.

315. ——, and Margery King of the same, spinster, on 14 Apr., 32 Eliz., at B., bewitched John Watson, who languished until 22 Apr. following, when he died at B. *Endorsed.* Billa vera.

Po se non cul nec re.

*Remitted from the General Sessions of the Peace holden at Hertford on* 13 *July,* 32 *Eliz.*

316. Joan White, wife of Thomas W. of Bushey, on 20 Dec., 32 Eliz., at B., bewitched Marion Man, daughter of William M. of B., who languished until 27 June following, when she died at B. *No endorsement.*

Po se non cul nec re.

*Gaol Delivery Roll*

Maria Burges cul m° p incantacoe rep p anno.

Thomas Kynge  
Margeria Kynge  } quieti modo omes et delibati.

Cul de antiquo.

317. Ellena Browne   cul adtunc p incantacone rep p anno.

1590.   Kent Summer Sessions and general gaol delivery holden
at Rochester on 16 July, 32 Eliz.  Writ dated 20 June,
32 Eliz.

318.  Elizabeth White of Boxely, spinster, on 10 June, 32 Eliz.,
at Plumstead, bewitched to death 1 cow valued at 30s. of the
goods and chattels of Heydon Burbage. *Endorsed.*  Billa vera.
Po se non cul.

319.  ——, on 11 Oct., 31 Eliz., at Estwicke, bewitched Alice
Whittingham, daughter of Hugh W., who languished until
14 Oct. following, when she died at E. *Endorsed.*
Po se non cul nec re.

1591.   Essex [Summer] Sessions.  [Commission dated 4 June,
33 Eliz.] [1]

320.  Ellen (or Helen) Graye of Dagenham, spinster, on 12 Feb.,
33 Eliz., at D., bewitched Anna Bixon, who languished until
30 Mar. following, when she died at D. *Endorsed.*  Billa vera.
Po se cul ca null   Judm.

321.  ——, on 22 Oct., 32 Eliz., at D., bewitched Richard
Foster in his body. *Endorsed.*  Billa vera.
Po se cul.

322.  ——, on 11 Sept., 29 Eliz., at D., bewitched to death
1 cow valued at 33s. of the goods and chattels of Henry Whood.
*Endorsed.*  Billa vera.
Po se cul.

323.  ——, on 28 Mar., 33 Eliz., at D., bewitched Ellen Playt,
who languished in her whole body. *Endorsed.*  Billa vera.
Po se cul.

324.  ——, on 7 Mar., 33 Eliz., at D., bewitched 4 gallons of
cream of the goods and chattels of John Horold so that it would
not make butter. *Endorsed.*  Billa vera.
Po se cul.

325.  Margaret Rooman of Bocking, spinster, on 5 May, 33 Eliz.,

---

[1] Attached inquisitions are dated 29 May and 1 July, 33 Eliz.

at B., bewitched to death a black cow valued at 40s., of the goods and chattels of Thomas Elmesteede of B. *Endorsed.* Billa vera.

Po se cul   Judm scdm formam statuti inde edit et puis.

326. Alice Crake of Frenchingfylde, spinster, on 29 Jan., 33 Eliz., at F., bewitched Thomas Symson, who languished until 3 Mar. following, when he died at F. *Endorsed.* Billa vera.

Po se non cul nec re.

327. Agnes Whilland of Dagenham, spinster, on 10 July, 32 Eliz., at D., bewitched to death 1 sow valued at 10s. of the goods and chattels of Richard Foster of D. *Endorsed.* Billa vera.

Po se non cul nec re.

328. ——, on 26 Dec., 33 Eliz., at D., bewitched Margaret Collopp. aged 4 yrs.. daughter of John C. of D.. who languished until 4 Jan following, when she died at D. *Endorsed.* Billa vera.

Po se non cul nec re.

329. ——, on 30 Apr., 32 Eliz., at D., bewitched to death a sorrell mare valued at 3l. 6s. 8d. and 1 yellow dun cow valued at 40s. of the goods and chattels of John Collopp of D. *Endorsed.* Billa vera.

Po se cul   Judm scdm formam statuti, inde edit et puis.

330. Juliana Cocke of Ashdon, spinster, on 20 Mar., 33 Eliz., at Lit. Walden, bewitched 3 horses valued at 6l., 2 cows valued at 4l., and 2 calves valued at 10s. of the goods and chattels of John Petite of which one horse and the cows and calves instantly died. *Endorsed.* Billa vera.

Po se cul   Judm scdm formam statuti inde edit et puis.

1591.   Surrey Summer Sessions and general gaol delivery holden at Kingston-upon-Thames on 8 July, 33 Eliz. Commission dated 4 June, 33 Eliz.

*Gaol Calendar*

331. Joan Guner missa ad gaol p Henr' Weston, mil. (*and others*) p incantacone.

332. Margaret Strangweys (*deleted*).

333. Margery Collyns of Wokɪng, spinster, on 31 Oct., 33 Eliz., at W., bewitched to death 1 ox valued at 3*l.* of the goods and chattels of William Westbroke. *Endorsed.* Billa vera.

Po se non cul.

### Gaol Delivery Roll

Margeria Collins and others } quieti modo omes & delibati.

Johanna Gunner { quia sup inquisicone . . . nihil mali v⁹sus eos aliquem comptum est dign̄ vlt⁹iori impꝑsonamento Io . . . delibet' modoꝑ ꝑclamacoem.

1591.    Sussex Summer Sessions and general gaol delivery holden at East Grinstead on 5 July, 33 Eliz. Commission dated 4 June, 33 Eliz.

334. Agnes Mowser of Fletchinge, spencer, on 29 Apr., 23 Eliz., at F., bewitched Anne Clemans, daughter of Henry C., armiger, who languished until 20 May following. *Endorsed.* Billa vera.

Po se cul    Judm scdm formam statuti inde edit et puis.

### Gaol Delivery Roll

Agnes Mowser cul m⁰ ꝑ incantacone    Judm scdm formam statuti et reꝑ⁹ ꝑ anno.

1592.    Essex Lent Sessions and general gaol delivery holden at Chelmsford on 2 Mar., 34 Eliz. Commission dated 24 Jan., 34 Eliz.[1]

335. Agnes Hales of Stebbing, spinster, on 23 Feb., 33 Eliz., at S., bewitched Elizabeth Pyper, who languished until 25 Feb. following, when she died at S. *Endorsed.* Billa vera.

Po se non cul de felon & murdro sed cul ꝑ fascinacone p̃dco Elizabethe Pyper    Judm scdm formam statuti in huioi casu nuꝑ edit & puis.

336. ——, on 12 Sept., 29 Eliz., at S., bewitched Mabel Scott, who languished until 20 Oct., when she died at S.

[1] In 1927 this file was bundled with those of 24 Eliz. (Assizes 35/24).

Po se non cul de felon & murdro sed cul p fascinacone p̃dco Mabelle Scott Judm scdm formam statuti.

337. Margery Dickes, otherwise Thatcher of Bradfeilde, spinster, on 9 July, 33 Eliz., at B., bewitched Martha Convin, daughter of John C. of B., who languished until 25 July following, when she died at B. *Endorsed*. Billa vera.

Po se non cul nec re.

338. ——, on 11 July, 33 Eliz., at B., bewitched Edward Warren, son of George W., who languished until 16 July following, when he died at B. *Endorsed*. Billa vera.

Po se non cul nec re.

339. ——, on 1 Mar., 32 Eliz., at B., bewitched 1 sow and 11 pigs which were consumed and wasted. *Endorsed*. Billa vera.

Po se non cul nec re.

340. Margaret Hogden of Witham, spinster, on 17 Dec., 33 Eliz., at W., bewitched Anne Gowers, wife of William G., who languished until 30 Aug. following, when she died at W. *Endorsed*. Billa vera.

Po se non cul nec re.

341. Elizabeth Boxer of Aveley, spinster, on 20 May, 33 Eliz., bewitched Benedict Clerk who languished until 18 July following, when he died at A. *Endorsed*. Billa vera.

Po se non cul nec re.

342. ——, on 26 June, 32 Eliz., at A., bewitched Richard Beldam, who languished until 1 Feb. following, when he died at A. *Endorsed*. Billa vera.

Po se non cul nec re.

343. ——, on 28 Sept., 32 Eliz., at A., bewitched Elizabeth Beldam, who languished until 15 Oct. following, when she died at A. *Endorsed*. Billa vera.

Po se non cul nec re.

1592. Essex Summer Sessions and general gaol delivery holden at Chelmsford on 10 July, 34 Eliz. Commission dated 26 May, 34 Eliz.

344. Anne Scott of Great Dunmowe, spinster, on 1 Jan., 33 Eliz., at Grt. D., bewitched Anne Swetinge, daughter of

John S., who languished until 13 Apr.. 34 Eliz.. when she died at Grt. D. *Endorsed.* Billa vera.

Po se cul ca null   Judm.

345. Audrea Mathewe of Great Dunmowe, spinster, on 1 Jan., 34 Eliz., at Grt. D., bewitched to death 1 cow and 1 calf of the goods and chattels of Henry Longe, gentleman. *Endorsed.* Billa vera.

Po se cul   Judm scdm formam statuti.
See 396, 397.

346. Agnes Draper of Great Dunmowe, spinster, on 1 July, 34 Eliz., at Grt. D., bewitched Alice Haueley, who became infirm, etc. *Endorsed.* Billa vera.

Po se cul.

*Inquisition taken at Chelmsford on 6 Apr., 34 Eliz.* [1592].

347. Jane Wallys of Stebbing, spinster, on 8 June. 33 Eliz., at S., bewitched William Brock, who languished until 15 June following, when he died at S. *No endorsement.*

Po se cul ca null   tri non p̃gñ m° & Judm.

348. ——, on 10 June, 33 Eliz., at S., bewitched to death 1 white mare valued at 40s., and 1 red cow, valued at 40s., of the goods and chattels of Thomas Shave at S. *No endorsement.*

Po se cul.

*Gaol Delivery Roll*

Audrea Mathewe ⎫ Cul modo p incantacone et rep̃ in p̃sona
Agnes Draper    ⎬ Judm scdm formam statuti inde . . .
                ⎭ edit et puis̃.

1592. Hertford Summer Sessions and general gaol delivery holden at Hertford on 7 July. 34 Eliz. Commission dated 26 May, 34 Eliz.

349. John Sely of Stansted, yeoman, on 31 Mar., 34 Eliz., at S., bewitched to death 40 hogs of the goods and chattels of John Spencer. *Endorsed.* Billa vera.

Po se non cul.

350. Mary Hamont of Walkerne, spinster, on 20 Mar., 34 Eliz., at W., bewitched to death 1 horse valued at 4l. of the goods and chattels of William Walby. *Endorsed.* Billa vera.

Po se cul   Judm scdm formam statuti scilt stare sup pilloriam quatuor tempibus anni.

351. ——, on 3 May, 34 Eliz., at W., bewitched to death 3 hogs valued at 30s. of the goods and chattels of William Bramfeild. *Endorsed.* Billa vera.

Po se cul   Judm scdm formam statuti.

352. ——, on 2 June, 33 Eliz., at W., bewitched to death 1 bay horse valued at 7l. 10s., 1 red cow valued at 50s. of the goods and chattels of William Bramfeild. *Endorsed.* Billa vera.

Po se cul   Judm scdm formam statuti.

### Gaol Delivery Roll

John Sely and others } Quieti modo omes et delibati.

Maria Hamont.  Cul modo ꝑ incantacone et reꝑ ꝑ anno. [A later roll states that she escaped from prison by negligence of the gaoler.]

1593.   Essex Lent Sessions and general gaol delivery holden at Chelmsford on 8 Mar., 35 Eliz.  Commission dated 5 Feb., 35 Eliz.

353  Alice Alberte of Felsted, spinster, on 25 July, 34 Eliz., at F., bewitched to death 22 sheep valued at 5l., 1 cow valued at 40s., 1 calf valued at 8s., and 1 pig valued at 8s., of the goods and chattels of Roger Wood. *Endorsed.* Billa vera.

Cul  Judm scdm formam statuti.

354. Elizabeth Esterford of Hedningham Sybbell, spinster, on 5 Dec., 34 Eliz., bewitched 1 sorrel mare, 1 sorrel bald horse, and 1 cow of the goods and chattels of Henry Spencer, which languished at H.

Non est in ꝑsona.

See 359, 360, 361.

### Gaol Delivery Roll

Alicia Albert   cul mº ꝑ fascinacone   Judm *etc.*

Cul de antiquo.

Alicia (*sic*) Mathewe } cul Julij xxxiiijº ꝑ fascinacone reꝑ ꝑ Agnes Draper        } anno.

1593.    Hertford Lent Sessions and general gaol delivery at Hertford on 5 Mar., 35 Eliz. Commission dated [5] Feb., 35 Eliz.

355. Ellen Browne of Buntingford, spinster, on 20 Nov., 35 Eliz., at B., bewitched Margaret Dellew, who languished until 1 Mar. following. *Endorsed.* Billa vera.

Po se non cul.

356. ——, on 21 Sept., 34 Eliz., at B., bewitched John Gates, who languished until the last day of February following at B. *Endorsed.* Billa vera.

Po se non cul.

1593.    Essex Summer Sessions and general gaol delivery holden at Chelmsford on 26 July, 35 Eliz. Commission dated [15] June, 35 Eliz.

357. Agnes Haven of Boreham, spinster, on 10 Apr., 35 Eliz., bewitched John Brett, who languished in divers parts of his body for a long time. *Endorsed.* Billa vera.

Po se cul.

358. ——, on 1 Sept., 30 Eliz., at B., bewitched Edith Hawes, who languished until 20 Dec. following, when she died at B. *Endorsed.* Billa vera.

Po se cul ca null  Judic.

359. Elizabeth Esterford of Sibill Heningham on 4 Dec., 33 Eliz., at H., bewitched 1 mare, 1 horse, and 2 cows valued at 10*l.*, of the goods and chattels of Henry Spencer. *Endorsed.* Billa vera.

Po se cul.

See 354, 360, 361.

360. ——, on 8 Mar., 27 Eliz., at S. H., bewitched Henry Bayford, who languished until 18 Mar. following, when he died at S. H. *Endorsed.* Billa vera.

Po se non cul nec re.

See 354, 359, 361.

361. ——, on 1 Dec., 27 Eliz., at S. H., bewitched Anne Biford, who languished until 28 Dec. following, when she died at S. H. *Endorsed.* Billa vera.

" THE STRANGE WOMAN AND HER SPIRITS A.D. 1621

(From a contemporary drawing. Brit. Mus Add. MS. 32496)

Po se non cul nec re.

See 354, 359, 361.

362. Margaret Saunder of Heningham Sible on 6 Apr., 33 Eliz., at H. S., bewitched Elizabeth Bragge, who languished in divers parts of his body for a long time. *Endorsed.* Billa vera.

Po se non cul.

363. Margaret Mynnet of Woodham Ferres on 10 Apr.. 35 Eliz., at W F., bewitched Joan Symond, who languished in divers parts of her body for a long time. *Endorsed.* Billa vera.

Po se cul.

364. ———, on 19 Apr., 35 Eliz., at W. F., bewitched Simon Fylpott, who languished until 26 Apr. following, when he died. *Endorsed.* Billa vera.

Po se cul ca null  Judm.

365. ———, on 31 Mar., 35 Eliz., at W. F., bewitched Joan Lorken, who languished until 6 Apr. following, when she died at W. F. *Endorsed.* Billa vera.

Po se cul ca null  Judm.

366. ———, on 1 Apr., 35 Eliz., at W. F., bewitched Isabella Lorken, who languished until 2 Apr. following, when she died at W. F. *Endorsed.* Billa vera.

Po se cul ca null   Judm.

367. Elizabeth Packman of Great Clafton, spinster, on 10 Feb., 35 Eliz., at Grt. C., bewitched Luke Crosse, who languished until 10 July following. *Endorsed.* Billa vera.

Po se non cul nec re.

### Gaol Delivery Roll

Agnes Haven
Margareta Mynne } cul modo omes Judicat' et S⁹ p coħ.

Elizabeth Esterford cul m° p incantacone  Judm scdm formam statuti.

Margareta Saunder
Elizabeth Packman } quieti modo omes & delibati.

Cul de antiquo.

Alicia Albert.   cul m⁹tij xxxᵗᵒ p incantacone reᵖ p anno.

1593.   Hertford Summer Sessions and general gaol delivery holden at Hertford on 20 July, 35 Eliz.  Commission dated 15 June, 35 Eliz.

368.   Joan Garrett of Hatfeld, spinster, on 30 Oct., 34 Eliz., at H., bewitched Margery Hawkes at H., who languished until 18 Nov., 35 Eliz., when she died at H.  *Endorsed.*  Billa vera.
Po se non cul nec re.

369.   ——, on 10 Apr., 34 Eliz., at H., bewitched Christopher Penyfather, who languished until 31 Oct. following, when he died at H.  *Endorsed.*  Billa vera.
Po se non cul nec re.

370.   ——, on 4 June, 33 Eliz., at H., bewitched to death 1 mare of the goods and chattels of William Marshall.  *Endorsed.* Billa vera.
Po se cul.

371.   ——, on 1 May, 28 Eliz., at H., bewitched Agnes Clark, who languished until 1 Aug., 33 Eliz., when she died at H.  *Endorsed.*  Billa vera.
Po se non cul nec re.

372.   ——, on 24 Aug., 33 Eliz., at H., bewitched Susanna Clark, who languished until 30 Jan. following, when she died at H.  *Endorsed.*  Billa vera.
Po se non cul nec re.

*Gaol Delivery Roll*

Johanna Garnett   cul m° p fascinacone & rep̃ p anno.

1593.   Kent Summer Sessions and general gaol delivery holden at Maidstone on 12 July, 35 Eliz.  Commission dated 15 June, 35 Eliz.

373.   Ellen Cheseman, wife of Nicholas C. of Ayllesforde, stonehewer, on 2 Apr., 25 Eliz., at A., bewitched William Englefeild of Hunton, stonehewer, who became decrepit in his right shoulder and shank.  *Endorsed.*  Billa vera.
Po se non cul nec re.

374. ——, on 17 Apr., 34 Eliz., at A., bewitched Lawrence Wells of A., tailor, who languished until 4 Feb. following, when he died at A. *Endorsed.* Billa vera.

Po se non cul nec re.

375. Joan Foster of Stansted, spinster, on 21 June, 26 Eliz., at S., bewitched Joan Lane, who languished until 23 June following, when she died at S. *Endorsed.* Billa vera.

Po se non cul nec re.

376. ——, on 10 Dec., 30 Eliz., at S., bewitched 1 mare of Robert Woldam, which languished until 16 Jan. following, when it died. *Endorsed.* Billa vera.

Po se non cul.

377. ——, on 31 May, 34 Eliz., at S., bewitched William Wodden, who languished until 24 June following. *Endorsed.* Billa vera.

Po se non cul.

378. ——, on 10 Nov., 34 Eliz., at S., bewitched Alice Woldam, who languished until 17 Nov. following. *Endorsed.* Billa vera.

Po se non cul.

379. Agnes Bigg of Rolvinden, spinster, on 31 May, 29 Eliz., bewitched Anne Hucksted, who languished until 7 June following, when she died at R. *Endorsed.* Billa vera.

Po se non cul nec re.

380. ——, on 10 Feb., 30 Eliz., at R., bewitched Cephas Bright, who languished until 24 Feb. following, when she died at R. *Endorsed.* Billa vera.

Po se non cul nec re.

381. ——, on 31 Oct., 34 Eliz., at R., bewitched Simon Nashe, who languished until 8 Apr. following, when he died at R. *Endorsed.* Billa vera.

Po se non cul nec re.

382. ——, on 2 Feb., 35 Eliz., at R., bewitched John Wilson, who languished until 5 Feb. following, when he died at R. *Endorsed.* Billa vera.

Po se cul ca null Judm.

*Gaol Delivery Roll*

Agnes Bygge    cul m<sup>o</sup> judicat' et S<sup>9</sup> p coʇ.

1593.    Sussex Summer Sessions and general gaol delivery
holden at East Grinstead on 16 July, 35 Eliz. Commission dated 15 June, 35 Eliz.

383.   Elizabeth Whighte of Balcome, spinster, on 10 Jan.,
35 Eliz.. at B.. bewitched Andrew Payne, who languished until
20 June following. *Endorsed.*   Billa vera.
Po se no cul.

384.   ——, on 20 Jan., 35 Eliz., at B., bewitched Joan Geale,
who languished until 3 July following. *Endorsed.*   Billa vera.
Po se non cul.

385.   ——, on 25 Feb., 35 Eliz., at B., bewitched Joan Vinall,
who languished until 3 June following. *Endorsed.*   Billa vera.
Po se non cul.

386.   ——, on 30 Nov., 34 Eliz., at B., bewitched Thomas
Vinall, who languished until 3 June following. *Endorsed.*
Billa vera.
Po se non cul.

1594.    Essex Lent Sessions and general gaol delivery holden
at Chelmsford on 18 Mar., 36 Eliz. Commission dated
25 Feb., 36 Eliz.

387.   Agnes Bett of Safferne Walden, spinster, on 6 Oct., 33
Eliz., bewitched Nicholas Whighte, who languished until 5 Jan.
following, when he died at S. W. *Endorsed.*   Billa vera.
Po se non cul nec re.

388.   ——, on 20 Feb., 35 Eliz., at S. W., bewitched to death
1 calf valued at 6*s.* 8*d.* of the goods and chattels of Edmund
Pettett. *Endorsed.*   Billa vera.
Po se non cul nec re.

389.   Elizabeth Garrett of Gosfeild, spinster, and Joan Garrett,
spinster. on 26 Dec.. 36 Eliz.. at G., bewitched Ralph Huntman.
who languished until 28 Dec. following, when he died at G.
*Endorsed.*   Billa vera.

Elizabeth Garrett : po se cul ca null Judm. Johanna Garrett : po se non cul nec re.

390. ——, ——. on 31 Dec., 36 Eliz., at [Stisted ?], bewitched Walsingham Cooke, who languished for a long time.

Elizabeth Garrerd : po se cul. Johanna Garrett ; po se cul ca null rep͌ p anno Judm scdm formam statuti.

391. Stephen Ingrave or Hugrave of Aberton, labourer, on 16 Mar., 36 Eliz., at Fingringh', bewitched to death 2 cows valued at 4*l*. of the goods and chattels of John Smithe. *Endorsed*. Billa vera.

Po se non cul nec.

392. ——, and Alice Hugrave of the same, spinster, on 30 Sept., 33 Eliz., bewitched Margaret Stanton, widow, who languished until 23 Dec., 35 Eliz., when she died. *Endorsed*. Billa vera.

Po se non cul nec re. [Both prisoners.]

393. Mary Belsted of Boreham, spinster, otherwise Mary Muldleton on 1 Nov. 32 Eliz., at B., bewitched to death a brown bay mare valued at 3*l*. and 4 hogs valued at 26*s*. 8*d*. of the goods and chattels of John Hare. *Endorsed*. Billa vera.

Po se cul Judm scdm formam statuti rep͌ p anno.

394. Anne Harrison of Thorpe, spinster, on 1 Oct., 33 Eliz., at T., bewitched Margaret Childerly, who languished until 15 Oct., when she died at T. *Endorsed*. Billa vera.

Po se cul ca null Judm.

395. ——, on 21 Sept., 35 Eliz., at T., bewitched Margaret Simondes, who languished until 29 September following, when she died at T. *Endorsed*. Billa vera.

Po se cul ca null Judm.

*Gaol Delivery Roll*

Elizabeth Garrett. cul mᵘ judicat' et Sᵍ p collu quousqᵣ &c.
Anna Harryson. cul mᵒ rep post Judicm : Weake evidence.
Maria Belsted } cul mᵒ p fascinacone. Judicm scdm formam
Johanna Garrett } statuti.
Agnes Bett } quieti modo omes et deliberati.
Stephus Hugrave }
    Cul de antiquo.

Elizabeth Esterford. cul Julij xxxv p fascinacoe rep̃ p anno.

Alicia Albert cul m⁹tij xxxvᵗᵒ p fascinacoe rep̃ tunc p anno : mortua officm　·　·

1594. Essex Summer Sessions and general gaol delivery holden at Brentwood on 8 Aug., 36 Eliz. Commission dated [1] June. 36 Eliz.

396. Awdria Mathewe of Great Dunmawe, spinster, on 10 Dec., 36 Eliz.. at Grt. D., bewitched Rebecca Gynne. daughter of George G., who languished until 28 Jan. following, when she died at D. *Endorsed.* Billa vera.

Po se cul ca null　Judm.

See 345, 397.

397. ———, on 20 Aug., 33 Eliz., at Grt. D.. bewitched Robert Underwood, who languished until 16 Feb., 35 Eliz., when he died at D. *Endorsed.* Billa vera.

Po se cul ca null　Judm.

See 345, 396.

398. Bridget Hayle of Thorpe, widow, on 5 Oct., 35 Eliz., at T., bewitched a bay mare valued at 30s. of the goods and chattels of Robert Swanson of T., husbandman, so that it wasted. *Endorsed.* Billa vera.

Po se cul ca null　Judm scdm formam statuti.

399. ———, and Elizabeth Hayle of Thorpe, daughter of Bridget H., spinster, on 22 Dec., 35 Eliz., at T., bewitched Richard Brande, labourer, who languished until 1 Mar., 35 Eliz., when he died at T. *Endorsed.* Billa vera.

Po se non cul nec re [both prisoners].

400. Anne Harvey of Mannyngtree. spinster, on 2 July. 35 Eliz., at M., bewitched Parnel Wooluett, who languished until 16 May following, when she died at M. *Endorsed.* Billa vera.

Po se cul ca null　Judm.

401. ———, on 26 Sept., 32 Eliz., at M., bewitched Elizabeth Bowle, who languished until 8 Nov. following, when she died at M. *Endorsed.* Billa vera.

Po se non cul nec re.

402. ——, on 25 Dec., 32 Eliz., at M., bewitched John Bowle, who languished until 7 Oct. following, when he died at M. *Endorsed*. Billa vera.

Po se non cul nec re.

*Gaol Delivery Roll*

Audria Mathewe } cul m⁰ Judicati et S⁹ p colł quousq̨ &c.
Anna Harvye

Brigitta Hayle { cul m⁰ fascinacone rep̃ p anno Judm scdm formam statuti.

Cul de antiquo.

Elizabeth Esterford { cul Julij xxvᵗᵒ p incantacoe Judicat et execut scdm formam statuti et m⁰ delib*ai*.

Johanna Garrett } cul m⁹tij xxxvjᵗᵒ p incantacone rep̃ p anno
Maria Belsted Judicm scdm formam statuti, &c.

Anna Harryson { cul m⁹tij xxxvjᵗᵒ p murdro p incantacoem rep̃ post Judicm " weake euidence ".

1595. Essex Lent Sessions and general gaol delivery holden at Chelmsford on 3 Mar., 37 Eliz. Writ dated 26 Jan., 37 Eliz.

403. John Cremer (*deleted*) of Ingrave, labourer, and Grace Trower of the same, spinster. on 30 Sept., 36 Eliz., at Kettingdon, bewitched to death 4 geldings valued at 12*l*. and 16 cows valued at 50*l*. of the goods and chattels of Richard Luckin. *Endorsed*. Billa vera p Gracia. Ignoramus p Joh'

Po se cul rep̃ p anno.

*Gaol Delivery Roll*

Gracia Trower cul m⁰ p incantacoe Judm scdm formam statuti &c., rep̃ p anno.

1595. Hertford Lent Sessions and general gaol delivery holden at Hertford on 28 Feb., 37 Eliz.

*Gaol Delivery Roll*

Cul de antiquo.

404 Alicia Games cul Julij xxxvjᵗᵒ p incantacoe rep p anno.

1595. Kent Lent Sessions and general gaol delivery holden at Rochester on 20 Feb., 37 Eliz. Writ dated 26 Jan., 37 Eliz.

405. Alice Jeken of Hinxell, spinster, on 10 Mar., 35 Eliz., at H., bewitched Arnold Fygg, who languished until 15 Feb., 37 Eliz., when he died at H *Endorsed.* Billa vera.

Po se non cul nec re.

1596. Hertford Lent Sessions and general gaol delivery holden at Hertford on 1 Mar., 38 Eliz. Writ dated 24 Jan., 38 Eliz.

406. Katherine Dewxburie or Dewesbury, wife of Nicholas D. of Warre, labourer, on 6 Sept., 37 Eliz., at W., bewitched Agnes Wattes, wife of Roger W. of W., butcher, who languished until 20 Oct. following. *Endorsed.* Billa vera.

Po se $Q^9$ n$^c$r.

407. ——, on 20 Mar., 33 Eliz., at W., bewitched Thomas Bromley, son of Richard B., who languished until 10 June following. *Endorsed.* Billa vera.

Po se cul repri ad gaol p vno anno.

408. ——, on 27 Aug., 37 Eliz., at W., bewitched Robert Cock, who languished until 20 Jan., 38 Eliz., when he died at W. *Endorsed.* Billa vera.

Po se $Q^9$ n$^c$.

### Gaol Delivery Roll

Kat$^9$ina Dewxbury cul p incantacone & repr p anno.

1596. Surrey Lent Sessions and general gaol delivery holden at Southwark on 16 Feb., 38 Eliz. Writ dated 24 Jan., 38 Eliz.

*Remitted from the General Sessions of the Peace holden at Croydon on Tuesday next after the feast of the Epiphany, 38 Eliz.* [13 *Jan.*].

409. Alice Marten alias Tosby of Blechingly, spinster, on 30 Apr., 35 Eliz., at B., bewitched to death 1 ox valued at 3*l.*, 1 ram valued at 6*s.* 8*d.*, 1 weather sheep valued at 6*s.*, 1 lamb valued at 3*s.* 4*d.*, of the goods and chattels of Edward Tyrry at B. *No endorsement.*

Po se $Q^9$ n$^c$r.

1596. Essex Summer Sessions and general gaol delivery holden at Brentwood on 15 July, 38 Eliz. Writ dated 12 June, 38 Eliz.

410. Agnes Smith of Stebbing, widow, on 10 Dec., 35 Eliz., at S., bewitched Alice Browne. wife of Richard B.. who languished until 24 Dec. following, when she died at S. *Endorsed*. Billa vera.

Po se Q$^9$ n$^c$r.

1596. Hertford Summer Sessions and general gaol delivery holden at Hertford on 19 July, 38 Eliz. Writ dated 12 June, 38 Eliz.[1]

411. Alice Crutch. wife of Thomas Crowtch of Grt. Trynge, labourer, on 28 Sept., 34 Eliz., at Grt. T., bewitched Hugh Balden, who languished until 1 Apr. following, when he died at Grt. T. *Endorsed*. Testes. Marry Montague. Billa vera.

Po se cul ca null S$^9$.

412. ——, on 4 July, 38 Eliz., at Grt. T., bewitched to death 1 horse valued at 50s. of the goods and chattels of Thomas Grace (*sic*). *Endorsed*. Testes Thomas Grave. Billa vera.

Po se cul ca null S$^9$

413. ——, on 26 Dec., 38 Eliz., at Grt. T., bewitched to death 1 horse valued at 4l. of the goods and chattels of Barnard Michael otherwise Search. *Endorsed*. Testes Barnard Mychell. Billa vera.

Po se cul ca null S$^9$.

1597. Surrey Lent Sessions and general gaol delivery holden at Southwark on 24 Feb., 39 Eliz. Commission dated 25 Jan., 39 Eliz.

414. Margaret Cooke of Kyngston-upon-Thames, wife of Peter C. of the same, husbandman, on 1 Jan., 38 Eliz., bewitched Joan Francke, who languished until 1 Feb. following, when she died at K. *Endorsed*. Billa vera.

Po se Q$^9$ n$^c$ r.

415. ——, on 1 Jan., 38 Eliz., at K., bewitched Joan Bounce, who languished until 1 Mar., 38 Eliz., when she died at K. *Endorsed*. Billa vera.

Po se Q$^9$ n$^c$ r.

[1] When examined by me in 1927 this file was bundled with those of 43 Eliz. (Assizes 35/43).

1597.    Essex Summer Sessions and general gaol delivery holden
at Brentwood on 30 June, 39 Eliz.  Writ dated 27 May,
39 Eliz.

416.  Alice Waren of Brentwood, spinster, on 22 June, 39 Eliz.,
at Southweld, bewitched William Leonard, who languished in
divers parts of his body. *Endorsed.*  Billa vera.

Po se cul repr p vno anno.

*Gaol Delivery Roll*

Alicia  Warren cul p incantacone repri in gaola p anno integro
& stabit sup pilloriam.

1598.    Essex Lent Sessions and general gaol delivery holden at
Chelmsford on 27 Feb., 40 Eliz.  Writ dated 24 Jan.,
40 Eliz.

417.  Robert Browning of Aldam, labourer, on 31 Jan., 40 Eliz.,
at Barfold, defrauded the King's subjects, persuading them that
by conjuration and invocation of evil spirits they might discover
hidden hoards of gold and silver, and regain lost goods. *Endorsed.*
Billa vera.

Po se cul ponat sup pilloriam.

1598.    Hertford Lent Sessions and general gaol delivery holden
at Hertford on 3 Mar., 40 Eliz. Writ dated 24 Jan.,
40 Eliz.

418.  Mary Taylor of Hartford, spinster, on 9  May, 38 Eliz.,
at H., bewitched Simon Grubb, who languished until  9  Oct.,
when he died at H.  *Endorsed.*  Jone Grub, Frauncis Grub.
Billa vera.

Po se cul ca null   S$^9$.

419.  ——, on 20 Aug., 28 Eliz., at H., bewitched to death
7 hogs valued at 20s. of the goods and chattels of Ralph Willow-
bye. *Endorsed.*  Ralph Willowby.  Billa vera.

Po se cul.  Repr ad gaol scdm formam statuti.

*Gaol Delivery Roll.*

Maria Taylor }
and others   } cul modo omnes p diu$^v$sis felonijs S$^9$ p collum.

1599. Hertford Lent Sessions and general gaol delivery holden at Hertford on 19 Mar., 41 Eliz. Commission dated 12 Feb., 41 Eliz.

*Remitted from the General Sessions of the Peace holden at Hertford on Monday next after the feast of the Epiphany, 41 Eliz. [8 Jan.].*

420. William Browne of Buntingford, in the parish of Leyston, locksmith, on 16 Dec., 41 Eliz., at B., bewitched Thomas Hantler of B., mercer, who languished until 30 Dec. following. *No endorsement.*

Po se Q$^9$ n$^c$ r.

1600. Essex Lent Sessions and general gaol delivery holden at Chelmsford on 28 Feb., 42 Eliz. Commission dated 24 Jan., 42 Eliz.

*Remitted from the General Sessions of the Peace holden at Chelmsford on 4 Oct., 41 Eliz.*

421. Isabella Whyte of Purley, spinster, on 20 July, 40 Eliz., at P., bewitched to death 1 ram lamb valued at 6s. 8d. and 9 pigs valued at 3s., of the goods and chattels of Thomas Ward. *No endorsement.*

Po se Q$^9$ n$^c$ r.

422. ———, on 30 Aug., 36 Eliz., at P., bewitched to death 1 black hewed cow valued at 3l. and 1 red cow valued at 3l. 6s. 8d. of the goods and chattels of T. W. *No endorsement.*

Po se Q$^9$ n$^c$ r.

1600. Hertford Lent Sessions and general gaol delivery holden at Hertford on 10 Mar., 42 Eliz. Commission dated 24 Jan., 42 Eliz.

*Inquisition taken at Chipping Barnett on 12 Feb., 42 Eliz.*

423. Alice Fulwood, wife of Peter F. of Chippinge Barnett, barber, on 5 Feb., 42 Eliz., at C. B., bewitched Marion Harwood in the back part of her head so that it was bruised from which bruising she instantly died.

[The indictment continues that at the time of the murder Alice had no goods nor chattels, lands, tenements, etc. Also the Constable on 9 Feb. at C. B. arrested the said Alice and had her in custody intending to bring her before the Justices for examination touching witchcraft and murder, but Alice on 9 Feb. from the custody of the Constable of her own account withdrew and herself feloniously rescued and escaped.    And that after the escape she had no goods, etc.]  *No endorsement.*

Po se Q$^9$ n$^c$r ad p$\tilde{\text{x}}$.  In gaol apud St Albones.

1600.    Essex Summer Sessions and general gaol delivery holden at Chelmsford on 30 June, 42 Eliz.  Commission dated 23 May, 42 Eliz.

424.  Rose Chapman of Water Belchampe, spinster. on 29 Apr., 41 Eliz., at W. B., bewitched John Payne, who languished until 4 Aug. following, when he died at W. B.  *Endorsed.*  Witnesses : Uxor William Payne, Uxor Peter Crainfeild, et Edward Cooe, gen.  Billa vera

Po se Q$^9$ n$^c$ r.

1600.    Hertford Summer Sessions and general gaol delivery holden at Hertford on 4 July, 42 Eliz.  Commission dated 23 May, 42 Eliz.

425. Joan Vaughan of Chesthunt, widow. on 12 Nov., 41 Eliz., at C., bewitched Alice Slowen, who languished until 25 Nov. following, when she died at C.  *Endorsed.*  For evidence : Thomas Slowin. Sara Slowin.    Billa vera.

Po se [*remainder illegible, probably* Q$^9$.]

426.  Alice Bakett of Grt. Gaddesden, spinster, wife of John B. of Grt. G., labourer, on 1 June, 40 Eliz., at Grt. G., bewitched to death 1 milch cow valued at 40s. of the goods and chattels of Thomas Wells.  *Endorsed.*  For evidence :  Thomas Welles. Billa vera.

Po se Q$^9$ n$^c$ r.

427.  Elizabeth Turlogg of Chesthunt on 10 Feb.. 42 Eliz.. at C., bewitched Alice Twygg, who languished until 30 June following.  *Endorsed.*  For evidence :  William Daunte, Alice Twygge.

Po se Q$^9$ n$^c$ r.

428.  ——, on 9 Oct., 41 Eliz., at C., bewitched Alice Havers, who languished until 9 Nov. following, when she died at C.

*Endorsed.* For evidence : Mary Aungell, Elizabeth Aungell, Alice Lowyn, Avice Hill, Agnes Wylkinson, Thomas Lowine.
Po se Q⁹ nᶜ r.

1601. Essex Summer Sessions and general gaol delivery holden at Chelmsford on 23 July. 43 Eliz. Commission dated 12 June, 43 Eliz.

429. Ursula Harvy of Ramsey. spinster, wife of Thomas H. on 14 Sept., 42 Eliz., at R., bewitched Thomas Gouldingham, who languished until 24 Sept., when he died at R. *Endorsed.* Witnesses : Jonas Gouldinge, Edward Gyles, Margery Sadler, John Lufkyn, Robert Sergiant. Billa vera.
Po se cul ca null S⁹.

430. ——, on 30 June, 42 Eliz., at R., bewitched Thomas Lacy, who languished until 30 June, 43 Eliz., when he died at R. *Endorsed.* Witnesses : Barberie Lacie, William Herd. Billa vera.
Po se cul ca null S⁹.

431. Anne Harris of Feeringe, spinster, on 25 Apr., 41 Eliz., at F., bewitched Anne Esterford. who languished until 10 July following. *Endorsed.* Witness : Anne Esterford. Billa vera.
Po se cul.

432. ——, on 27 Apr., 42 Eliz., at F., bewitched Anne Kyes, who languished until 20 July following. *Endorsed.* Anne Kyes. Billa vera.
Po se cul.

433. —— on 10 May, 40 Eliz., at F., bewitched Mary Smyth, who languished until 20 July following. when she died at F. *Endorsed.* Margaret Smithe. Billa vera.
Po se cul ca null S⁹.

434. Helen Alyer otherwise Ayleard of Black Notley, widow, on 17 June, 43 Eliz., at B. N., bewitched Sarah Brewer, spinster, who languished until 29 June following, when she died at B. N. *Endorsed.* Philip Brewer. Billa vera.
Po se Q⁹ nᶜ r.

435. ——, on 6 Aug.. 41 Eliz., at B. N., bewitched Elizabeth

Bones, who languished until 7 Jan. following, when she died at B. N. *Endorsed.* William Bonas. Billa vera.

Po se Q$^9$ n$^c$ r.

436. Clemence Vale of Fearing, spinster. wife of John Vale. on 3 Oct., 42 Eliz., at F., bewitched Mary Gibbs, daughter of John G., who languished until 6 Jan. following, when she died at F. *Endorsed.* Witness: John Gybes. Billa vera.

Po se cul ca null   S$^9$.

437. Lucy Eltheridge of Thorpe, widow, on 2 Apr., 43 Eliz., at T., bewitched John Braxted (or Brasted), who languished until 5 Apr. following, when he died at T. *Endorsed.* Witness: William Braxted. Billa vera.

Po se cul ca null   S$^9$.

438. ——, on 31 Mar., 43 Eliz., at T., bewitched Robert Braxted, who languished until 6 Apr. following, when he died at T. *Endorsed.* Witness: William Braxted. Billa vera.

Po se cul ca null   S$^9$.

439. ——, on 14 Oct., 42 Eliz., at T., bewitched to death 10 white weather sheep valued at 5s. each, and 10 ewes valued at 4s. of the goods and chattels of Geo. Clarke. *Endorsed.* Witness: George Clarke, Samuel Danniell, George Clarke. Billa vera.

Po se cul.

440. Magdalen Purcas of Panfield, spinster, wife of John P. on 10 Feb., 41 Eliz., at P., bewitched John Badcock, son of Robert B., who languished until 20 Mar. following, when he died at P. *Endorsed.* Robert Badcock. Billa vera.

Po se cul ca null   S$^9$.

1601.   Hertford Summer Sessions and general gaol delivery holden at Hertford on 20 July, 43 Eliz. Commission dated 12 June, 43 Eliz.

441. Sarah Assar of Lit. Munden, spinster, on the last day of Feb., 43 Eliz., at Lit. M., bewitched Mary Irelande, who languished until 20 Mar. following, when she died at Lit. M.

*Endorsed.* The evidence Robert Ireland, Susan Ireland, Ellen Gibson. Billa vera.

Po se Q⁹ nᶜ r.[1]

442. Mercy Hill of Barley, spinster, on 10 Nov., 42 Eliz., at B., bewitched Grace Ollivere, who languished until 10 Apr. following, when she died at B. *Endorsed.* Evidence : Edward Olyver. Billa vera.

Po se cul p t'ns. Q⁹ p murdro ħet iudm scdm formam statuti.

443. ——, on 20 Aug., 42 Eliz., at B., bewitched Anne Ollivere, who languished until 2 Apr. following, when she died at B. *Endorsed.* For evidence ; Edward Olyver. Billa vera.

Po se cul.

444. ——, on 10 June, 42 Eliz., at B., bewitched 1 black cow valued at 40s. of the goods and chattels of Roger Brayne. *Endorsed.* For evidence : Roger Braine. Steven Hawke, Mʳ. Doctor Ryllett. Billa vera.

Po se cul.

1602. Essex Lent Sessions and general gaol delivery holden at [Brentwood] on 25 Feb., 44 Eliz. Commission dated 20 [Jan.], 44 Eliz.

445. Anne Hyble of Shawforde, widow, on 1 Jan, 44 Eliz., at S., bewitched Mary Woode, daughter of Nicholas W., who languished until 14 Jan. following, when she died at S. *Endorsed.* Witnesses : Nicholas Woode, Margery Woode, Jane Woode, William Dawson. Billa vera.

Po se cul ca null repri quousq₃ &c.

446. Anne Wyrght of Hatfeild Broadoke, spinster, on 2 Jan., 44 Eliz., at H. B., bewitched John Clement, who languished until 8 Feb. following, when he died at H. B. *Endorsed.* Witnesses : William Clement, Margaret Clement, Jane Ringer otherwise Lucas, Anne Crabbe. Billa vera.

Po se Q⁹ nᶜ r.

---

[1] Although acquitted of witchcraft Sarah Assar, upon an indictment of stealing an " ashe clothe " valued at 10d. was found guilty. The gaol delivery roll is wanting, but doubtless she suffered the usual penalty for petty larceny, *i.e.* to be publicly " whipped until her body be bloody ".

1602.    Essex Summer Sessions and general gaol delivery holden at Chelmsford on 19 July, 44 Eliz.  Commission dated 4 June, 44 Eliz.

447.  Elizabeth Pegge of Braintree, widow, on 18 June, 44 Eliz., at B., bewitched to death a black milch cow valued at 3*l.* and 1 red pied cow valued at 3*l.* of the goods and chattels of Laurence Rachell.  *Endorsed.*  Laurence Rotchell.  Billa vera.

Po se cul het iudm scdm formam statuti.

448.  ——, on 30 June, 42 Eliz., at B., bewitched Joan Parman, who languished until 30 Aug. following.  *Endorsed.*  Jone Pardman.  Billa vera.

Po se cul het iudm scdm formam statuti.

449.  ——, on 30 Sept. 42 Eliz., at B., bewitched Sarah Wilbore, who languished in divers parts of her body until the day of taking this inquisition.  *Endorsed.*  Sarah Wilbore. Billa vera.

Po se cul het iudm scdm formam statuti.

450.  Audrey Pond of Old Saling, spinster, wife of Robert P. of the same, labourer, on 29 May, 44 Eliz., at O. S., bewitched to death 1 sorrel horse of the goods and chattels of John Sorell. *Endorsed.*  John Sorell.  Billa vera.

Po se cul ca null   S⁹.

451.  ——, on 6 Dec., 44 Eliz., at O. S., bewitched Thomas Cutt, who languished until 2 Jan. following, when he died at O. S. *Endorsed.*  Eme Cutt, William Elsinge, Richard Wenden, Walter Pratt, John Emson, George Bisshopp.  Billa vera.

Po se cul ca null   S⁹.

1602.    Sussex Summer Sessions and general gaol delivery holden at Horsham on 12 July, 44 Eliz.  Commission dated 14 June, 44 Eliz.

452.  Robert Stockton of Dallington, labourer, on 20 May, 43 Eliz., at D., bewitched William a Jeames, who languished until 17 Apr. following, when he died at D.  *Endorsed.*  Testes Tobias Ferall, John Rosse, Thomas Richardes, Robert Adames, Richard Carpenter.  Bila vera.

Po se Q⁹ nᶜ r.

See No 472.

N. D.   Kent Lent Sessions.   [Evidently about 1603.] [1]

453. Fridgwith Symons of Smarden, widow, on 28 Oct., 44 Eliz., at S., bewitched Thomas Jorden, son of Henry J., who languished until 7 Mar., 45 Eliz., when he died at S. *Endorsed.* Testis. Henry Jorden. *Billa vera.*

Po se Q ncr.   ad largu triabat' ad px.

454. ——, on 7 July, 43 Eliz., at S., bewitched Elizabeth Gardner, daughter of Allan G., who languished until 30 July following, when she died at S. *Endorsed.* Testis. Mary Gardner. *Billa vera.*

Po se Q⁹ ncr.   ad largu.

455. ——, on 1 May, 41 Eliz., at S., bewitched Richard Swayland, son of Nicholas S., who languished until 14 June following, when he died at S. *Endorsed.* Testis. Isabell Swaysland. *Billa vera.*

Po se Q' nc.   ad largu triabat' ad px.

## James I, 1603–1624

1603.   Essex Summer Sessions and general gaol delivery holden at Brentwood on. . . .   Commission dated 25 June, 1 Jas. I.

456. Margery Wilson of Black Notley, widow, on 10 Dec., 42 Eliz., at B. N., bewitched Mary Rust, who languished until the 10 Mar. following, when she died at B. N. *Endorsed.* *Billa vera.*

Po se cul ca null S⁹.

457. ——, on 14 May, 1 Jas. I, at B. N., bewitched to death 1 brown cow valued at 40*s.* of the goods and chattels of Thomas Goodaye. *Endorsed.* *Billa vera.*

Po se cul ca null S⁹.

[1] Indictments Nos. 453–5 are possibly of the last year of Elizabeth's reign.   I found them in a miscellaneous bundle (Assizes 35/333).

458. ——, on 28 May, 44 Eliz., at N., bewitched Bridget Bruer, who languished until 26 July following. *Endorsed.* Billa vera.

Po se cul ca null S⁹.

459. John Banckes of Newporte Ponde, yeoman, on 4 Dec., 45 Eliz., at N. P., bewitched Blanch Nicholls, daughter of Henry N., who languished until 27 Feb. following, when she died at N. P. *Endorsed.* Witnesses. Henry Nicolls, Anne Nicolls. A testimonial from the neighbours for suspicion " throf hereunto annexed ". Billa vera.

Pose Q⁹ nre f . . . batt bon.

460. Joan Roath or Wroth of Grt. Bentley, spinster, on 20 June, 1 Jas. I, at Grt. B., bewitched 1 brown milch cow valued at 4*l.* and 2 red milch cows valued at 4*l.* each of the goods and chattels of John Blackborne. *Endorsed.* Witness : John Blackborne. Billa vera.

Po se cul ca null S⁹.

461. ——, on 10 Dec., 42 Eliz., at Grt. B., bewitched John Bysshopp, who languished until the last day of February following, when he died at Grt. B. *Endorsed.* Bishop. Billa vera.

Po se cul ca null S⁹.

462. Anne Horne of Halsted, spinster, on 6 Feb., 45 Eliz., at H., bewitched to death 2 hens valued at 12*d.*, 2 chickens valued at 8*d.* of the goods and chattels of Robert Norman. *Endorsed.* Robert Norman witnessing. Billa vera.

Po se Qᵉ nc recessit.

1603. Hertford Summer Sessions and general gaol delivery holden at Hertford . . . Commission dated 25 June, 1 Jas I.

### *Gaol Calendar*

Agnes Whittenbury comiss's p Philippū Butler mit p suspicōne venefic̃.

463. Agnes Whittenbery of Auston, spinster, wife of Robert R., on 25 Mar, 43 Eliz., at A., bewitched Joice Newland, who

languished until 30 Apr. following. *Endorsed.* For evidence. Elizabeth Benn. Joyce Newland. Billa vera.

Po se cul iudm.

464. ——, on 31 May, 1 Jas I, at Aston, bewitched to death 2 hogs of the goods and chattels of Francis Combes. *Endorsed.* For evidence—Isabel Combes. Billa vera.

Po se cul iudm.

465. ——, on 31 Dec., 45 Eliz., at Auston, bewitched Thomas Hills, who languished until 1 Mar. following. *Endorsed.* For evidence.—Thomas Hills.

Po se cul iudm.

1603. Kent Summer Sessions and general gaol delivery holden at Maidstone on 29 Sept., 1 Jas. I. Commission dated 25 June, 1 Jas. I.

466. Anne Wynchester of Westram, spinster, wife of George W., labourer, on 30 Sept., 38 Eliz., at W., bewitched Anne Masters, who languished until 14 Oct. following. *Endorsed.* Testes. William Masters, Anne Masters vx eius. Audery Stace, Stephen Turke. Billa vera.

Po se Q$^9$ n$^c$ r.

467. ——, on 30 June, 42 Eliz., at W., bewitched John Preston, who languished until 1 Sept. following, when he died at W. *Endorsed.* Mathew Thornton. Billa vera.

Po se Q$^9$ n$^c$ r.

468. ——, on the last day of February, 43 Eliz., at W., bewitched Jane Harris, who languished until 31 Oct. following, when she died at W. Thomas Harris test. *Endorsed.* Billa vera.

Po se cul ca null S$^9$.

469. George Winchester of Westram, labourer, and Anne W., on 30 Sept., 41 Eliz., at W., bewitched Margaret Steddolph, who languished until 1 Aug. 44 Eliz., when she died at W. *Endorsed.* Annes Steddolpe testes. Billa vera.

George Winchester. Po se Q$^9$ n$^c$ r. Anne Winchester. Po se cul ca null.

1605.    Kent Lent Sessions and general gaol delivery holden at
Rochester on 4 Mar., 2 Jas. I.  Commission dated
23 Jan., 2 Jas. I.

470.  Charity Hills, wife of William H. of Brenchley, black-
smith, on 20 Nov., 1 Jas. I, at Horsemanden, bewitched Nicholas
Holmwood, son of George H. of H., who languished until 3 May
following, when he died at  H.  *Endorsed.*  George Homewood jur.
Billa vera.

Po se Q$^9$ n$^c$ r.

471.  ——, on 13 July, 1 Jas. I, at B., bewitched William
Moyse, son of Edmund M. of Brenchley, who languished until
20 July following, when he died at B.  *Endorsed.*  Edmund
Moyse.  Billa vera.

Po se Q$^9$ n$^c$ r.

1605.    Sussex Summer Sessions and general gaol delivery holden
at East Grinstead on 8 July, 3 Jas. I.  Commission dated
1 June, 3 Jas. I.

472.  Robert Stikden of Dalington, chandler, on 20 May,
2 Jas. I, at D., bewitched Margaret Carpenter, who languished
until 10 June following.  *Endorsed.*  Billa vera.

Po se Q$^9$ n$^c$ r.

See No. 452.

N.D.  Kent.  [Evidently after Dec., 1605.[1]]

473.  Mary Mercye of Mylton, spinster, on 30 June, 3 Jas. I,
at M., bewitched Alice Gates, who languished until 6 July
following, when she died at M.  *Endorsed.*  Agnes Sare, Margaret
Church, Bennet King, Elizabeth Sheffe, Alice Young, Joan
Hope, Thomas Ramsey, Thomas Richardes, William Gore,
Jo : Safron.  Billa vera.

Po se cul ca null  S$^9$.

474.  ——, on 10 Feb., 1 Jas. I, at M., bewitched John Sawyer,
who was greatly vexed in divers parts of his body until 10 Mar.

[1] Indictments Nos. 473–4 are from the miscellaneous bundle
Assizes 35/333.

following, when he died at M. *Endorsed.* Testis. Agnes Sare. Billa vera.

Po se cul ca null  S⁹.

1606. Hertford Lent Sessions and general gaol delivery holden at Hertford on 28 Mar. [4 Jas. I]. Writ dated 12 Feb., 3 Jas. I.

475. Joan Vaughan of Cheshunt, widow, on 20 Nov., 3 Jas. I, at C., bewitched Alice Cheare, who languished until 1 Apr., 4 Jas. I. *Endorsed.* For evidence. Alice Cheare, Alice Cheare, jur. Smeth [*very indistinct*]. Billa vera.

Po se Q⁹ nᶜ r.

1606. Hertford Summer Sessions and general gaol delivery holden at Hertford on 1 Aug., 4 Jas. I. Commission dated 21 June, 4 Jas. I.[1]

476. Alice Stokes of Raystone, spinster, on 2 Dec., 4 Jas. I. at R., bewitched Richard Bland, who languished until 25 Aug. following, when he died at R. *Endorsed.* For evidence John Bland. Billa vera.

Po se cul ca null  S⁹

477. ——, on 7 July, 1 Jas. I, at R., bewitched John Rumbold, who languished in divers parts of his body. *Endorsed.* For evidence John Rumbold. Billa vera.

p̄donat'

478. Christiana Stokes of Raystone, spinster, on 22 Jan., 3 Jas. I, at R., bewitched Roger Gybbons, who languished until 9 June following, when he died at R. *Endorsed.* For evidence. Judith Gybbons, Elizabeth Farron. Billa vera.

Po se cul ca null  S⁹

479. ——, on 20 Dec., 36 Eliz., at R., bewitched John Peirse or Hogg, who languished until 15 Jan. following, when he died at R. *Endorsed.* For evidence. James Youlden. Billa vera.

Po se cul ca null  S⁹.

---

[1] Contemporary pamphlet, see p. 284. I find no trace of John Harrison and her daughter, who were sentenced to death at these Assizes.

480. ——, on 5 Jan., 41 Eliz., at R., bewitched Jane Wakefeild, who languished, etc. *Endorsed.* For evidence. Jane Wakefield. Billa vera.

pdonat'.

1607.    Essex Lent Sessions and general gaol delivery holden at Chelmsford on 23 Mar., 4 Jas. I. Writ dated 23 Jan., 4 Jas. I.

481. Blanche Worman of Mousam, in the parish of Chelmsford, spinster, on 20 Mar., 3 Jas. I, at M., bewitched Thomas Hall, who was consumed and wasted and yet is. *Endorsed.* Test. William Hall. Billa vera.

Po se cul ca null   $S^9$.

482. ——, on 1 Apr., 2 Jas. I, at M., bewitched Jane Sellyn, who was consumed and wasted and yet is. *Endorsed.* George Sellin. Billa vera.

Po se cul ca null   $S^9$.

483. ——, on 7 Jan., 4 Jas. I, at M., bewitched Leonard Goodin of M., who languished until 1 Feb. following, when he died at M. *Endorsed.* Test. John Goodin. Billa vera.

Po se cul ca null   $S^9$.

484. ——, on 1 Nov., 4 Jas. I, at M., bewitched Bridget Cole, wife of William C., who was consumed and wasted and yet is. *Endorsed.* Test. William Cole. Billa vera.

Po se cul ca null   $S^9$.

485. ——, on 3 May, 4 Jas. I, at M., bewitched Thomas Browne of M., who languished until 12 Aug. following, when he died at M. *Endorsed.* Test. Browne. Billa vera.

Po se cul ca null   $S^9$.

486. ——, on 18 Aug., 4 Jas. I, at M., bewitched Joan, wife of Edward Mault, who was consumed and wasted and yet is. *Endorsed.* Test. Edward Mault. Billa vera.

Po se cul ca null   $S^9$.

487. Anne Harvye of Coxall, widow, on 16 Mar., 4 Jas. I., at C., bewitched Margaret Aliston, wife of Robert A., who was

wasted and consumed and yet is. *Endorsed.* Test. Robert Alleston. Billa vera.

Po se Q$^9$ nc r.

1607. Essex Summer Sessions and general gaol delivery holden at Chelmsford on 20 July, 5 Jas. I. Commission dated 26 June, 5 Jas. I.

488. Edwin Haddesley of Willingale, yeoman, on 10 June, 4 Jas. I, at Goodester, bewitched Joan Platt, wife of Robert P., who was wasted and consumed and yet is. *Endorsed.* Testes : Joan Platt, John Harvye. Billa vera.

Po se Q$^9$ nc r.

489. ——, on 7 May, 35 Eliz., at Stansted Mountfitchett, bewitched John Grace, who languished until 2 June following, when he died at S.M. *Endorsed.* Testes : Jo: Lucken. Billa vera.

Po se Q$^9$ nc r.

1608. Hertford Summer Sessions and general gaol delivery holden at Hertford on 8 July, 6 Jas. I. Commission dated 27 [May], 6 Jas. I.

490. Agnes Smith of Asshwell, widow, on 10 Oct., 3 Jas. I, at A., bewitched John Barley, the younger, aged 4 yrs., son of John B., the elder, who languished until 17 Oct. following, when he died at A. *Endorsed.* John Barley. Billa vera.

Po se Q$^9$ nc r.

See 491, 518, 527.

491. ——, on 1 Feb., 5 Jas. I, at A., bewitched Susanna Warren, daughter of Thomas W., who was wasted and consumed and yet is. *Endorsed.* For evidence Thomas Warren. Billa vera.

Po se Q$^9$ nc r.

See 490, 518, 527.

1609. Essex Summer Sessions and general gaol delivery holden at Chelmsford on 24 July, 7 Jas. I. Commission dated 20 June, 7 Jas. I.

*Gaol Calendar*

Alicia Bust ꝓ mand̄ Thome Waldegrave ar̄ ꝓ suspicone del Witchcraft.

492. Anna Feild ꝓ mand̄ eiusdem ꝓ suspicone Witchcraft.

493. Mary Wade of Paswic, spinster, wife of Edward W., on 25 Apr., 7 Jas. I, at Coggeshall, bewitched Grysagon Parker, who was "pyned and lamed" *Endorsed.* Thomas Aylett, John Mare. Billa vera.

Po se cul ca null     Repri pᵗ. iudicm ꝓ p̃gñ.

494. ——, on 4 Apr., 6 Jas. I, at Bradwell-juxta-Coggeshall, bewitched Elena Stebbinge, who was "pyned and lamed". *Endorsed.* Ellen Stebbinge, John Maie, Thomas Aylett. Billa vera.

Po se cul ca null     Repri pᵗ. iudicm ꝓ p̃gñ.

495. ——, on 25 Apr., 7 Jas. I, at Coggeshall, bewitched Grace Lacye, who was "pyned and lamed". *Endorsed.* Thomas Aylett, John Maye. Billa vera.

Po se cul ca null     Repri pᵗ. iudicm ꝓ p̃gñ.

496. ——, on 31 Aug., 6 Jas. I, at C., bewitched Mathia Deane, wife of James D., who was "pined and lamed".

Po se cul ca null     Repri pᵗ. iudicm ꝓ p̃gñ.

497. Alice Buske (Bust in gaol calendar) of Alphamstone, widow, on 5 July, 7 Jas. I, at A., bewitched John Polley, who languished until 7 July following, when he died at A. *Endorsed.* William Pollie, Mary Pollie, John Pollie, James Pollie, William Rayner, John Myller. Billa vera.

Po se cul ca null Sꝰ.

*Gaol Delivery Roll*

Alicia Buske   Sꝰ ꝓ coll quosꝗ &c.
Maria Wade   repr in gaol sine ball.

1610. Essex Lent Sessions and general gaol delivery holden at Chelmsford on 7 Mar., 7 Jas. I. Commission dated 3 Jan., 7 Jas. I.

498. Anne Prentice of Bocking, widow, on 8 June, 7 Jas. I, at B., bewitched Edward Freman, who was wasted and consumed

and yet is. *Endorsed.* Test. Edward Freeman, William Clealand. Billa vera.

Po se non cul nec re.

499. Katherine Lawrett of Colne Wake, spinster, on 22 Aug., 7 Jas. I, at C. W., bewitched Susan Kynge, who languished until 29 August following, when she died at C. W. *Endorsed.* Test. John Lawrett, William Lawrett, Henry Allum, William Kinge, Constance Kinge, Agnes (*Annis*) Taylor & Agnes (*Annis*) Cooke. Billa vera.

Po se cul ca null  S⁹.

500. ——. [*No date*], at C. W., bewitched to death 1 horse valued at 10*l.* of the goods and chattels of Francis Plaile. *Endorsed.* Test. Francis Playle, John Lawrett, William Lawrett, Henry Allum. Billa vera.

Tri  Po se cul ca null  S⁹.
*Full Latin transcript and English version, p. 87 supra.*

501. Anne Pennyfather of Lit. Totham, spinster, wife of Thomas P., on 23 July, 6 Jas. I, at Grt. Totham, bewitched Robert Thorocke, who was wasted and consumed and yet is. *Endorsed.* Robert Barnard. William Purr, Robert Hunter. John Austen. Billa vera.

Po se non cul nec re.

502. ——, on 6 Nov., 6 Jas. I, at Grt. T., bewitched Mary Clarke with intention to hurt and destroy, etc. *Endorsed.* Witnesses : Nicholas Clark, Agnes (Annis) Garling, Thomas Hawkins, Robert Brocas, William Purr, Robert Thorrocke, Robert Hunter, John Austen. Billa vera.

Po se non cul nec re.

503. Lucy Buttler of Halsted, spinster, on 6 Aug., 7 Jas. I, at H., bewitched Elizabeth Mault, who languished until 27 Sept. following, when she died at H. *Endorsed.* Test. William Malt. Billa vera.

Po se non cul nec re.

504. ——, on 1 Feb., 5 Jas. I, at H., bewitched Joan Springe,

wife of John S., who languished until 1 June, 6 Jas. I, when she died at H. *Endorsed.* Witness : John Sprigg. Billa vera.

Po se non cul nec re.

505. Winifred Stowers [Steward in gaol calendar] of Halsted, spinster, wife of John S., on 15 Oct., 7 Jas. I, at H., bewitched Grace Gest, wife of John G., who was wasted and consumed and yet is. *Endorsed.* Test. John Gest, Ann Jolly, Susan Berry. Billa vera.

Po se non cul nec re.

1610.    Hertford Lent Sessions and general gaol delivery holden at Hertford on 23 Mar., 7 Jas. I.  Commission dated 23 Jan., 7 Jas. I.

506. Margery Raye of Barkhamsted, wife of Ralph R., on 1 Oct., 7 Jas. I, at B., bewitched Elizabeth Humfrey, who languished until 14 Feb. following, when she died at B. *Endorsed.* Testimonis. Agnes Humphry et Tobie Raye. Billa vera.

Po se cul ca null    Judm S$^9$.

1610.    Essex Summer Sessions and general gaol delivery holden at Chelmsford on 16 July, 8 Jas. I.  Commission dated 8 June, 8 Jas. I.

507. Alice Pitches of Stysted, widow, on 31 Jan., 6 Jas. I, at Black Notley, bewitched Grace Sharpe, wife of George S., who languished until 1 May following, when she died at B. N. *Endorsed.* Test. Margery Cooke, Thomas Stampe, William Ellis, John Farsser. Billa vera.

Po se non cul nec re.

1610.    Hertford Summer Sessions and general gaol delivery holden at Hertford on 20 July, 8 Jas. I.  Commission dated 8 June, 8 Jas. I.

508. Agnes Sutton of Estwick, spinster, wife of Edward S. on 1 June, 3 Jas. I, at E., bewitched Audrey Sewell, who languished until 20 July following, when she died at E. *Endorsed.* Billa vera.

Po se non cul nec re.

509. Agnes Sutton of Bishop's Hatfeild, spinster, wife of Edward S., on 20 Apr., 8 Jas. I, at B. H., bewitched Elizabeth Munke, who was consumed and wasted and yet is. *Endorsed.* Billa vera.

Po se cul ca null repr p$^t$. iudicm.

1611. Essex Lent Sessions and general gaol delivery holden at Chelmsford on 2 Mar., 9 Jas. I. Commission dated 24 Jan., 9 Jas. I.

510. Richard Jonn of Northokenden, labourer, and Anne, his wife, on 20 Nov., 9 Jas. I, at N., bewitched and destroyed 1 horse of the goods and chattels of —— Prentisse. *Endorsed.* Testis. John Garret, John Harrodyne. Billa vera.

Richard Jonn   Po se po se Q$^9$ p hoc.   S$^9$ sup aliud indcament.

Anna Jonn est tam infirma q̃d non potest loqui. morit' ante q'm triat̃ fuit.

511. ——, ——, on 20 Nov., 9 Jas. I, at N., did consult with, entertain, employ, feed, and reward divers evil spirits, namely, one called "Jockey", one called "Jacke", and one called "Will", with the intention of killing and stealing horses, sheep, and other animals of their neighbours. *Endorsed.* Testes. John Garret, John Harrodyne. Billa vera.

Richard Jonn   po se cul ca null   S$^9$.

Anna Jonn est m$^o$ tam infirma q̃d non potest loqui morit', ante triat fuit.

*Gaol Delivery Roll*

Ric$^9$us Jon   S$^9$ p coll quousq, &c.

1611. Kent Lent Sessions and general gaol delivery holden at Maidstone on 14 Feb., 8 Jas. I. Commission dated 23 Jan., 8 Jas. I.

512. Katherine Howlett of Staplehurst, widow, on 5 July, 8 Jas. I, at S., bewitched Dorothy Hoade, who languished until 16 July following, when she died at S. *Endorsed.* Jur. John Hoad. Billa vera.

Po se non cul nec re.

*Inquisition taken at General Sessions of the Peace holden at Canterbury Castle on Tuesday next after the feast of Epiphany, 8 Jas. I [8 Jan., 1611].*

513. Sibil Ferrys of St Lawrence, widow, on 1 Mar., 7 Jas. I, at St L., bewitched Jane Nortcliffe, wife of John N., who languished until 1 June following.

Vacat quia non valet in lege virtute statuti inde nup edit.

*Full Latin transcript and English version, p. 88 supra.*

1612. Essex Summer Sessions and general gaol delivery holden at Chelmsford on 20 July, 10 Jas. I. Commission dated 12 June, 10 Jas. I.

514. Alice Batty of Toppesfeild, spinster, wife of William B., on 6 May, 5 Jas. I, at T., bewitched John Reade, who languished until 5 Mar. following, when he died at T. *Endorsed.* Test. Grace Wayte. Christopher Reade. Elizabeth Reade. Billa vera.

Po se Q⁹ nc r.

515. ——, on 1 Jan., 9 Jas. I, at T., bewitched Christopher Reade, who was wasted and consumed and yet is. *Endorsed.* Test. Christopher Reade. Billa vera.

Po se Q⁹ nc r.

516. ——, on 1 Sept., 8 Jas. I, at Haverell, bewitched Martha Laver, who languished until 1 Dec. following, when she died at Haverell. *Endorsed.* Testis. Edward Laver. Billa vera.

Po se Q⁹ nc r. Alicia Battye.

1612. Hertford Summer Sessions and general gaol delivery holden at Hertford on 24 July, 10 Jas. I. Commission dated 12 June, 10 Jas. I.

517. Agnes Smith of Ashwell, widow, on 1 Sept., 9 Jas. I, at A., bewitched 1 bay horse and 1 black horse of the goods and chattels of George Arnold which " were destroyed ". *Endorsed.* Test. George Arnold, Thomas Willson. Billa vera.

Po se non cul nec re  Georg Arnold.

See 490, 491, 526.

1613. Essex Lent Sessions and general gaol delivery holden at Chelmsford on 15 Mar., 10 Jas. I. Commission dated [23] Jan., 10 Jas. I.

518. Robert Parker of Toppesfeild, gentleman, on 5 Nov., 10 Jas., at T., by charms and sorceries attempted to hurt and destroy Thomas Browne. *Endorsed.* Billa vera.

Po se cul & het iudicm scdm formam statuti.

*Full Latin transcript and English version, pp. 89–90 supra.*

519. John Cornell of Borley, joiner, and Robert Parker of Toppesfeild, gentleman, on 5 Nov., 9 Jas. I, at T., bewitched Thomas Browne, the younger, who languished until 25 July, 10 Jas. I, when he died at T. *Endorsed.* Testes. Thomas Browne, Mary Browne, Christopher Roote, Elizabeth Bateman, Maryett Greene, Elizabeth Greene. Billa vera.

Po se $Q^9$ nc r [both prisoners].

520. ——, on 3 Aug., 10 Jas. I, at T., bewitched Thomas Browne, the elder, who was wasted and consumed and yet is. *Endorsed.* Testes. Thomas Browne, Mary Browne, Samuel Edwards, Edward Cracherwood. Billa vera.

Po se $Q^9$ nc r [both prisoners].

1613. Hertford Lent Sessions and general gaol delivery holden at Hertford on 12 Mar., 10 Jas. I. Commission dated 23 Jan., 10 Jas. I.

521. George Adowins of Flamsted, otherwise George Clothier of F., labourer, and Sarah, his wife, on 6 Mar., 10 Jas. I, at F., bewitched Hugh Adownes, who languished until 13 Mar. following, when he died at Caddington. *Endorsed.* Test. Helen Androwe, Robert Adownes, Henry Boteler, ar.. John Walker, Henry Osmond, Philip Godfrey, John Sutton, Thomas Lea. Billa vera.

George Adowins Po se cul ca null $S^s$. Sarah Adowins Po se $Q^9$ ncr.

522. Thomas Hamond of Appesden, husbandman, and Agnes, his wife, on 30 Nov., 10 Jas. I, at A., bewitched Henry Chapman who languished until 9 Feb. following, when he died at A.

*Endorsed.* Test. Elizabeth Chapman. Billa vera [for Agnes]. Ignoramus pro Tho. Hamond.

Agnes Hamond. Po se.

523. ——, ——, on 10 Oct., 6 Jas. I. at A., bewitched 3 horses of the goods and chattels of Edward Parker. *Endorsed.* Test. Edward Parker. Billa vera.

Po se Q⁹ [both prisoners].

### *Gaol Delivery Roll*

Georgius Adownes. S⁹ p coℏ quousq̃ &c̃.

Thomas Hamond ⎫
Sara Adowne    ⎬ Quieti & delib⁹ant'.
               ⎭

Agnes Hamond. repri sine baℏ p suspicõne incantacõnis.

1614.    Hertford Lent Sessions and general gaol delivery holden at Hertford on 7 Mar., 11 Jas. I. Commission dated 24 [Jan.], 11 Jas. I.

### *Gaol Delivery Roll*

524. Lyon Gleane. To be sett in the stockę & whipped & sent to Boston suspected for a coniurer.

1615.    Essex Lent Sessions and general gaol delivery holden at Chelmsford on 6 Mar., 12 Jas. I. Commission dated 23 Jan., 12 Jas. I.

525. Grace Tabour of Stooe Marris, spinster, on 1 June 12 Jas. I, at S. M., bewitched to death 2 black cows valued at 40s., each of the goods and chattels of Edward Meade. *Endorsed.* Test. Edward Meade. Billa vera.

Po se Q⁹.

1615.    Hertford Lent Sessions and general gaol delivery holden at Hertford on 10 Mar., 12 Jas. I. Commission dated 23 Jan., 12 Jas. I.

526. Anne Smith of Ashwell, widow, on 1 Nov., 12 Jas. I., at A., bewitched Frances Ashelyn, who was wasted and consumed and yet is. *Endorsed.* William Knott, Anne Wrangle, William Hasillwood, Clement Gunwill. Billa vera.

Po se repri sine tri. . . .

See 490, 491, 517.

[An attached paper gives the names of eleven witnesses.—
Testes : Anne Wrangle, Clement Gunnill, Hugh German, Robert
Nicolls, William Hazelwood, Alice Boone, Thomas Brayne,
Nicolas Baynard, Peter Rolfe, William Knott, Mr. Marshall.]

527. ——, on 1 Mar., 10 Jas. I, at A., bewitched to death 1
red roan horse valued at 8l. of the goods and chattels of Clement
Gunnell. *Endorsed.* Test. Clement Gunnill. Billa vera.

Po se cul het iudicm scdm formam statuti.

*Gaol Delivery Roll*

Anna Smyth. Guilty for distroying a horse by wichcraft &
het iudcm scdm formam statuti.

1616. Essex Lent Sessions and general gaol delivery holden
at Brentwood on 4 Mar., 13 Jas. I. Commission dated
23 Jan., 13 Jas. I.

528. Blanche Prisley of Navestock, widow, on 1 Feb., 13 Jas. I,
at N., did receive, entertain, and feed evil spirits with the
intention of hurting and destroying subjects of the king in their
bodies and souls. *Endorsed.* Testes : Mary Bett, Joan Marler,
Margaret Finche, Elizabeth Course, Leonard Midwiffe, Elizabeth
Darbie, Katherine Tompson, Julia Pryor, widow, Mary Reinoldes,
widow, Phillis Green, John Turnor, Winifred Norris, William
Maple, John Finche, Jonas Ryvett, William Abbotte, Elizabeth
Dise. George Colforde. Billa vera.

Po se Q⁹ nc.

529. Anne Prisley of Navestock, spinster, on 1 Feb., 13 Jas. I,
at N., did receive [*as above with same witnesses, etc.*].

Po se Q⁹ nc r.

530. Katherine Prisley of Navestock, spinster, on 1 Feb.,
13 Jas. I, at N., did receive [*as above with same witnesses, etc.*].

Po se Q⁹ nc r.

1616. Hertford Lent Sessions and general gaol delivery holden
at Hertford on 8 Mar., 13 Jas. I. Commission dated
23 Jan., 13 Jas. I.

531. Anne Smyth of Ashewell, widow. on the last day of February, 7 Jas. I, at A., bewitched Thomas Wrangle, who languished until the last day of February, 10 Jas. I, when he died at A. *Endorsed.* Test. Anne Pecock. Billa vera.

Po se    Repri sine [*illegible*].

1616.    Essex Summer Sessions and general gaol delivery holden at Chelmsford on 15 July, 14 Jas. I. Commission dated [1 June] 14 Jas. I.[1]

532. John Godfrie of Lamborne, glover, on 19 Apr., 13 Jas. I, at Chigwell, bewitched John White, who languished until 24 Apr. following, when he died at C. *Endorsed.* Test. Elizabeth White, Ursula Saltmarshe, Jane White. Billa vera.

Po se Q$^9$ nc r.

533. Sarah Godfrie of Lamborne, spinster, wife of John G., on 12 Aug., 11 Jas. I, at Staplesford, bewitched to death 1 brown horse valued at 5*l.* of the goods and chattels of John Allam, *Endorsed.* Test. John Allam. Billa vera.

Po se Q$^9$ nc r.

534. ———, on 7 Aug., 11 Jas. I, at Staplesford, bewitched to death 1 gray mare valued at 6*l.* of the goods and chattels of John Allam. *Endorsed.* Test. John Allam. Billa vera.

Po se Q$^9$ nec r.

535. ———, on 31 July, 11 Jas. I, at S., bewitched to death 1 hog valued at 20*s.* of the goods and chattels of John Allam. *Endorsed.* Test. John Allam. Billa vera.

Po se Q$^9$.

536. ———, on 15 Aug., 11 Jas. I, at S., bewitched 1 gray nag valued at 3*l.* of the goods and chattels of John Allam. *Endorsed.* Test. John Allam. Billa vera.

Po se Q$^9$.

537. Margaret Lambe of Southokenden, spinster, wife of Elie L., on 2 Mar., 13 Jas. I. at S., did consult with and entertain evil

---

[1] Partly illegible. The writ is dated 1 May, 14 Jas. 1.

spirits. *Endorsed.* Test. Richard Nayler, Agnes Nayler. Billa vera.

Po se Q⁹ nc r.

538. Susan Barker of Upminster, spinster, wife of Henry B., on 28 Sept., 13 Jas. I, at U., did take up a skull out of a grave, etc., with the intention of using the skull to bewitch Mary Stevens. *Endorsed.* Test. Anne Stevens. Billa vera.

Po se Q⁹ nc r.

*Full Latin transcript and English version, p. 90 supra.*

539. ——, on 10 Feb., 13 Jas. I, at Hornechurche, bewitched Mary Stevens, who was wasted and consumed and yet is.

Po se Q⁹ nc r.

540. ——, on 7 Apr., 14 Jas. I, at U., bewitched Edward Ashen, the elder, who languished until 11 May following, when he died at Hornechurch. *Endorsed.* Francis Rand, esquire, Ann Ashen, William Stevenns, Thomas Dyason.

Po se cul ca null S⁹.

541. ——, on 20 Feb., 12 Jas. I, at H., bewitched Edward Ashen. the younger, who languished until 3 Feb. following, when he died at H. *Endorsed.* Agnes Ashen, Catherine Coppin, Mary Dyason, Margaret Ashen. Billa vera.

Po se cul ca null S⁹.

*Gaol Delivery Roll*

Susanna Barker S⁹ p collum quousq, &c.

1617. Sussex Lent Sessions and general gaol delivery holden at East Grinstead on 3 Mar., 14 Jas. I. Commission dated 23 Jan., 14 Jas. I.

542. Margaret Pannell of Salehurst, spinster, wife of Thomas P., on 10 June, 14 Jas. I, at S., bewitched Joan Cannard, who was wasted and consumed and yet is. *Endorsed.* Joan Cannard. Billa vera.

Po se Q⁹ nc r.

543. ——, on 1 July, 11 Jas., I, at S., bewitched Thomas

P

Comp*ar*, who was wasted and consumed and yet is.  *Endorsed.*
Thomas Comp'. Joan Young. Billa vera.

Po se Q⁹ nc r.

544. ——, on 1 Jan., 7 Jas. I, at S., bewitched to death 1 sow
valued at 8*s.* and 8 pigs valued at 16*s.* of the goods and chattels
of Thomas French. *Endorsed.* Anne Frenche. Billa vera.

Po se Qˢ.

1618.  Essex Lent Sessions and general gaol delivery holden at
          Chelmsford on 2 Mar., 15 Jas. I.  Commission dated
          23 Jan., 15 Jas. I.

545. Mary Holt of Lit. Lees, widow, on 25 Apr., 9 Jas. I,
at Lit. L., bewitched Margaret Ellis, who languished until 1 May
following, when she died at Lit. L. *Endorsed.* Test. William
Ellis. Billa vera.

Po se cul ca null Sⁿ Repri pᵗ iudicm.

546. ——, on 9 Sept., 12 Jas. I, at Lit. L., bewitched Margaret
Bright, who was wasted and consumed and yet is. *Endorsed.*
Testes. Margaret Bright, Tabitha Bucklee, Susan Robiohn.
Billa vera.

Po se cul ca null Sⁿ Repr pᵗ iudicm.


*Gaol Delivery Roll*

Maria Holt   cut modo p murdro p incantaconem & repri post
          iudicm in gaola sine bałł.

1618.  Hertford Lent Sessions and general gaol delivery holden
          at Hertford on 6 Mar., 15 Jas. I.  Commission dated
          23 Jan., 15 Jas. I.

547. Joan Messenger of Barkhamsted Mary, spinster, on
1 Feb., 13 Jas. I, at B. M., bewitched Elizabeth Poope, who
languished until 30 Apr., 14 Jas. I, when she died at B. M.
*Endorsed.* William Poope, Ann Grover. Billa vera.

Po se Q⁹ nc r.

548. ——, on 18 Mar., 12 Jas. I, at B., bewitched William
Cocke, who languished until 18 Mar., 13 Jas. I, when he died at

B. M. *Endorsed.* John Hopkins, Ellen Cocke, Ann Grover, Henry White. Billa vera.

Po se Q⁹ nc r.

549. ——, on 27 Oct., 15 Jas. I, at B. M., bewitched to death 2 stoned horses valued at 8*l.* of the goods and chattels of Miles Wodd. *Endorsed.* Miles Wodd. Billa vera.

Po se Q⁹ nc r.

1618. Hertford Summer Sessions and general gaol delivery holden at Hertford on 24 July, 16 Jas. I. Commission dated 5 June, 16 Jas. I.

550. Alice Nashe of Barkeway, widow, on 12 Jan., 16 Jas. I, at B., bewitched Margaret Bishopp, who languished until 5 Feb. following, when she died at B. *Endorsed.* William Bishoppe, Elizabeth Dowse, Susan Fitche. Billa vera.

Po se Q⁹ nc r.

551. Margaret Hullett of Barkewaie, wife of Richard H., on 7 Sept., 14 Jas., at B., bewitched Henry Braie, who languished until 12 Sept. following, when he died at B. *Endorsed.* Susan Fitche, Agnes Braie, Susan Dewe, Judith Osladd, Agnes Newnham. Billa vera.

Po se Q⁹ nc r.

1619. Essex Lent Sessions and general gaol delivery holden at Brentford on 8 Mar., 16 Jas. I. Commission dated 23 Jan., 16 Jas. I.

### Gaol Calendar

552. Anne Byford comytted by Sr John Deane for witchcraft. [Indictment wanting.]

### Gaol Delivery Roll

Anna Byford [and others] Delibent' p pclam.

1620. Essex Lent Sessions and general gaol delivery holden at Chelmsford on 6 Mar., 16 Jas. I. Commission dated 24 Jan., 17 Jas. I.

553. Margaret Greene of Fownes, widow, on 22 Dec., 17 Jas. I, at F., bewitched Lawrence Fannyng, the younger, who languished

until 27 Dec. following, when he died at F. *Endorsed.* Lawrence Fannynge, Susan Fannynge, Joan Allyn, Mary Wethers. Billa vera.

Po se Q⁹ nc r.

1621.    Essex Lent Sessions and general gaol delivery holden at Chelmsford on 12 Mar., 18 Jas. 1. Commission dated 18 Jan., 18 Jas. 1.

554. Elizabeth Parnsbye of Ricklynge, spinster, wife of William P., labourer, on 20 Apr., 18 Jas. I, at Ellsnam, bewitched John Tuer, doctor of laws, who was wasted and consumed and yet is. *Endorsed.* Abdias Tuer, clerck, Mr. Doctor Tuer, Hester Wade, John Shepred. Billa vera.

Po se Q⁹ nc r.

555. Anne Hewghes of Grt. Leighes, widow, on 24 June, 13 Jas. I, at Grt. L., bewitched John Archer, who languished until 24 June following, when he died at Grt. L. *Endorsed.* John Steele, M^{tris} Buckle, Richard Oddin, Ann Kent, William Wallit. Billa vera.

Po se Q⁹ nc r.

556. ——, on 1 Aug., 17 Jas. I. at Grt. L., bewitched Thomas Meade, who was wasted and consumed and yet is. *Endorsed.* Thomas Meade. Billa vera.

Po se Q⁹ nc r.

557. ——, on 1 Feb., 17 Jas. I, at Lit. L., bewitched Margaret Bright, who was wasted and consumed and yet is. *Endorsed.* Margaret Brighte. Billa vera.

Po se Q⁹ nc r.

558. ——, on 1 Mar., 17 Jas. I, at Grt. L., bewitched to death 1 pied cow valued at 3*l.* of the goods and chattels of Richard Edwardes. *Endorsed.* Richard Edwardes. Billa vera.

Po se Q⁹.

## Charles I, 1625–1648

1626.    Essex Lent Sessions and general gaol delivery holden at Chelmsford on 20 Mar., 1 Chas. I. Commission dated 23 Jan., 1 Chas. I.

559. Helen Pedder of South Halsted, spinster, wife of John P., husbandman, on 1 June, 1 Chas. I, at S. H., bewitched Christiana Norman, who became decrepit and so remained until the taking of this inquisition. *Endorsed.* Elizabeth Byne, Margaret Atmer, John Norman, Susan Harvye, Robert Ward. Billa vera.

Po se Q⁹ nc r.

560. ——, on 1 Nov., 1 Chas. I, at S. H., bewitched Mildred Norman, who languished until 7 Nov. following, when she died at S. H. *Endorsed.* John Norman. Billa vera.

Po se Q⁹ nc r.

561. ——, on 8 Feb., 1 Chas. I, at S. H., bewitched to death 4 hens and 3 capons of the goods and chattels of John Norman. *Endorsed.* Susan Harvey, John Norman, Elizabeth Byne. Billa vera.

Po se Q⁹ nc r.

1626. Kent Lent Sessions and general gaol delivery holden at Maidstone on 2 Mar., 1 Chas. I. Commission dated 12 Feb., 1 Chas. I.

*Gaol Calendar for Maidstone Prison*

562. Anna Gunn vid. suspected for a witch.

[Indictment wanting.]

1626. Essex Summer Sessions and general gaol delivery holden at Chelmsford on 12 July, 2 Chas. I. Commission dated 23 June, 8 Chas. I.

563. Dennis Nash of Springfeild, spinster, on 1 May, 2 Chas. I, at S., bewitched Samuel Forster, the younger, aged 18 years, who was debilitated. *Endorsed.* Samuel Forster, Joseph Prentice. Robert Oddy, John Potter, jur. Billa vera.

Po se non cul nec re.

*Gaol Delivery Roll*

Dennis Nash is now acquitted of felony and witchcraft, and must be delivered paying her fees.

From detached indictments in same bundle.[1]

[1] The date given in No. 568 points to this file being part of that for the Summer Sessions, 2 Chas. I, but the prisoners' names do not correspond with those on the gaol delivery roll of that assize.

564. Joan Freeman of Harlow, widow, on 24 Mar., 1 Chas. I,
at Great Parringdon, bewitched Dorcas Nayler, who languished
until the day of taking this inquisition. *Endorsed.* Joshua Nayler,
Elizabeth Walker. Billa vera.

Po se Q⁹ nᶜ r.

565. Dorothy Hills of Weathersfeild, widow, on 1 May.
14 Jas. I, at W., bewitched Jane Flemyng, who languished until
10 Mar. following, when she died at W. *Endorsed.* John
Flemynge, Katherine Skoling, Judith Atkin, Marie Saunders,
Elizabeth Dowset. Billa vera.

Po se Q⁹ nᶜ r.

566. ——, on 20 Nov., 1 Chas. I, at W., bewitched Thomas
Wright, who was killed at W. *Endorsed.* Katherine Skoling,
Judith Atkin, Mary Saunders, Elizabeth Dowset. Billa vera.

Po se Q⁹ nᶜ r.

567. Katherine Kinge of Shaulford, widow, and Anne West,
of Shaulford, widow, on 1 Jan., 1 Chas. I, at S., bewitched Anne
Willett, who languished until 1 Feb. following, when she died at
S. *Endorsed.* Peter Willett. Billa vera.

Po se Q⁹ nc r [both prisoners].

568. Katherine Kinge, etc., " *decimo die instantis mensis Julij,*"
2 Chas. II, at S., bewitched Mary Thorpe, who was wasted and
consumed and yet is. *Endorsed.* James Thorpe. Billa vera.

Po se cul ca null   S⁹.

1627.   Essex Summer Sessions and general gaol delivery holden
        at Chelmsford on 9 July, 3 Chas. I. Commission dated
        25 May, 3 Chas. I.

*Gaol Calendar*

The presentment of the names and facts of the prisoners.

Barbara Auger sent in by Sʳ. Nicholas Coote and accused for
wichery.

569. Barbara Awgar of Upminster, widow, otherwise called
Barbara Bright on 4 May, 21 Jas. I, at U., bewitched Andrew
Parslowe, who languished until 22 May following, when he died
at U. *Endorsed.* Frances Wagstaffe. Billa vera.

Po se Q⁹ nᶜ r.

570. ——, on 30 Aug., 1 Chas. I, at Hornechurch, bewitched Mercy (*Mersiam*) Perry, wife of Thomas P., who languished until 8 April, 3 Chas., when she died at H. *Endorsed.* Thomas Perrey. Billa vera.

Po se Q⁹ nᶜ r.

571. ——, on 20 Oct., 2 Chas. I, at H., bewitched John Perry, aged 4 yrs., son of Thomas P., who languished until 23 Oct., when he died at H. *Endorsed.* Thomas Perrey. Billa vera.

Po se Q⁹ nc r.

1628.　Essex Lent Sessions and general gaol delivery holden at Brentwood on 10 Mar., 3 Chas. I. Commission dated 23 Jan., 3 Chas. I.

*Gaol Calendar of Prisoners in the Castle of Colchester*

572. Anna Freeman for witchcrafte.

[Indictment wanting.[1]]

1630.　Essex Summer Sessions and general gaol delivery holden at Chelmsford [2] on 7 July, 6 Chas. I. Commission dated 28 May, 6 Chas. I.

573. Dionisia Josselyn of Grt. Canfeild, widow, on 1 May, 2 Chas. I, at Grt. C., bewitched Joan Judd, who was wasted and consumed. *Endorsed.* Katherine Judd. Billa vera.

Po se Q⁹ nc r.　repri p batt.

See No. 576.

1630.　Surrey Summer Sessions and general gaol delivery holden at Kingston-on-Thames [3] [July, 6 Chas. I]. Commission dated 28 May, 6 Chas I.

574. Margery Brotherton of Reygate, spinster, wife of Francis B., yeoman, on 1 Oct., 18 Jas. 1, at R., bewitched John, infant son of Thomas Crust, who languished until 20 Oct., when he died at R. *Endorsed.* Anthony Best, John Fuller, William

---

[1] Probably " not found " by the Grand Jury.

[2] Brentwood in margin of commission. The venue is not mentioned on the gaol delivery roll.

[3] Southwark in margin of commission. In 1927 this file was in bundle Assizes 35/171.

Life and his wife, Anne Wonham, John Boules, and Katherine, his wife, Alice Locksley, Robert Ridlie, John Richardson, Edine Greege, John Glover, Elizabeth Ames, Alice Plege, Barbara Ware, Mary Morer, Joan Hurlock, Mary Saunders, Jasper Fuller, Sibil, his wife, Margaret Pullen, Ann Ware, Robert Lewes, Thomas Cruste, and Ann, his wife, Mary Smith, Richard Perrin, Lucy White, William Beckwith, Susan Beckwith, Alice Heath, Susan Richardson, Jane Mason. *Billa vera.*

Po se cul ca null S⁹ Repri pᵗ iudicm.

575. Margery Brotherton and Elizabeth Brotherton of Reygate, spinster, on 1 Mar., 20 Jas. I, at R., bewitched Elizabeth Beckwith, aged . . . , daughter of William Beckwith, who languished until the 14th of the same month, when she died at R. *Endorsed.* Twenty-nine witnesses first above-named. *Billa vera.* Ignoramus p Elizabeth Beckwith (*sic*).

Po se cul ca null S⁹ Repri pᵗ iudicm.

1631. Essex Lent Sessions and general gaol delivery holden at Brentwood on 17 Mar., 6 Chas. I. Commission dated 24 Jan., 6 Chas. I.

576. Dionisia Josselyne of Grt. Canfield, widow, on 1 Apr., 1 Chas. I, at Grt. C., bewitched Joan Judd, who languished until 19 Oct., 6 Chas. I, when she died at Grt. C. *Endorsed.* Katherine Judd, Francis Samon, Joan Greygoose, Ellen Sabyn. *Billa vera.*

Po se Q⁹ nᶜr.

See No. 573.

1631. Kent Summer Sessions and general gaol delivery holden at Maidstone on 20 July, 7 Chas. I. Commission dated 10 June, 7 Chas. I.

577. Katherine Younge of Ash-juxta-Sandwich, spinster, wife of John Y., labourer, on 1 May, 21 Jas. I, at A., bewitched Mary Randall, widow, who was wasted and consumed. *Endorsed.* Joseph Welles, Mary Randall, Vyncent Rynoldes, John Richardson, Mildred Carter, Mary Dye, Sara Vynge, Henry Harfleete, Thomas Addames, George Welles. *Billa vera.*

Po se cul ca null S⁹.

578. ——, on 1 May, 4 Chas. I, at Ash, bewitched Dorcas Welles, aged 5 yrs., daughter of Joseph Welles, who languished until 1 June following, when she died at A. *Endorsed.* Same witnesses. Billa vera.

Po se cul ca null S⁹.

579. Martha Younge of Ash-juxta-Sandwich, spinster, on 1 Apr., 7 Chas. I, at A., bewitched Anne Lacy, aged 4 yrs., daughter of Thomas Lacy, who was wasted and consumed. *Endorsed.* Daniel Pryor, Mary Lacy, William Carleton. Billa vera.

Po se Q⁹ nᵉ r.

*Gaol Delivery Roll*

Katerina Younge   repri vsq ad px.

Martha Younge⎫
  and others  ⎬ Quieti & delibent'.

1634. Essex Lent Sessions and general gaol delivery holden at Chelmsford on 26 Feb., 9 Chas. I. Commission dated 23 Jan., 9 Chas. I.

580. Jane Prentice or Hanby of Harwich Town on 1 Aug., 22 Jas. I, at H., bewitched Cecilia Feild, wife of William F., who languished until 20 October, 22 Jas., when she died at H. *Endorsed.* William Feild. Billa vera.

Po se Q⁹ nc r.
See 588.

*Gaol Delivery Roll*

Jana Pretice als Hanleye [and others]   delibent'.

1635. Kent Summer Sessions and general gaol delivery holden at Maidstone on 8 July, 11 Chas. I. Commission dated 29 May, 11 Chas. I.

581. Mary Butler of Seavenooke, spinster, on 20 Aug., 8 Chas. I, at S., bewitched Katherine Smyth, who was consumed and wasted. *Endorsed.* William Smyth, Elizabeth Wallys. Billa vera.

Po se Q⁹ ncr.

582. ——, on 1 Apr.. 1 Chas. I, at S., bewitched Christopher Patchett, who languished until 1 June, 4 Chas. I, when he died at S. *Endorsed.* Edward Patchett. Billa vera.

Po se Q⁹ nc r.

583. ——, on 1 July, 7 Chas. I., at S., bewitched Bridget Marshall, who languished until 1 June, 10 Chas. I, when she died at S. *Endorsed.* Richard Marshalle. Billa vera.

Po se Q⁹ nᶜr.

1636. Kent Lent Sessions and general gaol delivery holden at Maidstone on 24 Feb., 11 Chas. I. Commission dated 23 Jan., 11 Chas. I.

584. Ellen Tislington of Horton Kirby, spinster, wife of George T. of the same, husbandman, on 1 July, 11 Chas. I, at H. K., bewitched Andrew Lewis, who was wasted. *Endorsed.* Francis Cornewell, Anne Cornwell, Thomas Lewis, Rachael Lewis, Rachael Browne, George Weller, Dionisia Clerke, Margaret Johnson, Elizabeth Staple. Billa vera.

Po se Qta nc r.

1636. Essex Summer Sessions and general gaol delivery holden at Chelmsford on 25 July, 12 Chas. I. Commission dated 7 June, 12 Chas. I.

585. Parnella Bontwood of Brayntree, widow, on 12 Jan., 11 Chas. I, at B., bewitched John Tibball, who languished until 15 Mar., 11 Chas. I, when he died at B. *Endorsed.* Margaret Tibball, Joan Vincent, Elizabeth Hutchin. Billa vera.

Po se Q⁹ nᶜ r.

1638. Essex Summer Sessions and general gaol delivery holden at Chelmsford on 26 June, 14 Chas. I. Commission dated 25 May, 14 Chas. I.

*Gaol Calendar of Prisoners in Colchester Castle*

Jane Prentice, widow.
586. Suzan Prentice, her daughter.
587. Elinor Witherill.

Comitted by Sʳ Harbottle Grimston, Kt. for that they were charged with fellony and witchcraft.

Anne Cate als Downes   committed, etc.

588. Jane Prentice of Harwich, widow, on 1 Mar., 13 Chas. I, at H., bewitched Ruth Hatch, who wasted until the day of taking this inquisition. *Endorsed*. Elizabeth Hatch, Emma Goodwin. Grace Evans. Billa vera.

Po se cul ca null. [*Below*.] Cul ca null repri sine iudico.
See 580.

589. ——, on 10 June, 14 Chas. I, at H., bewitched William Shawe, who languished until 20 June following, when he died at H. *Endorsed*. William Shawe, Emma Goodwyn, Grace Evans. Billa vera.

Po se Q^{ta} n^c r.

590. Anne Cade or Downes of Grt. Holland, spinster, on 10 Apr., 14 Chas. I, at Grt. H., bewitched Susan Rawlinson, who languished until 18 Apr., 14 Chas. I, when she died at Grt. H. *Endorsed*. John Rawlinson, Jane Teespyn, Agnes Feverell, Anne Harris. Billa vera.

Po se Qta n^c r.
See No. 615.

[Gaol delivery roll and indictments Nos. 586–7 wanting.]

1639. Surrey Lent Sessions and general gaol delivery holden at Southwark on 6 Mar., 14 Chas. I. Commission dated 23 Jan., 14 Chas. I.

591. Margery Reynold of Wrecklesham, widow, on 1 Sept., 11 Chas. I, at W., bewitched Margaret Baylie, who languished until 20 Aug., 13 Chas. I, when she died at W. *Endorsed*. John Baylie, Agnes Reynold, George Lockyer. Billa vera.

Po se Q^9 nc r.

592. ——, on 27 Mar., 11 Chas. I, at W., bewitched to death 1 red cow valued at 3*l*. of the goods and chattels of John Baylie at W. *Endorsed as No. 591*.

Po se Qta.

1639. Essex Summer Sessions and general gaol delivery holden at Chelmsford on 29 July, 15 Chas. I. [Commission dated 14 June, 15 Chas. I.]

*Calendar of Prisoners in Gaol at Colchester Castle*

593. Anne Lamperill. widowe. comitted by Edward Eltonhead, Esq., for beinge accused and suspected to be a witch.

594. Robert Garnett, comitted by William Lynne. Esq., for putting his trust in witches and conversing with them to the greate dishonour of God.
[Indictments Nos. 593–4 are wanting.]

*Gaol Delivery Roll*

Anna Lamperell. deliu⁹ed by proclamacon.

Roɓtus Garnett, hee was comitted for conversing with witches and must bee set att worke in the howse of correccon one weeke and then bee deliu⁹ed.

1641. Essex Lent Sessions and general gaol delivery holden at Chelmsford on 5 Mar., 16 Chas. I. [Commission 23 Jan., 16 Chas. I.]

595. Anne West, the elder, of Lawford, widow, on 11 Mar., 16 Chas. I, at L., bewitched to death 1 white sow hog valued at 10s. of the goods and chattels of Thomas Harte. *Endorsed.* Thomas Harte. Billa vera.
Po se Qta nc r.
Triaĩ fuit p jur'm pɳie ad px̃ gaole deliɓaconem put patet iɓm.

1641. Hertford Lent Sessions and general gaol delivery holden at Hertford on 18 Mar., 16 Chas. I. Commission 23 Jan., 16 Chas. I.

596. Elizabeth Peacock of Barkhampsɬed St Peeters, spmster, wife of George P., yeoman, on 24 July, 16 Chas. I, at B., bewitched Ellen Webb, who languished until 3 Aug. following, when she died at B. *Endorsed.* Daniel Webb, Mary Kenninge, Mary Sarman, Mary Wate, Eliza Chaplyn. Billa vera.
Po se Q⁹ nᶜ r.

*Gaol Delivery Roll*

Elizabeth Peacock. Shee is acquitted for murther by witchcrafte but must remaine in gaole till shee finde good sureties to appeare att the next gaole deliu^ye & in the meane tyme to bee of the good behaviour.

1642. Essex Lent Sessions and general gaol delivery holden at Chelmsford on 3 Mar., 17 Chas. I. Commission dated . . . 17 Chas. I.

*Calendar of Prisoners in Gaol at Colchester Castle*

597. Anne Wace. Shee was comitted by S^r. Thomas Bowes, Knt. accordinge to an order which he received from the last Assizes whereby it doth appear that the said Anne standeth indicted of witchcraft and the Courte was further informed that she is a very dangerous pson amongest her neighbours and not able to find very good and sufficient sureties for her appearance at these Assizes.

[Indictments wanting.]

1642. Essex Summer Sessions and general gaol delivery holden at Chelmsford on 18 July, 18 Chas. I. [Commission wanting.]

598. Mary Webb of Hatfeild Broadoake, spinster, wife of Hugh Webb, labourer, on 20 May, 18 Chas. I, at H. B., bewitched Susanna Hycoockes, wife of Richard H., who languished until 5 June following, when she died at H. B. *Endorsed.* Richard Hiccocks, Ellen Skingle, Ann Smee, Sarah Hutley. Billa vera. Po se non cul n^er.

1645. Essex Summer Sessions and general gaol delivery holden at Chelmsford on 17 July, 21 Chas. I. Commission dated 20 June, 21 Chas. I.[1]

[1] A true and exact Relation of the severall Informations, Examinations, and Confessions of the late Witches arraigned . . . and condemned at the late Sessions, holden at Chelmsford before the Right Honorable Robert, Earle of Warwicke, and severall of his Majesties Justices of Peace, the 29 of July, 1645. London 1645. *Collection of Tracts*, printed by J. R. Smith, 1838.

*Calendar of Prisoners in Gaol*

1. Elizabeth Hare
2. Margarett Moone
3. Mary Johnson
4. Mary Greencliffe
5. Anne West
6. Elizabeth Clarke
7. Anne Leech
8. Elizabeth Goodinge
9. Sarah Hateinge
10. Mary Hockett
11. Elizabeth Harvey
12. Joyce Bonds
13. Susanne Cocke
14. Margarett Landishe
15. Sarah Bright
16. Hellen Clarke        These are accused for sorcery & witchcrafte.
17. Anne Cate als Maidenhead
18. Alice Dixon
19. Joane Cooper [*rectius* Anne]
20. Rebecca Jonas
21. Dorothey Brooke
22. Dorothey Walters
23. Mary Wyles
24. Hellen Bretton
25. Mary Starlinge
26. Susanne Wente
27. Bridgett Mayors
28. Anne Thurston &
29. Mary Coppen
30. Anne Cooper [*rectius* Joan]
31. Rose Hallybread        These beinge accused for sorcery and witchcrafte are
32. Elizabeth Gibson &        dead in gaole.
33. Mary Cooke

*Coroner's Inquests*

Rose Hollybread of Chich St Osyth, aged about 65, died 11 June, by the visitation of God. Inq. 12 June, 21 Chas. I.

Elizabeth Gibson, wife of Thomas G. of Thorpe-infra-Socam, farmer, aged about 40 years, died 1 June, by the visitation of God. Inq. 2 June, 21 Chas. I.

Joane Cooper of Grt. Clackton, widow, aged 80, died 27 May, by the visitation of God. Inq. 28 May, 21 Chas. I.

Mary Cooke of Langham, widow, aged 60, died 29 May, by the visitation of God. Inq. 30 May, 21 Chas. 1.

599. Helen Bretton of Curby, spinster. wife of Thomas B., husbandman, on 20 July, 19 Chas. 1, at C., bewitched Henry Giles, son of William G., bricklayer, who languished until 21 July following, when he died at C. *Endorsed.* Ellen Mayors, Elizabeth Hunt, Jane Gates, Thomas Psalter, Richard Cole, John Hill, William Giles. Billa vera.

Po se cul ca null    S⁹ p collū &c̃.

600. Margery Grew of Walton-in-Sooken, spinster, wife of John G., husbandman. on 20 July, 20 Chas., at W., bewitched John Munt, son of Samuel M. of W., who instantly died. *Endorsed.* John Pamant, Samuel Munt, Helen Mager, Elizabeth Hunt. Billa vera.

Po se cul ca null    S⁹ sup at Ind.

601. ——, on 20 Sept., 20 Chas. I, at W-in-S., did entertain, etc., an evil spirit in the likeness of a bird called a jay, etc. *Endorsed.* Samuel Munt, John Panant, Ellen Mayor, Elizabeth Hunt. Billa vera.

Po se cul ca null    S⁹ p collū &c̃.

602. Anne Leach of Mysley, widow, on 25 June, 20 Chas. 1, at Maningtree, bewitched John Edwardes, infant son of Richard E. of Maningtree, gentleman, who languished until 5 July following, when he died at M. *Endorsed.* Matthew Hopkins, John Sterne, Richard Edwards, Susan Edwardes, Billa vera.

Po se cul ca null    S⁹ p collū &c̃.

603. Elizabeth Clarke of Maningtree, spinster, on 25 June, 20 Chas. I, at M., bewitched John Edwardes, son of Richard E. of M., who languished until 5 July following, when he died at M. *Endorsed.* [Same witnesses as No. 602.] Robert Tayler, Edward Parsley. Billa vera.

Po se cul ca null    S⁹ p collū &c̃.

604. ——, on 30 Dec., 20 Chas. I, at M., did entertain, etc.,

four evil spirits, one of them in the likeness of a young white cat called " Holt " : another in the likeness of a " Sandee Spannell " called " Jeremarye " : another in the likeness of a greyhound called " Vineger Tome " : another in the likeness of a black rabbit called " Sacke and Sugar ", so that she might practice witchcraft. *Endorsed.* Matthew Hopkins, John Sterne, Edward Parsley, Mary Phillipps. Frances Mills, widow. Billa vera.

Po se cul ca null S$^9$ sup. al Indcament. *See* Plate 6.

605. Rebecca Jonas of St Osith, widow, on 1 July, 18 Chas. I, at St O., bewitched Katherine Bumpstead, spinster, who instantly died. *Endorsed.* George Eatoney *clericus.* Billa vera.

Po se cul ca null   S$^9$ sup al Ind.

606. ——. on 1 July, 18 Chas. I, at St O.. bewitched Thomas Bumpstead, yeoman, who instantly died. *Endorsed.* George Eatoney *clericus,* Elizabeth Parker, Rose Hankine, Ellen Mayers, Priscilla Brigges. Billa vera.

Po se cul ca null   S$^9$ p collū &c̃.

607. Rebecca West of Lawford, spinster, on 1 June, 20 Chas. I, at L.. did entertain, etc., three evil spirits, one in the likeness of a grey cat called " Germany " : another in the likeness of a white cat called " Newes " : another in the likeness of a young man called " her husband ", so that she might practice witchcraft. Billa vera. John Cutler, Thomas Hart. Billa vera.

[No pleading, verdict, or sentence.]   *See* Plate 6.

608. Anne West of Lawford, widow, on 1 Aug., 15 Chas. I, at L., bewitched John Cutler, son of John C., yeoman, who instantly died. *Endorsed.* John Cutler, John Everrard, Rebecca West. Billa vera.

Po se cul ca null   S$^9$ p collū &c̃.

609. ——. on 10 July, 20 Chas. I, at Maningtree did entertain, etc., evil spirits in the likeness of a dog and of a kitling, etc.

A WITCH HUNTER AND HIS VICTIMS, A.D. 1647
(See Indictments Nos. 604, 607)

From *Discoverie of Witches*

*Endorsed.* John Cutler, John Everrard, John Eedes *clericus*, Thomas Hart. Billa vera.

Po se cul ca null S⁹ al Indcament.

610. Margaret Moone of Thorpe, widow, on 1 July, 16 Chas. I, at T., bewitched Joan Cornewell, daughter of Henry C. of T., yeoman, who languished until 1 Oct. following, when she died at T. *Endorsed.* Henry Cornewell, Beavis *V*incent, Thomas Barles. Billa vera.

Po se cul ca null S⁹ p collū &c̃.

611. ——, on 25 June, 20 Chas. I. at T., bewitched John Edwardes, infant son of Richard E. of Manningtree, who languished until 5 July following, when he died at M. *Endorsed.* Henry Cornewell, Beavis Vincent, Thomas Barles. Billa vera.

Po se cul ca null S⁹ p collū &c̃ sup al indicament.

612. ——, on 20 May, 19 Chas. I, at T., bewitched to death 1 black cow valued at 3*l.* of the goods and chattels of Thomas Cooker. *Endorsed.* [Same witnesses as No. 611.] Billa vera.

Po se cul S⁹ sup al ind.

613. Mary Sterling of Langham, spinster, wife of John S. of L., yeoman, on 17 May, 21 Chas. I, at L., did entertain, etc., two evil spirits each in the likeness of a mole, etc. *Endorsed.* Francis Mills, Isaac Bemish, Grace Norman. Billa vera.

Po se cul ca null S⁹ p collū &c̃.

614. ——, on 10 Jan., 20 Chas. I, at L., bewitched Robert Potter of L., yeoman, who languished until 9 Feb. following, when he died at L. *Endorsed.* Widow Mills, Grace Norman, John Sterne, Thomas Read, Matthew Hopkins, Henry Talbott, Elisha Cole, Isaac Bevis. Billa vera.

Po se non cul nᶜr S⁹ sup al Ind & repri pᵗ Judicm.

615. Anne Cate of Holland, spinster, on 7 May, 15 Chas. I, at H., bewitched Susanna Rowlinson, daughter of John R. of Holland, butcher, who languished until 10 May following when she died at H. *Endorsed.* Edward Darrell, John Alderton, Samuel Ray, John Rowlinson, Christopher Fuller, Frances

Throten, — Freeman, widd., Ellen Mayers, widd., Elizabeth Hunt. Billa vera.

Po se cul ca null   S⁹ p collū &c̃.

See No. 590.

616. Anne Cade or Maidenhead of Grt. Holland, spinster, on 10 May, 20 Chas. I, at Grt. H., bewitched Grace Ray, wife of Samuel R. of Grt. H., yeoman, who languished until 10 June following, when she died at Grt. H. *Endorsed.* John Aldarton, Samuel Wray, Frank Drawton, . . . Freeman, *vid.*, George Barney, William Freeman, John Rawlinson. Billa vera.

Po se cul ca null   S⁹ sup al Indcament.

617. Alice Dixon of Wivenhoe, widow, on 20 Mar., 15 Chas. I, at W., bewitched Thomas Mumford, son of John M., of W., husbandman, who languished until 20 July, 16 Chas. I, when he died at W. *Endorsed.* Margaret Mumford. Billa vera.

Po se cul ca null   S⁹ p collū &c̃.

618. Mary Johnson of Wivenhoe, spinster, wife of Nicholas J. of W., seaman, on 8 Apr., 21 Chas. I, at W., did entertain, etc., three evil spirits, two in the likenesses of rats, and one in the likeness of a mouse, etc. *Endorsed.* Ellen Mayors, Elizabeth Hunt, Anne Darrell, Priscilla Briggs. Billa vera.

Po se cul ca null   S⁹ p collū &c̃.   Repr⁹ post Judicm.

619. ——, on 20 June, 19 Chas. I, at W., bewitched William Durrell, son of George D., of Fingrigoe, seaman, who languished until 25 June following, when he died at F. *Endorsed.* Anne Durrell, Priscilla Brigs, Ellen Mayor, Elizabeth Hunt. Billa vera.

Po se non cul nᶜ r.

620. ——, on 20 June, 19 Chas. I, at W., bewitched Elizabeth Occlam, daughter of Daniel O. of W., who languished until 23 June following, when she died at W. *Endorsed.* Elizabeth Occlam. Billa vera.

Po se non cul nᶜr.

621. Joan Rowle of Lee, widow, on 1 Feb., 20 Chas. I, at L., bewitched Rachael North, daughter of John N., who was

" wounded and consumed ". *Endorsed.* Rachael North, . . . Dreamer, Anne Chapill, *Samuel* Read, Martha Barnad, Ellen Emere, Elizabeth Osborne, Mary Lam. Billa vera.

Po se non cul n^c r.

622. ——, on 6 July, 19 Chas. I, at L., bewitched Rachael North, daughter of John N., who languished until 20 July following, when she died at L. *Endorsed.* [*Same witnesses as No.* 621.] Billa vera.

Po se non cul n^c r.

623. ——, on 1 July, 19 Chas. I, at L., bewitched John North of L., who languished until 7 July following, when he died at L. *Endorsed.* [*Same witnesses as No.* 621.] Billa vera.

Po se non cul n^c r.

624. Mary Coppin of Curby, spinster, wife of John C., husbandman, on 20 July, 20 Chas. I, at C., bewitched Alice Astin, daughter of William A. of C., bricklayer, who instantly died. *Endorsed.* Ellen Mayors, Elizabeth Hunt, William Astin. Billa vera.

Po se cul ca null S^9 p collū &c̃. [Reprieved G.D.R.]

625. Ellen Clarke, wife of Thomas C. of Manningtree, mason, on 5 Apr., 19 Chas. I, at M., bewitched Anne Parsley of M., spinster, who languished until 5 May following, when she died at M. *Endorsed.* Matthew Hopkins, Susan Edwards, John Sterne, Grace Norman, Edward Parsley. Billa vera.

Po se cul ca null S^9 p collū &c̃.

626. Sarah Bright of Maningtree, widow, on 25 June, 20 Chas. I, at M., bewitched Anne Woolvett, daughter of Henry W. of M., mason, who languished until 27 June following, when she died at M. *Endorsed.* Winterflood, *vid.,* vx Henr. Woolvett, Applegate, vid., Eliza Potter, vid. Billa vera.

Po se cul ca null S^9 p collū &c̃.

627. Elizabeth Goodwyn of Manningtree, spinster, wife of Edward Goodwyn of M., labourer, on 15 June, 20 Chas. I, at M., bewitched John Edwardes, infant son of Richard E., gent., who languished until 5 July following, when he died at M.

*Endorsed.* Susanna Edwardes, Rebecca West, Mary Philipps. Billa vera.

Po se cul ca null   S⁹ p collū &c̃.

628.  ——,¹ on 5 Oct., 20 Chas. I, at M., did entertain. etc., two evil spirits each in the likeness of a young cat, one named " Mouse " and the other " Pease ". *Endorsed.* Susanna Edwardes, Matthew Hopkins, Grace Norman, Jonathan Freelove, John Sterne.   Billa vera.

Po se cul ca null   S⁹ p collū &c̃.

629. Dorothy Waters of Clacton, spinster, wife of Robert W. of C., labourer, on 2 June, 21 Chas. I, at C., did entertain, etc., an evil spirit in the likeness of a dun coloured mouse, etc. *Endorsed.*  Joseph Longe, Richard Cole.   Billa vera.

Po se cul ca null   S⁹ p collū &c̃.   Repri pt Judicm.

630.  Elizabeth Heare of Grt. Clacton, spinster, wife of Thomas H. of Grt. C., yeoman, on 2 Apr., 21 Chas. I, at C., did entertain, etc., an evil spirit in the likeness of a squirrel, etc.  *Endorsed.* Roger Himpson, Joseph Knights.   Billa vera.

Po se cul na null   S⁹ p collū &c̃.

631. Mary Wiles of Grt. Clacton, widow, on 3 Feb., 14 Chas. I, at Grt. C., bewitched Anne de Greate, daughter of Michael de G. of Grt. C., yeoman, who instantly died.  *Endorsed.* Joseph Longe, Richard Cole, Ellen Mayors, Elizabeth Hunt. Billa vera.

Po se cul ca null   S⁹ p collū sup al indcament.

632.  ——, on 20 Dec., 20 Chas. I., at Grt. C., bewitched Anthony Blowers, son of Edward B. of Grt. C., yeoman, who instantly died.  *Endorsed.*  Edward Blowers, Joseph Longe, Richard Cole, Ellen Mayers, Elizabeth Hunt, Priscilla Brigges. Billa vera.

Po se cul ca null   S⁹ p collū &c̃.

633.  ——, on 3 Feb., 14 Chas. I, at Grt. C., bewitched George Fossitt of Grt. C., yeoman, who was greatly wounded and

¹ She is here described as Elizabeth Goodine, wife of Edward G., cordwainer.  The gaol delivery roll has Gooding.

consumed. *Endorsed.* Richard Cole, Joseph Longe, Alexander Bryon, Ellen Mayers, Elizabeth Hunt, Anne Martyn. Billa vera.

Po se non cul n$^c$ r.

634. Anne Cooper of Grt. Clackton, spinster, wife of John C. of Grt. C., labourer, on 10 Apr., 21 Chas I, at Grt. C., bewitched James Curstissurre, son of John C., who languished until 11 Apr. following, when he died at Grt. C. *Endorsed.* John Curstifarre, Joseph Longe. Billa vera.

Po se cul ca null S$^9$ p collū &c̃.

635. ———, on 12 Apr., 12 Chas. 1, at Grt. C., bewitched Mary Knights, aged 5 yrs., daughter of John K., who languished until 20 May following, when she died at Grt. C. *Endorsed.* Joseph Longe, Roger Hempsson, Ellen Mayers, Elizabeth Hunt, Anne Martyn. Billa vera.

Po se non cul n$^c$ r.

636. ———, on 3 Mar., 21 Chas. 1, at Grt. C., did entertain, etc., three evil spirits each in the likeness of a mole called " Winne ", " Jezo ", " Pa*nne* ", etc. *Endorsed.* Joseph Longe *clericus*, Anne Martyn, Roger Hempsson. Billa vera.

Po se non cul n$^c$ r.

637. Anne Therston of Grt. Holland, spinster, wife of Edward T. of Grt. H., husbandman, on 1 May, 20 Chas. I, at Grt. H., did entertain, etc., two evil spirits, one in the likeness of a bird, and the other in the likeness of a mouse, etc. *Endorsed.* Samuel Wray, John Alderton. Billa vera.

Po se cul ca null S$^9$ p collū &c̃ Repri p$^t$ Judicm.

638. ———, on 10 May, 20 Chas. I, at Grt. H., bewitched to death 1 black cow valued at 5s. (*sic*) of the goods and chattels of John Aldurton of Grt. H., yeoman. *Endorsed.* John Aldurton, Samuel Wray. Billa vera.

Po se non cul nc r.

639. Susan Cocke of Chette St Osith, spinster, wife of John C. of C. St O., husbandman, on 1 Feb., 20 Chas. I, at C. St O., did entertain, etc., an evil spirit in the likeness of a

yellow cat, etc. *Endorsed.* Rose Handkin, Elizabeth Parker, George Eatoney. Billa vera.

Po se cul ca null    S⁹ p collū &c̃.

640. Joyce Boones of Chette St Osith, spinster, wife of William Boones of C. St O., yeoman, on 1 Feb., 20 Chas. I, at C. St O., did entertain, etc., two evil spirits one called " Jockey ", and one called " Rugge ", etc. *Endorsed.* [*Same witnesses as No.* 639.]   Billa vera.

Po se cul ca null    S⁹ p collū &c̃.

641. Margaret Landish of Chette St Osith, spinster, wife of William L. of C. St O., husbandman, on 25 Apr., 21 Chas. I, at C. St O., bewitched Thomas Bragge, who was consumed and wasted. *Endorsed.* Robert Turner, Elizabeth Parker, Rose Handkins.   Billa vera.

Po se cul ca null    S⁹ p collū &c̃.

642. Sarah Hatyn or Hating of Ramsey, spinster, wife of William H. of R., tailor, on 10 June, 16 Chas. I, at R., bewitched Lionel Jefferson, who languished until 10 July following, when he died at R. *Endorsed.* Robert Hayward, William Joy. Billa vera.

Po se cul ca null    S⁹ p collū &c̃.

643. ——, on 20 May, 17 Chas. I, at R., did entertain, etc., two evil spirits each in the likeness of a mouse. *Endorsed.* Bridget Reynolds, Joan Taylor, Mary Edwards, Mary Phillipps, William Jay, Robert Hayward.   Billa vera.

Po se cul ca null    S⁹ sup at Ind.

644. ——, on 17 May, 17 Chas. I, at R., bewitched Thomas Greene, who languished until 20 July, 17 Chas. I, when he died at R. *Endorsed.* [*Same witnesses as No.* 643.]

Po se cul ca null    S⁹ sup at Indcament.

645. Elizabeth Harvy of Ramsey, widow, on 14 Apr., 21 Chas. I, at R., did entertain, etc., three evil spirits each in the likeness of a red mouse. *Endorsed.* [*Four witnesses first named*

# APPENDIX I.

## Essex Gaol Delivery Roll, Summer 1645.[1]

Essex ss

Delibaco gaole dni Regis com su Essex tent apud Chellmsford in eodm com dic Jovis decimo septimo die Julij Anno regni dni nri Caroli dei gra Angli Scocie ffranc & hibnie Regis fidei defensoris &c vicesimo primo coram Robto comite Warwici Johe Barrington milite & Barronetto Martino lumley milite & Barronetto Henrico Holcroft milite Henr Mildmay de Wanstead milite Wilto Conyers Ar & alijs socijs suis Justic dci dni Regis ad gaolam suam com su Essex pd de prisonibz in ea existen deliband assign.

---

Robtus Griffeth p roboria. hee was attainted att Sumer Assizes in the xviijth of his matie: reigne for seuerall robberies in the highway but was reprived by a speciall warrant from his matie & was then ordered to remaine in gaole without baile & must remaine in gaole according to the said order

Maria Ashwood p murdr spui Shee is attainte for the murder aforesaid att the last gaole deliuerye but was reprived after judgmt: & must remaine in gaole vntill the next gaole deliuerye

Franciscus Smyth hee is attainte for two seuerall robberies but is reprived from execucon by the space of tenn daies next ensuinge this 22th day of July 1645. And if before that time nee pcure not a further reprive hee is then to be executed:

Maria Coppine. Shee is attainte for murder by witchcrafte but was reprived after judgmt vppon desire of Mr Gray the minister & must remaine in gaole without baile vntill the next gaole deliuerye.

Elizabeth Codwell. Shee is attainte for murthernge of her bastard child but because shee is found by a jury of matrons to bee with quicke child execucon of her is to bee staid vntill one month after her deliuerye & then execucon to bee done of her.

Jacobus Langden. hee is acquitted of two seuerall robberies in the highway but must remaine in gaole vntill hee find good suerties to appeare att the next gaole deliuerye & in the meantime to bee of the good behaviour

Edrus Orton. hee is comitted for that hee is vehementlie suspected to have robbed vppon the highway & must remaine in gaole without baile vntill the next quarter Sessions to bee holden for this County & then to bee bailed if the court shall thinke fitt to appeare att the next gaole deliuerye to bee holden for this county & in the meanetime to bee of the good behaviour

Johanna Rowle. Shee is acquitted vppon three seuerall murders by witchcraft but must remaine in gaole vntill snee find very good baile for her psonall appearance att the next gaole deliuerye & in the meanetime to bee of the good behaviour.

Anna Bragg She was formlie comitted by Sr Thomas Bowes for suspicon of murthering her bastard child but because none to psecute agt: her Sr Thomas Bowes is desred to examine this businesse & to baile her if hee shall thinke fitt to appeare att the next gaole deliuerye & to bee of the good behaviour.

Matheus Pett als Powell. hee was comitted by Robert Smith Esq, for diuers misdeameanors & must bee sett att worke in the howse of correccon vntill the next Sessions to bee holden for this county.

Willus Gilford. Ignoramus. hee is deliuered by pclamacon.

[To face page 231]

---

Samuel Nayler p furacone eque
Thomas Bristowe p duobz spadon
Johes Page p cons
Johes Creede p burglar
Johes ffreake p combust domoz
Susanna Went p fo spirit malu
Brigitta Mayers p cons
Elizabeth Harvey p cons
Susan Cooke p cons
Dorothea Waters p cons
Anna Thurstone p cons
Maria Johnson p cons &
Maria Sterlinge p cons

> Theise are attainte for the seuerall offences aforesaid and were reprived after jugdmt and must remaine in gaole without baile vntill the next gaole deliuerye.

---

Francu hamond p equa
Thomas Moore p murdro
Ricus Sheppd p burglar
Henr Mills p octo ovibz
Thomas Jackson p quinq porcis &
Willo Peakine p ove val xjd.

> Theise are aquitted for the seuerall felonies aforesaid & may be deliuered payinge their fees

---

Maria Greeneliffe
Dorothea Brooke &
Patiencia Peake

> Theise bee deliuered by pclamacon but must find good suerties to appeare att the next gaole deliuerye & in the meantime to bee of the good behaviour

---

Elizabeth Clarke p murdro & fo : spirit
Annan leach p murdro p incantacon
Rebecca Jonas p duobz murdris incantacon
Hellena Bretton p murdro
Margaret Grewe p murdro & spirit
Margaret Moone p duobz murdr
Anna Cade als Maidenhead p cons
Ellena Clarke p cons
Sara Bright p cons
Elizabeth Goodine p murdr & fo. spirit
Anna West p murdr & fo : spirit
Sarah hatinge p murdr duobz & fo
Maria Wiles p duobz murdr
Anna Coop p murdr
Alicia Dixon p murdr
Margaret landish p vastac in corpore
Elizabeth Hare p fo : spiritu malu
Mariana Hockett p cons &
Jocosa Boones p cons
Thomas Jones p lo val. xxs.
Johes Wattson p lo val ijs &
Wiltus Chapman p duobz vxor'

> These are attainte for the seuerall offences aforesaid & must bee hanged by the necke vntill they be dead.

> Theise had their clergie werebranded in the hand & may bee deliuered.

---

[1] Assizes 35/86. Essex file. This gaol delivery roll is endorsed on the list of bailiffs and constables.

*in No.* 643.] John Batteny, John Felgate. Francis Stock, John Battley. Billa vera.

Po se cul ca null   S⁹ p collū &c̃.

646. Mary Hockett of Ramsey, widow, on 14 Apr., 21 Chas. I, at R., did entertain three evil spirits each in the likeness of a mouse, called " Littleman ", " Prettyman ", and " Daynty ". *Endorsed.* [*First six witnesses named in No.* 645.] John Sterne. Billa vera.

Po se cul ca null   S⁹ p collū &c̃.

647. Bridget Mayers of Holland, spinster, wife of George M. of H., seaman, on 6 May, 21 Chas. I, at H., did entertain an evil spirit in the likeness of a mouse called " Prickeares ". *Endorsed.* John Alderton. Samuel Ray. John Rawlinson, John Basslitt, Frances Throten, . . . Freeman, vid., Ellen Mayers, Bridget Hunt, Dorothy Waltas. Billa vera.

Po se cul ca null   S⁹ p collū &c̃.

648. Susanna Went of Langham, widow, on 1 Apr., 20 Chas. I, at L., did entertain, etc., two evil spirits each in the likeness of a black mole, etc. *Endorsed.* Widow Mills, Grace Norman, Anne Wright, Matthew Hopkins, Nicholas Freeman. Billa vera.

Po se cul ca null   S⁹ p collū &c̃.

### *Gaol Delivery Roll*

### See Appendix I opposite.

[Nearly three years later Mary Coppinge, Bridget Mayers, Anne Thurston, Mary Johnston, and Mary Starlinge were still in prison according to the roll of the gaol delivery held at Chelmsford on 22 Mar., 23 Chas. I [1648]. Assizes 35/88. They were to be kept in gaol until delivered by due course of law. Assizes 35/89.]

### 1647. Essex Lent Sessions and general gaol delivery holden at . . Commission dated 12 Feb., 22 Chas. I.

649. Nicholas Leech of Maningtree, labourer, on 16 Mar., 22 Chas. I, at M., bewitched Anthony Snelling, son of Anthony S.,

who languished until 2 Apr., 23 Chas. 1, when he died at M. *Endorsed.* Anthony Snelling, Susan Snelling. Ignoramus.

650. Helen Disse of Redgewell, spinster. wife of John D. of R., labourer, on 20 Feb., 21 Chas. I, at R., bewitched Elizabeth Manwood, wife of William M., who languished until 10 Aug., 22 Chas. I, when she died at R. *Endorsed.* William Manwood, William Wade, Henry Warren. Ignoramus.

1647. Kent Lent Sessions and general gaol delivery holden at Maidstone on 22 Mar., 22 Chas. I. [Commission dated 12 Feb., 22 Chas. I.]

651. Hester Browne of Higham, widow, on 20 Aug., 21 Chas. I. at H., bewitched to death a black cow valued at 5*l.* of the goods and chattels of Thomas Harvy of H., yeoman. *Endorsed.* Thomas *H*odrey, Elizabeth Pare, Mary *B*eane.

Po se non cul Q<sup>a</sup>.

652. ——, on 6 Sept., 22 Chas. I, at H., bewitched to death a sorrell horse valued at 8*l.* of the goods and chattels of Thomas Peachey of H., yeoman. *Endorsed.* Thomas Pechey, Mary Beane, Widdow Peare. Billa vera.

Po se non cul Q<sup>a</sup>.

653. ——, on 20 Mar., 21 Chas. I, at H., bewitched to death 2 white ewe sheep valued at 10*s.* each of the goods and chattels of Thomas Wakelyn of H., yeoman. *Endorsed.* Thomas Wakelyn, Mary Beane, Elizabeth Pare. Billa vera.

Po se non cul Q<sup>a</sup>.

654. ——, on 1 Oct., 20 Chas. I, at H., bewitched to death a grey gelding valued at 40*s.* of the goods and chattels of William Browne of H., yeoman. *Endorsed.* William Browne, Elizabeth Pare, Mary Beane. Billa vera.

Po se non cul Q<sup>a</sup>.

655. ——, on 11 Mar., 20 Chas. I, at H., bewitched Elizabeth Rothery, daughter of William R. of H., labourer, who languished until 12 Mar. following, when she died at H. *Endorsed.* William Rothery, Mary Beane, Elizabeth Pare. Billa vera.

Po se non cul Q<sup>a</sup>.

1647. Surrey Lent Sessions and general gaol delivery holden at . . . Commission dated 12 Feb., 22 Chas. I.

656. Anne Jackson [erased] of the parish of St Saviour's, Southwark Borough, widow, on 1 Feb., 22 Chas. I, at St S., bewitched Sarah Gilbert, wife of George G., who languished until 14 Feb., 22 Chas. I, when she died at St S. *Endorsed.* Anne Burnham, Lettice Gately, George Hewett, George Gilbert. Ignoramus.

1647. Essex Summer Sessions and general gaol delivery holden at Brentwood on 11 Aug., 23 Chas. I. Commission dated 12 July, 23 Chas. I.

657. Jane Lavender of Navestocke, spinster, wife of Francis L. of N., tailor, on 20 June, 23 Chas. I, at N., bewitched Margaret Cole, spinster, who was wasted and consumed. *Endorsed.* Joan Cole, Sarah Wyer. Billa vera.
Po se non cul n$^{cr}$ Q$^a$.

658. ——, on 1 Jan., 22 Chas. I, at N., bewitched Anne Hawkes, who languished until 1 Apr., 23 Chas. I, when she died at N. *Endorsed.* Thomas Hawkes, Winifred Norris, Ruth Sherbolt. Ignoramus.

659. Francis Lavender of Navestocke, yeoman, on 1 Jan., 19 Chas. I, at N., bewitched Mary Peirce, wife of Richard P., who languished until 1 Mar., 19 Chas. I, when she died at N. *Endorsed.* Thomas Hawkes, Richard Peirce, Winifred Norris, Ruth Sherbolt. Billa vera.
Po se non cul n$^{cr}$ Q$^9$.

660. ——, on 1 July, 23 Chas. I, at N., bewitched Sarah Wyer, wife of John W., who was wasted and consumed. *Endorsed.* Sarah Wyer, Joan Cole, John Stapler, Robert Crabbe, William Small. Billa vera.
Po se non cul n$^{cr}$ Q$^9$.

661. ——, on 20 July, 23 Chas. I, at N., bewitched to death 2 calves of William Hone of N., yeoman. *Endorsed.* William Hone. Ignoramus.

1647.  Hertford Summer Sessions and general gaol delivery
holden at Hertford on 16 Aug., 23 Chas. 1.  Commission
dated 12 July, 23 Chas. I.

662.  Margaret Burby of Barley, widow, on 20 May, 19 Chas. I,
at B., bewitched Thomas Skepp, who languished until 10 Sept.,
19 Chas. I, when he died at B.  *Endorsed.*  John Witham,
Henry Witham, Stephen Rusted.  Billa vera.

Po se non cul n$^{cr}$ Q$^a$.

663.  ——, on 1 May, 23 Chas. I, at B., bewitched Robert
Pattin, who was wasted and consumed.  *Endorsed.*  Robert
Pattin, Hester Skippe, Jane Winne, Susan Welles, Maria Cropp-
well, Elizabeth Rayner.  Billa vera.

Po se non cul n$^{cr}$ Q$^a$.

664.  Elizabeth Browne of Chesthunt, spinster, wife of William
B., glover, on 1 July, 14 Chas. I, at C., bewitched Mary Addams,
wife of Thomas A., who languished until 14 May, 17 Chas. I,
when she died at C.  *Endorsed.*  Thomas Addams, Sarah
Manssefeild, Katherine Yates, Sarah Pecksely, Mary Rashe.
Billa vera.

Po se cul ca null  repr ante Judic.

665.  Margaret Cotterell of Lit. Munden, spinster, wife of
Robert C. of Lit. M., gentleman, on 1 Mar., 7 Chas. I, at M.,
bewitched Lady Anne Holmes, wife of Henry H. of M., knight,
who was wasted and consumed in her body and legs.  *Endorsed.*
Lady Anne Holme.  Ignoramus.[1]

1648.  Kent Summer Sessions and general gaol delivery holden
at Sevenoaks on 5 Sept., 24 Chas. 1.  [Commission
dated 15 June, 24 Chas. I.]

*Gaol Delivery Roll*

666.  Anne Radwell for witchcraft . . . Attainted of seu$^9$all
felonyes att former gaole deliu$^9$yes and must bee
kept in gaole without bayle.
[Indictment wanting.]

---

[1] At the same Assizes Robert Cotterell, *aurifaber*, was indicted
for stealing household articles of Lady Holme, 1 July, 18 Chas. I.

## Commonwealth, 1649-1659

1649.   Essex Summer Sessions and general gaol delivery holden at Chelmsford on 26 July, 1649.  Commission dated 12 June, 1649.

*Gaol Calendar*

667.   Ruth Stephens   she was comitted by Sr John Barrington. Knight and Barronett and charged with suspition of witchcrafte.   Shee is dead.

1649.   Kent Summer Sessions and general gaol delivery holden at Maidstone on 10 July, 1649.   Commission dated 12 June, 1649.

668. Sarah Kempsely of Breadhurst, spinster, wife of John K. of B., on 1 Mar., 1648 [1649], at Rayneham, bewitched to death 1 grey " rooned " gelding valued at 8*l.*, 1 black mare valued at 3*l.*, 1 white gelding valued at 3*l.*, 1 dun gelding valued at 5*l.*, 1 black heifer valued at 3*l.*, 1 red heifer valued at 3*l.*, 1 red and white cow valued at 6*l.* of the goods and chattels of John Hartly of R., yeoman. *Endorsed.* John Hartly, Thomas Sorte. Billa vera.

Po se non cul Q$^a$.

669. ——, on 10 Feb., 1648 [1649], at R., bewitched Jane Hasnett, wife of John H. at R., who was wasted and consumed. *Endorsed.* Jane Hasnett.  Ignoramus.

670. Susan Morefeild of Boughton Bleane, widow, on 16 June, 1649, at B. B., bewitched George Shrubshall, who was " wasted and distempered ". *Endorsed.* William Shrubshall. Billa vera.

Po se non cul n$^{cr}$ Q$^a$.

671. ——, on 5 Sept., 23 Chas. I. at B. B.. bewitched Alice Waller, daughter of Mark W., who languished until 1 Oct., 23 Chas. I, when she died at B. B. *Endorsed.* Mark Waller, William Hilles. Billa vera.

Po se non cul n$^{cr}$ Q$^a$.

1650.   Hertford Lent Sessions and general gaol delivery holden at Hertford on 11 Mar., 1649 [1650].   Commission dated 4 Feb., 1649 [1650].

672. William Litchfeild of Yardley, labourer, and Prudence Litchfeild, his wife, on 10 June, 24 Chas. I, at Y., bewitched 1 black cow valued at 6*l.* of the goods and chattels of William Halfehead of Y., yeoman, which was wasted and consumed. *Endorsed.* William Halfehead, Frances Burges. Billa vera adver' Prudence L. Ignoramus adver' W. L.

[No plea, verdict nor sentence.]

673. Anne Man of Ashwell, widow, on 20 May, 24 Chas. I, at A., bewitched to death 4 bay geldings valued at 10*l.* each of the goods and chattels of Thomas Plumer of A., yeoman, *Endorsed.* William Plumer, Frances Burges, John Blewett, John Boothes. Billa vera.

Po se non cul.

### *Gaol Delivery Roll*

Prudence Lichfeild indicted of witchcraft and trespass to remain in gaol till she find sufficient sureties to appear at the next gaol delivery to be holden for this county.[1]

1650.    Essex Summer Sessions and general gaol delivery holden at Chelmsford on 10 Aug., 1650. Writ dated 3 July, 1650.

674. Elizabeth Balden of Knebworth, widow, on 10 Apr., 1650, at K., bewitched to death 1 bay gelding valued at 10*l.* of the goods and chattels of Richard Milton. *Endorsed.* Richard Milton. Billa vera.

Po se non cul.

### *From a Miscellaneous Bundle* [2]

675. Mary Welby of Newport Pond, widow, on 10 May, 1650, at K., bewitched 1 gray horse valued at 10*l.* of the goods and chattels of Richard Milton. *Endorsed.* Richard Milton, Frances Burges. Ignoramus.

---

[1] I found this entry in bundle Assizes 35/92. indictment No. 672, being in bundle Assizes 35/90.

[2] Possibly of later date.

676. Elizabeth Whitlocke of Grt. Chesterfeild on 20 Sept., 1649, at Grt. C., bewitched Roger Rayner, who languished until 10 Oct., when he died at Grt. C. *Endorsed.* Alice Rayner, Margaret Reynolds, Katherine Basse, Jane Rookes, Dorothy Glover, Elizabeth Swallow, Helen Reynolds, Frances Burges. Ignoramus.

677. Deborah Naylor of Elsingham, widow, on 20 Sept., 20 Chas. I, at E., bewitched John Pakeman, who languished until 10 Mar. following, when he died at E. *Endorsed.* John Crabb, Trew Wade. Ignoramus.

1650. Surrey Summer Sessions and general gaol delivery holden at Croydon on 29 July, 1650. Writ dated 3 July, 1650.

*Gaol Calendar*

678. Lucy Norman committed upon suspicion of witchcrafte. [Indictment wanting.]

1651. Essex Lent Sessions and general gaol delivery holden at Chelmsford on 5 Mar., 1650 [1651]. Commission dated 5 Feb., 1650 [1651].[1]

*Gaol Calendar*

Joane Waight   shee was comitted by Thomas Cooke of Chishull Esq[r] beinge charged to have vsed the Arte of Witchcrafte and to have a familiar spirit come to her and sucke her as hathe bene deposed before the said Justice.

679. Joan Wayte of Grt. Barneston, spinster, wife of Robert W. of B., labourer, on 29 Aug., 1650, at Audleyend, did entertain, employ, and feed an evil spirit called a butterfly. *Endorsed.* Francis Burges, William Cane, Humfrey Bright, Randall Nottage, Margery vx eius, Margaret Otley. Ignoramus.

*Full Latin transcript, p. 91 supra*

680. ——, on 10 May, 1649, at Grt. B., bewitched Dorothy Wood, spinster, who was greatly wasted. *Endorsed.* [Same witnesses as No. 679.] Ignoramus.

[1] Assizes 35/91, but the gaol calendar was found in Assizes 35/92.

*Gaol Delivery Roll*

Delivered by proclamation and may be discharged paying  . .
fees.

**1651.**    Surrey Summer Sessions and general gaol delivery
holden at Kingston-on-Thames, on 16 July, 1651.
Commission dated 7 June, 1651.

681. Susan Smith,[1] wife of William S. of Reigate, labourer.
Susan Humfrey of Reigate, widow, and Alice Tapner of Reigate,
widow, on 20 Mar., 1650 [1651], at R., bewitched Jonas
Humphrey, who was much weakened, wasted and consumed.
*Endorsed.* Jonas Humfrey, Gilbert Swayne, Giles Thornton.
Alice Baker, Robert Smith, William Mathew.   A true bill ag^t
all but Susan Smith ag^t whom we doe not find the Bill.

Pu se not guilty nor fly [Humfrey and Tapner].

682. Frances Heyward, wife of Richard H. of Lambeth,
labourer, on 10 Jan., 1650 [1651], at L., bewitched Elizabeth
Bull, wife of John B., who was wasted and consumed.   *Endorsed.*
Sworne. John Griffen, John Bull, Margaret Griffen, Mary
Clare, Joyce Holman, Elizabeth Smith, Anne Bowman, Mary
Cooper, Goodwife Swabey, — Morgan.   A true bill.

Pu se not guilty nor fly  disch.

**1652.**    Essex Summer Sessions and general gaol delivery holden
at Chelmsford on 4 Aug., 1652.   Commission dated
30 June, 1652.

*Gaol Calendar*

Elizabeth Hynes.   Shee was comitted by Sir Thomas Bowes
Knt., beinge charged for that shee hath confessed
of her selfe that shee entertaynes twoe impes or
evill spirittes in the shape or likenes of kittlinges
and that the said kitlinges each night come to
her and suck of her body.

683. Elizabeth Hynes of Thorpe, spinster, on 11 Apr., 1652, at
T., employed two evil spirits one in the likeness of a white kitten
called Bes and another in the likeness of a black kitten called

---

[1] Her name is deleted, the bill not being found.

Katt. *Endorsed.* Thomas Marsh, Judith Ealey, Henry King, Abraham Barrell, Ruth Marsh, Mary Porter. We doe not find this to be a true bill.

1652. Kent Summer Sessions and general gaol delivery holden at Maidstone on 27 July, 1652. Commission dated 30 June, 1652.[1]

684. Susan Pickenden of Halden, spinster, wife of John P. of H., labourer, on 28 Oct., 1648, at H., bewitched Elizabeth Lowes, daughter of William L., aged about 17 yrs., who languished until 8 Mar. following, when she died at H. *Endorsed.* Elizabeth Lowes. Wee doe finde this to be a true bill.

Pu se guilty noe goodes hanged.

685. ——, on 26 May, 1652, at H., bewitched Anne Taylor, aged about 11 yrs., daughter of Dorothy T., widow, who languished until 26 June following, when she died at H. *Endorsed.* Margaret Riggaby, Dorothy Taylor, Elizabeth Lowes, Mary Hely, Daniel Holland. Wee finde this to be a true bill.

Pu se not guilty nor fly Acq$^t$.

686. ——, on 2 Feb., 1648 [1649], at H.. bewitched Thomas Holland, aged 23 yrs., who languished until 2 Apr., 1650, when he died at H. *Endorsed.* Daniel Holland. Wee doe finde this to be noe true bill.

687. Thomas Willson of the Isle of Grayne, labourer, and Jane W., his wife, on 1 Apr., 1648, at I. of G., bewitched 3 white hogs valued at 10s. each, and 33 quarters of wheat of the goods and chattels of Robert Clifford, which were wasted and consumed at I. of G. *Endorsed.* Robert Clifford. Wee finde this to be a true bill.

Pu se guilty imprisonment according to the statute, &c. [Both prisoners.]

[1] A Prodigious and Tragicall History of the Arraignment, Tryall, Confession, and Condemnation of six Witches at Maidstone, in Kent. at the Assizes there held in July, Fryday 30. this present year; 1652. Before the Right Honorable, Peter Warbuton. . . Collected from the Observations of E. G. Gent, a learned person, present at their Conviction and Condemnation. London. 1652. *Collection of Tracts*, printed by J. R. Smith, 1838.

688. William Reynolds of the Isle of Grayne, victualler. Thomas and Jane Wilson [*as above*], on 29 May, 1649, at I. of G., bewitched 70 sheep of the value of 18*l*. of the goods and chattels of Robert Clifford, which were wasted and consumed at I. of G. *Endorsed*. Katherine Westley. Elizabeth Smyth, Nicholas Marchant, Christopher Lycence, Robert Clifford, Anthony Christian, Robert Hewsted, Thomas Tatnum, Elizabeth Clerke, Mary Barpett.

Pu se guilty imprisonm$^t$ for the space of one whole yeare without bayle and once in every quarter stand in the pillory, &c. [All three prisoners.]

*Gaol Calendar of Prisoners at Maidstone Gaol*

| | |
|---|---|
| Anne Ashbye otherwise Cobler | |
| Anne Martyne | ——Witchcraft confest. |
| Susan Pickenden | |
| Mildred Wright | |
| Anne Willson | Suspicon of Witchcraft. |
| Thomas Goddard | |
| Agnes Haytoe | |
| Mary Browne | |
| Mary Reader | Suspicon of Witchcraft. |

689. William Reynolds of the Isle of Grayne, labourer, and Elizabeth, his wife, spinster, on 22 Nov., 1651, at I. of G., bewitched John Lancaster, aged about 40, who languished until 22 Jan. following, when he died at I. of G. *Endorsed*. Emlyn Kirby, Elizabeth Owen, Martha Symondes. We doe finde this to be a true bill.

Pu se not guilty nor fly  Acq$^t$. [W.R.  No plea for Elizabeth, nor is she mentioned in the gaol delivery roll.]

690. Thomas Creede of Cranebrook, feltmaker, and Dorothy Avery of C., widow, on 1 Nov., 1648, at C., bewitched 10 " setts of oade " of the value of 60*l*. of the goods and chattels of Thomas Ferror, which were impaired and destroyed. *Endorsed*. Thomas Werrall, Thomas Weller.  We finde this to be a true bill.

Pu se not guilty dd.

691. Thomas Creed on 1 June, 1652, at C., bewitched to death 1 white mare and 1 dun mare valued at 6*l.* each of the goods and chattels of William Lambe. *Endorsed.* William Lambe, Mary Lambe, Anne Austen. We find this to be a true bill.

Pu se not guilty nor fly Acq\.

692. ——, on 14 Mar., 1651 [1652], at C., bewitched to death 1 grey mare valued at 7*l.* of the goods and chattels of Richard Harvey. *Endorsed.* Richard Harvey, Elizabeth Harvey. We finde this to be a true bill.

Pu se not guilty nor fly Acq.

693. Mary Reade of Lenham, widow, on 22 Dec., 1648, at L., bewitched Valentine Emmes of L., husbandman, who instantly died. *Endorsed.* Frances Gessell, Richard Tharpe, Richard Pecke, John Clerke, William Weldish, Elizabeth Stedman. We finde this to be a true bill.

Pu se guilty noe goodes hanged.

694. Anne Ashby of Cranebrook otherwise called Anne Cobler of C., spinster, and Anne Martyn, spinster, on 19 May, 1652, at C., bewitched Elizabeth Wilding, aged 3¾ yrs., daughter of Richard W., who languished until 11 July, when she died at C. *Endorsed.* Richard Wilding, Lettice Wilding, Joane Vincmube, Michael Reynolds. We doe finde this to be a true bill.

Pu se guilty noe goodes hanged.

695. Anne Ashby, Anne Martyn, Mildred Wright otherwise Writh of C., spinster, Anne Wilson of C., widow, and Mary Browne of C., widow, on 19 Apr., 1652, at C., bewitched Elizabeth Osborne, wife of Alexander O., who languished until 15 July, when she died at C. *Endorsed.* Alexander Osborne, Mary Amett, Michael Reynolds, Robert Cooke. We doe finde this to be a true bill.

Pu se guilty noe goodes hanged (A.A. and A.M.). Pu se guilty noe goodes hanged and reprived after by order of Parliam\. (M.W. and A.W.) Pu se guilty noe goodes reprived before Judgm\. (M.B.)

R

696. ——, ——, ——, ——,[1] on 4 Dec., 1651, at C., bewitched a female infant aged 10 days, which languished until 14 Dec. following, when it died at C. [Same endorsement, pleas, verdicts, and sentences.]

697. Agnes Heightoe of Benenden, spinster, wife of Jervis H., labourer, on 20 May, 1649, at B., bewitched to death 10 pigs valued at 15d. each of the goods and chattels of Richard Atkin. *Endorsed.* Richard Atkin, Mary Budds. We doe finde this to be noe true bill.

698. Alice Rayzell of Halstow, spinster, wife of Nicholas R., husbandman, on 27 Sept., 1651, at Upchurch, bewitched Phebee Hinckly, aged 3 yrs., daughter of Robert H., who languished until the 6 Nov., when she died at U. *Endorsed.* Thomas Iles, Robert Hinckly.   We doe finde this to be noe true bill.

*Gaol Delivery Roll*

| | |
|---|---|
| Anne Ashby or Cobler<br>Anne Martin<br>Mildred Wright<br>Anne Wilson<br>Mary Read<br>Susan Pickenden | Theis are attainted of sev⁹al felonies . . . & witchcraftes & must be seu⁹ally hanged by their necks untill they be dead. |
| Thomas Creed<br>Dorothy Avery | Theis are acquitted & may bee delivered paying their fees. |

Mary Browne is convicted of witchcrafte for murdering Eliz. Osburne and is reprived by the Court before Judgm^t. but must bee safely kept in gaole till she bee thence deliv⁹ed by due course of lawe.

| | |
|---|---|
| William Reynoldes<br>Thomas Wilson<br>Jane Wilson | They are convicted of witchcraft. Every of them must suffer imprisonment for 1 year without bayle. To be pilloried every quarter in some market town upon the market day or such time as any fair shall be kept there stand openly upon the pillory by the space of six hours and there every of them shall openly confesse his or her error and offence. (*Abstract only.*) |

[1] Mary Browne is omitted in this indictment.

699. Thomas Goddard
700. Goddard Gresham
} Suspected of witchcraft and are to remain in gaol without bayle till they shall be delivered by due course of law.

Agnes Heightoe
701. Stephen Godley
} They must remayne in gaole till they find suretyes to appeare at the next generall delivery and in the meantime to be of the good behaviour.

[At the following assizes (Lent, 1653) Heightoe and Godley were delivered. Gresham and Goddard were to remain in gaol until bailed. Mary Browne was not mentioned.]

1653. Essex Lent Sessions and general gaol delivery holden at Chelmsford on 24 Mar.. 1652 [1653]. Commission dated 4 Feb., 1652 [1653].

702. Susan Haveringe of West Tilbury, widow, on 2 June, 20 Chas. II, at W. T., bewitched to death 3 bay colts valued at 4l. of the goods and chattels of Robert Smyth. *Endorsed.* Robert Smyth. We find this to bee noe true bill.

703. ——, on 25 Mar., 1652 [1653], at W. T., bewitched Thomas Maple, aged 4 yrs., who languished until 24 Apr. following, when he died at W. T. *Endorsed.* Thomas Maple. We find this to bee noe true bill.

704. Elizabeth Wyndell of W. T., widow, on 20 June, 1646, at W. T., bewitched Joan Jervis, wife of Cornelias J. of W. T., yeoman, who languished until 10 July following, when she died at W. T. *Endorsed.* Cornelius Jervis, Mary Griffen. We finde this to be noe true bill.

[Presumably some bills were also " found " as according to a gaol delivery roll of later date Haveringe and Windell " were to remain in gaol according to the Kalendar of the Sessions held for this County in October last until these assizes ".]

1653. Kent Lent Sessions and general gaol delivery holden at Maidstone on 14 Mar.. 1652 [1653]. Commission dated 4 Feb., 1652 [1653].

705. Ellen or Eleanor Howell of Bruckland, widow, on 20 Oct., 1649, at B., bewitched Lucy Berridge, wife of John B., who languished until 26 Oct. following, when she died at B. *Endorsed.* John Berridge. Peter Maplesden, Edward Paine, George Kennett, John Pannett (sicke), Edward Evans, Jane Leuy (sicke), Elizabeth Pannett, Elizabeth Knight, Bartholomew Treble, Thomas Stephens, Elizabeth Goldsmyth. Wee finde this to be a true bill.

Pu se & Sum 1653 [1] not guilty nor fly Acq<sup>td</sup> Acq^td.

706. ———, on 1 Mar., 1646 [1647], at B., bewitched Jane Dibden, wife of Richard D., who languished until 3 May following, when she died at B. *Endorsed.* Jane Leauey, Edward Payne. Wee finde this to be a true bill.

Pu se & Sum 1653 [1] not guilty nor fly Acq<sup>ted</sup>.

707. Ellen Howell, spinster, on 20 Sept., 1652 [lower down 20 Dec.], at B., bewitched to death 2 mares valued at 10*l.*, 2 black cows valued at 10*l.*, 3 white sheep valued at 30*s.*, of the goods and chattels of Peter Maplesdenn. *Endorsed.* Peter Maplesdeane. Wee finde this to be a true bill.

Pu se not guilty nor fly Acq<sup>ted</sup>.

708. ———, on 12 Jan., 1652 [1653], at B., bewitched Anne Pannett, aged ¾ yr., who languished until 13 Jan. following, when she died at B. *Endorsed.* Elizabeth Pannett. Wee find this to be a true bill.

Pu se not guilty nor fly Acq<sup>ted</sup>.

709. Susan Lovell of Cranbrook, widow, on 3 Jan., 1652 [1653], at C., bewitched William Baker of C., labourer, who languished until 30 Sept. following, when he died at C. *Endorsed.* Mary Baker, Symon Dent, Alice Dent. Wee find this to be a true bill.

Pu se not guilty nor fly Acq<sup>ted</sup>.

710. ———, on 26 Aug., 1652, at C., bewitched Mary Dence,

---

[1] There was evidently a delay in the trial of Ellen Howell. She was discharged from Maidstone gaol in the summer of 1653.

aged 9 yrs., who was weakened, pined, and lamed. *Endorsed.*
Alice Dence, Mary Baker. Wee find this to be a true bill.
Pu se not guilty nor fly Acq<sup>ted</sup>.

1653. Essex Summer Sessions and general gaol delivery holden
at Chelmsford on 28 July, 1653. Commission dated
22 June, 1653.

### Gaol Calendar

711. Benjamyn Brand for sorcery he is to remayne in gaole
for 12 months according to the Kalendar of the
last sessions.

Mary Hurst she was comitted by Isaack Aleyn, Esq<sup>r</sup>. beinge
charged to be a witche and by witchcraft to have
hurt Isaack (*sic*) Hodge of Nevenden, yeoman.

712. Mary Hurst of Nevendon, spinster, on 24 May, 1653,
at N., bewitched William Hodge, who was wasted, consumed,
etc. *Endorsed.* William Hodge, John Crosse, Thomas Austen,
Sarah Allen, Richard Landell, Hester Rymes. Wee finde this
a true bill.
Pu se guilty noe good℘ reprived before Judgm<sup>t</sup>.

### Gaol Delivery Roll

Mary Hurst convicted of ffelony by witchcraft reprived before
Judgm<sup>t</sup>. & must remayne in Gaole vntill shee shalbe
delivered by due course of lawe.

1654. Essex Summer Sessions and general gaol delivery holden
at Chelmsford on 19 July, 1654. Commission dated
13 June, 1654.

713. Anne Clarke of Waltham Holicross, spinster, wife of
Stephen C. of the same, labourer, at W. H., bewitched Mary
Legg, spinster, who was wasted, consumed, etc. *Endorsed.*
Anne Sherbert, Edith Legg, John Legg. Wee doe not find this
bill to be true.

714. ——, on 20 Aug., 1645, at W. H., bewitched Philip Blott,
who languished until 21 Aug., 1647, when he died at W. H.
*Endorsed.* Benjamin Shelley, Ann Sherberte, Edith Legg,

John Legg, Henry Blott.   Wee doe not find this bill to be true.
See 713, 721, 722.

1654.    Kent Summer Sessions and general gaol delivery holden
at Maidstone on 24 July, 1654.   Commission dated
13 June, 1654.

715.   Helen Shells of How, spinster, on 20 Apr., 1654, at H.,
bewitched John Miller, who was wasted, consumed, etc.
*Endorsed.*   Jane Ward, John Miller, Diana Turner, John Miller,
jun., Elizabeth Miller, Richard Phipps.   Wee finde this to be
a true bill.
Pu se not guilty nor fly   Acq$^{td}$.

716.   Anne Rabbett of Staplehurst, widow, on 1 Aug., 1651,
at S., bewitched to death 1 gelding valued at 12*l* of the goods
and chattels of William Tolhurst.   *Endorsed.*   William Tolhust,
Richard Kingsnoth, Susan Hartnupp.   Wee finde this to be
a true bill.
Pu se not guilty.

717.   ——, on 1 Sept., 1653, at S., bewitched Anthony Reeve,
son of John R., aged 3 mos., who languished until 4 Sept.
following, when he died at S.   *Endorsed.*   John Reeve.   Wee
finde this to be a true bill.
Pu se not guilty nor fly   Acq$^{td}$.

1654.    Sussex Summer Sessions and general gaol delivery holden
at Horsham on 28 July, 1654.   Commission dated
13 June, 1654.

718.   Jane Shoebridge of Withiam, spinster, on 30 Dec., 1652,
at W., bewitched Mary Muddle, spinster, aged 12 yrs., who was
wasted, consumed, etc.   *Endorsed*   Sarah Muddle, Thomas
Sayker, Robert Turner, John Seavenocke, William Shenfeild,
Benjamin Caute, Richard West the turnekey.   We find this to
be a true bill.
Pu se not guilty nor fly   Acq$^{td}$.

719.   Clement Shoebridge of Withiham, widow, on 1 Jan.,
1650 [1651], at W., bewitched Benjamin Caught, who was wasted,

consumed, etc. *Endorsed.* Benjamin Caught, Sarah Muddle, Robert Turner. Wee find this to be a true bill.

Pu se not guilty nor fly  Acq<sup>td</sup>.

720. ——, on 30 Dec., 1653, at W., bewitched Mary Muddle, spinster, aged 13 yrs., who was wasted, consumed, etc. *Endorsed.* Sarah Muddle, Thomas Sayker, Robert Turner, John Seavenocke, William Shenfeild, Anne Hart, Benjamin Caught.  Wee finde this to be a true bill.

Pu se not guilty nor fly  Acq<sup>td</sup>.

1655. Essex Lent Sessions and general gaol delivery holden at Chelmsford on 26 Mar., 1654 [1655]. Commission dated 13 Feb., 1654 [1655].

721. Anne Clarke of Waltham Hollicrosse, spinster, wife of Stephen C. of the same, labourer, on 29 Mar., 1654, at W. H., bewitched Mary Legg, spinster, who languished until 29 July following, when she died at W. H. *Endorsed.* John Legg, Zachary Crofton, Edward Golding, Elizabeth Legg, Jane Wood, Susanna Bridges, John Legg, jun., Mary Michaell, Jane Wooddall. We find this to be a true bill.

Pu se not guilty nor fled  Acq<sup>ted</sup>.

722. ——, on 10 June, 1648, at W. H., bewitched Philip Blott, who languished until 20 Aug. following, when he died at W. H. *Endorsed.* Henry Blott, Mary Blott. Edith Legg. Frances Burges [and the nine witnesses named in No. 721]. We find this to be a true bill.

Pu se not guilty nor fled  Acq<sup>ted</sup>.

See 713, 714, 721.

1655. Surrey Lent Sessions and general gaol delivery holden at Southwark on 7 Mar., 1654 [1655]. Commission dated 13 Feb., 1654 [1655].

723. Elizabeth Hatton of Darking, widow. on 20 Apr., 1654, at D., bewitched Elizabeth Stone, wife of William S., who languished until 11 May following, when she died at D. *Endorsed.* Anne Newman, Elizabeth Stente, Margaret Barnham, Eleanor

Prior, John Harman, Elizabeth Hooker, Elizabeth Moore, William Hooker. We find this a trew bill.

Pu se guilty noe goods to bee hanged.

*Gaol Delivery Roll*

Elizabeth Hatton attainted of ffeloney . . . & must bee hanged, etc.

1655.    Kent Summer Sessions and general gaol delivery holden at Maidstone on 7 Aug., 1655. Commission dated 4 July, 1655.

724. Margaret Walters of Kingsnorth, spinster, wife of William W. of K., labourer, on 1 Jan., 1649 [1650], at K., bewitched William Happer, who languished until 27 Apr., 1650, when he died at K. *Endorsed.* Susan Ashdale, Frances Markewicke, Thomas Bateman, Margaret Bateman. We finde this to be a trew bill.

Pu se not guilty nor fled   Acq^ted.

1656.    Kent Lent Sessions and general gaol delivery holden at Maidstone on 17 Mar., 1655 [1656]. Commission dated 12 Feb., 1655 [1656].

725. Elizabeth Misselbrook of Orpington, spinster, wife of Thomas M. of O., labourer, on 20 Dec., 1655, at O., bewitched Thomazine Wickes, spinster, who languished until 16 Mar. following, when she died at O. *Endorsed.* Nicholas Wickes, Emma Wickes, David Polly, Robert Boomer, Susan Savadge, Richard Browne. We find this to be a true bill.

Pu se not guilty nor fled   Acq^ted.

1657.    Essex Lent Sessions and general gaol delivery holden at Chelmsford on 9 Mar., 1656 [1657]. Commission dated 3 Feb., 1656 [1657].

726. Mary Symons of Much Totham, spinster, wife of William S. of the same, labourer, on 10 Aug., 1656, at M. T., bewitched John Amett, who was wasted, consumed, etc. *Endorsed.* Thomas Amett. We find this not to be a true bill.

1657. Kent Lent Sessions and general gaol delivery holden at Maidstone on 17 Mar., 1656 [1657]. Commission dated 3 Feb., 1656 [1657].

727. Mary Allen, the younger, of Gowdherst, spinster, on 30 Nov., 1656, at G., did feed and employ an evil spirit in the likeness of a black dog with the intent, etc. *Endorsed.* George Weldish, Thomas Francis, Robert Tamken, Walter Tickner. Wee find this to bee a true bill.

Pu se guilty noe good? to bee hanged.

### Full English transcript, p. 91 supra

728. Mary Allen, the elder, of Gowdherst, spinster, wife of Stephen A. of G., labourer, on 20 Nov., 1656, at G., did feed and employ an evil spirit in the likeness of a black dog with the intent, etc. *Endorsed.* [Four witnesses named in No. 727.] Mary Allen, the younger, George Busbridge, Stephen Garrett, Matthew Browne, Elizabeth Clarke William Sadler, Elizabeth Weldish, Thomas Read. Wee find this to bee a true bill.

Pu se guilty noe good? to bee hanged.

### Gaol Delivery Roll

| | |
|---|---|
| Mary Allen, the elder<br>Mary Alen, the younger | These are attainted of . . . witch-crafts and must bee severally hanged by their necks untill they be dead. |

1657. Surrey Lent Sessions and general gaol delivery holden at Southwark on 25 Mar., 1657. Commission dated 3 Feb., 1656 [1657].

729. Mary Wallis of Guildford, spinster, wife of John W. of G., husbandman, on 20 Aug., 1654, at G., bewitched Nicholas Wallis, aged 7 yrs.. who languished until 13 Oct. following, when he died at G. *Endorsed.* Nicholas Wallis, John Wallis, Ellen Wallis, Lettice Wallis, Anne Steaning, Anne Rogers. Wee doe find this a trew bill.

Pu se guilty noe good? to bee hanged.

*Gaol Delivery Roll*

Mary Wallis. Shee is attainted of Murder by Witchcraft. To remaine in gaole without baile untill . . . delivered by due course of lawe.

[She was still in prison 22 Mar., 1657–8.]

1657. Kent Summer Sessions and general gaol delivery holden at Maidstone on 7 July, 1657. Commission dated . . June, 1657.

730. Judith Sawkins of Aylesford, widow, on 20 Dec., 1656, at A., bewitched Mary Meadowes, daughter of Elizabeth M., aged 12 yrs., who was wasted, consumed, etc. *Endorsed.* Mary Birchall, Elizabeth Meadowes. Mary Smythe (not sworne), Ellen Jarvis (not sworn), Margaret Taylor, Mary Fletcher, Elizabeth Kingsmad, Alice Lott, Sarah Bly, Dorothy Shipster, Elizabeth Haynes, Katherine Austen, James Aylett, Abraham Benstead, Elizabeth Edwards, Mary Smyth. Richard Stanford, Elizabeth Edwards Wee find this to be a true bill.

Puse guilty noe goode to bee hanged. xxix^th March, 1658.
See No. 733.

731. Anne Dadds of Woodchurch, widow, on 19 Feb., 1656 [1657], at W., bewitched Thomas Eley, aged 2¾ yrs., who languished until 5 Mar. following, when he died at W. *Endorsed.* John Eley, Joan Chittenden, Hester Smith, Alice Evans. Wee find this to be a true bill.

Puse not guilty nor fled.

732. ——, on 19 Feb., 1656 [1657], at W., bewitched Elizabeth Eley, wife of John E., who languished until 5 Mar. following, when she died at W. *Endorsed.* [Witnesses as in No. 731.] Wee finde this to bee a true bill.

Puse not guilty nor fled.

*Gaol Delivery Roll*

Judeth Sawkins, 7 Apr., 1657, shee stands indicted for witchcraft and for burneinge a barne and corne. To be kept in gaole without baile until delivered by due course of lawe.

[She was hanged 30 Mar., 1658. Gaol D. R.]

1658. Kent Lent Sessions and general gaol delivery holden at Maidstone on 30 Mar., 1658. Commission dated 9 Feb., 1657 [1658].

733. Judeth Sawkins of Alesford, widow, on 7 June, 1656, at A., bewitched Frances Long, wife of Edward L., who languished until 15 July, when she died at A. *Endorsed.* Frances Duke, Alice Latt, Dorothy Shipster, Elizabeth Meadowes, Jane Wyatt. Ursula Bensted, Richard Stanford, William Swanne. Wee find this to be a true bill.

Pu se not guilty nor fled   Acqtted.

See No. 730.

1658. Hertford Summer Sessions and general gaol delivery holden at Hertford on 30 July, 1658. Commission dated 28 June, 1658.

734. Agnes Gardiner of Bennyngton, spinster, wife of Christopher G. of B., labourer, on 3 July, 1658, at B., did feed, employ, and entertain two evil spirits, one in the likeness of a black cat and the other in the likeness of a toad. *Endorsed.* John Wallis, Henry Walker, Abraham Hurst, Thomas Norwood, John Chapman, Joseph Noone, John Kent. Wee find this a true bill.

Puse not guilty nor fledd. Acq^td & dd.

735. ——, on 3 July, 1658, at B., bewitched Marcy Spencer, at B., who was wasted and consumed. *Endorsed.* [Names of witnesses as No. 734.] We find this not to be a true bill.

1659. Essex Summer Sessions and general gaol delivery holden at Chelmsford on 1 Aug., 1659. Commission dated 23 June, 1659.

736. William Bones of Finchingfeild. labourer. Abraham Bones of the same, labourer, and Mary Warner of the same, widow, on 10 Aug., 1658, at F., bewitched Sarah Smith, spinster, who was wasted, consumed, etc. *Endorsed.* Sarah Smith, Gilbert Harrington, James Harrington. Alice Stebings. Alice Saymes. Hanna Hills. Wee finde this a trew bill.

W. Bones dead.

Pu se not guilty nor fled. Acq^tted [both prisoners].

*Gaol Calendar*

737. Alice Warner shee was comitted by Dudley Templer Esq$^r$. for witchcraſte.

738. Anne Woolward of Chelmsford, spinster, wife of Alexander W. of C., labourer, on 2 May, 1659, at C., bewitched John Adams, the younger, who was wasted, consumed, etc. *Endorsed.* John Adams, Edward Hittison, William Hittison, —— Sturgion, Elizabeth Clarke, Thomas Babor, Thomas Harte, Thomas Gray, Elizabeth Fuller, Elizabeth Spight. Noe trew bill.

## Charles II, 1660-1684

1660. Kent Lent Sessions and general delivery holden at Maidstone on 12 Mar., 12 Chas. II. Commission dated 23 Jan., 12 Chas. II.

739. Mary Sharpe of Queenborough, widow, and Anne Cooper of the same, widow, on 22 Sept., 12 Chas. II, at Q., bewitched to death 1 grey mare valued at 4$l$. of the goods and chattels of Henry Seages. *Endorsed.* Henry Seages, Abraham Parkes. Billa vera.

Po se non cul [both prisoners].

740. ——, ——, on 20 Sept., 12 Chas. II, at Q., bewitched 1 black cow valued at 3$l$ of the goods and chattels of Henry Seager. *Endorsed.* [Names of witnesses as No. 739.] Billa vera.

Po se non cul [both prisoners].

741. Mary Sharpe, etc., on 1 Sept., 12 Chas. II, at Q., bewitched John Robinson, who languished until 12 Sept. following, when he died at Q. *Endorsed.* Richard Thomson, Susan Cooper, Anne Man, William Johnson. Billa vera.

Po se non cul n$^{cr}$ Q$^a$.

1660. Essex Summer Sessions and general gaol delivery holden at Chelmsford on 17 Sept., 12 Chas. II. Commission dated 10 July, 12 Chas. II

*Gaol Calendar*

742. Elizabeth Huntsman. She was committed by Thomas Smyth Esq$^r$. beinge charged to have used the diabolicall art of witchcraſte.

Bridgett Weaver. She was comitted by S Thomas Bowes, Knt., for that shee upon her exaiacon hath confessed that shee hath cherrished and suckled an impe.

743. Bridget Weaver of Harwich, spinster, wife of Geoffrey W. of H., labourer, on 11 Feb., 12 Chas. II, at H., did entertain and feed an evil spirit in the likeness of a bird. *Endorsed*. Daniel Smyth. Billa vera.

Po se non n$^{cr}$ Q$^a$.

*Gaol Delivery Roll*

Elizabetha Huntsman. Delivered by proclamation and must be discharged paying . . . fees.

Bridgitta Weaver. Acquitted. must be discharged paying . . . fees.

1660. Surrey Summer Sessions and general gaol delivery holden at Kingston-upon-Thames on 3 Sept., 12 Chas. II. Commission dated 10 July, 12 Chas. II.

*Gaol Delivery Roll*

744. Joanna Neville . . . 1660 for murder by witchcraft. Must be kept in gaole until delivered by due course of lawe.

1662. Essex Lent Sessions and general gaol delivery holden at Chelmsford on 15 Mar., 14 Chas. II. Commission dated 23 Jan., 13 Chas. II.

745. Anne Silvester of Orsett. wife of William S. of the same, labourer, on 24 Feb., 14 Chas. II, at O., did entertain, employ, and feed two evil spirits in the likeness of two whelps. *Endorsed*. John Elston, Mary Elston, Lucy Bently, Anne Clovell. Billa vera.

Po se non cul n$^{cr}$ Q$^a$.

746. ——, on 24 Feb., 14 Chas. II, at O., bewitched Mary Elston, spinster, who was wasted, hurt, etc. *Endorsed*. [Names of witnesses as No. 745.] Billa vera.

Po se non cul n$^{cr}$ Q$^a$.

1663. Essex Lent Sessions and general gaol delivery holden at Chelmsford on 22 Mar., 15 Chas. II. Commission dated 23 Jan., 14 Chas. II.

*Gaol Calendar (damaged)*

747. . . . lley, widowe, dead

748. [Sarah Houg]hton, spinster

comitted by Sir Robert
Kempe, knight, for that
they . . . . witchcrafte
confessed that the have
tormented and pyned . . .
children of one . . .

1663. Essex Summer Sessions and general gaol delivery holden
at Brentwood on 13 August, 15 Chas. II. Commission
dated 19 June, 15 Chas. II.

*Gaol Calendar*

Sarah Houghton   attaint of felony & witchcrafte   Shee was
reprieved after judgmᵗ. And is since dead.

1664. Kent Lent Sessions and general gaol delivery holden at
Maidstone on 2 Mar.. 16 Chas. II. Commission dated
23 Jan., 15 Chas. II.

749. Alice Rasell of Newington, widow, wife of . . . R. of the
same, labourer, on 20 July, 12 Chas II, at N., bewitched John
Browne of N., aged 16 yrs., who languished until 8 Feb.,
Chas. II, when he died at N. *Endorsed.* Susan Ogles, Thomas
*A*crive, John Budd, William Browne, Mary Ford, Thomas
Blissenden, Mary Ogles   Billa vera.

Po se non cul nᶜⁱ Qᵃ

1664. Surrey Lent Sessions and general gaol delivery holden at
Southwark on 22 Feb., 16 Chas. II. Commission dated
23 Jan., 15 Chas. II.

750. Elizabeth Lewes of Putney, spinster, wife of Robert L.
of the same, gent., Elizabeth Lewes, daughter of Robert L.,
and Anne Hollingworth, spinster, wife of William H. of the same,
labourer, on 13 Dec., 15 Chas. II, at P., bewitched Naomi
Fisher, wife of William F., who was wasted, consumed, etc.
*Endorsed.* Robert Milner, William Milner, Mary Cole, Naomi
Fisher, Owen Cooke, Katherine Fisher, Anne Boughton, Mary
Houlton, James Emberdon, Ellen James, Erasmus Feltman in
medicinis docto', Joan Franckham, Margaret Ashfeild, Sarah
Randall, Joan Jewell. Ignoramus.

751. ——, on 13 Dec., 15 Chas. II, at P., bewitched James Fisher, aged 9 yrs.. who was wasted. consumed, etc. *Endorsed*. [Names of witnesses as No. 750.] Ignoramus.

752. Elizabeth Lewes, etc., on 28 Aug., 15 Chas. II, at P., bewitched Mary Smith otherwise Cutt of P., who languished until 1 Sept. following, when she died at P. *Endorsed*. Phillis Bourton, Margaret Ashfield, Mary Cole, Jane Williams, Owen Cooke, Naomy Fisher, Robert Miller, junior, Robert Miller, senior, Katherine Fisher, Mary Houghton. Vera billa.

Po se non cul n<sup>cr</sup> Q<sup>a</sup>.

1664. Essex Summer Sessions and general gaol delivery holden at Chelmsford on 8 Aug., 16 Chas. II. Commission dated 10 June, 16 Chas. II.

### *Gaol Calendar*

Robert Coppynge   he was committed by Sir Hobert Barrington. Knight, for takinge away the life of William Slater of Woodham Ferris by witchcrafte.

753. Robert Copping of Woodham Ferryes, labourer, on 8 May, 16 Chas. II, at W. F., bewitched William Slater, who languished until 10 May following, when he died at W. F. *Endorsed*. Margery Slater, John Aylett, Richard Jeffery, Edward Bonham. Ignoramus.

### *Gaol Delivery Roll*

Robert Copping ⎱ delivered by proclamation and must be
and others ⎰ delivered paying their fees.

1666. Essex Lent Sessions and general gaol delivery holden at Chelmsford on 2 Apr., 18 Chas. II. Commission dated 23 Jan., 17 Chas. II.

754. Martha Driver of Barking, widow, otherwise Martha Chalke, on 4 Nov., 17 Chas. II, at B., bewitched John Stevens, aged 5 yrs.. who languished until 8 Nov. following, when he died at B. *Endorsed*. Josiah Best, Elizabeth Best, John Bird, Thomas Crofts, Richard Emmes, Jane Grymes, Rebecca Best, Judith Lake. Billa vera.

Po se non cul n<sup>cr</sup> Q<sup>a</sup>.

1665.    Surrey Lent Sessions and general gaol delivery holden at Guildford on 19 Mar., 18 Chas. II.    Commission dated 23 Jan., 17 Chas. II.

755. Elizabeth Wood of Dorking, widow, and Mary Walker of Dorking, widow, on 29 Mar., 17 Chas. II, at D., bewitched Thomas Bothell. who languished until 4 Apr. following, when he died at St. Saviour's, Southwarke. *Endorsed.* Robert Holloway, Simon Smyth, Anne Newman, William Lee, Samuel Bothell, John Terry, Richard Sumersell, John Price, Sarah Sheppard, Robert Newman, Maria Bothell, Margaret Bothell. Billa vera.

Po se non cul n$^{cr}$ Q$^a$. [Both prisoners.]

756. Elizabeth Wood of Dorking. widow. on 10 Dec., 14 Chas. II, at D., bewitched Ephraim Bothell, aged 12 yrs., who languished until 23 Dec. following, when he died at D. *Endorsed.* Mary Bothell. Ignoramus.

1669.    Kent Summer Sessions and general gaol delivery holden at Rochester on 27 July. 21 Chas. II.    Commission dated 11 June, 21 Chas. II.

757. Anne Buddle of River, spinster, wife of William B., labourer, on 24 May, 21 Chas. II, at R., bewitched Mary Southouse, spinster, aged 17 yrs., daughter of John S. of R., tailor (*scissor*), who languished until 6 June following, when she died at R. *Endorsed.* John Southouse, Margery Southouse, William Pelham, Sarah Pelham, John Kingmill, Jane Buddle, Elizabeth Bennett. John Roberts, Richard Clarke, Robert Carter. Billa vera.

Po se non cul ne se retrax  Quiet &c.

1670.    Surrey Lent Sessions and general gaol delivery holden at Southwark on 28 Feb., 22 Chas. II.    Commission dated 3 Feb., 22 Chas. II.

758. Mary Middleton of Roderhith, spinster, wife of Thomas M., labourer, on 10 Sept., 21 Chas. II, at R., bewitched Thomas Doe, who languished until 9 Jan., 21 Chas. II, when he died at

R. *Endorsed.* Elizabeth Bloomfeild. Elinora Carter, Mary Metherell, Elizabeth Jones, Grace Parsons. Billa vera.

Po se non cul n<sup>cr</sup> Q<sup>a</sup>.

1670. Essex Summer Sessions and general gaol delivery holden at Brentwood on 18 July, 22 Chas. II. Commission dated 3 June, 22 Chas. II.

*Gaol Calendar*

| | |
|---|---|
| Sara Ladbrooke<br>Margaret Lach<br>John Wood | committed by Sir Thomas Bowes, Knt., being suspected to be guilty of witchcraft. |
| Joane Crumpe | comitted by Henry Pert esq. being accused by severall psons for bewitching one Thomas French to death and also for bewitching of one Robert Thompson of Brookestreet. |

759. Margaret Leech of Bradfeild, widow, on 1 Nov., 20 Chas. II, at B., bewitched Martha Nash, who languished until 8 Nov. following, when she died at B. *Endorsed.* Daniel Nash. Billa vera.

Po se non cul n<sup>cr</sup> Q<sup>a</sup>.

760. Sarah Ladbrooke of Bradfeild, widow, on 20 Mar., 21 Chas. II, at B., bewitched Dorcas Fall, who languished until 25 Mar. following, when she died at B. *Endorsed.* Thomas Heyward, Robert Smart. Billa vera.

Po se non cul n<sup>cr</sup> Q<sup>a</sup>.

761. John Wood of Bradfeild, labourer, and Sarah Ladbrooke of the same, widow, on 20 Oct., 20 Chas. II, at B., bewitched Richard Forrest, who languished until 20 Oct. following, when he died at B. *Endorsed.* Elizabeth Forrest. Billa vera.

J. W. Po se non cul n<sup>cr</sup> Q<sup>s</sup>. S. L. Po se non cul n<sup>cr</sup> Q<sup>a</sup>.

762. John Wood of B., labourer, on 12 Nov., 18 Chas. II, at B., bewitched Susanna Palmer, who languished until 12 Nov. following, when she died at B. *Endorsed.* Henry Palmer. Billa vera.

Po se non cul n<sup>cr</sup> Q<sup>s</sup>.

763. Joan Crumpe of Weale, widow, on 10 Nov., 21 Chas. II, at W., bewitched Eleanor French, wife of John F. of W., farmer, who languished until 26 June following, when she died at W. *Endorsed.* John French, Dorothy Wybrough, William Scott, Priscilla Scott, Elizabeth Crouch, Joan Jelfe, Dorothy Fillybrowne, Margaret Tompson, Thomas Sampford, Priscilla Rapley. Billa vera.

Po se non cul n$^{cr}$ Q$^a$.

1670.   Kent Summer Sessions and general gaol delivery holden at Maidstone on 12 July, 22 Chas. II. Commission dated 3 June, 22 Chas. II.

764. Sarah French of Gowdhurst, widow, on 1 June, 22 Chas. II, at G., bewitched John Allen, aged 4½ yrs., who languished until 3 June, 22 Chas. II, when he died at G. *Endorsed.* William Allen, Robert Bassocke, John Hemberry. Billa vera.

Po se non cul n$^{cr}$ Q$^a$.

1671.   Kent Summer Sessions and general gaol delivery holden at Maidstone on 8 Aug., 23 Chas. II. Commission dated 23 June, 23 Chas. II.

765. Katherine Barren or Barrett of Woolwich, widow, on 10 July, 23 Chas. II, at W., " did consult, covenant with, entertain, imploy, feed and reward " a certain evil spirit in the likeness of a rat, etc *Endorsed.* Thomas Bonnett, Samuel Ladbrooke, Mary Merrett, Anne Hodgskins, Anne Medcapp, Margaret Short, Mary Keeper, Elizabeth Kennett, Thomas Cocke, Mary Bridges, Richard Turpentine, William Sawood, William Cyphlett, Joan Pruen, Mary Cyfleete, Katherine Bonnicke. Billa vera.

Po se non cul n$^{cr}$ Q$^a$.

1674.   Hertford Summer Sessions and general gaol delivery holden at Hertford on 6 Aug., 26 Chas. II. Commission dated 20 June, 26 Chas. II.

766. Susan England of Westbarkhamsted, widow, on 20 June, 25 Chas. II, at B., bewitched Thomas Gold the younger, who languished until 5 Apr. following, when he died at W. *Endorsed.* Thomas Gold, John Gold, Mary Ward, Elizabeth Puddeford,

Anne Bird, Anne Gold, Edward Gold [possibly other names torn off]. Billa vera.[1]

Po se non cul n$^{cr}$ Q$^a$.

1675. Essex Lent Sessions and general gaol delivery. [Commission dated 3 Feb., 27 Chas. II.]

767. Elizabeth Gynn, wife of William G., of Grt. Dunmow, labourer, on 10 July, 26 Chas. II, at Grt. D., bewitched Edmund Treddar, aged 9 yrs.. son of Roger T. of Grt. D.. labourer, who languished until 6 Jan. following, when he died at Grt. D. *Endorsed*. Rosamund Treddar, Elizabeth Goddard, John Stokes. Philip Clarke. Ignoramus.

1675. Kent Lent Sessions and general gaol delivery holden at Maidstone on 17 Mar., 27 Chas. II. Commission dated 3 Feb., 27 Chas. II.

768. Mary Brice of Chatham, spinster, on 1 May, 21 Chas. II, at C., bewitched Mary Addes, wife of Edward A., who languished until 10 Dec. following, when she died at C. *Endorsed*. Edward Addes, Robert Yardly. Billa vera.

Po se non cul n$^{cr}$ Q$^a$.

769. Mary Brice of St Nicholas, Rochester, widow, on 28 Sept.. 26 Chas. II. at St N. bewitched Henry Packman, who was wasted and consumed. *Endorsed*. Elizabeth Hill. Henry Packman, Nicholas Burwash, Anne Watson, Anne Bishopp, Sarah Baker. Billa vera.[2]

Po se non cul n$^{cr}$ Q$^a$.

1676. Kent Lent Sessions and general gaol delivery holden at Maidstone on 14 Mar., 28 Chas. II. Commission dated 18 Feb., 28 Chas. II.

---

[1] Susan England was also indicted for murdering Thomas Gold by throwing him upon the ground on 20 Aug., 23 Chas. II. She was acquitted.

[2] Mary Brice, widow, was also charged with assaulting Mary Wirrall with a broom and killing her, and by another indictment with burning household goods of Nicholas Burwash. In both cases a verdict of not guilty was returned.

770. Anne Neale of Milton, near Gravesend, widow, on 20 Mar., 24 Chas. II, at M., bewitched William Eason, who languished until 27 Mar. following, when he died at M. *Endorsed.* Walter Rynn. Ignoramus.

771. ——, on 5 July, 24 Chas. II, at G., bewitched Elizabeth Morgan, aged 6 wks., daughter of Roger M. and Jane, his wife, who languished until 20 July following, when she died at G. *Endorsed.* Jane Haselby. Ignoramus.

772. ——, on 1 Apr., 24 Chas. II, at G., bewitched Walter Warren, aged 13 mos., who languished until 1 July, when he died at G. *Endorsed.* Thomas Warren. Ignoramus.

1678.    Kent Lent Sessions and general gaol delivery holden at Maidstone on 11 Mar., 30 Chas. II. Commission dated 3 Feb., 30 Chas. II.

773. Jane Watts of St Nicholas, Rochester, spinster, wife of John W. of the same, labourer, on 5 Mar., 30 Chas. II, at R., bewitched Anne Huggins, aged 16 yrs., who was wasted, consumed, etc. *Endorsed.* Anne Huggins, John Batty, Margaret Day, Elizabeth Hartridge, Anne Benson, Anne Staines. Billa vera.

Po se non cul n^{cr} Q^a.

1679.    Kent Summer Sessions and general gaol delivery holden at Maidstone on 29 July, 31 Chas. II. Commission dated 20 June, 31 Chas. II.

774. Mary Foster, wife of John F., of St Lawrence in the Isle of Thanet, cordwainer, on 15 July, 29 Chas. II, at St L. bewitched Margery Rigden, aged 9 weeks, daughter of Henry R. and Sarah, his wife, who languished until 19 July following, when she died at St L. *Endorsed.* Sarah Rigden, Frances Williams, Martha Glover, Parnell Bourn, Elizabeth Sheerman, Jane Moverley, Anne Joad, Elizabeth West, Henry Rigden. Billa vera.

Po se non cul n^{cr} Q^a.

775. ——, on 4 Apr., 30 Chas. II, at St. L., bewitched Michael Jordan, who was wasted and consumed. *Endorsed.* Michael

Jordan, Isabel Jordan [and the six last-named witnesses in No. 774]. Billa vera.

Po se non cul n$^{cr}$ Q$^a$.

1680. Sussex Summer Sessions and general gaol delivery holden at Horsham on 22 July, 32 Chas. I. Commission dated 11 June, 32 Chas. I.

776. Alice Nash, wife of Thomas N. of Battell, labourer, on 19 Feb., 32 Chas. II. at B., bewitched Elizabeth Slater, aged 2½ yrs., daughter of William S., who languished until 21 Feb. following, when she died at B. *Endorsed.* William Slater, Mary Tyhurst, Ellen Grayline. Billa vera.

Po se non cul n$^{cr}$ q$^a$.

777. ——, on 19 Feb., 32 Chas. II, at B., bewitched Anne Slater, aged 5½ yrs., daughter of William S., who languished until 22 Feb. following, when she died at B. *Endorsed.* [Names of witnesses as No. 776.] Billa vera.

Po se non cul n$^{cr}$ q$^a$.

1681. Kent Lent Sessions and general gaol delivery holden at Maidstone on 15 Mar., 33 Chas. I. Commission dated 3 Feb., 33 Chas. I.

778. Anne Blundy otherwise Blundell of Strode, widow, on 5 Feb., 33 Chas. II, at S., bewitched Mary Griffin, aged 14 days, dau. of John G. and Anne, his wife, who languished until 7 Feb. following, when she died at S. *Endorsed.* Anne Griffin, Judith King, Mary Warham, Hama Shancke. Billa vera.

Po se non cul n$^{cr}$ q$^a$.

779. Thomas Whiteing of How, labourer, on 20 Jan., 32 Chas. II, at H., bewitched Sarah Curtis, spinster, who was wasted, consumed, etc. *Endorsed.* Robert Boyer, Joseph Miller, Sara Curtis, William Burman, John Ellis, Sims Beadell, Bridget Gilbert, Joan Stephens, Thomas Haley, Robert Witherley, Robert Beadle, Dr. Faber, Dr. Hooker, Dr. Robinson, Anne Seares, Faber Armitage, William Tucke, Barbara Cena, Ann Sears, William Werren. Ignoramus.

1681.    Kent Summer Sessions and general gaol delivery.  Commission dated 3 June, 33 Chas. II.

780. Elizabeth Scott of Cranbrook, widow, on 25 Apr., 31 Chas. II, at C., bewitched John Colman, who languished until 2 May, 33 Chas. II, when he died at C. *Endorsed*. Mary Colman, Samuel Bradshaw, Anne Butler. Ignoramus.

1682.    Surrey Lent Sessions and general gaol delivery holden at Southwark on 23 Mar., 34 Chas. II.[1]

781. Joan Butts of Astead, widow, on 1 Mar., 34 Chas. II, at A., bewitched Elizabeth Burridge, spinster, who was wasted, pined, etc. *Endorsed*. Elizabeth Farborough, John Tuer, Esther Tuer, Joan Watever, Bartho*lomew* Chelsham, Thomas Bourne, Henry Foreman, Nicholas Hawkins, Elizabeth Burridge, jun., Robert *P*otts, Elizabeth Blake, Robert Somers, Henry Luffe, Elizabeth Burridge, sen., Nicholas Gealle, Thomas Reynolds, Margaret Howell, John Rogers. Billa vera.

Po se non cul n$^{cr}$ q$^{a}$.

782. Joan Butts of Ewell, widow, on 4 Oct., 32 Chas. II. at E., bewitched Mary Farborough, who languished until 12 Oct. following, when she died at E. *Endorsed*. Henry Farborough, Elizabeth Farborough. Billa vera.

Po se non cul n$^{cr}$ q$^{a}$.

### James II, 1685-1688

1686.    Kent Lent Sessions and general gaol delivery holden at Rochester on 8 Mar., 2 Jas. II.

783. Deborah Hayward of Chilham, spinster, on 26 Aug., 2 Jas. II, at C., bewitched Elizabeth Viney, spinster, who was wasted, consumed, etc. *Endorsed*. Elizabeth Viney, Martha Gull, Elizabeth Young, Anne Packham, Anne Wood, John Dale, Stephen Dynes, William Hukins, Jane Hukins. Billa vera.

Po se non cul n$^{cr}$ Q$^{a}$.

[1] Strange and Wonderfull News from Yowell in Surry (1681) ; An Account of the Tryal and Examination of Joan Buts (1682).

## William III, 1689-1701

1690. Kent Lent Sessions and general gaol delivery holden at Maidstone on 11 Mar., 2 Wm. & Mary. Commission dated 1 Feb., 1 Wm. & Mary.

784. Elizabeth Mathewes. wife of William M. of Woolwich. labourer, on 20 Aug., 36 Chas. II, at W., bewitched a male infant, born of the body of Joan Dodd, wife of William D., which then and there died. *Endorsed.* Joan Dodd, Henry Trimme, Katherine Eagles, Elizabeth Collington, William Burman, Elizabeth Burley. Billa vera.

Po se non cul n$^{cr}$ Q$^a$.

785. ——, on 4 Nov., 35 Chas. II, at W., bewitched a male infant born of the body of Joan Dodd, wife of William D., which then and there died. *Endorsed.* [Names of witnesses as in No. 784.] Billa vera.

Po se non cul n$^{cr}$ Q$^a$.

1692. Kent Summer Sessions and general gaol delivery holden at Maidstone on 12 July, 4 Wm. & Mary. Commission dated 27 May, 4 Wm. & Mary.

786. Jane Bussey, wife of David B. of Bobchild, labourer, on 21 May, 4 Wm. & Mary, at B., did consult, covenant with, etc., 3 evil spirits in the likenesses of mice. *Endorsed.* John Linsey, Debora Bishopp, Elizabeth Brenthly. Billa vera.

Po se non cul ncr Qa.

787. Frances Graves of Tong, widow, on 25 Mar., 4 Wm. & Mary, at T., did consult, covenant with, etc., 4 evil spirits in the likenesses of mice. *Endorsed.* Anne Wildish, John Webb, Deborah Bishop, Elizabeth Brenchly. Billa vera.

Po se non cul ncr Qa.

788. Elizabeth Bird, wife of Robert B. of Newnham, labourer, on 23 June, 4 Wm. & Mary, at B., did consult, covenant with, etc., 4 evil spirits in the likenesses of mice. *Endorsed.* Rosamond Morgison, Frances Lorman, John Cibballs, Margaret Willis, Mary Colegate, Deborah Bishop, Elizabeth Brentsly. Billa vera.

Po se non cul ncr Qa.

1698.    Kent Lent Sessions and general gaol delivery holden
at Maidstone on 21 Mar., 10 Wm. III.  Commission
dated 23 Jan., 10 Wm. III.

789. Mary Clerke of Ashford, spinster, on 30 Oct.. 10 Wm. III.
at A., bewitched Philip Howard, the younger, aged 13 yrs.,
who was wasted, consumed, etc. *Endorsed.*  Elizabeth Reeve.
Billa vera.

Po se non cul ncr Qa.

1701.    Surrey Summer Sessions and general gaol delivery holden
at Guildford on 28 July, 13 Wm. III.  Commission
dated 20 June, 13 Wm. III.[1]

790. Sarah Moredike, wife of Edward M. of the parish of
St Saviour, Southwark, labourer, otherwise Sarah M., widow,
on 1 Apr., 12 Wm. III at . . . bewitched Richard Hathaway,
who was wasted, consumed, etc. *Endorsed.*  James Remington.
Richard Habard, Jane Michell, Richard Hathaway, jur., Thomas
Welling, jur., Thomas Bridges, jur., Laurence Kelly, jur.,
Millicent Chapman, Christiana Blewitt, John Wright, jur.,
John Thompson, Elizabeth Bran, Edward Dell, Gervase
Francklyn, Richard Horne, Anne Eaton, Elizabeth Willoughby.
Billa vera.

Po se non cul ncr Qª.

### Gaol Delivery Roll.

Sara Moredike . . . acquitted . . . and must be delivered paying
her fees.

[1] A Full and True Account of the Apprehending and Taking of
Mrs. Sarah Moordike, Who is accused for a Witch, Being taken near
Paul's Wharf . . . for having Bewitched one Richard Hetheway
. . . With her Examination before the Right Worshipful Sir Thomas
Lane, Sir Oven Buckingham, and Dr. Hambleton in Bowe-lane.
1701.
A short Account of the Trial held at Surry Assizes, in the Borough
of Southwark, on an Information against Richard Hathway . .
for Riot and Assault.  London, 1702.
The Tryall of Richard Hathaway, upon an Information For being
a Cheat and Imposter.  For endeavouring to take away the Life
of Sarah Morduck, For being a Witch at Surry Assizes . . . London,
1702.

Richard Hathaway haveing false accused Sara Moredike of Witchcraft Without any reason or colour for the same & ꝑtending himselfe to be bewitched by her must remaine in gaole till he shall find sureties before one or more of his ma^{ts} Justices of peace of this County for his psonall appearance at the next Assizes & Gen^{9}all Gaole deliu^{9}y to be holden for this county to answer &c., and in the mean time to be of the good behaviour.

# APPENDIX II

## The Discovery of Witches

compiled by Michael Dalton " partly out
of the book of discovery of the Witches that were
arraigned at Lancaster, anno 1612 before Sir James
Altham & Sir Edward Bromley, Judges of Assize
there, and partly out of M. Bernard's
Guide to Grand Jurymen ".

1. These witches have ordinarily a familiar or spirit, which
appeareth to them ; sometimes in one shape, sometimes in
another, as in the shape of a man, woman, boy, dog, cat, foal,
fowl, hare, rat, toad, &c. And to these their spirits they give
names, and they meet together to christen them (as they speak).
*Ber.* 107. 113.

2. Their said familiar hath some big or little teat upon their
body, and in some secret place, where he sucketh them. And
besides their sucking, the Devil leaveth other marks upon their
body, sometimes like a blue spot or red spot, like a flea biting ;
sometimes the flesh sunk in and hollow (all which for a time may
be covered, yea taken away, but will come again, to their old
form). And these the Devils marks be insensible, and being
pricked will not bleed, and be often in their secretest parts, and
therefore require diligent and careful search. *Ber.* 112, 219.

These first two are main points to discover and convict these
witches ; for they prove fully that those witches have a familiar,
and made a league with the Devil. *Ber.* 60.

So likewise if the suspected be proved to have been heard to
call upon their spirit, or to talk to them, or of them, or have
offered them to others. So if they have been seen with their
spirit, or seen to feed some thing secretly ; these are proofs they
have a familiar, &c.

3. They have often pictures of clay or wax (like a man, &c.
made of such as they would bewitch) found in their house, or
which they roast, or bury in the earth, that as the picture
consumes, so may the parties bewitched consume.

267

4. Other presumptions against these witches ; as if they be given to usual cursing and bitter imprecations, and withall use threatnings to be revenged, and their imprecations, or some other mischief presently followeth. *Ber.* 61, 205.

5 Their implicit confession ; as when any man shall accuse them for hurting them or their cattle, they shall answer, " You should have let me alone then " : or, " I have not hurt you as yet " : these and the like speeches are in manner of a confession of their power of hurting. *Ber.* 206.

6. Their diligent inquiry after the sick party, or coming to visit him or her, unsent for ; but especially being forbidden the house.

7. Their apparition to the sick party in his fits.

8. The sick party in his fits naming the parties suspected ; and where they be or have been, or what they do, if truly.

9. The common report of their neighbours, especially if the party suspected be of kin, or servant to, or familiar with a convicted witch.

10. The testimony of other witches, confessing their own witchcrafts, and witnessing against the suspected. that they have spirits or marks ; that they have been at their meetings ; that they have told them what harm they have done, &c. *Ber.* 212, 223.

11. If the dead body bleed upon the witches touching it.

12. The testimony of the person hurt, upon his death.

13. The examination and confession of the children (able and fit to answer) or servants of the witch, especially concerning these six observations, sc. If the party suspected have a familiar, or any teat, or pictures ; her threatenings and cursings of the sick party ; her enquiry after the sick party ; her boasting or rejoicing at the sick parties trouble. Also whether they have seen her call upon, speak to, or feed any spirit, or such like, or have heard her foretel of this mishap, or speak of her power to hurt, or of her transportation to this or that place, &c.

14. Their own voluntary confession (which exceeds all other evidence), sc. of the hurt they have done, or of the giving of their souls to the Devil, and of the spirits which they have, how many, how they call them, and how they came by them.

15. Besides, upon the apprehension of any suspected, to search also their houses diligently, for pictures of clay. or wax, &c., hair cut, bones. powders, books of witchcrafts, charms, and for

pots or places where their spirits may be kept, the smell of which place will stink detestably.

Now to shew you further some signs, to know whether the sick party be bewitched.

1. When a healthful body shall be suddenly taken, &c. without probable reason, or natural cause appearing, &c. *Ber.* 169.

2. When two or more are taken in the like strange fits, in many things.

3. When the afflicted party in his fits doth tell truly many things, what the witch, or other persons absent are doing or saying, and the like.

4. When the parties shall do many things strangely, or speak many things to purpose, and yet out of their fits know not any thing thereof.

5. When there is a strength supernatural, as that a strong man or two, shall not be able to keep down a child, or weak person, upon a bed.

6. When the party doth vomit up crooked pins, needles, nails, coals, lead, straw, hair, or the like.

7. When the party shall see visibly some apparition, and shortly after some mischief shall befall him. *Ber.* 173.

# APPENDIX III

## Slander

## CASES IN THE COURTS OF COMMON PLEAS AND KING'S BENCH

During the prevalence of the witch-mania, many malicious accusations of felonious witchcraft were made, and such statements were, of course, actionable. In some cases it is to be noticed that the authorities, civil [1] or ecclesiastical,[2] took cognizance of the defamation and bound over the slanderer. More generally it was left to the injured party to take the necessary action. The complaint of Jaquet, duchess of Bedford, in 1478, has already been noticed briefly, and is an example of procedure among peers.[3] Persons of lower rank cleared their characters by bringing suit in the Courts of Common Bench and King's Bench. Numerous examples of such causes might be discovered on the rolls by an industrious searcher. An example from each court is given here in full and may be of interest, since nothing of the kind seems to have appeared as yet in print.[4]

The first case, Swayne v. Atkinson, taken from the records of the Court of Common Pleas, is typical of many others and speaks for itself. The damages claimed are small, viz. £100.

[1] For instance in 1669 John Allen, the elder, of Stondon, was indicted for saying " Jone Mills is a witch and did bewitch the ale of Matthew Parnell ". *Hertf. Co. Sessions Rolls*, i, 217. See also the case of Richard Hathaway, *supra*. At the Cheshire Assizes, Apr., 1657, Edward Wilson and Joan Taylor were bound over for swearing that a certain man was betwitched by a woman witch. Punishment according to the ordinance against swearing. P.R.O., Chester 21/4, p. 362.

[2] Several cases from the Courts of Durham are noted in Depositions, Surtees Society, 1845, pp. 27, 33, 84.

[3] See p. 41 *supra*.

[4] With the exception of one case recently printed by me in *Ewen of East Anglia and the Fenland*, p. 69.

COMMON PLEAS. SWAYNE *v.* ATKINSON. C. P. 40, 2704, m 1351. *Trinity,* 1658.

Yorkshire. Richard Atkinson late of Holbecke in the county aforesaid, yeoman, was attached to answer Rosamond Swayne of a plea of trespass upon the case, &c. And whereupon the said Rosamond by James Catterall, her attorney, complaineth that whereas the said Rosamond is a good, true, faithfull, honest and religious pson of this Commonwealth of England from the time of her nativity hitherto and hath dureing all that time been reputed esteemed and noted to bee of a good conversacon and condicon as well amongst her neighbo<sup>rs</sup> as all other the good people of this Commonwealth of England with whom shee hath had any conversation or acquainetance and was never stained with the guilt of any kinde of Witchcrafte, Inchantement, charmes or sorceries or any other such like notorious crimes whatsoever. Nevertheless, the said Richard not being ignorant of the premisses but malitiously intending and contriving not onely to deprive the said Rosamond of her good name, fame, and credditt but alsoe to bring her into danger of the losse of her life and forfeiture of all & singuler her goods and chattels the twentieth day of ffebruary in the yeare of our Lord one thousand six hundred fifty and seaven att Holbecke of his meare malice did speake utter publish and pnounce of, to, and concerning the said Rosamond in the presence and hearinge of divers good people of this Commonwealth being neighbours and acquaintances of the said Rosamond these false, feigned, scandelous, malitious and opprobrious wordes following, that is to say, thou (meaning the said Rosamond) art a witch and did take my sonnes limies from him (meaning one Leonard Atkinson his sonn) by reason of the speaking, publishing, and pnounceing of which false, faigned, scandelous, malitious and approbrious wordes the said Rosamond is not onely much impaired in her good name, fame, and creddit, but also hath been compelled to expend severall somes of money to cleare her inocenty herein to the damage of the said Rosamond of one hundred poundes. And thereupon shee bringeth her suite, &c.

And the said Richard by Samuel Brogden, his attorney, cometh and defendeth the force and injuiry when, &c., and sayth that he is not guilty of the pmisses above upon him imposed in manner and forme as the said Rosamond above hath complained against him and of this he puts himself upon the Country, and the said Rosamond likewise.     Therefore the Sheriffe is commanded that he cause to come here from the day of the holy Trinity in three weeks, twelve, &c., by whom, &c.,   And who neither, &c., to make a jury, &c., because as well, &c.

The second illustration will provide a much more important example, and a few preliminary investigations add to the interest.

According to a petition of Henry. earl of Stirling and others in the House of Lords, 27 June, 1660, it appears that " Sir Peter Vanlore, the elder, in his lifetime settled the Castle and parks of the Devizes in Wiltshire on Lady Mary Powell and the heirs of her body, with remainder to his own right heirs, but Sir Edward Powell, late husband of Lady Powell, who for sixteen years had separated himself from the company of his wife, did about 5 Sept.. 1651. with William Hinson *alias* Powell, his nephew. now a member of Parliament, Thomas Levingstone. Anne, his wife, and others, by force and false pretences possess themselves of the house where Lady Powell then lay dying, on feigned actions arrested and hurried away her servants, kept her house in a warlike manner with armed men, and having by force secluded from her all persons but themselves, procured her to acknowledge a fine of the property mentioned above, to the use of Sir Edward and herself for life with remainder to the use of the defendants, Thomas Levingstone, Anne, his wife, and their heirs. Lady Powell died on the 6th Oct., 1651, whilst still under the same restraint, the fine by ante date and false entry was made a fine of Trinity term, 1651." [1]

Among those who conceived a violent enmity towards Mrs. Anne Levingstone was Abraham Vandenbemde. who with others, left no stone unturned to secure her destruction, the steps taken resulting in the execution of a disinterested third party. According to a contemporary pamphlet, in December, 1651, the Confederates repaired to one Joan Simpson and offered her 10*l*. in hand, and 500*l*. more in Hilary term following, if she would swear that Mrs. Levingstone had used sorcery and witchcraft to take away the life of Lady Powell. On 10 Jan. following, one Anne Hook (who pretended herself to be a cunning woman) being employed by the Confederates, persuaded her thereunto by offering her 120*l*. and half the money which Vandenbemde and another were to give her and her husband for making their

[1] Hist. MSS. Comm.. 7th Rep.. pt. i. p. 110.

affidavits. Simpson, however, " abominating so wicked a practice to take away an innocent gentlewomen's life, discovered the plot." Notwithstanding that a writ of supplicavit issued out of Chancery to bind the Confederates to good behaviour, they continued to employ Hook, to procure the desired witnesses. Accordingly, Hook went to one Joan Peterson, living in Spruce Island near Wapping. This Peterson is said to have been an able practitioner in physic, and was also suspected of being a worker of black magic. Joan Peterson was offered 100*l*., and asked to swear that she had given certain powders and bags of seeds to Mrs. Levingstone to help her in her law suits, and to provoke unlawful love. Joan refused to do what was required, and to obviate the possibility of another exposure, the Confederates designed a further scheme. Accordingly on 7 Mar. they obtained a warrant from a justice of the peace named Waterton for the apprehension of Joan Peterson, and search of her house for images of clay, hair, and nails. Strict examination and diligent enquiry revealed nothing of an incriminating nature. The Confederates, however, carried her before Waterton, where Vandenhemde, Collet, a solicitor, and others sat with the Justices' Clerks to take her examination. Interrogated touching her usage of witchcraft and sorcery to take away the life of Lady Powell of Chelsea, she answered that she never used sorcery or witchcraft. nor had she ever heard of Lady Powell, except when not long before one Anne Hook (an Irish woman) came to her with one Goodwife Garland to persuade her to make an oath against Mrs. Levingstone. Whereupon the Justice, " contrary to law " says the pamphleteer, gave an order to search her. The searchers found nothing on her body which might create the least suspicion of her being a witch, whereupon the Justice took bail for her appearance at the next Sessions. On the 14th March following (being the Sabbath day) by the Confederates' means Joan was again apprehended and re-examined, and to encourage her to confess she was told that she need not fear as her life was not aimed at, but evidence was desired to support an accusation against Mrs. Levingstone, who had obtained Lady Powell's estate, and thereby undone 36 persons of her kindred. Joan replied that she never knew, nor heard of the said Lady Powell, otherwise as aforesaid ; and that she had not heard from the said Mrs. Levingstone for above a year before that time. Then she was searched again in a most unnatural and barbarous

T

manner by four women whom the Confederates had brought with them. One of the women told the Justice that there was a " teat of flesh in her secret parts more than other women usually had ". Accused was then committed to New Prison and from thence to Newgate, where she was left to " the ordering and mercy of one Brocks, a keeper there and an agent of the Confederates ".

On 5 Apr. two bills of indictment were preferred against Joan Peterson at Hick's Hall, and found by the grand-jury. The first indictment according to a pamphlet was to the effect that she had conspired with another gentlewoman to administer a potion or posset to Lady Powell, who soon after the drinking died. The second charge was for bewitching one Christopher Wilson. On 6 Apr. Joan Peterson " was arraigned before Mr. Recorder (who was of counsel for the conspirators), and on the 7th of Apr. was tried ; at which trial the said Confederates (who before had spent three weeks' time at Wapping in procuring witnesses) were present, with three Counsellors to prosecute the said Peterson. Then the Court proceeded upon the first indictment, which was for bewitching the Lady Powell to death ; whereupon many women persons of mean degree (and of ill fame and reputation) were produced against her, and interrogated by the said Counsel, according to the briefs delivered unto them, wherein all the witnesses' testimonies, written before hand. And being asked what she had to say for her self ? (upon her knees) she took God to witness that she never knew the Lady Powell nor the house where she dwelt, nor was any wise guilty of her death ; and delivered a paper of such witnesses as she had to defend her, desiring that they might be called, whereupon Dr. Bates, and Dr. Colledon, physicians, together with Mr. Stamford, and Mr. Page, surgeons, and divers other persons of good quality, testified the disease, manner of sickness, and the cause of the said lady's death, which were the dropsy, the scurvy, and the yellow jaundice, and that they wondered how she was able to live so long [about 80], having most of these diseases growing on her for many years before ; amongst which evidences the innocency of Mrs. Levingstone, formerly by the Confederates maliciously aspersed and bespattered, was now fully vindicated, to their great astonishment, trouble, and disgrace."

The verdict recorded was " not guilty noe flying ", and the Court proceeded to the second indictment. The anonymous recorder states that this charge was of " bewitching one Christopher Wilson (who doth not himself complain of any such thing, but the Confederates only), and the only material evidence that then was against her, was one Margaret Austin (who had formerly been a wandering person, but was in charity taken up. relieved, and kept, by the said Joan Peterson, until she perceived that the said Austin had purloined some of her goods out of her house) and two witnesses more ; the substance of whose testimony was as followeth. That the said Wilson, having been a long time sick, and hearing that the said Peterson had done good to many, sent for her to come to him, who accordingly did, and administered means for his recovery, which at first was conceived to do him good ; but he afterwards relapsed, and the reason that was urged to induce the Court and Jury to believe that he was bewitched, was, that during his sickness, she sent to him for moneys for her physic : to whom answer was returned that he could then send her none. Whereupon it was then deposed that she did reply, that he had better have sent her monies, for he should be ten times worse than ever was ; And that afterwards he became very ill again, and remained languishing. Many other witnesses were produced ; but could only swear to generalities, hear-says, and most absurd and ridiculous impertinences ; then being by the Court demanded what she could say for her self ? she desired that such witnesses as she had then there present, might be called (some of which durst not appeare because that the said Mr. Waterton (as the witnesses themselves do and will affirm) had threatened to send them to Newgate, if they did appear). Whereupon several witnesses were called, and being demanded what they could say for the prisoner, they began to tell, that they had known her for a long time, and that she had done many cures, and much good among the neighbours, but never knew that she did any ill ; But the officers of the court interrupted them saying (in a taunting manner) are you for a witch ? and is this all you can say ? and so turned several of them away before they could be further heard. Then one came to the court (a stranger to the prisoner) and offered to depose, that one in black, called Thomas Southwick (known to be servant to Thomas Crompton another of the Confederates) stood in the Sessions yard, offering money to strangers there. to come in and swear that the said Peterson was a witch, and amongst the rest offered to give her money if she would do the same, but he, being called for, could not be had, nor would appear, although Colonel Okey, and some other Justices upon the Bench desired the Recorder to take notice of it, and to give order that the said Thomas Southwick might be brought into court."

Upon this second indictment a verdict of guilty was brought in. Joan Peterson pleaded pregnancy, but was found not to be quick with child, although several physicians affirmed that she was in that condition. On the 6 Apr. the innocent (if we may believe our authority) woman was condemned to die. After that the Confederates and their agents went to her and offered her a reprieve or pardon if she would confess that Mrs. Levingstone had employed her to make away the life of the Lady Powell, to which she replied she could not, because it was altogether false. One of the said Confederates urging her again to say something against Mrs. Levingstone, she told him he was a rogue, and gave him a blow on the face, which made his nose bleed."

Joan Peterson steadfastly refusing to perjure herself, was on the 12th Apr. brought to the place of execution (Tyburn), when the Ordinary, nine or ten times, earnestly pressed her to confess something against Mrs. Levingstone. "The Executioner told the Ordinary he might be ashamed to trouble a dying woman so much, to which he replied, he was commanded so to do, and durst do no otherwise."

Joan Peterson having been thus done to death, Anne Levingstone shortly afterwards [Easter term, 1652] brought into the court of the Upper Bench a bill complaining against Sir Sigismond Alexander, Abraham Vandenbemde, Thomas Crompton, Thomas Collett (the lawyer), and the other persons mentioned in the above account, and putting her damages at what must have been a very great amount in 1652, namely 20,000*l*. The result of this slander action does not appear. Various suits touching the ownership of the Wiltshire property continued in the courts for 10 years, with the result that the fine was vacated by an Act of Parliament, which received the royal assent on the 19th May, 1662.

An entry in the Upper Bench roll relating to a trial for alleged perjury provides some account of this slander action It has become detached from the Keeper's section, and is now bound in the wrong order.

UPPER BENCH (KEEPERS. &c.).    K.B. 27, 1759.    (Between membranes 687 and 688.)    *Michaelmas, 1653.*

Middlesex.    Before this time that is to say upon Tuesday (to wit) the twelfth day of July in the year of our Lord One thousand six hundred fifty three at the sessions of the publique peace held for the County of Middlesex at Hickeshall in St John Street in the said County Before Sr John Thorowgood Knt., Josias Berners. and John Hooker, esquires, and others their fellows Justices assigned to keep the publique peace in the said Countie   And also to hear and determine divers felonies trespasses and other misdoings committed in the same county upon the oath of twelve jurors it was p̃sented That whereas in Easter Term in the year of our Lord one thousand six hundred fifty and two before the keepers of the liberty of England by authority of parliament in the Upper Bench at Westminster came Thomas Levingston & Anne, his wife, by Francis Gregge, their attorney, And then and there brought into the Court of Upper Bench their Bill against Sir Sigismond Alexander, Knight, Abraham Vandenbemde, Thomas Crompton, gent., Thomas Collett, gent., Thomas Garland & Elizabeth, his wife, Richard Hooke & Anne, his wife, John Austin & Margaret, his wife, Christopher Muckley & Thomas Southwicke being in the Custody of the Marshal &c., of a plea of trespass upon the Case And there were pledges of prosecuting, that is to say, John Doo & Richard Roo, which said Bill followeth in these words ∫∫ Midd.   Thomas Levingston esquire, & Anne, his wife, complain of Sir Sigismond Alexander, Knight, [*and the others named*] being in the Custody of the Marshal of the Marshalsea of the Keepers of the liberty of England by authority of Parliament before the same Keepers in the upper Bench for That whereas the said Sir Sigismund Alexander [*and the others named*] having wicked devillish and malicious intent not only to take away the good name and fame of the said Anne Levingston but utterly to ruin destroy and take away the life of the said Anne Levingston without any just cause (she being an innocent pious and just person of this Commonwealth) the sixth day of April in the year of our lord one thousand six hundred fifty & two at the parish of St Clements Dane in the County aforesaid did falsely & maliciously confederate plot conspire combine together with oaths p̃misses bonds & other engagements each to other and with other meanes practices and machinations to cause the said Anne to be indicted arraigned and condemned to death for causing and procuring (as they the said Sir Sigismund Alexander [*and the others named*] did then and there falsely and maliciously pretend) Dame Mary Powell th . . . late before deceased and late wife of Sir Edward Powell, Knight and Baronet, to be distroyed with witchcraft sorcery poison or one of them ; whereas the said Anne Levingston was never guilty of those or any such like abominable and execrable crimes or practices or any of them. Whereupon the said Thomas Levingston & Anne, his wife, said that they were damnified to the value of Twenty thousand pounds. And thereupon they bring their suit &c. And whereas Afterwards that is to say in the term of St Michael in the year of our lord One thousand six hundred fifty and two before the Keepers of the liberty of England by authority of Parliament in the upper Bench at Westminster came as well the said Thomas Levingston & Anne, his wife, by their attorney aforesaid As the said Sir Sigismond Alexander, Knight, [*and the others named*] by Henry Fauntleroy their Attorney came & did defend the force and injury when &c. And did say that they were not guilty thereof And of this they did put themselves upon the Country And the said Thomas Levingston and Anne, his wife, thereof likewise &c. Therefore a jury thereupon was to come before the Keepers. *etc.* on Monday next after the eight days of St Hilary then next following And who neither &c. to recognize &c. Because as well &c. The same day was given to the parties aforesaid there &c. Afterwards

between the parties aforesaid the plea aforesaid the jure aforesaid was respited before the Keepers, *etc.*, until Saturday next after eight days of the holy Trinity in the year of our lord one thousand six hundred fifty & three unless Henry Rolle Chief Justice assigned to hold pleas before the said Keepers, *etc.*, on Friday next after the said eight days of the holy Trinity at Westminster in the great hall of Pleas there according to the form of the Statute &c. should first come for default of Jurors &c. Whereas Afterwards that is to say on the aforesaid Friday next after the said eight days of the holy Trinity that is to say the seventeenth day of June in the year of our lord God one thousand six hundred fifty three abovesaid at Westminster aforesaid in the County of Middlesex aforesaid before the aforesaid Henry Rolle then & yet chief Justice assigned to hold pleas before the Keepers, *etc.*, there being then associate unto himself Edward

Cantrell, gent., according to the form of the Statute &c. came as well the aforesaid Thomas Levingston & Anne, his wife, as the aforesaid Sir Sigismond Alexander, Knt., [*and the others named*] by their Attorney aforesaid And the Jurors of the Jury aforesaid, that is to say, Sir John Poole, Baronet, Arthur Newman, gent., Edward Rogers, esquire, Francis Flaxmore, esquire, Francis Awsiter, esquire, John Allanson, esquire, Thomas Paltocke, gent., William Chambers, gent., William Smyth, gent., John Baldwyn, esq., William Browne, gent., & Robert Butler, gent., being likewise called came and were elected tried & sworn to say the truth of and upon the premisses One Susan Rocke late of Wappinge in the parish of White Chappell in the County of Middlesex, spinster, otherwise called Susan Rocke the wife of William Rocke of the parish aforesaid, mariner, on the aforesaid Friday the seventeenth day of June in the year aforesaid before the aforesaid Henry Rolle then Chief Justice as aforesaid having associated unto him Edward Cantrell according to the form of the statute &c. at Westminster aforesaid in the county of Middlesex aforesaid in the great hall of pleas there was produced as witness on the behalf of the said Thomas Levingston & Anne, his wife, plaintiffs in the cause aforesaid then depending between the said parties And was then and there sworn upon the holy Evangel of God to say the truth and nothing but the truth in the premises put in issue as aforesaid she the said Susan Rocke not having the fear of god before her eyes but being moved & seduced by the instigation of the devil And the lawes of England little regarding nor the penalties in the same contained in anyways fearing And her oath aforesaid in that behalf taken little esteeming then and there in the cause aforesaid then depending as aforesaid in suite between the parties aforesaid by her own proper act & consent falsely maliciously wilfully & corruptly upon her oath aforesaid before the aforesaid Henry Rolle, *etc.*, did say depose swear & give in evidence to the Jurors aforesaid so as aforesaid tried chosen & sworn to try the issue aforesaid between the parties aforesaid in manner and form aforesaid joyned That the Black Silke Tabby Gowne, two Silver Salts, & two silver spoones which Joan Peterson (one Joan Peterson lately executed for a witch who was also suspected to have bewitched Dame Mary Powell lately deceased to death) had of the plaintiff Anne Levingston was given unto her (Joan Peterson) by Robert Levingstone (a supposed kinsman of the said Thomas Levingston) for helping him the said Robert Levingston to buy wines & fruit of Elizabeth Garland (a neighbour of the said Joan Peterson) after the time that the said Robert Levingston bought a parcel of wines & fruit of the said Elizabeth Garland and not for any bags which the said Anne Levingston had of the said Joan Peterson nor for any manner of sorcery or witchcraft to be used upon the said Dame Mary Powell, Whereas in truth and in deed the Black silke Tabby Gowne, *etc.*, which Joan Peterson had of the plaintiff Anne Levingston was not given unto her the said Joan Peterson by the said Robert Levingston for helping him the said Robert to buy wines & fruit of Elizabeth Garland And whereas in truth & in deed the same Gowne, *etc.*, were given to the said Joan Peterson before the time that the said Robert Levingston bought a parcel of wines and fruits of the said Elizabeth Garland & not after And whereas in truth & indeed the same Gown, *etc.*, were given to the said Joan Peterson for certain bags which the said Anne Levingston had of the said Joan Peterson and for sorcery & witchcrafte to be used upon the said Dame Mary Powell; And so the said Susan Rocke the aforesaid seventeenth day [of] June in the year abovesaid at Westminster in the County of Middlesex aforesaid before the aforesaid Chief Justice in manner & form aforesaid by her own proper Act & consent aforesaid in cause aforesaid falsely wilfully & corruptly did comitt wilful & corrupt perjury to the great damage of the said Sir Sigismund Alexander [*and the other defendants named*] And against the publique peace &c. Which said Indictment the Keepers, *etc.*, afterwards for certain causes have caused to be determined &c. By which it was commanded to the Sheriff of the County aforesaid that he should not omit &c. but cause her to come & answer &c. And even now, that is to say upon Monday next after the three weeks of St Michael in the self same Term before the Keepers, *etc.*, comes the aforesaid Susan Rock by Ambrose Broughton, her attorney, And having heard the Indictment aforesaid she saith that she is not guilty thereof. And thereupon she put herself upon the Country; And Andrew Broughton, esquire, Coroner and Attorney of the said Keepers, in the Court of the said Keepers before them the said Keepers in the Upper Bench aforesaid who for the said Keepers in this part doth follow likewise, &c. Therefore let a Jury therein come before the said Keepers, *etc.*, on Monday next after the eight days of St Martin

And who &c. to acknowledge &c. Because as well &c. The same
day is given as well to the aforesaid Andrew Broughton, esq.,
who followeth, &c. As to the aforesaid Susan Rocke &c. At
which said Monday, *etc.*, before the aforesaid Keepers, *etc.*,
Come as well the aforesaid Andrew Broughton, esq., who
followeth &c. As the aforesaid Susan Rocke by her Attorney
aforesaid  And the Sheriff returned the names of Twelve Jurors
whereof none &c. Therefore it is commanded to the Sheriff
that he omit not &c., but distrain them by all their lands, &c
And that of their issues &c  And that he have their bodies before
the said Keepers, *etc.*, in the eight days of St Hilary wheresoever
&c before the beloved & faithful Henry Rolle Cheif Justice
Assigned to hold pleas before the said Keepers, etc. if sooner upon
Tuesday the nine & twentieth day of November at Westminster
*etc.*, according to the forme of the statute &c. he shall come for
want of Jurors &c  Therefore the Sheriff must have their bodies
&c. to acknowledge in form aforesaid. The same day is given as
well to the aforesaid Andrew Broughton, esq., who followeth,
&c. As to the aforesaid Susan Rocke &c.

# APPENDIX IV

## List of Witches not mentioned in Indictments

**1560.** Kent. Mother Bushe, late of St John's, suspected to be a witch. Visitation of the Archdeacon of Canterbury. *Archæologia Cantiana.* xxvi, 31.

**1566.** Essex. " One masons wief of Boram who was a witche " advised that she should confess nothing, " for yf thow dust, thow wolt dyve for hit ; and thowe wilt turne thy neighbowrs to troble." *Precedents*, by W. H. Hale, p. 147.

**1570.** Essex. Malter's wife of Theydon Mount and Anne Vicars of Navestock, suspected witches. examined by Sir Thomas Smith. Several depositions. *Life of Sir Thomas Smith*, by J. Strype, 1820, pp. 97–100.

**1570–1.** Canterbury. Several witches imprisoned. Mother Dungeon presented by the grand jury. *A History of Witchcraft*, by Prof. W. Notestein, p. 386.

**1570–1.** Folkestone, Kent. Margaret Browne, accused of unlawful practices, banished from town for seven years, and to be whipped at the cart's tail if found within six or seven miles of town. *Descriptive and Historical Account of Folkestone*, by S. J. Mackie, p. 319.

**1574.** Kent. Old Alice of Westwell, a ventriloquist, arraigned and convicted. *Discoverie of Witchcraft*, by R. Scot (ed. 1886), p. 104.

**1575.** Essex. " Widowe Jackson. a witch." *Precedents*, by W. H. Hale, p. 157.

**1576.** Essex. James Hopkinne of Hornchurch confessed that he went to Mother Persore, at Navestocke, " a conninge woman, to know by what me[a]ns his masters cattell was bewytched." *Precedents*, by W. H. Hale, p. 163.

**1577.** Essex. Henry Chittam of Gt. Bardfield charged for coining of false money and conjuring. *Acts Privy Council*, N.S., ix, 391 ; x, 8, 62.

1577. Sussex. Sessions of the Peace at Seaford. The grand jury presents Joan à Wood for being a witch (*venefica*). *Memorials of Seaford* (Suss. Arch. Soc., vii, p. 98).

1578. Sussex. Tree, bailiff of Lewes, and Smith of Chinting, to be examined touching conjuration. *Acts Privy Council*, N.S.. x, 220.

1579. Surrey. Simon Pembroke of Southwark suspected to be a conjuror, brought to the parish church of St. Saviour's to be tried by the " ordinarie judge for those parties ". fell dead before the opening of the trial. *Chronicles* (Holinshed, 1586), iii, 1271.

1580. Kent. Richard Yeorke of Stoale, a conjuror to be apprehended. *Acts Privy Council*, N.S., xii, p. 22. Several other practisers of conjuration in London named.

Essex. Humfrey Poles of Malden to be apprehended for conjuracion. *Ibid.*, p. 34.

Essex. Nicholas Johnson of Wodham Mortimer said to have practised sorcery. *Ibid.*, p. 251.

1582. Kent. Goodwife Swane of St John's in Thanet, vehemently suspected by the church authorities, to be a witch, boasting " that she can make a drink. which she saith if she give it to any young man that she liketh well of, he shall be in love with her ". *Archæologia Cantiana*, xxvi, 19.

1583. Kent. Ellen Bamfield of St Peters in Thanet vehemently suspected by the church authorities to use witchcraft. *Ibid.*, xxvi, 45.

1585. Essex. John Shonnke, the elder, of Romford, " detected for that he wente to faither Parfoothe for helpe for his wief : whiche Parfoothe is suspected to be a wiche." John says that he went to him to help his wife, and would do the same again. Afterwards he confessed " himself hartelie sorie for sekinge mans helpe. and refusing the helpe of God." *Precedents*, by W. H. Hale, p. 186.

1586. Kent. Joan Cason tried before the mayor of Faversham, and condemned to death for invocation of wicked spirits. Depositions. *Chronicles* (Holinshed, 1586), iii, 1560.

1592.  Essex.  A Colchester indictment is preserved.  Margaret
        Rand of Colchester, spinster, on 28 Nov.. 35 Eliz.,
        bewitched Judith Lingwood, wife of John L. of C.,
        tailor, at C., who languished until 7 Dec. following, at
        C. *Endorsed.*  Billa vera.
        Po se non cull.  Stowe MSS. 840, f. 42.

1595.  Herts.  Contemporary pamphlet mentioned by Lowndes
        (*Bibliographer's Manual*, 1968).
        The Arraignment and Execution of 3 detestable
        Witches, John Newell, Joane his wife, and Hellen
        Calles, two executed at Barnett, and one at Braynford,
        1 Dec., 1595.

1597.  Kent.  Visitation of the Archdeacon of Canterbury.
        St Lawrence in Thanet.  " Sibilla Ferris, the wife of
        Henry Ferris, that there is a fame in their parish that
        she is a witch, but saith herself is not guilty of any
        such offence."  *Archæologia Cantiana*, xxvi, 32.

1599.  Essex.  Tailer, a wizard of Thaxted, is mentioned in the
        Proceedings in the Court of the Archdeaconry of Essex.
        *Precedents*, by W. H. Hale, p. 219.

1602.  Essex.  Darrel mentions Alice Bentley tried at Quarter
        Sessions held at Saffron Walden, 13 Apr., 1602, for
        bewitching Susan Boyton who was possessed.  *A Survey
        of Certaine Dialogical Discourses*, p. 54.

Temp. Eliz. Kent.  Pardon to Alice S. for bewitching a cow and
        pigs at Northfleet.  Bodleian, Rawlinson MSS., C. 404,
        f. 205*b*.

1606.  Herts.  Joan Harrison and her daughter are said to have
        been hanged for witchcraft at Royston, according to
        a contemporary pamphlet reprinted by W. B. Gerish,
        1909.
        The most Cruell and Bloody Murther committed by
        an Innkeeper's Wife . . . With the severall witchcrafts
        and most damnable practises of one Johane Harrison
        and her Daughter upon severall persons, men and
        women at Royston, who were all executed at Hartford
        the 4th of August last past.  1606.  London.  Printed
        for William Ferebrand and John Wright.  1606.

1644.  Kent.  " The widow Drew hanged for a witch."  *Collections
        for an History of Sandwich*, by W. Boys, p. 714.

1645. Sussex. Martha Bruff and Anne Howsell ordered by the " mayor of Rye and others " to be put to the ordeal of water. *Hist. MSS. Comm. Reports,* xiii. pt. iv. 216. See p. 67 *supra.*

1645. Kent. A contemporary pamphlet is entitled : The Examination, Confession, Triall, and Execution of Joane Williford, Joan Cariden, and Jane Hott : who were executed at Faversham, in Kent . . all attested under the hand of Robert Greenstreet, Maior of Faversham. London, 1645. *Collection of Tracts,* printed by J. R. Smith, 1838.

1649. Herts. The names of two executed witches are obtained from a contemporary pamphlet : The Divels Delusions or A faithfull relation of John Palmer and Elizabeth Knot two notorious Witches lately condemned at the Sessions of Oyer and Terminer in St Albans, 1649.

1651. Essex. A Colchester indictment is preserved. John Lock of Colchester, weaver, on 8 Nov., 1651, at C., did take upon himself, witchcraft etc. to declare and make known to one William Fayrcloth of C., weaver, the place where he should find certain yarne which had been stolen from him, etc. *Endorsed* Witnes. Elizabeth Fayrcloth, William Moore theld, sworne. This is a true bill.

> Confest and adiudged to remaine in the Gaole of Moothall for one whole year from henceforth and in the meantyme to be set on the pillorie once in every quarter of the said yeare upon a market day according to the statute.
>
> Stowe MSS. 840, f. 32.

1659. Herts. Information was laid against Alice Free of Little Hadham for bewitching Frances Rustat to death. Hertfordshire County Sessions Rolls, i, 126, 127, 129.

1661. Herts. Frances Bailey of Broxbourne complained of abuse by those who believed her to be a witch. *Ibid.,* i, 137. See also p. 52, *supra.*

1694. Kent. Ann Hart of Sandwich convicted, but escaped punishment in consequence of an act for a general and free pardon which passed in 1695. *Collections for an History of Sandwich,* by W. Boys, p. 718.

# APPENDIX V

## A SCOTTISH INDICTMENT[1]

1633, 29 May.

Intrat upon pannell Marion Richart, *alias* Layland, for the pointis of witchcraft, sorcerie, and divination, and utheris underwrittin.

In the first ye, the said Marion ar indyted and accuised of contraveining the tenour of the Act of Parliament maid be our umquhile dread soverane lady Mary be the grace of God Quein of Scotland with the advyse of hir thrie Estaites in hir nynth parliament that quher they being informit of the hevie and abominable superstition used be divers of the leidges of this realme be using of wichcraftis, sorceries, and negromancie, and credence givin thairto in tymes bygane. againes the law of God, and for avoiding and away putting of all sic superstition in tyme cuming it wes statute and ordainit be the Queines Majestie and thrie Estaites forsaid that na persone or persones of quhatsomewer estait, degrie or condition they be of, tak upon hand in any tymes therafter to use any maner of wichcraftis, sorcerie or negromancie, or give themselvis furth to have any sic craft or knowledge thairof, thairthrow abusand the people, under the paine of death. And trew it is that ye, the said Marion, have contraveined the tenour of the said act be using and practising of wichcraftis, sorceries and divinationes, and of giving of yourself furth to have sic craft and knowledge, and in keiping companie and society with the devill, and thairthrow abusand the people at diverse and sundrie tymes and places in maner following, and therfoir and for airt and part of the said abominable superstition used and practised by yow aught and sould be adjudged to the death : And in speciall ye, the said Marion, are indyted and accused for airt and part [abetting] of the said abominable superstition for that sex or sevin yeires since James Fischer, your oy [grandchild], being keiping Manse Smythis swyne, went up into ane auld hous called the house of

[1] *The Register of the Privy Council of Scotland*, 1633, p. 551.

Howing Gremay to saife himselfe from a cold showir that wes raining and quhen he cam in to the saide old hous he saw yow and Kathereine Miller sitting thair and the devill, in liknes of a black man, sitting betuixt yow, and the said Katherine cryed fearclie ' Tak him for he will tell upone us ' ; bot ye wold not suffer and said ' Let him alane for na body will beleive him.' And upon the morning therafter the said James, your oy, told Manse Smyth, his master, that he had seine yow and Katherine Miller and the devill together in the old hous. And lykwayes that night, whilk ye and the said Katherine wer in the stockis befor your now cuming to the toun, the said Katherine said unto you, ' Yea, plaige of God upon thy oy, for if thow had done to him that quhilk I baid the he had not bein troubling us now ' ; quhilks pointis will be sufficiently provin and therfor rank wich cannot now deny.

Secondly, ye, the said Marion, are indyted and accuised for airt and part of the said abominable superstition in that fyve or six yeires since Elspeth Sandesone contractit ane hevie disease in so much that sho wes quyt bereft of all hir sences for ane long space, ye, coming to the said Elspethis hous, made ane water quhilk ye call ane remedie for forspeaking and tooke water into ane round cope and went out into the byre and took sumthing out of your purse lyk unto great salt and did cast therin and did spit thrie severall tymes in the same and ye confest yourselfe when ye had so aundit in bitt (quhilk is ane norne tearme), that is to say, ye blew your breath thairin ; and thairafter ye sent it to the said Elspeth with the servand woman of the house and bad that the said Elspeth sould be waschin tharin, hand and feite, and scho sould be as heall as ever sho wes ; as also ye said to the servant woman that ye send with the water that if scho told it agane scho should never thryve, and so soone after as scho reveilet it scho died, quhilk death was wrought be your deid, and quhilk also ye confest before the session at Sanday [Orkney] and therfor rank wich cannot now deny.

Thirdly, ye, the said Marion, ar indyted and accuised for airt and part of the said abominable superstition in that ther wes a poore wyfe with yow who wes travelling of cheild in your hous and desyred a sope milk with yow, quhilk ye on nawayes wold give ; therfoir the said poor woman sent to Robert Dreveris hous (quhilk wes in that same bigging) to get a sope milk quhilk the said Robertis wyfe sent unto hir ; and immediatlie thairefter the said Robertis wyfe lost the profeit of hir wholl milk. Quharfor she cam into yow and did lament for her profeit that she wantit. Ye ansuerit and said, ' Go thy way to the sea and tell nyne boares of the sea cum in, that is to say, nyne waves of the sea, and let the hindmost of the nyne ga back againe and the nixt thairafter tak thrie loofullis of the water and put within thy stoupe and quhen thow comes home put it within thy kirne and thow will get thy profeit agane ' ; quhilk ye, rank wich, cannot also deny.

Fourthlie, ye ar indyted and accuised for airt and part of the said abominable superstition in that Helein Hamiltoun, spous to James Keith, and all hir houshold being straited with dreuth for the space of tuentie dayes or ane moneth that no drink could quench the same, and the said Heleine and hir husband alledging yow for the great drew that they had upon ane Sunday ye cam to the said Heleines hous and fetchit with yow ane mutchkin of small aill in ane chopping can and offerit to the said Heleine and hir familie to drink, bot the said Helein refuisit to drink it, bot ye urgit it more and more upon hir and saide, ' I have ane sonsay hand and my mother befoir my day,' and made everie on of them to drink therof, and immediatlie before the nixt Sonday thair thrist was eisit and the heavy weicht that wes upon them the tyme of thair great thrist and dreuth wis taken away, quhilk ye, rank wich, cannot also deny.

Fyftly, ye, the said Marion, are indyted and accuised for airt and part of the said abominable superstition in that ye cam to William Fothringhame his house benorth to get almis, and his wyf not being at leasure to give yow alms ye went to the dure and sayde, as ye went, that schie should loss als meikle schortly ; and aught dayes after that his best kow died, quhilk wes done be your deid, quhilk ye, rank wich, cannot also deny.

Saxtly, ye, the said Marion, ar indyted and accuised for airt and part of the said abominable superstition in that ye cam to Stronsay (Orkney) to Margrat Thomesones hous, and the said Margrat had nyne ky quhilk wes not ridin and ye said unto hir, ' Give me almis and befoir this day aucht dayes ilk kow on your aught sall be riddin ' ; quhilk almis ye resavit from the said Margrat and befoir that day aught dayes ilk kow that she had wes riddin quhilk fell out even according as ye spaik, quhilk ye rank witch cannot also deny.

Sevinthlie, ye, the said Marion, ar indyted and accuised for airt and part of the said abominable superstition in that ye did wasch the feit of James Davidsones kat into his bait water becaus he could get no fisch that yeir, saying that the said James in tyme cuming wold get more fisch in respect of your work in wasching of the cates feit in his bait water ; and quhen ye had waschin the cat thairin ye did tak the water wherein the cat wes waschin and did cast it out after him quhen he did go to the sea, quhilk point, ye, rank wich, cannot allso deny.

Eighthly, ye, the said Marion, ar indyted and accuised for airt and part of the said abominable superstition in that about fyve or six yeires since ye cam to David Jokis hous who wes going to the sea and wes making moane that he had gottin no fisch that yeir ; ye ansuerit and sayde that micht be easily mendit, and called for the thing that geid about the fyre, quhilk wes the cate, and said that ye wold wasch the cates heid and feit into the water quherin the bait wes to be leiped and said that ye wald tak that water and cast it about him and upon him and into his sea caschie and into his bait coubie, and quhen he cam to the sea he sould get fisch enoch, quhilk ye, rank witch, cannot deny.

Attour, ye ar indyted and accuised for airt and part of the said abominable superstition in that ye cam to Stronsay about tua or thrie yeires since in sumer and asking almis fra Andro Couper, skipper of ane bark, he said to yow, " Awa wich, carling, devill a farthing ye will fa " ; quherupon ye departed wery offendit. And, incontinently, he going to sie, the bark being under saill, he ran mad and wold have luppin ovirburd an his sone, seing him, gat him in his airmes and held, quherupon the seiknes imediatly left him and his son ran mad. And Thomas Patersone, seing him tak the madnes and the father to turne weill, ane dog being in the bark, to [oke the] dogg and bladded him upon the sone his shoulders and therafter keist the said dog in [the sea], quharby these in the bark wer saifed, quhilk being done all the doggers at the sey . . . landyeris for feir gave yow abundantly, quhilk all wes done be yowr witchcraft and . . . quhilk ye cannot deny.

And generallie ye ar indyted for airt and pairt of using and practising of witchcraftis, sorceries, divinationes and charmis, as is particularlie abovewrittin, and giving your selfe furth to have sic craft and knowledg, thairby abusing the people, and that by your cursingis and imprecationes ye wrong and hurt man and beist, quhilk evill ar brocht to pas be the power and working of the devill, your master, and therfoir aught and should underly the law and be adjudged to the death thairfoir and in exampill of utheris to do the lyk.

29 May, 1630. The haill assyse, all in ane voice, be the mouth of the chancellar fyllis the pannell in the first. the secund anent the watter and chairme, the third, the sext, the aught and nynt, and clengis hir of the fourt, fyft, and sevint poyntis, and referris sentence to the judge and dome to the dempstar.

A YORKSHIRE TERROR A.D 1621

(From a contemporary drawing, Brit. Mus., Add MS. 32496)

# APPENDIX VI

## Depositions (17th Century)

### (Brit. Mus. Add. MS 27402, fos 104–121)

[This MS. is not easily read and the transcriber has found it necessary to omit several words entirely, while other uncertain readings are printed in italics. A few depositions which did not relate to accusations of witchcraft have been left out.]

---

These Examinations of Wizards and Witches (com: Suffolc :) in August 1645 were not long since given me by John Thruston of Hoxne Esq$^r$ whose Ancestors were Justices of the Peace for the said County : and these Depositions might probably be taken by some one of them. *M.S.*

Alicia Warner de Rushmere ffrely beeinge at her liberty confessed that she had enterteined certeine euill sperits w$^{ch}$ had succed her and that she imployed them to carry lice to one Wrights wife and to one barnies and the s$^d$. weamen weare lousie according as she confessed. Billa vera.

Sara Warner de Rushmere de eadē sister to Ali. Billa vera.

Elizabeth Greene de Winckfield, vid. Jo Browneinge testu that she confessed the day after her app$^r$hendinge that she was a witch and he askeinge her how she knew it & she ansd she knew it by the tokens found about her. he askinge her how these tokens came she sd that goody Wright of Stradbrooke sent her 3 imps w$^{ch}$ she found at home like 3 chickings and these sucked her & made those teats. She called these imps Giles Alse & Bes & further the deuill appeared to her like a man one night when she was in bed a slepe and nipped her by the neck and wak$nd$ her and that he took her by the hand & asked her if she wold serve him, but she did not confes that she did assent, but sd he drew 3 drops of blood of her arme & shewd the place where he drew it & th$^t$ he asket her to kepe some imps w$^{ch}$ she told him she

291

wold and after, she succled her 3 imps as beefore she refused the money the diuell offered her. Rich Aldus testatur vt ante. Billa vera.

Elizabeth Fillet de Wetherden. John Spinke testatur that about 7 years since this acc'ed beinge angry w^{th} his man for not mendinge her shoes he did often times see a rat that did troble him in his shop but he cold never kil it and beinge rosolued to shote it cold se it no more. After he saw a mowle run about his shop but he cold not get. After this accu. lieinge bedered stroke her kep and this informant's wife beinge told of it sayd she shold lie and rot before she wold come at her if she weare her keep. psently after, this woman had a child taken w^{th} a stronge fit of sicknes and the day after the sicknes it had lice about it but shisninge the lininge it was cleere frō the lice. Tho gardiner . . . Tho. Janings testatur. that her told that the searcher was come to towne and he asked her if she wold be searched and she sd let the honest wemen come and she wold be content and she further sayd the divell tempted her to kill her selfe and she shold auoyd this standell. Ignoramus.

Grace Gunburgh vxor de eadem. John Waller testatur. That in the time of watchinge he saw a door creepe upon her head in the time of her watchinge. James May testatur. that he saw a fly in the time of her watchinge and he burnt it as he thought. The searchers sd she had marks. Ignoramus.

Elizabeth Hobert that the day after her attach. Maninge testatur that the diuell appeared to her about 30 years since like a black boy and drew blood against her will at her back after wd at the same time she couenanted w^{th} him that he shod have her body and soule and wold auenge her of those that angered her and that he wold furnish her w^{th} money but never pformed it. Further that wished her cosen Hobart harme and he fell lame and so continued till he died w^{ch} was w^{th}in 3 days after she was questioned. John Hayward, that after the diuel had god blod of her he asked her to forsake god & Ch. and she consented to him upō pmise y^{t}. she shold want nothinge and bee reuenged and then she confessed she had imp *tht* mad *loose* and that her imps did suck twice or 3 a week but had not beene w^{th} her this fornight & further vt ante. Billa vera.

Richardus fforeman de Stowmarket⎫ Testatur Sterne.
Williā Keeble de Stowmarkt.        ⎭    Ignoramus.

Margaret *Powell* vxor. John Curtise test. that she confessed after 6 days watchinge that she had *3* imps sent her from Mother Browne and that they had fed on her severall times. there names weare bes. nan and joane, and that they had sucked her the past Saturday. Billa vera.

Eli[zabeth] Richmond vxor de Bramford after 6 days watchinge confessed. teste. M^r Curtise that the deuill came to her and imbraced her and asked her to love him and trust in him and wold defend her and curse her enemies and she asked him who he was and he sd y^e pfit Daniell and he told her she must forsake god & the Church and that she must not goe to Church to heaue the . . . w^cn she pmised upon her troath she wold doe and after this, beinge angrie w^th one goody turnis she wished the plague on her and she died within 6 weeks and as she thought it was upō her curseinge. quere.

Ailicea Marsh vx deadē after 3 days & nights spake to Will Itiles & desired him to come to her about 3 o 4 after for she had something she wold confes to him, he came to her accordincgely & she confessd that the deuill came to her in the likenes of a cat and desired her sowle but she wold not giue it him, but she gave him her body & after this he had the use of her body & so depted. After this he appeared and brought her a wrightincge and he drew blood of her and she marked it w^th the blod he drew from her, and that he sent 3 imps that shold doe any thinge for her and that she imployed those imps to kill certeine hogs and that she succled these imps theyr names weare dic Tom & Will. She cofessed she killed Simsons son and Simson further testified that his hog died at that time.

Goody Smith Hen. Sanford wit. after 3 nights watchinge. She confessed to him y^t she had cursed 2 childeren of Parkers and that they languished immediately an did giue thē apples and wish they might doe him hurt and died w^thin one quarter of a yeare and concerneinge one fulcher's child that beeinge disconted that iat was not woanen she went and touched the child in the cradle and imediately it sprung up in the cradle and beinge take w^th strange fits and imediately died that her imps hange in her secret parts in *a bag* and her husband saw it.

and that these imps sucked on her. billa vera.

and that she granted to his couenant.

Payne de eadē testatur in the 3 night after watchinge that he beinge at plowgh curseinge &c., the deuill appeared to him like a dog and required him to forsake god and Christ w^ch he consented to. Joh. Curtise testatur about 30 years since vt ante but upō his appe' he bad him avoyd satō upō the 2 apperance w^ch was some years after he made a covenant w^th him vt ante.

Sterne testa that after 8 days watchinge, the deuill tempted him to hange him selfe and that 20 years since *he* thought the diuell appeared to him and he syd the diuill tempted him to give him his sowle and he sd I resined my sowle frely from god & I give it freely to the diuill.

John Chambers de eadē John Curtise testatur, after 3 days that about 12 years the deuill told him in the shape of a boy that if he wold follow his directiō and make a covenant w^th him he shold want no thinge and that he brought a wrightinge to him to him and he drew blod of his finger and sined the covenant and the diuell pmisd to find him 3 imps w^ch accordingely he receiued, and imployed these imps to kill a bullock of widman and an horse of an other mans and he sent his imps richard to kill one Smiths horse and it died, and he sent his imp John to kill one Smith's child and it died.

Testatur Smith that Ch confessed freely that he was the cause that sent two toads to his wife as she was dressinge of her child and that he came aback to his howse to see if the toads had done that he sent them for and that the child w^ch she was then dressinge did forthwith languish and die.

Lidea Taylor vxor, John Beoment testatur that she was app[rehended] the 30 of July and about the   day of August she confessed that she was a witch & that she had 2 imps the one like an owle the othe like a blackburd and that by these means she killed one *Berts* cattell and that he and all his howse weare the worse for her and that her imps counselled her to steale and that they counselled her to kill her selfe, and that the diuill did appear to her in the night and wold haue had . . . w^th her but she called her husband ; Ed. Cattinge testatur idem , John Barlet sd she came to his howse upō the Tuesday night, &c. Ignoramus.

Margaret Legat de Playford, Will Wels testatur, that about 7 years since he fallinge out w^th the *sone* of Mar. Legate his child fell sick and askinge the deuise of a Phisitia in ipswitch cold find no cause of the desease, the child still continueinge sick Cryed out it thought it was stunge w^{th} wasps, soone after this Legate came to this infor mants howse upō *he* thretened if she came there any more he wold through her in to the riuer he beeinge a miller, yet after this she came to his howse and although he reuiled her yet she came into his howse and sate upon his bed, and after he forced her out of his howse she fell downe and asked him forgiuenes.

Eadem testatur Clerke that she sd to this infor. that she was a damned creature and if she had not beene taken she shold haue done much harme. Alicia *E*ayth testatur idem vt ante.

Mar. *J*ason sayth that whilst this accusant was watchinge one of her imps like a mowle came to her and sucked her in the secret pts.

John Wilkinson testatur that she after 3 days watchinge sd that she had a thinge *liuyd* by her like a child but she neuer saw it nor neuer heard it speake. Ignoramus.

An Ellis de Metingham    Tho. Hudson sd that vpō a falling out w^{th} *w^hoathis woman* he was lame and so continued but lately changeinge his surgeō he doth now begin to mend. I͡g.

ffides Mils vxor de ffresingfield    Jno Goodinge testatur that after two nights watchinge she confessd she had 3 birds some called them imps theyr names Tom Rob*ur* and John and that these imps did on her and that she gaue one of these birds to one of Tho. Aldus child w^{ch} breake out w^{th} 21 soars and died that she sent 2 of her birds to 2 of pages child and had both likewise soars and one of them died and that she sent one of her birds to goodmans locks w^{ch} caused one of his cows to skip ouer a stile a burst her neck w^{ch} happened accordingely and that Tom caused John Wolnose horse to throw him in the water, & Robt caused Aldus his cart to stand fast on the playne grownd, and that the diuell drew blod of her and writ w^{th} it but what he wright she knew not.

Laurence Caluer testatur vt ante. [No return.]

Anna Marsh de Tattingstone she beeinge watched 2 days & 2 nights thretened those that had thus vsed her she wold be reuenged of them testatur  . . that one of these watchers haueinge two small childeringe at home alone w^{th} a fier vpō the harth one of theyr cloaths fell on fire, and was so burnt that *so* it died of it. Ignoramus.

Susanna Smith de Rushmere, vxor.  Robt Mayhew testatur the next day after her app^rhensiō confessed that 18 years since the diuill appeared to her like a red shaged dog and tempted her to kill her childeren but she stroue w^th him 24 howers before he went frō her but she wold not kill them, but beinge desired to relate further of her witchcraft there rise two swellings in her throate so that she cold not speake, but he comeinge to her the next night she confessed that the diuill did againe appeare to her in likenes of a black bee and told her that she shold bee attached the next day and that if she confessed any thinge she shold die for it and beinge demanded why she wold eate nothinge there beinge good meate ꝑuided for her she said the diuell told her she shold neuer eate nor drinck acgaine but they then ꝑvided and brought her meate and w^th much tremblinge she got some downe and further sd that the diuell came to her in the likenes of a black bee and went in to her body and there continued vntill that [*paper clipped*] that she wold not confes vntill he went from her againe but after that he was gone she confessed that she had sined a couenant w^th the diuell at his first appearance and sined it w^th a cross and after that the diuell writ her name to that couenant to w^ch she had made that marke and that the diuell had so told her weare there a rusty knife in the roome wheare w^th she might kill her selfe and they looked in that place & found such an old knife as she discribed but she sd that she cold not kill her selfe because they wa . . . in the roome.  Rich Marnin testatur vt ante.  billa vera.

Ellen Crispe vxor de Sweslinge : Hen. Minstrell testatur that the parents of this woman and this woman have been formerly counted and commonly reputed for a witch.  Tho. Sier testatur that upō denyinge of the husband of this accusant a loade of *h*ay he had one of his cows as gaue nauglty milke of two of her teats and since hath dried up.  Ignora.

Margeret Mixter vid. de Shotley.  Elizabeth Maī testatur that the 3^d. night she seemed *to* bee very sick and semed to haue very strainge fits and desired to ruck downe or ly downe and such fits she had seuerall nights and after they ꝑceived her in those fits immediately this informant searched her and cold playnely ꝑceiue that her teats weare newly sucked and that she wiped of the fresh blod frō the end of her teats w^th her finger, and she confessed that one Japhery *W*ods sent her a toad some 6 years since and it sucked on her thygh, and after that the toade came into her woll basket, and in the time of her watchinge she cryed out & sd that Satan was w<sup>th</sup>in her and prayed thē that watched w<sup>th</sup> her to hold her body & to worke downe Saten w<sup>ch</sup> they . . . and she after thancked thē and sd they had done her greate good and had wrought Satan out of her and when it Satan was w<sup>th</sup> in her beinge asked how he came into her she sd that on Wod sent it and that it came like a mowse to her and they shold it goe away like a mowse againe, & that this Wods sent the toade to her. Jo. looke testatur vt ante. Sara Wods testatur that she standinge by the accus. saw a thinge come from vnder her coats in likenes and shape of a beauer brush and passed vnder neath a chest but cold not find what became of it and *they* chardgeinge her that was one of her imps she sd no it was one of her neybors chickinges Billa vera.

Eade Iteru quod filiu cuiusdē Ja. Pullen occidit. billa vera.

Susan Marchant de Hintlesham, vid. John Easte testatur that she being attached upō the Sunday at night but haueinge 2 or three howers *of* the Munday at night she confessed to this infor. that she 3 imps theyr names Antony blackfast and will, the 2 first like rabets and they sucked on her and the other like a crow and that she dry nursed and that she haue had these 28 years, and that the crow tempted her to strike a cow lame of her brother Jaferies, w<sup>ch</sup> she did, the first time the diuill appeared to her was as she was milkeinge of a cow and singeinge of a Psalme, and asked why she sunge Psalmes for she was a damned creature and from that time she received her imps. Rich. Glamfield, testatur that vpō the Munday she confessed that the diuill did appeare to her in the shaddow of a man, and beinge a milkeinge and singeinge as befor the deuill told her she had renounced God Ch. and her Baptisme and desired of him if she had done so she might know it by some sine and all that day after what so euer she sa . . . and from that time she had her imps vt ante. billa vera.

Briget Bigsby de eadē. testatur Rich Glamfield, that she confessed freely w<sup>th</sup>out watchinge, the first day that she was a witch & that her grandmother had made her so and that about 3 weeks after the last sessions there came 2 mise as she lay by the fier and scratched her by the foote & drew blood on her & that she was affraid and told her grandmother of it who bad her not be affraid but ent⁹teine thē and she shold be auenged of all her enemies, and upō the thursday after the came againe and drew tokens wᶜʰ weare found about her and at that time she heard a voyce speake to her wᶜʰ bad her denie god & Ch. and he wold be a husband to her but she denied it and saw not who it was that spake it, her imps told her theyr names Joweare John & Naturall, and have sucked 5 times since she had them, they told if she wold grant to theyr couenant she shold neuer rest day nor night. billa vera.

Susanna Stegold de eadē, testatur   John Easte, testatur, that after that the marrage of her first husband the diuill came into her and beinge asked how she knew it she sd that she knew it for she had pigs and one of thē beinge more rauenous thē other she wished it might neuer eate againe and immediately it died and after her husband beinge a bad husband she wished he might dept from her meaneinge as she sd that he shold die and p̃sently after he died mad. and when this informant went frō her there followed a dor after him wᶜʰ this accusant sayth was an impe wᶜʰ she sent after him but it cold doe him noe harme and beinge in the . . . art she cryed out, oh ! my deare husband, but beinge asked whither she bewitched him to dead or noe, and sd she wished ill wishes to him and what so euer she wished came to pas. Jaffer Ward sayth that the day after her appʳhensiō she confessed she had 3 imps. Rich Glanfield testatur that she sd the killinge of her own pig was to try her skill. billa vera.

Joanna Potter deadē testatur Glan. that she confessed the day after her attachinge that she had 4 imps and had sent 2 of them to her granchild, and that she had made a couenant wᵗʰ the diuill and fetched blud at her nose and sined the couenant the diuill brought to her & that she imployed her imps to kill certeine fowls and she confessed to him that one of her imps his suck her at the time she talked wᵗʰ him. billa vera.

Maria Dacō. de Playford ipse confitetur  billa vera.

Eliza. Southerne de Dunage, testatur Mʳ. Browne minister that she confessed wᵗʰ 24 howers after her attã that upō a fallinge out wᵗʰ mother Collit about a years since, some two nights after she concieued the diuell was sent to her by this mother Collit in the shape of a crabfish wᶜʰ came into the bed to her and nipt her & fetcht blod &c., and afterwards spake to her & demanded of to seale a covenant vt allia copi p̃mise to prouide for her against all want where upō she yelded vnto him, at his next appearance he lay w^th her  She saw not *his* shape but onely felt round . . . and cold like a stone  Speakeinge to her in a shrill voice promiseinge to *guide* for her and beinge a pedler if weare at any time late the deuill allways helpt her home.  She met the diuell midsomer last like a black boy 10 years old by a whitethorne as she went to Westleton and there he ꝑmised her 2s. 6d. and he had not then but she shold haue it the next time she came that way but he fayled of his promise, he met her indeed, but complayned of the hardnes of the times the boy was hary though yonge she say [she] wold haue confessed this the night before but the diuell wold not her the ministe vsed no other argument to make her confes the *ontly*by sayinge doe wronge yo^r selfe but cleare yo^r consience ;  the couenent she sealed was to expire at 14 years . . . w^ch was but fower years since.  Tho. Spatchet testatur, vt ante   bill vera.

Prissilla Collit vx de ead  Tho Spatchet. afte 3 nights & days watcheinge after an howers slepe, in a sicknes about 12 years since the diuell tempted to make away w^th her childeren or else so shold allways continue poore, and he then demanded a couenant of her w^ch she did deny, but she carried one of her childeren and layd it close to the fyer to burne it, and went to bed againe and the fier burnt the hare and the head lininge and she heard it cry but cold not have power to helpe it, but one other of her children pulled it away and the next time the diuell came to her he demanded her to seale the couenant vt alias and she consented to him against her will and sealed it w^th her blod, and she *sent* him to destroy a bottome of one godmā harpers at newcastle and that he returned answeare that he had done it, he promised her she shold find 10s. in whin bush for sealinge the couenant but she neuer had it, & that she went from Dunage to Bostone in 2 days and the diuell told her she shold not goe up past the knees but she went up to the neck and if a boate had [not] come by by chance she had beene drowned for there weare 3 men in the boate & they cold all hardly pull her upō into the boate the diuell held her downe so fast in the water.  Testatur vt ante M^r Browne clerk :  and further that she cold change her imps into any shape the diuell gave he so much powers and that she wold haue beene gone to skape searchinge but she had not the power, this she wold haue related a day and a night before but the diuell wold not let her.  billa vera.

1. Tho. Ratlif nup de Shelly. In p incantatione. Tho. Monticute testatur that he beeinge fellynge of a tree this Ratclife came to gather chips and denied her and immediately w^th one our this deponent was full of strange lice beeinge beefore this cleare & haueinge put on a cleane shirt the day beefore ; George Waterbury test. that vpō seuerall fallinge out w^th her he haue sufferred seuerall strange losses of his cattell as his hoggs dieinge . . . beeinge pfectly well beefore this difference. Abigall Brigs sayth that after she had beene in custody 6 days but not kept eyther from sleepe or foode neyther was she walked at all in this time. she confessed that a month after the death of her husband there came one to her in the shape of her husband and lay heuy upon her & she asked him if he wold kille her & he answeared in the voyce of her husband no I will bee a loueinge husband to you, and beeinge further demanded if she wold confess no more concerneinge this appeareance she answered she was stopped and cold not but confirmed that that w^ch she had sayd was true. Prissilla Brigs sayth she searched her & found two teats : Sterne test. that she confessed that she had beene a common curser & it had often fallen out accordinge as she wished, & further that her malice had brought her to what she was come to, but wold confes she was a witch, & further that she consented to that man w^ch appeared to her to bee her husband after her consent he pmised her she shold bee reuenged of all her enimies but she sd she found Satan a liar. [No return.]

2. John Lowis In. p incatatione, testatur Ca Kno. That after his swiminge at fframinghā he confessed in his psence, he haueinge showen his markes to this deponent that the bigest of his imps Tho. for he had 7 *Flo* bess and mary did suck at this teate, but beeinge asked if he had made any contract sd not but Tō had sometimes moued in a hollow voyce to that purpose. he beeinge asked *how* longe these imps had sucked, sd 5 years and he sd to Ton who came first to him asked if he shold suck he sd *when* goody . . . mother Sherewod weare weary of him he shold suck of him. & further he sd the water was inchanted by an other witch, teste daniel Rayner that Lowis confessed he imployed his yellow imp to doe all the hurt he cold at Sea betwene Yarmouth & Winterton and that he had beene the death of many cattell and that these imps did force him to imploy thē about some euill action. Nath Man. of Branson testatur he that upō a fallinge out w^th M^r. Lowis & M^r. Lowis thretinge him he went for a

warrat to bind him to the pease and that imedeately after M<sup>r</sup>. Lowis came to this deponents wife who haueinge a child w<sup>th</sup> her he wold giue her 2s. 6d. to buy it somethinge and immediately after this mony receiued the child fell sick languished and though it eate the meate yet it gathered no strength but so continued vntill it died : 34 :

1. Maria Bush de Bactō In. vt ante freely. taken on the munday confessed that night & teusday morninge, teste M<sup>r</sup>. Maltin, that ye deuill did appeare to her in ye shape of a man about 15 yer since and *3* we. after the death . . , and had after, the vse of her body. the first time he lay w<sup>th</sup> her was that he sent her 3 imps the one like a whelp, the other like mise, and she had imployed these imps to kill 3 cows and 20 turkies of M<sup>r</sup>. Pritimans, and this because he tooke her collection from her & for this cause killed 2 cows of goodman Garnams w<sup>ch</sup> they . . . as they told her, & that she sent one imp like a toade to Eli. Heath to tormenter because she wold not giue he *relife* and this to torment her continally w<sup>ch</sup> it wold haue done if she had not . . . . her ; and that these 3 imps did suck upon 3 seuerall teats in her secret pts, vera.

2. Margaret Benet de eade vt ante teste M<sup>r</sup>. Maltin frely vt ante, con. that the deuill met her as she came frō Newtō w<sup>th</sup> a long cloake, and she knew him by his feete, it was in the day time he asked her to for sake Ch. and bee ruled by him and she shold bee reuenged of all that angered her, and that she yelded to this motiō. and that she was aduised by the diuell to take of the hayer of the back of the wid. Hoggards cows and giue it . . . her imp kit and she did whereupō one cow died and the other languished : she nourished this imp *kik* once a month and the last time it succed she sayd it was iust immedeately beefore she was searched and that the divell in the shape of a man at the first . . . carried her body ouer a close into a thicket of bushes and there lay w<sup>th</sup> her and after scratched her hand w<sup>th</sup> the bushes and took her hand into his hand and writ vpon a black patch but she knew not what, and that she sent her imp kit to goody garnham to make he cow giue her a sownd *p*unch *but* not to kill her and it did accordingely and this because she refused to let her haue a pint of butter, and killed diuers other cattell, & vera.

3. Ellen Greenelif the wife of K. G. de eade vt ante. freely immediately after *ap.* cō that he mother did send her 3 imps that

after she had thē she oftene tempted to kill herselfe and whilst these imps was with her she wished that garnā *c*ow might bee lame & that Hogard meare might be lame, because he went for the searcher, and they both fell but and she did imploy thē to send lice to M<sup>r</sup>. Lockwod w<sup>ch</sup> he w*a*s and that about one years since in the night the deuill came to bed to her & was cold but had not the vse of her body, and y<sup>t</sup> time profered her if she wold forsake god and Ch. and trust in him she *w*old want no thinge and appeared to her the Sunday beefore she was attached, in the shape of a boy and told her if she confessed he wold teare her in peaces w<sup>ch</sup> did much affright her.  vera.

4. Eli : Watcham de eadē vt ante, igno.

5. Margaret *T*ray vx de Ofton.  In quod diabolica arte et incantatione murdro Anna Price &c.

6. Sibilla Greene vxor.  de Wickā vt ante that vpō search she had very apparent teats and that Winter's wife did confes vpō examinatiō that she had he imps from her.  ignoramus.

7. Joane Balls vx. de eadē vt ante after watchinge frō thursday vntill Saturday.  after she had heard that he daughter had confessed beefore ; she confessed that she had sent two imps like mise to her daughter and bad her she shold not bee affrayd of them and that she was trobled w<sup>th</sup> such things as did suck her but she never saw them and that there beeinge 3 teats found about her she sayd she wold not say how many imps she had but sd she had not above 3, and so she wold haue confessed to M<sup>r</sup>. Willan the thursday beefore she was watched, but the diuell came to her and wold not suffer her & M<sup>r</sup>. Wellan beeinge alone at that time that he beeinge alone w<sup>ch</sup> he conceived there was some euill sperit in *r*ome and aduised to say her prayers and defie the deuill and she did it and confessed that the diuell ansd she cold not hirt her beecause he did not feare him. this woman pfessed anabaptisme, and runner after the new secks, teste M<sup>r</sup>. Willa. Ck. and vpō Saterday moneinge she confessed that one of her imps had succed her that day morneinge and it did appeare by the search of some weomen at that time that it was so.  vera.

8. Maria Brame de eadē vt ante. likewise upō the fryday & after on the Saterday that she had received 2 things like mise that her mother Jo. Balls had sent her and had her not bee afraid of them for if she had thē she shold neuer want and bee

reuenged on her enemies, and that in the night time 2 days after her mother had psuaded her to receive them they came and succed her in the night time, but she was so affrayd of thē that she durst neuer toutch thē w^th her hand and they had tempted her diuerse times to denie Ch. and God but she had not consented, and that she had neuer imployed thē and that she had had them not aboue a fortnight beefore, she further confesseth that on friday at night her watchers and her selfe beeinge a sleepe the imps came to her and skeard her out of her sleape and she rucked downe and sucled them. billa vera.

9. Mary the wife of Winter de eadem vt ante, sayd that she had had things that did troble her but she cold not confes and sd she was sure she was cleare 5 weeks since, and if she had any things they came tor frō mother greene, teste M^r. Willan and that she had certeine tokens found about her upō her searchinge, teste Mary read ; vera.

10. Anna vxor Ellis qd p incantationes consumsisset corpus . . Tho Hudson. testatur A Hudson that her some falling out w^th her he fell lame a fortnight after. Ignoramus.

11. Elizabeth Man vxor quod p incañ occidisset anne man, test James Stannar et vxor eius, that after a fallinge out w^th man she had immediately a child sick and and beeinge trobled w^th a was or bee all the while about it it continued shreekeinge and crieinge two days vntill it died and that the mother of this child vpon a fallinge out w^th this man was immediately taken sick and lame so that she faynt to bee carried into the howse ; and that the searchers found teats and the marks of a witch, and that day that this deponent went w^rh this woman to the searchers, when she came home at night one of her childerin was taken w^th a strainge fit of shrekeinge and clawinge at theyr faces when they wold hold it in theyr armes. and so held in this fit vntill midnight. and haue had 3 such fits since , and that her mother was hanged for a witch ; vera.

fframinghā

12. Ellen Driuer de eadē vt ante Robt Wayts that after 3 days and 2 night watchinge she confessed she had 2 imps did suck on her and that deuill appeared to her like a man &^rthat she was married to him in one . . . parishes and that he liued with her 3 years and that she had 2 childeren by him in that time w^ch weare changelings, teste Wayts con. et Ed. Weeding she sd

further that it was 60 years since the diuell wooed her to marry him and it was the n*ect* time of his comeinge beefore agreed to him after she wer married he had the carnall vse of her but was cold, and inioyned her beefore marrage to denie god and Christ. and she sd that she did not know that any of his neybours did euer see him, she further sd that beeinge in bed w^th him she felt of his feet and they weare clouen, and he liued w^th her 2 years and then he died as she thought, and that it was her pride was the cause that made her consent to him   vera.

13. Mary vxor Scrutton de eadē Ed. Weeteinge, the first night she was takē, she had 3 imps that succed her seuerall times this 3 or 4 month some times 2 o 3 in a day and that they kept a sqeakeinge and that one night she heard them on the plan . . . er and she told her husband there weare mise & answeared you *company* w^th witches & yo^r plagued. w^th some of theyr emps, that the deuill appeared to her twise once like a beare, once like a cat, and that she tempted her in a hollow voyce to kill her child, and as she was comeinge home lately the deuill met her like a man and took her by the arme but wold not confes what he sd to her.  vera.

14. Mary Edwards quod inter. Eli Smith test. Ber. Brandin that after Mary Edwards had giuen this El. an apple w^th in a fortnight after the child fell sick, and so continued and good while and then died Igno.

15 Iterū quod fran. Wood inter vt ante testa. Elsa Woods sayd that Mary Edwards tooke a way a hat from fran. Woods and this Elis. Woods tooke the hat frō the sd Mary and after wards this child fell sick and died.  Igno.

16. Iterū quod Robt. Pallant.  Marie trasy testatur quod mother Wyard in her confession sd she met w^th her and told her y^t he ha*d* killed Robt. Pallard and Mary Edwards sent him him to doe it, Marienie May testatu. that this Edwards came to her masters howse and she gaue her some milke but not so much as she desired and she went away mumblinge and the next day Robt. Pallard, beeinge well in *t*he armes of a mayd seruant sheake out fearfully and was lame of one sid and the next day died.  vera.

16 (*sic*). Elizabeth Warne. quod inter Joh Butterā ; Jo: Butter testa. that vpō fallinge out w^th womā about a howse rent the child was taken w^th strange fits of the cramp, and this woman

came told them an *a*pple of a thistle might doe it good. and she gaue it one w<sup>ch</sup> it did weare & it is wis after wards well and afterwards goeinge to fframingham it was taken w<sup>th</sup> other strange fits.  Ignora.

17. Elisabeth Warne de eadē p incantatione, after 3 days & nights watchinge she confessed that  pride and lustfullnes had brought her to this, and desired ishe might bee  walked apace for she had the deuill w<sup>th</sup>in them.  billa.

18. Anna Moats the wife of Robt. freely, w<sup>th</sup>out watchinge w<sup>th</sup> in two ours, confessed that she had 2 imps & that she had seuerall times sent to mak them kill diuers of Canvis cattell and they did so. and beeinge asked if she had not toutcht his body she asked againe if she wold not burne her, & they answeared noe, but the company pressinge in she confessed no more but that these imp did suck her in those.  test. M<sup>r</sup>. Trase, Jo. Caluer, that the diuell did appeare first to her when she was a lone in her howse and after she had beene curseinge of her husband and her childeringe and that she gaue her consent to make her couenant w<sup>th</sup> the deuill.  vera.

19. Margaret vxor Bayts de eadem vt ante after 2 or 3 days Watchinge coñ when she was at work she felt a thinge come vpon her legs and go into her secret pts and nipped her in her secret pts where her marks weare found, and an other time when she was in the Church yard she felt a thinge nip her againe in those parts & further that she had but two teats and they might be made at once suckinge.  Teste Weeteinge.  Mary Trasy sayth y<sup>t</sup> Marga Bayts before any watchinge confessed to her that there came a thinge to her in the likenes of a mouse and ran vnd<sup>9</sup> her coats & sucked her, and that it sucked her a nother time & that it had sucked her twice since the time of attachment.  Igno.

20. Anna Palmer de eadē vt ante the first night she was takē. that she had two imps like turkicocks the one she called great tur. & the other little.  teste Weedinge.  Mary gunnell sayth that about 8 years since Mother Palmer came to the howse of Robt. Wayts w<sup>ch</sup> home she then liued and then desired to giue her a pot of beare but they denied to giue her any and she went a way thretinge she might want a cup of beare her selfe eare longe & after this they cold make no beare that wold last aboue 3 weaks after this.  Igno.

21. Anne Vsher de eadē after 2 nights watchinge confessed that about a year sine she felt a thinge like a small cat come ouer her legs once or twice & that it scratched he mightily after that she felt 2 things like butterflies in her secret pts w^th w*t*chings dansings and suckinge & she felt them w^th her hands and rubbed thē and killed them, and an other time when she sate a spinge a powlcat skipt in to her lap and spake to her and sd if she wold deny Ch. god, &c. he wold bringe her wittles w^ch she after consented, but he neuer brought her anythinge after, after her consent, he drew blod off her hand beeinge 2 or 3 drops w^ch dropped on the stole but know whither he dropt on to the paper or licked it up and that he appeared 2 or 3 times to her in the likenes of a cat but did not contes further.  vera.

22. Mary Becket de eadē vt ante, after 2 nights watchinge confessed that the diuell did appeare to her in the likenes of a man and told her her sins weare so great that there was no heuen for her she sayd that ther weare 2 things flew aboue her bed like dors and she beat them downe, after this she fell a sleepe and when waked her felt them come up her thy and sucked her and drew two teats and once, teste Weedinge.  Igno.

23. Margaret Wyard de eade vt ante, after 2 or 3 nights watchinge sd that 7 years since the deuill appeard to her in the likenes of a calfe and told her he *was* her husband and asked her to have the vse of her body w^ch then she did denie, after this he came to her in the shape of handsome yonge gentleman w^th yelloow hayre and black cloaths & often times lay w^th her and had the carnall vse of her but wld pforme the *St* of a man & she obserued he had a clouen foote, & he made her denies god and Ch., and came and brought wrightings in her hand and fetcht blood of her thygh and Catched it in a thinge & writt in the paper *he* was then like a man he told a month since that a man and a woman shold come to search for wit[ches] but bad her not feare them for he told her she was his, & sd that he wold bee searched two, & bad her not reueale any thinge, and when she began to confess the deuill beat her downe he was like a shaddow, but she was now glad she had got time to confes, she sd she had 7 imps like *flies*, dors, spiders, mise, & she had but fiue teats and when they came to suck they fight like pigs with a sow.  After ward she sd she had one like a toade the diuell told her there weare some witches had gold rings on theyr fingers.  The deuill bad her kill Sheldrak's child and that he told her mother mother chi*n*ery

had *sent* her to doe it, & he asked her to blast M^r. Mase his corne but she sd she wold n[ot] and then he an[swered] he wold and sd Mother Neuill ioyned w^th him, teste Weedinge, Mary Trasy. Billa vera.

24. Margeria With alias Chim*n*y quod int̃ filiũ John Sheldrake. Mary *T*rasy testatur quod Mother man told her that the diuell told her he had killed this child and that mother Chimny sent him to doe it. Tho ffisher testur that after a fallinge out w^th her Sth that he had a yonge child taken the next day w^th strange fits and whilst it had these fits it came out full of blew spots & when the fit left it they weare not seene and w^th one month died & the corps beeinge dead wold not grow stif allthough it layd 18 howers vnburied, she told him that deuill did desire her to serue him but she did refuse and that M^r. Lowis did come to her and bad her neuer confes any thinge about witchcraft. teste Hopkins She sd the deuill tempted her to blast M^r. Mases corne w^ch she denied & he sd that he wold, and she bad him doe, and he did it and sd that mother neuell ioyned w^th her. test Weedeinge. Igno. quo ad murd. Billa vera quoad incanta.

25. Anna Sherewod de eadē vt ante . . . testatur. Igno.

26. Susanna D*exe* de Westrope pro incantatione. sayd after 2 days watchinge, she met w^th a little white doge 3 in the same place. 2 at the noone day once at twylight & she was affrayd of it, beeinge asked whiter she was the cause of the sicknes of Tho. Mills or noe shee lift vp her hands and wayled & sd she was and that was the cause of her greefe and w^th all related the fashiō of his sicknes and places of his greefe w^ch was accordingely as she related and beeinge asked how she did it she sd she had spoake a naughty word and that she had wished a wife a *cros*, and beinge asked how she knew the man was sick she sd because he was not a church and beinge how she knew that lyinge sick she sd her daughter told her who denyed that she did not tell her, and did again confes this very thinge beefor the Justices : billa vera.

27. Francis Wildes of Blaxall.

[Unfinished.]

---

In. Maria vxor Nath. Bacō de Chatishā quod demone societatis sua admisit et duos mali spiritus fouebat sub forma mascis et nigri auis ad mala intentiones contra Statu. Hopkins testatur q$^d$ p$^r$d Maria nihil. Ed. Smith sayth that he was the first man that had the sd Mary in custody after her accusatiō for a witch & afterneth that she confessed as soone as he taken confessed she had 2 imps sent her by mother Cortnell and that she had sucled them twise & imployed them to kill crows. Moses Rayner. Rayner. that she did succle 2 imps vpon the fast day after Mid Somer. Ann Alderman de Chatisham vt ante. Rich Glam et Rayner testatur, that she confessed thie first day she was app$^r$hended w$^{th}$out, &c. that she had 3 imps, grashopp, mouse, squirrill and that she was a witch & had so beene allmost 8 years & that she had these imps frō mother Cotnell that met the diuell seuerall times in field once like a man and once like a dog & vrged to seale her couenant but she refused and that the diuell lay w$^{th}$ her and was cold, & for refuseinge to seale the couenant *that* the deuill wronge of her finger & that she seuerall times succled her imp and that she sent her imp Tho to kill her daughter and he did kill her and that she wished her sons child cold in the mouth & it died likewise. vera.

Natha Bacō, vt ante. by confes before M$^r$. Jen. that he had seald a couenant w$^{th}$ his blod w$^{th}$ the deuill & that the deuill promised him 14 p an . . . after 2 years that he was attached w$^t$ a fortnight, that he had 2 imps frō mother shipper & that he succled them at his brest and that he had sent the one for salt & the other for oatemell, the deuill came in the shape of a ruge dog when he came to him, teste Moses Rayner.

Rebecca vxor ffran Morris de eadē vt ante : confessed beefore any violence, watchinge, or other threts, the deuill came to her about 3 weeks agoe the deuill came to her in likenes of a little boy and desired a couenant accordinge to the former, and she consented to his desire but denied to seale the couenant and the day after he sent her 3 imps and that she had succled them twise, & that she imployed thē to kill a cat, a dog, & a hen. Ed. Smith. Moses Rayner testibus.
Maria fuller de Combs vt ante confi post pena, vera.

Maria vxor Rich. Cloues de Yoxford freely confessed upon the first attachment confessed that the deuill came to her in the shape of a little boy and that she made a couenant w$^{th}$ the deuill and imployed her imps in generall seruice but not in murder. billa vera.

Margeria Sparā de Mendam, confessed w<sup>th</sup> out watchinge &c., that she had 3 imps will Tom like blackbird and nan like a white moll, the white one came to her when she was a mayd and the othe 2 came after the death of her ffather, the 2 blackones she sent after her husband beeinge a solier to ptect him, and the white one to sea git his liueinge ; that she met the deuill in the wood in the likenes of a black man & that the Deuill told him (*sic*) that there wold come a man to her to search for her imps and that she shold send them a way, and that beefore this she was tempted by Satā to kill M<sup>rs</sup>. Jacob, and she bad him doe and that M<sup>rs</sup>. Jacob did die but not so soone as she expected, that she is a lewd womā sildome come to Church. test. Jacob Neech.

Katerine Tooly of Westleton vt ante freely w<sup>th</sup> in 6 howers after attachment, that the deuill came to her in the shape of a black boy about 2 years and a halfe agoe he desired a renounceinge &c., & she consented to it, and she gaue him her hand to draw blod to confirme it, w<sup>ch</sup> he did, and he left two imps w<sup>th</sup> her, Jackly & pybold, after, vpon a fallinge out w<sup>th</sup> her some, Jackly asked her what he shold doe for her she bad him goe and set the marks of a witch on him and he did it as did appeare, after, vpō a difference w<sup>th</sup> M<sup>r</sup>. Driuer minister she sent iackly to meete him as he was to goe (to prach) frō Celsol to Westleton, and strike him and his horse dead, and the imp required blod of her to doe it but he returned to her & told he cold not doe it he had no power ouer him, and the reason was because he serued god, teste M<sup>r</sup>. Driuer. After this Jacly told her that there was a bushell of rusty mony in S<sup>r</sup>. Robt Brooks Closet & he wold fetch her some but she did not. Robt. Hak*en* teste. vera.

Tho Eeuerard de Holsworth vt ante and Mary, his wife, confesseth when he was a prentise goinge vpon arrant w<sup>th</sup> a dog w<sup>th</sup> him a black dock like a water dog crossed the way w<sup>ch</sup> skipped ouer a hij row and made no noyse, w<sup>ch</sup> made him affrayd and when he came at the place wher the deuill crossed the way the howne whined and wold not come over the way and then he went back and carried him ouer and when he was ouer the howne twistered about his legs whined and made him much a ffrayed & that he cold not looke against the light when *he* came at the house whither he was agoeinge, and the man that dwelt there told him that dog had beene seuall times seene there but sent him an other way home when he came home he layd downe to sleepe and drempt that somethinge crep vpō vpon his legs and go to his shin, and then he waked and felt it and it was like a rabbet and this asked him if he wold loue it and if he wold denie god Ch. &c. but he refused then, but consented to it after ward, when he met it in the field, and yᵗ it scratcht him under his ear and got blood of him & syd now it had what it wold haue. that he had teats and that the imps sucked at those teats, that he sent his imps to kill a deere and a rotten sheepe . . . *I*rish John Wods *his* children and his owne granchild he wᵗʰ his wife killed, teste Mʳ. Swaine. Hen Thurston. vera.

Mariana the daughter of Thō Everard vt ante, confesseth. billa vera.

Sara Spindler de Holsworth confesseth that she had thre imps one like a bird & 2 like a mowle and had imployed thē to seuerall murders.

Jana Linstead vt ante ; and vpō attachment freely confessed that she had enterteined imps meg, ioane, and nage wᶜʰ did vsually suck her but did put her to noe payne put her into a shakeinge & feare and that sent one of her imps to hinder a baker frō bakeinge his breade wᶜʰ accordingely happened, and sent an other to kill the daughter of one clarke wᶜʰ she did, further she met wᵗʰ the deuill in the shape of a man who wold haue lyen wᵗʰ her but she denied him wherevpō he thretned her but did her noe hyrt, vera.

Eli. Hubard vt ante, confes after watchinge frō Saterday vntill tewsday at night she confessed she had enterteined 3 imps wᶜʰ she had sucled, and had sent one of them to kill John Taylors child, and the child died accordingely and one Rich. Lo*ws* child she killed & Robt. Newmans : all this she denied wᵗʰ in 6 howers, yet vpō thursday after she freely vpō her knees beginge pdon of them she had thus wronged, she confessed it all againe, beside seuerall cattell, that she had had these 3 imps 12 years. billa vera.

Jacobus More vt ante, freely wᵗʰout watchinge, confesseth that had beene wᵗʰ Euered at Holsworth and he pswaded him to take one of his imps wᶜʰ he refused but after he sent it to him by his daughter & then receiued it, then the diuell appeared to him in the likenes of a boy in the day time and pswaded him to forsake god Christ, &c., and he consented to it and he drew blode to seale the couenant, after, he went to his brothe who gaue him an other imp, and this imp he carried w<sup>th</sup> him to Bungay where he imployed this imp to kill his brother Witt More, for refuseinge to pay him a legacy w<sup>ch</sup> Witt More accordingely died. that he ioyned w<sup>th</sup> his brother Euerard and sent an imp to destroy a field of corne, w<sup>ch</sup> returned him answear that it was done, and that his sister Euerard required his imp nan to send w<sup>th</sup> 2 of her husbands to send to Pr. Ru w<sup>ch</sup> accordingely he deliuered and haue not seene since w<sup>ch</sup> is allmost 3 years since, billa vera.

Margaret Eccleston de Linstead vt ante, vpō the testimony of Smith that vpō a differrence w<sup>tn</sup> his daughter Jane Smith and this Ecclestone she thretned a reuenge and forth w<sup>th</sup> immediately this Jane Smith fell lame, and after vpō a second thret she payne increased and after Ecclestone came to her and layd her hand vpō Janes head and told her if she pleased she wold ask her forgiuenes but she puttinge her by refuseinge to let her toutch her she grew worse & worse for 2 or 3 days and then died, vpō the testimony of Chr. Legate she confessed that she had an imp that did suck on her and wold often vrge her to imploy it in doeinge hyrt and that she sent it Jane Smith and it killed her, and that she wold haue called her imp frō *Jan* Smith againe and saued her life but she cold not for she came too late, and after that she did witnes to her husband that all she had confessed was true & that she had fownd *else* since her confession. Teste Tho. looke. billa vera.

An Smith of Glemham and Mary Smith, vt ante, after two days and two nights watchinge confessed and againe confessed the same beefore M<sup>r</sup> Bacō after a day & nights sleepe, that they couenanted w<sup>th</sup> the deuill and had received seuerall imps and imployed them in the distruction of seuerall cattell & sold and trafficked for 2 of her imps, the one she sold for 2s., the other for 18d. that she sent one imp to lame goody Barker and *get diffe* betwixt her husband and her selfe, and had sold one impe to Bet Bray of Stradbrook and an other to an arnoll of the same and that her sone haue one imp w<sup>th</sup> him in the army and his resolued to goe to the king's pty w<sup>th</sup> it. billa vera.

Marie Sexton vt ante vpo cofession freely that (in the a sicknes w<sup>ch</sup> she had about 8 weeks) since a rug dog came to her and this dog set he was sent frō Ipswitch and that this dog did draw blood of her tounge and at the seconod time of the appearance of this dog the dog required if she wold reuenge her selfe of the Constables that had carried her to Ipswitch vpō misdeameanor but she refused to consent and that she suclet her impe twise in one weeke. billa ver.

Rachell Sextō vt ante, ffreely, that in the time of sicknes there appeared to her a thinge like a mowse, came upō her brest lyinge in bed and thretned her, but she gaue noe consent to the enterteinement of it. ign.

An *Barker* de eadē vt ante. ffre. confess. that about 2 years since there came to her a little dun dog and syd to he if you will cleaue to me thou shalt *want* nothinge & told her shee shold find mony vnde a *stap* in the hall garden but she found none, at the 2 time of his appearance he drew bloode frō her greate toe where wᵗʰ he writ her name wᵗʰ her consent, haueinge a pap ɪn his hand as she thought & further a month since beeinge the thancks giueinge day she went to Prior and asked him for some wry wᶜʰ denied and the spirit asked her if he gaue her any She told him no he answeared he had as good and wᵗʰin 3 or 4 days after, the man died very strangely, and at a nother time she found a *cist* in . . . yard wᶜʰ the dog desired and she gaue it him. billa vera.

Anna Driuer. the wife of francis vt ante nihil confite.

Ailicea vxor Rich. Glamfield de eadē nihil confitetur.

Margerie Blaks de eadē vt ante nihil confitetur.

Ellen Bishop, Rosa Clamfield, Tho Clarke, Marierie Blake de eadem omnes vt ante non confitet.

Rebecca Prick de Belstead vxor Will vt ante, after fower days, confessed she had 2 imps and that she had entered a couenant and enterteined the imps after. vera.

Anna Wright of Stradbrooke. vera.

Jane Riuet of Cobduck. vera.

Mary Godard of Belstead. vera.

Susan Manners de Copduck vt ant, after watchinge frō munday vntill weddensday she confessed that she had received 2 imps sis & kate frō her grandmother and that she cryed out if her grandmother for destryinge her selfe & all her kindered. teste. Rob. Hitchcock that these imps succed her. test Tho. Bull.

Alice Muntford vt ante de eadē against her it wast testified by the searchers that Mother Philips and Mother Mills sayd that some teats that weare found about her weare witches markes.

Mary Skipper de eadē vt ante, that after watchinge frō munday vntill weddesday she confessed that deuill appeared vnto her in the shape of a man after her husbands death and told if she wold enter a couenant w<sup>th</sup> him he wold pay her debts and he wold carrie her to heauen and that she shold neuer want, w<sup>ch</sup> she did & sined it w<sup>th</sup> her blod, and that he left her 3 imps and that she imployed one to kill lanes child and killed it, & that the deuill bad her goe church and make a greate show but if she attended diligently he wold nip her she felt of a weake after and that the deuill haue constantly had the use of her euer since, but she felt him allways cold.  teste.  Robt Hitchcok, vera Rebecca *U*stwod.

Judith Kettle of flowtō post watch. confessed she had fower imps tit, gray, tray, rob, & th<sup>t</sup> she succled these imps 7 yeare. vera.  teste the . . .

# APPENDIX VII

## Depositions (18th Century)

### (Hardwicke Papers : Add. MS. 35838, f. 404)

Depositions against some supposed witches before the Grand Jury at the Assizes at Leicester, Sept. 1717. The bill was not found so the trial did not come on. Sir G. Beaumont, Foreman, made this Extract, and gave it Lord Parker, Judge of the Assize. His Lordship brought the Extract to Kensington and this is a true copy of it. F. Barnard.

An Extract of the informations of 25 persons at Leister assizes against an old woman her son and daughter for witchcraft, the two former of which were then in prison and comitted for the said crime.

These informants all depos'd that all the supposed witches had severally their thumbs & great toes ty'd togather & that they were thrown so bound into the water, & that they swam like a cork, a piece of paper, or an empty barrell, tho : they strove all they could to sinck.

Divers of these informants depos'd that during strange illness of severall persons who were bewitched as they were well assured by those persons or some of them they had the Minister to pray by them without any good effect at all, but applying to a cunning man or white witch they were directed to put the afflicted party's water into a bottle and set it near the fire which accordingly they frequently did and cork$^d$. it well and ty'd down the cork w$^{th}$ 20 rounds of packthread, notwithstanding which the water w$^d$. always give a crack like a gun, & the cork fly out leaving the bottle and pack thread as it was, while the water was in the bottle the afflicted parties had ease but upon its bursting out their pains & illness return'd.

The good women who gave information depos'd, that for experiment sake they used to stew their own water so, but their's would never crack or fiz or fly away like the other, but would symmer as quietly when it was heated as any spring water.

When the patients urine was set to stew by the fire some one of the witches was allways observed to come into the room sometimes in the shape of a cat & sometimes a dog who would run in panting as if he was upon a hard chase, and these dogs and cats would come in tho : the doors and windows were shut and all passages except keyholes & chimneys stopt & could never be catch<sup>d</sup> but would grin furiously, and approaching near the bewitch'd persons give them great pain and so vanish.

Another remedy used and prescribed by the cunning man was to put rosemary balm and mary gold flowers in a bagg to the patients brest as a charm and to give them inwardly a decoction made of the same in a quart of ale & their own blood w<sup>ch</sup> medesine was once put into an earthen pot and laid up safe yet stolen out of the pot invisibly by the witches, and the pot itself was seen to fly of its own accord with a great violence from a shelfe in the house against a cow in the yard and dashed into a thousand pieces.

But the most infallible cure was to fetch blood of the witches w<sup>ch</sup> was constantly practis<sup>d</sup> and with good success but the witches would be so stubborn that they were often forced to call the constable to bring the assistance of a number of persons to hold them by force to be blooded.

The old woman's skin was so tough that they could get no blood of her by scratching so they used great pins & such instruments for that purpose.

One of the bewitch'd persons vomited up a great quantity of gravell and dirt and thatch of a house and stones which were so big, that it was incredible how they could come out of any chritian mouth.

Severall of the informants depos'd that they themselves had been bewitch'd and afflicted after this manner & besides had seen and felt great black bees to come out of their own & other peoples noses & mouths, w<sup>ch</sup> bees could not be struck down or taken but would make a terrible humming & then fly up y<sup>e</sup> chimney.

Another young maiden voided downwards by the help of a midwife, and with as much pain as if it had been a child birth a great number of stones of a large size the stones themselves were produced and shew'd as evidence, and the midwife & girl and her mother all swore to the truth of the fact. A young woman who dyed as was supposed bewitch<sup>d</sup> to death had monstrous wounds upon her body which appeard to be the bites of some human teeth, and others like the gnawing of dogs and the informants did depose, that the old woman that was accused of witchcraft, might have no teeth w<sup>ch</sup> she could thus bite & gnaw with, yet her son and daughter had.

Searching the old witch publickly before a great number of good women in their town, they deposed there were found in her secret parts two white pieces of flesh like paps and some swore they were like the teats of an ewe, & some like the paps of a cat.

# APPENDIX VIII [1]

The Examination and confession of certain Wytches at Chensford in the Countie of Essex before the Quenes maiesties Judges, the xxvi daye of July Anno 1556 At the Assise holden there as then, and one of them put to death for the same offence, as their examination declareth more at large.

*The examination of them with their confession before Doctor Cole and master Foscue at the same Sise verbatum, as nere as coulde be gathered, and firste of Elizabeth Frauncis who saide as here foloweth.*

Fyrst she learned this arte of witchcraft at the age of xii yeres of hyr grandmother whose nam mother Eue of Hatfyelde Peuerell, disseased. Item when shee taughte it her, she counseiled her to renounce GOD and his worde and to geue of her bloudde to Sathan (as she termed it) whyche she delyuered her in the lykenesse of a whyte spotted Catte, and taughte her to feede the sayde Catte with breade and mylke, and she dyd so, also she taughte her to cal it by the name of Sathan and to kepe it in a basket.

When this mother Eue had geuen her the Cat Sathan, then this Elizabeth desired firste of the sayde Cat (callinge it Sathan) that she might be ryche and to haue goodes, and he promised her she shoulde—askinge her what she would haue, and she sayde shepe (for this Cat spake to her as she confessed in a straunge holowe voice, but such as she vnderstode by vse) and this Cat forthwith brought shepe into her pasture to the number of xviii, blacke and whyte, whych continued with her for a tyme, but in the ende dyd all weare away she knewe not howe.

Item, when she had gotten these shepe, she desired to haue one Andrew Byles to her husband, which was a man of some welth, and the cat dyd promyse she shold, but that he sayde she must fyrste consent that this Andrew shuld abuse her, and she so did.

[1] Illustrated pamphlet in the Archiepiscopal Library at Lambeth, Printed by Philobiblon Society (*Miscellanies*, vol. viii). See indictment No. 17.

And after when this Andrew had thus abused her he would not mary her, wherfore she willed Sathan to waste his goodes, which he forthwith did, and yet not beyng contentid with this, she wild him to touch his body whych he forthewith dyd whereof he died.

Item, that euery time that he did any thynge for her, she sayde that he required a drop of bloude, which she gaue him by prycking herselfe, sometime in one place and then in an other, and where she pricked her selfe there remayned a red spot which was styl to be sene.

Item, when this Andrew was dead, she douting her selfe with childe, willed Sathan to destroye it, and he bad her take a certayne herbe and drinke it, whych she did, and destroyed the childe forthwyth.

Item, when she desyred an other husbande he promysed her an other, naminge this Frauncis whom shee nowe hath, but said he is not so rich as the other, willynge her to consent vnto that Frauncis in fornycation which she did, and therof conceaued a daughter that was borne within a quarter of a yere after they were maried.

After they were maryed they liued not so quietly as she desyred, beinge stirred (as she said) to much vnquietnes and moued to swearing and cursinge, wherfore she willed Sathan her Cat to kyll the childe, beinge aboute the age of half a yere olde, and he did so, and when she yet founde not the quietnes that she desyred, she wylled it to lay a lamenes in the leg of thys Frauncis her husbande, and it did in this maner. It came in a morninge to this Frauncis shoe, lying in it lyke a tode, and when he perceived it puttinge on his shoe, and had touched it with his fote, he being sodenly amased asked of her what it was, and she bad him kil it and he was forthwith taken with a lamenes whereof he can not healed.

After all this when shee had kept this Cat by the space of xv or xvi yeare, and as some saye (though vntruly) beinge wery of it, she came to one mother Waterhouse her neyghbour (a pore woman) when she was going to the oven and desired her to geue her a cake, and she wold geue her a thing that she should be the better for so long as she liued, and this mother Waterhouse gaue her a cake, where vpon she brought her this cat in her apron and taught her as she was instructed before by her grandmother Eue, telling her that she must cal him Sathan and geue him of her bloude and bread and milke as before, and at this examination woulde confesse no more.

*Mother Waterhouse of Hatfylde peuerell of the age of lxiiii yeares
being examined the same day confessed as followeth, and the
xxix daye suffered.*[1]

Fyrst she receyued this cat of this Frances wife in the order
as is before sayde, who wild her to cal him Sathan, and told her
that yf she made muche of him he would do for her what she wolde
haue him to do.

Then when she had receyued him she (to trye him what
he coulde do) wyld him to kyll a hog of her owne, which he dyd,
and she gaue him for his labour a chicken, which he fyrste
required of her and a drop of her blod. And thys she gaue him at
all times when he dyd anythynge for her, by pricking her hand
or face and puttinge the bloud to hys mouth whyche he sucked,
and forthwith wold lye downe in hys pot againe, wherin she kepte
him, the spots of all the which priks are yet to be sene in her skin.

Also she saythe that another tyme being offended with one
Father Kersye she toke her catte Sathan in her lap and put hym
in the wood before her dore, and willed him to kyll three of this
father Kersyes hogges. whiche he dyd, and retourning agayne
told her so. and she rewarded hym as before. wyth a chicken
and a droppe of her bloud, which chicken he eate vp cleane as he
didde al the rest, and she cold fynde remaining neyther bones
nor fethers.

Also she confessed that falling out with one widdow Gooday
she wylled Sathan to drowne her cow and he dyd so, and she
rewardid hym as before.

Also she falling out wyth another of her neyboures, she killed
her three geese in the same maner.

Item, shee confessed that because she could haue no rest
(which she required) she caused Sathan to destroye the brewing
at that tyme.

Also beying denyed butter of an other, she caused her to lose
the curdes ii or iii dayes after.

Item fallinge out with an other of her neybours and his wife,
shee wylled Sathan to kyll him with a bludye flixe, whereof he
dyed, and she rewarded him as before.

Likewyse shee confessed, that because she lyued somwhat
vnquietly with her husbande, she caused Sathan to kyll him,
and he doid so about ix yeres past, syth which tyme she hath
lyued a widdow.

[1] See indictment No. 18.

Also she said that when she wolde wyl him to do any thinge for her, she wolde say her Pater noster in laten

Item, this mother Waterhouse confessed that shee fyrst turned this Cat into a tode by this meanes, she kept the cat a great while in woll in a pot, and at length being moued by pouertie to occupie the woll, she praied in the name of the father and of the sonne, and of the holy ghost that it wold turne into a tode, and forthwith it was turned into a tode, and so kept it in the pot without woll.

Also she said, that going to Brackstede a lyttle before her apprehentyon, this Sathan wylled her to hye her home, for she shulde haue great trouble and that shee shoulde be eyther hanged or burned shortly, more at this tyme she woulde not confesse.

*Jone Waterhouse daughter to this mother Waterhouse, beinge of the age of* xviii *yeres, and examined confesseth as foloweth.*[1]

Fyrst that her mother this laste wynter woulde haue learned her this arte, but she lerned it not, nether yet the name of the thinge. She saith she neuer saw it but once in her mother's hand, and that was in the likenes of a tode, and at that time comming in at a sodeyn when her mother called it oute to worke some thynge withall, she herde her to call it Sathan, for shee was not at any time truely taught it, nor did neuer exercise it before this tyme as foloweth :

Item she confessed that when her mother was gone to Breackstede, in her absence lacking breade, she went to a gyrle a neybours chylde, and desired her to geue her a pece of brede and cheese, whiche when denied and gaue her not, or at the least not so muche as wolde satisfye her, shee goinge home dydde as she had seene her mother doe, callynge Sathan, whiche came to her (as she sayd) she thoughte out of her mothers shewe from vnder the bedde, in the lykenes of a great dogge, demaundynge what she wolde haue wherewithall she beyng a fearde, sayd she wold have him to make such a gyrle a ferd naminge this gyrle, then asked hee her what she wolde geue hym, and she saide a red kocke, then sayde hee no, but thou shalt geue me thy body and sowle, whereby she beinge soore feared, and desyrous to be rydde of hym, sayd she wold : And herewith he went to this gyrle in the lykenes of an euyll fauoured dogge with hornes on his head, and made her very muche afearde, and dothe yet haunt her, nowe can not these witches (as they saye) cal hym in agayn, because

[1] See indictment No. 19.

they dyd not let hym out. And more (sayth shee) she never dydde, but this her doinge was the reuealyng of all the rest.[1]

FINIS

The Second Examination and Confession of mother Agnes Waterhouse, and Jone her daughter, vpon her arainement, with the questions and answeres of Agnes Browne the childe, on whom the spirite haunteth at this present, deliberately declared before Justice Southcote and Master Gerard the quenes atturney the xxvii day of July Anno 1566, no lesse wonderful then most true.

*The Confession of Agnes Waterhowse the xxvii daye of July in Anno 1566 at Chelmsforde before Justice Southcote and M. Gerard the quenes atturney.*

Fyrst being demaunded whether that shee were gyltye or not gilty vpon her araynement of the murtheringe of a man, she confessed that she was gilty, and then vppon the euidence geuen agaynst her daughter Jone Waterhouse, she sayde that she hadde a white Cat, and wylled her cat that he shuld destroy many of his neyghbours cattell, and also that he shoulde kyll a man, and so he dyd, and then after she must go ii or iii mile from her house, and then she toke thoughte howe to kepe her catte, then she and her catte concluded that he the sayde Catte wolde become a tode, and then she shuld kepe him in a close house and geue hym mylke, and so he wolde continue tyll she came home againe, and then being gone forth, her daughter hauing ben at a neyghbour's house there by, required of one Agnes Browne, of the age of xii yeres or more, a peece of breade and cheese, and the sayde Agnes saide that shee had none, and that she had not the key of the milkhouse dore, and then the sayde Jone went home and was angry with the said Agnes Broun and she saide that she remembred that her mother was wonte to go vp and downe in her house and to call Sathan Sathan she sayde she wolde proue the like, and then she went vp an downe the house and called Sathan, and then there came a black dogge to her and asked her what she woulde haue, and then she saide she was aferd and

[1] Imprynted at London by Willyam Powell for Wyllyam Pickeringe dwelling at Sainte Magnus Corner, and are there for to be soulde Anno 1566, the 13 August.

Y

sayd, I wold haue thee to make one Agnes browne afrayde, and then he asked her what she wold giue him and she saide she wold geue hym a red kock, and he said he wolde haue none of that, and shee asked him what he wolde haue then, and he sayde he wold haue her body and soule, and so vpon requeste and feare together she gaue him her body and soule, and then sayde the quenes atturneye *Howe vvylt thou do before God*    O my Lord, I trust God wyll haue mercy vpon mee, and then he saide *thou saiste vvell*, and then he departed from her, and then she saide that she herde that he made the sayde Agnes Browne a fearde.

The said Agnes Brown was then demaunded and called for, and then she came in, and beinge asked what age she was of she sayde she thoughte she was xii yeres old, and then the quenes atturney asked her what shee could say, and then shee saide that at suche a day, naming the daye certayne that shee was chirning of butter and there came to her a thynge lyke a black dogge with a face like an ape, a short taile, a cheine and a syluer whystle (to her thinking) about his neck, and a peyre of hornes on his heade, and brought in his mouth the keye of the milke-house doore, and then my lorde she saide, I was afearde, for he skypped and leaped to and fro, and satte on the toppe of a nettle, and then I asked hym what he wolde haue, and he saide he woulde haue butter, and I saide I had none for him and then he saide he wolde haue some or he went, and then he dyd run to put the keye. into the locke of the mylkehouse dore, and I sayde he sholde haue none, and he sayde he wolde haue some, and then he opened the dore and went vppon the shelfe, and there vpon a new chese laid downe the key, and being a whyle within he came out againe, and locked the dore and said that he had made flap butter for mee, and so departed, and then she saide shee tolde her aunte of it, and then she sent for the priest, and when he came he bad her to praye to God, and cal on the name of Jesus, and soo the nexte day my lord he came again to me with the keye of our milkehouse dore in his mouthe, and then I saide in the name of Jesus what haste thou there, and then he layed downe the key and sayde that I spake euyll woordes in speakyng of that name, and then hee departed, and so my aunte toke up the key, for he had kept it from vs ii dayes and a nyghte, and then we went into the milkhouse and there we dyd se the print of butter vpon the chese, and then within a few daies after hee came againe with a beane pod in his mouth, and then the queenes atturney asked what that was, and so the other Justices declared, and then shee sayde my lorde I saide in the name of Jesus what hast thou there, and so then he laid it downe and saide I spake euil wordes and departed and came agayne by and by with a pece of breade in his mouth, and I asked hym what he wold haue, and he sayde butter it was that he wold haue, and so he departed, and my lord I dyd not see hym noo more tyll wenseday laste, whiche was the xxiiii day of July, why said the quenes atturneye was he with the on Wenseday last. ye she said. what did he then to thee sayde he, my lorde saide shee he came with a knyfe in his mouthe and asked me if I were not dead, and I saide No I thanked God, and then hee sayde if I wolde not dye that hee wold thrust his knife to my harte but he wold make me to dye, and then I sayde in the name of Jesus lay down thy knyfe, and he sayde he wolde not departe from his sweete dames knyfe as yet, and then I asked of hym who was his dame, and then he nodded and wagged his head to your house mother Waterhouse, then the queenes attourneye asked if she sayde Agnes Waterhouse what she saide to it, then she demanded what maner knife that it was, and Agnes Browne said it was a daggar knife, there thou liest saide Agnes Waterhouse. why, quod the quenes atturney, mary my lord (quod she) she saith it is a daggar knife and I haue none such in my house, but a greate knyfe, and therein she lieth, yea yea, ·my lord quoth Jone Waterhouse she lieth in that she saith it hadde a face like an ape, for this that came to mee was like a dogge, well sayde the quenes attourney, well, can you make it come before us nowe, if ye can we will dyspatche you out of prison by and by, no saith saide Agnes Waterhouse I can not, for in faith if I had let hym go as my daughter did I could make hym come by and by, but now I have no more power ouer him, then said the queenes atturneye, Agnes Waterhouse when dyd thye Cat suck of thy bloud neuer saide she, no saide hee, let me se, and then the jayler lifted up her kercher on her heade, and there was diuerse spottes in her face and one on her nose. then sayde the quenes atturney, in good faith Agnes when dydde he sucke of thy bloud laste, by my fayth my lord sayde she, not this fortnyght, and so the jurye went together for that matter.[1]

[1] Imprinted as above.

*The ende and last confession of mother Waterhouse at her death, whiche was the* xxix *daye of July. Anno* 1566.

Fyrste (beinge redi prepared to receiue her death) she confessed earnestly that shee had bene a wytche and vsed suche execrable sorserye the space of xv yeres, and had don many abhominable dede. the which she repented earnestly and unfaynedly, and desyred almighty Gods forgeueness in that she had abused hys most holy name by her deuyllishe practyses, and trusted to be saued by his most vnspekeable mercy. And being demaunded of the by standers, shee confessed that shee sent her Sathan to one Wardol, a neibour of hers, beinge a tayler (with whom she was offended) to hurte and destroye him and his goodes. And this her Sathan went therabout for to haue done her wyll, but in the ende he returned to her agayne, and was not able to do this myschiefe, she asked the cause, and he aunswered because the said Wardol was so strong in fayth that he hadde no power to hurte hym, yet she sent hym dyuerse and sundry time (but all in vayne) to haue mischeuid hym. And being demaunded whether she was accustomed to go to church to the common prayer or deuine seruice, she saide yea. and being required what she dyd there she saide she did as other women do, and prayed right hartely there, and when she was demanded what praier she saide, she aunswered the Lordes prayer, the Aue Maria, and the belefe, and then they demaunded whether in laten or in englyshe, and shee sayde in laten, and they demaunded why she saide it not in englyshe but in laten. seing that it was set out by publike aucthoritie and according to Goddes word that all men shoulde pray in the englyshe and mother toung that they best vnderstande, and shee sayde that Sathan wolde at no tyme suffer her to say it in englyshe, but at all tymes in laten : for these and many other offences whiche shee hathe commytted, done and confessed. shee bewayled. repented, and asked mercy of God, and all the worlde forgyuenes and thus she yelded vp her sowle, trusting to be in joye with Christe her Sauiour, which dearely had bought her with his most precious bloudde. Amen.[1]

[1] Imprynted as above.

# INDEX OF NAMES

The figures in italic type refer to the numbers of indictments (pp. 117–264), and those in roman type to the numbers of the pages.

L

Lach. *See* Leech.
Lacy (Lacie, Lacye). *430, 495, 579*
Ladbrooke. *760, 761, 765* ; 257
Lake, *754*
Lakeland, 30
Lambe (Lam), *537, 621–3, 691*
Lambert, *15, 187*
Lambeth, Surr., *682*
Lambourne (Lamborne), E., *120, 532, 533*
Lamperill, *593* ; 220
Lancaster, *689*
Landell, *712*
Landish (Landishe), *641,* App. I ; 222
Lane (Lanne), *202, 375*
Langden, App. I
Langham, E., *613, 614, 648* ; 223
Larkyn, *248*
Latt. *See* Lott.
Latter, *9, 10*
Lavender, *657–61*
Laver, *516*
Lawe, *214, 232* ; 13
Lawford, E., *193, 194, 595, 607, 608*
Lawrett, *499, 500* ; 87, 88
Lawsell, *270*
Layland, 286
Layston (Leyston), H.. *420*
Lea. *See* Lee.
Leach. *See* Leech.
Lee (Lea), *521, 755*
Lee. *See* Leigh.
Leech (Lach, Leach, Lech), *602, 649,* App. I ; 10, 222, 257
Legat (Legate), 294, 295, 311
Legg, *716, 717, 721, 722*
Leicester, Leic., 314
Leigh (Lee, Lees, Leighes, Leighs), Grt. and Lit., E., *200, 201, 258–60, 545, 546, 555–8, 621–3*
Lenham, *K. 693,*
Lennox, Countess of, 42
Leonard, *416*
Leper, *216, 218*
Lessingwell, *299*
Letherdall, *160*
Lever, 38
Levy (Leauey), *705, 706*
Levingstone, 272, 273, 276–80
Lewen, *38*
Lewes (Lewis), *574, 575, 584, 750–2*
Lewes, Suss., 283

Leyston. *See* Layston.
Life, *574, 575*
Lightbone, 33
Lingarde, *35*
Lingwood, 284
Linsey, *786*
Linstead, 310
Linstead, Suff., 311
Litchfeild (Lichfeild), *672* ; 236
Litlebury (Lyttelberie), *220, 221* ; 155
Littlehare. *See* Lyttelhare.
Lock, 285, 295. *See also* Looke.
Locksley, *574, 575*
Lockwod, 302
Lockyer, *591, 592*
London, *265*
London (City), 80, 170
Long (Longe), *345, 629, 631–6*
Looke, 297, 311. *See also* Lock.
Looman, *255*
Loppam, *25*
Lorken, *365, 366*
Lorman, *788*
Lott (Latt), *730, 733*
Lovell, *709, 710*
Low, 310
Lowes (Lowis, Lowys), *3, 4, 684, 685* ; 65, 300, 301, 307
Lowine (Lowyn), *428*
Lucas, *446*
Lucken (Luckin), *403, 489*
Lucton, E., *300*
Ludd, *281*
Luffe, *781*
Lufkyn, *429*
Lumey (Lumley, Lumney), *226, 227,* App. I ; 155
Lycence, *688*
Lynne, *594*
Lyttelberie. *See* Litlebury.
Lyttelhare, *24* ; 79

M

Mager, *600*
Magicke, 111
Maidenhead, *616,* App. I ; 222
Maidstone, K., *11, 12, 13, 116*
Main, 296
Malden, 283
Maldon, E., *67–9, 119*
Malt (Mault), *486, 503*
Malter, 282
Maltin, 301
Man, *316, 673, 741,* 300, 303, 307
Manderston, Berw., 42

T

*Printed in Great Britain by Stephen Austin & Sons, Ltd., Hertford.*

CPSIA information can be obtained at www.ICGtesting.com
Printed in the USA
LVOW07*1429240315

431819LV00016B/195/P